# THE
# CHURCH'S
# STORY

# THE
# CHURCH'S
# STORY

## A History of
## Pastoral Care and Vision

BY
PETER LYNCH

**Pauline**
BOOKS & MEDIA
Boston

**Library of Congress Cataloging-in-Publication Data**

Lynch, Peter, 1945—
    The church's story : a history of pastoral care and vision / Peter Lynch.
        p. cm.
    Includes bibliographical references and index.
    ISBN 0-8198-1575-6 (alk. paper)
    1.  Pastoral theology—Catholic Church—History. 2.  Pastoral care—
History.  I. Title.
    BX1913.L96 2005
    253′.09—dc22

                                    2005005491

Cover art: Masolino da Panicale (1383–1447). *Curing the Crippled and the Resurrection of Tabitha.* Scala / Art Resource, NY

"P" and PAULINE are registered trademarks of the Daughters of St. Paul.

Copyright © 2005 Peter Lynch

Published by Pauline Books & Media, 50 Saint Pauls Avenue, Boston, MA 02130-3491.

www.pauline.org

Pauline Books & Media is the publishing house of the Daughters of St. Paul, an international congregation of women religious serving the Church with the communications media.

1 2 3 4 5 6 7 8 9                         11 10 09 08 07 06 05

Dedicated to the memory of my friend
John Ouvrier (1916 - 2001)
who helped me better to realize
that the pastoral challenges of our day
can be properly understood
only in the spectrum of the Church's history
and tradition.

# Contents

# Introduction

Pastoral care among Christians is the practical response of the Church, motivated by a faith in Jesus Christ, to the great variety of human needs experienced by individuals and communities. These needs vary. Some of them are basic, such as food, health care and shelter. Other needs are associated with feeling valued, having one's human rights respected and knowing that one is part of a loving and just community. And pastoral care is also about fostering a person's needs that are associated with spiritual growth and wholeness.

Traditionally, pastoral care has taken the biblical image of the shepherd for its name, inspiration and guide to continuing the mission of Jesus in the world, the shepherd-pastor looking after the flock. The symbol of the shepherd is common to both the Jewish and Christian Scriptures and rich in meaning. Yet the shepherd imagery runs the risk of fostering dependency and submissiveness. Sheep are not the most intelligent of creatures. Today, pastoral care places emphasis upon the empowerment of individuals and communities to free themselves from all that is oppressive, 'that the creation itself will be set free from its bondage to decay and will obtain the freedom of the glory of the children of God' (Rom 8:21).

This book is about the two thousand year history of the Christian community, especially the Roman Catholic community, in its efforts to engage in pastoral care. It is a short history of the Church but a history viewed specifically through the lens of pastoral care. This work, then, does not aim to be an overall history of the Church but a history with a more specific focus. While the emphasis throughout this book is that of the Catholic story of pastoral care, nevertheless, this story is frequently situated within the broader developments of pastoral care within other Christian Churches, especially those following the Protestant Reformation of the sixteenth century. Eastern Christianity flourished throughout the first millennium and its story of pastoral care, as it developed then, is unfolded in the earlier chapters of this book. Less attention is given to pastoral care within the Eastern Churches in the latter part of the book that deals with the second millennium. This is a tale yet to be told in a form easily accessible to Catholic and Protestant Christians of the West. In a concise history of pastoral care, such as this book offers, the range of topics and events addressed is necessarily selective. Some readers may be disappointed in discovering that particular ministries and the events that influenced and motivated them are absent. It is not possible to address in its entirety the vast scope of pastoral care and its long history in a book of this size. Omissions are inevitable.

Pastoral care has often been described as 'the cure of souls', a ministry of healing in the broad sense. The term denotes a concern for the emotional, moral and spiritual dimensions within the life of an individual. Within the Catholic tradition, this is to be seen in the continuing importance given to the sacrament of penance, namely the confession of sin, and priestly absolution. This sacrament, along with efforts of practical charity, became one of the most emphasized forms of pastoral care. In fact, sacramental forms of ministry have always played an essential part in Catholic pastoral life.

In more recent years in Catholic life, as in Protestantism, pastoral counseling and spiritual direction have grown in importance as a means of attending to the 'cure of souls', ministries not confined to priestly ministration. This is just one illustration of how pastoral care has broadened from being understood as the particular work of ordained ministers to now include lay ministry in its many forms. Increasingly, women experience the call to pastoral care. And, as will be told in the pages that follow, religious orders of women and men have constantly made a special and significant contribution to pastoral care in the Catholic tradition. Typically, they emerged to meet new pastoral challenges. While today religious orders have gone into sharp decline in many parts of the Church, new forms of lay pastoral care have developed in their place. This is just another example of how pastoral care is forever evolving. In Catholic life, the teaching office of the papacy, too, has had a fundamental role to play in setting the direction for pastoral care and receives considerable attention in this book.

Just how to define pastoral care is a matter of some conjecture. Is it mainly about practical charity, together with attention to personal guidance in ethical and spiritual matters? Or is pastoral care something much broader? This book adopts the latter understanding. This wider meaning of pastoral care, as developed throughout the following ten chapters, covers many aspects of the Church's life. These include a pastoral concern for fostering unity within the Christian community amidst doctrinal conflict and practices that threaten to tear it apart, a recurring crisis throughout the Church's long history. In fact, this was the most pressing pastoral concern within the New Testament Church in the time of St Paul as the first generations of Christians struggled for an identity, doctrine and way of life that was distinct from Judaism yet connected to it. Pastoral care, in the broader sense, is not only about alleviating individual deprivation through charitable action. It is also passionately concerned for social justice, working to remove the unjust causes of human suffering. And this book attempts to situate missionary endeavors within the broader description of pastoral care as Christians sought to awaken peoples of other cultures and religions to the message of Christ. How Christians went about drawing in new peoples into their community, how they related and presented the gospel to human beings so different from themselves is also part of the story of pastoral care in its many forms. Yet in today's more interconnected world – increasingly under the threat of religious disharmony and violence – Christians have been challenged to reassess their understanding and manner of relating to people unlike themselves.

The book begins the history of pastoral care with the Church as it took shape soon after the resurrection of Jesus rather than starting with the ministry of the historical Jesus as we meet him in the four Gospels. The book is about the story of the Church guided, for those who believe, by the Spirit of the risen Christ. But the Church is always influenced by the world in which it finds itself: political events, social and economic changes, intellectual movements, and theological developments. The conversion of the Roman emperor Constantine in the early fourth century resulted in a whole new context for pastoral care. Christians, once a persecuted minority in need of encouragement amidst their fears of a brutal death, were soon to constitute the official state religion that was to become medieval Christendom. Political changes inevitably result in a different style of pastoral care. Exploration of the New World beyond Europe; princes and states struggling to free themselves from the secular powers of the Roman papacy at the time of the Reformation amidst the birth of new theological ideas to combat superstition; the birth of a new Catholic Church brought about by the reforms of the Council of Trent; the Enlightenment that emphasized human reason and scientific observation at the expense of ecclesiastical and divine authority; the French Revolution that gave birth to the quest for human rights and freedoms; the industrial revolution that created the exploitation of a new working class within a transformed economy; atheistic communism with its brutal crushing of human freedom; nazism and its horrors; mass migration of peoples in search of a better life abroad; the sexual revolution and feminism that altered the nature of human relationships; globalization and its impact upon modern life; and damage inflicted upon the environment that threatens the very existence of life in all its diversity; and, finally, the philosophy of postmodernism that has led to a very different understanding of reality itself: these are among just some of the events that have caused profound change concerning the nature of human needs and methods required for pastoral care to respond to them. The post-Vatican II Church has had to refashion itself to respond to the new world order.

Such changes within the wider world all brought about greater reflection within the Church as it found itself continuously in new circumstances. The books of the Old and New Testaments, the works of the early Church Fathers, the great Ecumenical Councils, Church teachings, liturgical texts, the writings of theologians: all have provided guidance in the way the Church has set its priorities and decided upon its methods of pastoral care. Theological thinking, as will be seen, is at the heart of pastoral care. The Church's guide as to what is normative versus what can change (biblical and systematic theology); the Church's understanding of its mission and its forms of recognized ministry (ecclesiology); the meaning of human sinfulness and what constitutes a good and holy life (Christian ethics); what it means to be saved (soteriology); pastoral care through worship (liturgy); the relationship the different Churches have to each other (ecumenism) and to other faiths (inter-religious dialog); and the process of making particular pastoral decisions that affect individuals and the wider world (practical theology): all these different but connected theological disciplines have given shape to pastoral care.

The sciences, in particular, have become increasingly important to the aims and methods of pastoral care. Psychology has helped in a better understanding of the nature of human behavior when it comes to assessing sinfulness and in providing methods for pastoral guidance and counseling. Sociology has assisted in understanding social change and the contribution of religion to the lives of human communities. Management theory has offered insight into the nature of leadership and how organizations can best function. Economics has given increased insight into the ways of bettering the lives of people materially as well as the possibilities present for exploitation. Anthropology has contributed to a more enlightened appreciation of the importance of culture within the self-understanding and lives of people. Biology has yielded greater information about the creation of life and the nature of sexuality and its effects upon human relationships. Ecology has revealed the interconnectedness of the natural world in all its forms and the threat posed when nature's delicate balance is upset.

It is always tempting for pastoral care to be influenced by the ever increasing body of secular knowledge and influences at the expense of its God-given values and mission. This is as true today for pastoral care as it was for the early Church Fathers and theologians of the medieval Church who sought wisdom in the philosophy of the ancient Greeks. Pastoral care has always looked to human guidance and its social environment while remaining rooted in its divine vision of things. It is necessarily incarnational. It is this ever-changing story that is taken up in the pages of this history of pastoral care, especially within the Roman Catholic tradition.

# Chapter 1

## Jews and Gentiles

Old Corinth is a quiet, sleepy little village. Elderly men sit at tables outside the few cafés on the square sipping strong, black coffee, complaining about what the politicians are up to in Athens, the capital, or arguing about the tactics used by their team in a recent soccer match. After all, it was Greece that gave the world democracy and competitive sport. Just up the road from the cafés one can see the ruins of ancient Corinth: crumbling marble columns, once part of grand public buildings and impressive temples to the gods. Rising some 1500 feet above the ruined city and providing its distinctive feature is the Acrocorinth, a craggy limestone mountain. Overlooking the square of this tranquil village is the small and simple Orthodox Church of the Assumption of the Virgin Mary. The congregation that worships in this church can trace its origins back to St Paul (d. *c.* 65), some two thousand years ago. It was in Corinth, and towns like it around the Mediterranean, that Christianity came into being.

A couple of miles away, by the seaport, stands the modern city of Corinth with its avenues of brightly lit shops, traffic and apartment blocks, characteristic of any large town or city of today. It developed in the nineteenth century because of earthquakes in ancient Corinth. In Paul's day, the port was the place known as Lechaeum. It was a very busy port. Here cargo was unloaded from ships, coming from the western Mediterranean, on to vehicles. Such shipments were then transported the two miles to waiting boats at the seaport of Cenchreae, on the eastern side of the narrow neck of land of this isthmus that divides the Gulf of Corinth from the Saronic Gulf. Smaller ships, crammed with their goods for trade, were even dragged across a grooved pavement of land to be relaunched on the other side. Corinth controlled this maritime crossroads. By doing so, the city was a place of enormous strategic and commercial importance in linking trade between the western and eastern sectors of the ancient world. The city was filled with sailors and travelers, seeking amusement during their stay. As well, the isthmus connects the Peloponnesus with the landmass of Attica and Thessalonica to the north. Corinth is well situated. It looks simultaneously in four different directions and has profited immensely from doing so.

Corinth was destroyed by the Romans in 146 BCE. It was rebuilt by Julius Caesar (100-44BCE) in 44 BCE and located in the Roman province of Achaia, of which it was the capital. Even as far back as Homer, the city had been described as wealthy.[1] While Roman colonies were founded and settled mainly by veterans from the Roman legions, Corinth, it seems, was different. Its colonists were of the poorer classes, most of them *libertini*, freed slaves.[2] Philo (*c.*20BCE-*c.*50CE)[3] alludes to the presence of Jews in Corinth before the year 40. Their worship of only the one God, Yahweh, made them distinctive in the Roman world. Corinth was known for its production of bronze and manufacturing of terracotta. The spoken language was Greek, but being such a cosmopolitan place, a diversity of tongues would have been heard in the forum. Yet Latin, the language uniting the Roman Empire, was used for official business.

The Isthmian Games, held in the spring every two years, also helped Corinth to become a place of importance, for it was from Corinth that the games were administered. They took place in the sanctuary of the god of the sea, Poseidon, at Isthmia. Athletes came from all parts of Greece to compete. These games were second in importance only to the Olympic Games. Like the Games at Olympia, the Isthmian Games held great religious significance. The spirit of competitiveness of the Isthmian Games gave birth to the proverb, 'Not for everyone is the voyage to Corinth.'[4] These games flourished until the late fourth century in Christian times when, like other pagan festivals, they were closed down by the Emperor Theodosius (379-95).

Despite the fact that the Greeks maintained an aversion to the bloody and cruel spectacles of the gladiatorial entertainments of the Roman world, such sporting shows were popular in rough and cosmopolitan Corinth by the end of the first century of the Christian Era (or Common Era, CE). In fact, Roman Corinth was considered 'spiritually and intellectually empty'.[5]

Just like any other place within the Roman Empire, a host of deities were worshiped. The Egyptian goddess, Isis, in her capacity as a sea goddess, was popular. A cult surrounded also the Ephesian fertility goddess, Artemis, with her multiplicity of breasts.[6] But in Roman Corinth it was the sanctuary of Asclepius, the god of healing, that particularly flourished. People would make pilgrimage there to be cured of their different ailments and diseases. The cult had its temple along with sleeping facilities, as adherents would await directions from the god in their dreams as to how they could be healed. One might compare the shrine to a modern health farm, but with the all-important added religious component of cultic acts. Devotees engaged in exercise, observed a strict diet, took baths and participated in different forms of relaxation.[7] But Corinth was a bawdy city, noted for its immorality, drunkenness, brothels and materialistic ways. Aristophanes (c.448-c.388BCE), an Athenian comic poet, invented the verb 'Corinthianize', meaning to engage in sexually promiscuous activities.

Corinth is a good place to begin the story of pastoral care as it has unfolded in the history of the Church that has emerged and developed following the life, death and resurrection of Jesus. It is one of the earliest Christian communities about which we know. Paul first came here sometime between 49 and 52CE and stayed eighteen months. He later wrote at least five letters to his troubled Corinthian Church, some of which correspondence makes up two books of the New Testament. We know Paul returned to the city on two more occasions. But why single out ancient Corinth to learn about the kind of pastoral care that characterized the infant Church?

From the writings of the New Testament, the Corinthian Church provides perhaps the most detailed description we have of the variety of problems and concerns that faced the early followers of Jesus, issues that had to be addressed in a pastoral way. Some of these difficulties were particular to Corinth. But many were common to the wider body of the Church at that time, communities scattered around the Mediterranean world. In Corinth we catch a glimpse, often a disturbing glimpse, of pastoral care as it was exercised in the infancy of the Church's life. So many of the concerns in Corinth had an impact upon the wider collection of Churches. So, then, what did happen in Corinth after Paul established his Church there? What were the pastoral concerns? How were they addressed? And what resulted? But this story, as it unfolds, will move us well beyond Corinth as we become immersed in the politics, intrigue, social behaviors, institutions, intellectual ideas, doctrine, and religious practices of a growing Church. Pastoral care usually finds itself inextricably bound up with such factors as these. It was as true in Paul's day as our own.

### A Church Divided

Paul was clearly the founder of the first Christian community at Corinth. When he first went there, it was a rapidly developing urban center. An ethnically diverse city of thousands of people, it had a definite cosmopolitan flavor and so was open to new ideas and religious movements. Paul arrived there from Athens and came in contact with Aquila and his wife, Priscilla, who had to flee Rome because of an edict of the Emperor Claudius (41-54 CE) expelling all Jews from the imperial capital. Like Paul, Priscilla and Aquila were tentmakers and they invited him to live and work with them (Acts 18:1-3). Paul soon made converts to the new faith in the risen Christ, a faith which he had professed after his conversion on the road to Damascus some fifteen years or so earlier (Acts 9:1-9).

As a tentmaker, Paul's workshop was possibly in the bustling marketplace that provided him with plenty of opportunities for contact with people to share his message about Christ. Here he would have led new converts to the gospel. Likewise, the house in which he was staying with Priscilla and Aquila, and others like it, during his extensive journeys, must have provided a venue for his missionary work. The Greco-Roman household could be a large one. As well as the immediate family, there might be relatives, slaves, laborers, tenants, business associates, all living under the same roof. Such was the setting for house churches in the early Christian world. And there was the synagogue where Paul could preach his new faith to potential Jewish converts.[8] It would appear that in Corinth there were more Gentile Christians than Jewish ones (1 Cor 12:2). Just how many Christians there came to be in Corinth during Paul's lifetime is difficult to assess. But the number must have been reasonably large.

What was the social composition of the Corinthian Church in Paul's time? From 1 Cor 1:26 it would seem that the majority in that Church were from the lower classes of society although in other places, in Paul's letters to that same Church, there are indications that there were some who possessed wealth and prestige. As we shall see, this gave rise to some problems. The presence of well-off persons in the Church can be assumed from Paul's letters. Some would indulge in large amounts of food and drink (1 Cor 11:17-34) compared to the 'poor people' (1 Cor 11:22). And others had houses large enough to accommodate the whole Christian community for purposes of its gatherings (1 Cor 16:19). It is generally agreed that there was a considerable degree of diversity within this Christian community.[9]

Paul's mission, while in Corinth, was not without incident. Some Jews took offence at his message and insulted him. Others reported him to the Roman proconsul, accusing him of inciting people to break the Jewish Law, a matter of no great interest to this Roman official (Acts 18:12-17). Paul, the volatile man that he was, let his enemies know what he thought of them and concentrated his efforts, instead, upon the Gentiles, a great many of whom, so Luke tells us in Acts, became baptized believers. So, too, did a man named Crispus, president of a synagogue, along with his whole household (Acts 18:8). But after one and a half years working and preaching the message of Jesus the Christ, Paul left Corinth for his headquarters in Antioch, accompanied by his friends Priscilla and Aquila (Acts 18:1-18). Paul was now to embark on his third great missionary journey.

But what was happening back in Corinth in Paul's absence? He had been keeping in touch with this Church by letter before the writing of the Corinthian Letters we have in the New Testament (1 Cor 5:9), urging his readers, among other things, to refrain from mixing with people living immoral lives. One can only assume that there must have been many such people in Corinth. Unfortunately, this correspondence has not come down to us. Other preachers had begun to visit. Among them was Apollos, a well-educated Jew steeped in Hellenistic Wisdom philosophy. He made an impression on the community there. Paul acknowledged the preaching and teaching of Apollos whom, he claims, watered what he had previously planted (1 Cor 3:5-6). Cephas, later to be known as Peter (d. *c.*64-67), may also have gone there, as well as Jews associated closely with the Jerusalem Church, a Church that identified the Christian movement squarely within the Jewish faith. This was to spell trouble.

### Leadership Factions in the Community

The Christian community in Corinth had become divided. People had developed conflicting loyalties and were gravitating towards different leaders. Paul got to hear about these damaging circumstances from Chloe's people (1 Cor 1:11). Bad news travels fast. A situation had developed that threatened to tear apart the infant Church. Paul was not pleased. Different factions within the community had emerged. Slogans developed: 'I belong to Paul'; 'I belong to Apollos'; 'I belong to Cephas'; and 'I belong to Christ' (1 Cor 1:12). In whatever context, political slogans like these tend to paint exaggerated contrasts and lead to divisiveness which can be party politics. And this is precisely what had happened at Corinth. Paul decided to act. From Ephesus, possibly in the fall of the year 54, he wrote a stern letter to his Corinthian brothers and sisters in which he addressed problems causing division within his beloved Church. This letter we know as First Corinthians, to be found in the New Testament. It is a letter that catalogues a whole checklist of problems within that Church. This is Paul's pastoral response to a Church in trouble some twenty years after the death and resurrection of Christ.

It seems that these slogans were rallying points for different theological teachings associated with different leaders. Yet, for Paul, the problem was less about the different forms of theology concerning esoteric Gnosticism or Jewish propaganda being propounded by such slogans. It was more about the situation of rivalry and jealousy within the community leading to an all too human situation of boasting and pride.[10] This is a false kind of wisdom, wrote Paul, which is opposed to the true wisdom of Christ. Drawing from the Jewish Scriptures, Paul challenged the Corinthians: if anyone wants to boast about this leader or that, then let that person boast about the Lord (1 Cor 1:31). Paul's method of pastoral care was one of admonition and correction.

Scholars argue that these disagreements among the factions in Corinth may well have arisen as a result of baptism.[11] Members of a household church baptized by a particular missionary are a ready-made group of supporters. And, as we have already seen, the household could be large. In all likelihood, wealthier and more prominent members of the church led large households. This facilitated a degree of dependence. Different household churches within the city, then, may have developed allegiances to different missionaries. And some, it seems, were not for Paul. Pastoral care has always had to address this very human situation of jealousy and pettiness. Paul dealt with it firmly and decisively.[12]

### Litigation Problems

But there were other sources of divisiveness in the Church at Corinth that caused Paul concern. Believers were engaged in civil litigation against each other (1 Cor 6:1-8). Such conflict among the brothers and sisters was not to be tolerated. Paul could be very blunt. In unflattering terms, he told them that they were once 'fornicators, idolaters, adulterers, male prostitutes, sodomites, thieves, the greedy, drunkards, revilers, robbers' (1 Cor 6:9-10). But now, as people possessing the Spirit of God, he expected more of them. If they have differences, let them settle them amicably within the community itself and not in the pagan courts.

### Troubles Concerning the Lord's Supper

The Lord's Supper, as it occurred in certain circles within Corinth, had become a source of complaint among some. It was causing tension and division within the Church. Paul attempted to sort out the problem by means, again, of admonition and pastoral guidance (1 Cor 11:17-34). In early Christian times, the ritual celebration of the eucharistic meal was carried out in a very different fashion from today. It looked like a meal. What, precisely, was the problem? From Paul's letter, one can't be certain as to the full nature of the difficulties. But it is possible to make some likely reconstructions.[13]

Some of the well-off members of the congregation began eating the preparatory meal before the whole community had assembled. As well, during the Lord's Supper itself, some were enjoying their own private food that was of better quality and failed to share it with all. In other words, distinctions of social status and wealth within the community determined the quantity and quality of food one was given in the eucharistic meal in some house churches of Corinth. Such practices of inequality of food distribution were not uncommon in Roman society when a host invited guests to a dinner or banquet. And Corinth was a Roman colony. The wealthier Christians, then, felt they were already doing their lower class Christian brothers and sisters a favor by inviting them into their home in the first place for the eucharistic meal. There was no reason why these people ought to expect the same quality food as the more well-to-do members of the Jesus community. This is one possible explanation of the complaints reaching Paul's ears.

Other explanations have been suggested for the reasons for division within the Lord's Supper. The evening would have begun with an ordinary meal of several courses followed by a period of drinking accompanied by music and conversation. During this time the religious ritual of the Eucharist - of eating and drinking the blessed bread and cup of wine - very likely took place. For this meal, people would bring their own food, a potluck supper so to speak. Hence it was not simply a banquet offered only by the host. The problem presented to Paul was that some believers came early and got on with the eating and drinking before everybody had arrived. Those who came later received insufficient food from what was on offer 'and one goes hungry and another becomes drunk' (1 Cor 11:21). The rich, then, had brought better quality food and drink. They consumed this before the poorer members of the community had arrived. These lower classes of people within the community may not have been invited to the earlier sitting or they were simply unable to arrive earlier. Slaves, for example, would have had greater time restrictions placed upon them by their owners. Paul gives his pastoral advice: 'If you are hungry, eat at home, so that when you come together, it will not be for your condemnation' (1 Cor 11:34). In other words, they should all come together to eat the meal equally or, alternatively, eat first at home before sharing the Lord's Supper itself.

Not only is there the above problem concerning disunity surrounding the Eucharistic meal. Amidst the celebration, people were eating and drinking too heavily, thus showing insufficient respect for the sacred ritual in which they were participating. Paul warned them sternly: 'Whoever, therefore, eats the bread or drinks the cup of the Lord in an unworthy manner will be answerable for the body and blood of the Lord' (1 Cor 11:27).

## Food Sacrificed to Idols

One other problem regarding disunity within the Corinthian Church was the eating of food that had previously been sacrificed to idols (1 Cor 8-10). In ancient times, food would be offered in sacrifice to the gods and then eaten later in a ritual meal. The Jews, too, had this practice in their communion sacrifices. This same idea, of course, is at the basis of the Christian Eucharist. What was causing dissension in Corinth about such matters? It may well have been class-based differences again within the Church that led to complaints reaching Paul.[14] Because meat was expensive, poorer people would seldom have eaten it. For the lower classes, meat was associated mainly with ceremonial religious feasts. On the other hand, the wealthier classes would have been accustomed to eating meat in a variety of social settings. As Christians who had rejected idol worship, many such people would have been reluctant to risk losing social contacts where consecrated meat would be served. Was this behavior a scandal to the less well-off in the Corinthian community? In Paul's language, there had arisen a conflict between the 'weak' and the 'strong'. Paul's arguments are complex and seemingly inconsistent with his stand on food previously offered to idols. What he is clear about is that the issue has caused division among the believers. Some in the community had taken offence at what they saw as scandalous behavior on the part of their fellow Christians and this had led to considerable ill feeling among them. Paul's pastoral solution is clear: whatever you do, avoid being offensive to others (1 Cor 10:31-32).

Paul's overall response to this divided and troubled Corinthian Church was to appeal for a unity based upon his theological conviction that baptized believers must live in love, the greatest of the spiritual gifts (1 Cor 13). This love must characterize the body of Christ. Whether Jew or Greek, slave or citizen, 'we were all made to drink of one Spirit', he reminded his people in Corinth (1 Cor 12:13). As Paul said, 'Now you are the body of Christ' (1 Cor 12:27). It is for this reason that they were to live as one, from being a divided Church to a Church living in the unity of Christ Jesus.

### 2 Corinthians 10-13: The 'Painful Letter'

Timothy made a visit to Corinth (1 Cor 16:10-11) to remind them of Paul's teachings concerning Christ and he found things far from good there. He reported back to Paul on the alarming state of affairs in Corinth. Paul, it seems, hurriedly returned to the city prompted by Timothy's worried reports on the situation. There was some sort of major confrontation with members of the Church and Paul returned to Ephesus. On his arrival, he wrote another letter (his third) that is contained in 2 Cor 10-13. Paul's feelings of rejection and humiliation are evident. This is the 'painful letter'. Again, the issue is that of disunity. A group of Jewish Christians attacked his apostolic authority. The reasons for their attack are not all that clear to us. In this letter, Paul threw down the gauntlet. The Corinthians were to choose between himself and these so-called 'super-apostles' (2 Cor 11:5) who boast of their achievements and who preach 'another Jesus than the one we proclaimed' (2 Cor 11:4). Paul told them he may be 'untrained in speech' (2 Cor 11:6) but his message was the truth. In this letter, Paul insisted that the credentials of a true apostle are not in spectacular acts and the power of this age but in weakness and suffering, as he had experienced. 'If I must boast, I will boast of the things that show my weakness' (2 Cor 11:30).

Paul was clearly very worried and hurt over affairs within this Church. He felt a strong sense of pastoral responsibility concerning its welfare. He decided he had to make yet a third visit to see what could be done in this divided community of believers (2 Cor 13:1). He was afraid that, on arrival, he would find these Corinthian Christians - the Church he founded - in a state of 'quarreling, jealousy, anger, selfishness, slander, gossip, conceit, and disorder' (2 Cor 12:20). It does not make for a pretty picture. His pastoral response, in the meantime, was the same as that found in his earlier letter, First Corinthians: to urge them to live in peace so as to experience among themselves the God of love and peace (2 Cor 13:11-13). Paul did return to Corinth for another visit and stayed in the area for three months (Acts 20:2-3), from where he wrote his Letter to the Romans in which his thinking on salvation in Christ, in relation to Judaism, is most thoroughly expressed.

### 2 Corinthians 1-9: The 'Conciliatory Letter'

After hearing more positive news from Titus about the Corinthians following his departure from that Church, he wrote them a conciliatory, fourth letter, embodied in 2 Cor 1-9. Biblical scholars are in general agreement that the New Testament Second Letter to the Corinthians is actually a composite of these two separate letters, assembled together by a later editor.[15] The second part of the New Testament book of Second Corinthians (2 Cor 10-13), then, was written prior to the first part (2 Cor 1-9).

Paul wrote a letter indicating reconciliation had taken place between himself and the Church there. What is certain is that the majority of the members of this Church had now turned against the ringleader of the movement opposed to Paul (2 Cor 2:6). Paul's pastoral care for a Church that has been torn apart by jealousies and power plays was to ask its members to forgive this man who had caused so much dissension and he, too, would forgive him.

## A Church Awaiting the End of Time

A second issue of pastoral concern in this infancy period of the Church's life arose from the firm and central belief of the earliest Christians that Christ was soon to return, the *parousia*.[16] It was central to Paul's theology, particularly in First and Second Thessalonians. As we shall see, the Corinthian Church provides us with good insight as to how this belief in the Lord's return affected the teaching and living of the message of those who professed faith in the crucified and risen Christ. These early followers of the way of Jesus felt sure this event was imminent.[17] In some of his writings, Paul seems to have expected Christ's return would happen within his own lifetime. At least this was his thinking in the earlier period of his missionary work. Yet, in other passages, he considered the possibility that he might die before the *parousia* of Christ were to come about. Paul's thought seems to change on the matter.[18] No doubt this change in outlook came about because of the passing of each year without its occurrence. Whatever the reason, the earliest Christians based their lives upon the hope that the risen and glorified Christ would return. In so doing, he would bring his work of salvation unambiguously to completion. A triumphant Lord would defeat the powers of evil beyond doubt; his people would be brought into perfect fellowship; and God would be seen by all to be fully sovereign over all peoples and the whole of creation.[19]

In chapter 15 of the First Letter to the Corinthians, Paul argued in great detail about the central place of Jesus' resurrection and its relationship to the end of time. Because Christ has been raised from the dead, he has provided the opportunity for all who have faith to be raised with him. 'For if the dead are not raised, then Christ has not been raised' (1 Cor 15:16). There will be a future resurrection of the dead for those who have put their hope in him, 'When all things are subjected to him ... so that God may be all in all' (1 Cor 15:28). It will be the time of the sounding of the last trumpet when 'the dead will be raised imperishable, and we will be changed. For this perishable body must put on imperishability, and this mortal body must put on immortality' (1 Cor 15:52-53).

This apocalyptic thinking, put before the Christian believers at Corinth, lies behind Paul's exhortations and teachings about ethical issues. His ethical program goes beyond the philosophical ways of thought of the ancient Greek and Roman world (1 Cor 1:17-25). Apart from Paul's teachings on the end of time, his pastoral solicitude as to how these Corinthians, and Christians of other Churches, should lead their lives in the here-and-now makes no sense. Paul's whole pastoral practice was dominated by his eschatology. To some extent, the many problems experienced by the Corinthian Church had arisen precisely because they had failed to recognize the limitations and dangers of life in an age that would soon come to an end.[20]

### Transitory Human Practices

There are two major consequences of Paul's apocalyptic thinking. First, his teachings about such human practices and institutions as celibate living, marriage, slavery, sex, household relationships between women and men, and parental relationships: these are all transitory. For Paul, 'the appointed time has grown short ... For the present form of this world is passing away' (1 Cor 7:29,31). Such human arrangements are in their last days and so are subordinate to the new order that will soon come about with the return of Christ in glory. All forms of earthly, historical existence would be terminated. So this human ordering of things is quickly fading. Paul, then, was no social visionary out to change the way in which society was to be socially structured. He remained firmly enclosed within the Greco-Roman world of the first century that ordered society upon values so different from our own. In this respect, Paul remained a man of his time. His point was that social arrangements, as we now know them, simply would become obsolete. The subordination of women to men; the social and economic custom of slavery; marriage compared to virginity: soon, these would all disappear, thought Christians in Corinth and Churches like it in the first century. Paul's own framework of time did not envisage an ethical or social program extending across a number of generations.[21] But, alas, the return of Christ and the passing of this world did not occur, as Paul and the earliest generations of Christians had expected. Life in the age of the Church was going to be for a much longer period of time than originally anticipated. Christians, over subsequent centuries, had to rethink these social arrangements in the light of the broader values of the gospel.

### Holy Lives Ready to Meet the Lord

A second consequence of Paul's thinking about the end is that it colors his entire outlook on virtue and morality. Awaiting this return of Christ ought to lead believers into living in ways that will find them ready to greet their Lord when he returns. Living in a time that is fast running out, Christians should prepare themselves so that they will be ready, suitably prepared, to share in the final glory. Paul instructed his Christians in Galatia, 'whenever we have an opportunity, let us work for the good of all, and especially for those of the family of faith' (Gal 6:10). From exhortations to his sisters and brothers in Corinth, we get further evidence of Paul's sense of how the endtime ought to impact on the way a person lives now. For Paul, to live in the body was to be exiled from the Lord. But every person would be called to give an account of his or her life in the law court of Christ when the end comes. For then, one will be exiled from the body (2 Cor 5:9-10). Matthew's parable of the ten bridesmaids awaiting the return of the bridegroom - some of whom were foolish while others were wise - takes up this thinking about the endtime and the return of Christ as a basis for moral behavior (Mt 25:1-13).

We can see, then, just how important apocalyptic thinking was in Paul's pastoral guidance as to how Christians were to live in this world. It is one of the most distinctive characteristics of the theology behind pastoral care in early Christianity. As the biblical scholar Ernst Käsemann once wrote, 'apocalyptic was the mother of all Christian theology.'[22]

### A Church Helping the Needy

Generally, we associate the term 'pastoral care 'most often with reaching out to people in some kind of need: the poor, the sick, the bereaved, the addicted, the disadvantaged and marginalized: people troubled in some way or another. Examples of assistance to individuals or groups of people of this kind are well represented in the life of the earliest Christian communities described in the New Testament.

The ideal of service, *diakonia*, is at the heart of ministry in the New Testament Churches. Apart from its most basic meaning of serving the needs of people, it is used also for service of the word (Acts 6:4);

service of the Spirit (2 Cor 3:7); service of justification (2 Cor 3:9); and the overall task of leadership (2 Tim 4:5).[23]

### Healing

Jesus gave much attention to performing healing miracles that were understood as signs of the irruption of God's kingdom into this world. Shortly later, in the life of the early communities of Jesus believers, it is mainly in the Book of Acts that we get some glimpse into this form of pastoral care. Here there are a number of accounts of healing: the lame (Acts 3:1-10; 14:8-10); a paralytic (Acts 9:33-34); the cure of a person with dysentery (Acts 28:8); as well as the raising of two people from the dead (Acts 9:36-41; 20:9-12).

How do we interpret these miraculous healing acts of pastoral care in New Testament times? First, people living in a period of time prior to the scientific age, when the laws of nature were inadequately understood, believed simply in the reality of miracles. Such miracles went unquestioned. They were taken for granted. In New Testament times, religious healers and their recipients had no difficulty in believing in a direct form of divine intervention for the cure of a particular illness. Second, in the New Testament accounts of miraculous healing, they are inseparably linked with faith. They are not just thought of as unexplainable wonders. They are 'signs' (John's Gospel uses the word *sēmeion*, meaning 'sign', to describe them), speaking of God's love and the coming of God's kingdom.

But that still does not answer the question as to what actually occurred. Of help to us here is John Meier's detailed and scholarly examination of the question.[24] His work is concerned with the miracle accounts of Jesus in the four Gospels but one might transpose his findings to the apostles' healing miracles, narrated by Luke in the book of Acts, as these are described within the life of the infant Church. In doing so, however, one cannot overlook the unique ministry of Jesus in the thinking of the New Testament compared to that of the apostles.

Meier makes it clear that he is unable, as a biblical historian, to decide the theological question as to whether these particular extraordinary deeds of Jesus were miracles. But given the fact that such stories are reported in the Gospels, he asks whether at least the core of these stories can be traced back to the time and ministry of Jesus (and, for our purposes here, to the apostles within the early Church). Meier is posing the question: did the historical Jesus (and, here, we include the apostles) actually perform startling, extraordinary deeds, ones that included healings, which were considered by himself and his audience to be miracles? Or did such stories come entirely from the creative, theological imagination of the early Church? That is, could they have come from the missionary needs of the early Church that read them back into a miracle-free ministry of Jesus? Meier's questions, then, are not about whether miracles actually happened but whether what were thought to be extraordinary events did really occur, rather than comprise later, made-up stories to be used for apologetic purposes.[25] Meier, after a painstaking examination of various criteria for historicity, reaches an affirmative answer for the healing miracles of Jesus.[26] The so-called nature miracles (such as Jesus walking on the water and the changing of water into wine at Cana) are more problematic and would appear, for Meier, to be a creation of the early Church for theological purposes.[27] But at least the extraordinary events of healing, in his view, were thought by the New Testament authors to have occurred at the time. But how a particular person interprets these healing miracles now is ultimately dependent on that person's own worldview or theological stance: whether they are regarded as divinely empowered deeds outside the ordinary laws of nature; psychosomatic illnesses susceptible to such influences as hypnosis or a charismatic religious personality; or the result of some other explanation. Healings, believed to be miraculous, do stand out in the time of the infant Church as one of the characteristic means of ministering to the sick. Yet, as we shall see, pastoral care of the sick will develop a diversity of approaches according to changing ideas and practices in human history about sickness and care.

At the same time, there is a reference in the Letter of James (Jas 5:14-16) to 'elders' anointing the sick with oil and praying over them, an isolated text in the New Testament that took on increasing importance in the historical development of sacramental anointing of the sick. This anointing and accompanying prayer of faith, James tells his readers, 'will save the sick, and the Lord will raise them up; and anyone who has committed sins will be forgiven' (Jas 5:15).

Within the New Testament there is an assumption, taken from Judaism, that affliction has sin as its ultimate cause. But there is evidence of a hesitation to ascribe the immediate cause of illness in every case to personal sin, as in the case of the man born blind where Jesus states that his blindness is neither the result of his sin nor that of his parents (Jn 9:2-3).

## Almsgiving

Within Jewish piety, almsgiving was important. The respected Rabbi Hillel had a teaching: 'The more charity, the more peace'. There were two principal forms of relief offered to the poor. The *tamhkūy*, the 'poor bowl' of food, was distributed every day among wandering paupers. And there was the *quppāh*, the 'poor basket'. This was a weekly distribution to the poor consisting of both food and clothing. In all likelihood, the earliest Christians adopted these forms of welfare. Judaism had its tithe for the poor, coming from the harvest produce in certain years. And at harvest time the poor had special privileges, accorded to them by the Law, that consisted of a right to things like grapes fallen on the ground and gleanings from the crops. A curious custom that existed in Jerusalem was the placing of gifts in the 'chamber of secrets' within the Temple for those of the poor who came from good families. Their secret form of support may well have given rise to Jesus' saying about the giving of alms in secret (Mt 6:4).[28]

We know of a woman living in Jaffa named Tabitha, or Dorcas in Greek, who was noted for her untiring kindness and care of the poor. After an illness of some kind she died and Peter was sent for. A number of widows were in the house grieving over this much-loved woman. Tearfully, these women proudly showed Peter clothes Dorcas had made that, in all probability, were to be distributed among the poor. This woman was rewarded for her good deeds by being raised to life by Peter (Acts 9:36-43).

## Widows

Widows were singled out for special care. There is the story that in the Jerusalem Church there were complaints over discrimination. The Hellenists, Jews from the diaspora who had migrated to Jerusalem, complained to the native Hebrews in the Church that their widows were being overlooked in the daily distribution of alms. The situation was unfair and these women were experiencing hard times. A young Hellenist named Stephen, of whom we will hear more, was chosen among seven well-respected men within the community to attend to the food distribution to all those who were in need (Acts 6:1-6).

Over time, the care of widows seems to have become better organized in the infant Church. In the First Letter to Timothy (5:3-16), reflecting a more structured Church than we saw at Corinth, we are given a fairly detailed insight into the situation of widows. There was an approved list of widows entitled to receive support. Such women must have established for themselves a reputation for living a holy life. It was expected that a widow would devote herself to prayer and good works, especially if she had no family of her own. A widow, then, was eligible to be enrolled into some kind of special ascetic order: she had to be at least sixty years of age, to have had only one husband and to be noted for her good works. To what extent they were considered to be engaging in some form of officially recognized ministry or order remains unclear. Younger widows appear to have been regarded with some suspicion, perhaps reflecting a growing asceticism surrounding sex and marriage. It was thought the younger widows might get carried away by passion and want to remarry. In fact, this is what they were advised to do, namely, to remarry. The pastoral ruling was given that they ought not to be enrolled in the special Order of Widows lest they be condemned for being unfaithful to their original vows. Misogyny begins to creep into the pastoral directions being given about widows. These younger women, we are told, were prone to idle gossip, constant chatter and likely to meddle in other people's affairs. In fact, they were advised that it was probably better that they remarry, have children and take care of a home, lest they provoke scandal. One final point we may consider about widows emerges from this early piece of Christian writing: there may well have been too many of them relying on support from the community, stretching its resources. We are informed that those widows having relatives should be supported by them, leaving it to the community to care for the genuine needy who had no means of family support.

### The Jerusalem Church Collection

As well as assisting individuals experiencing financial hardship, there was help directed towards whole communities, a kind of corporate system of welfare. In the midst of all his problems with the Church of Corinth, Paul was concerned about finalizing efforts to raise money to help the Jerusalem Church that was in real financial difficulties. Just as he had instructed the Church in Galatia, Paul informed the members of the Church of Corinth that they were to set aside money, on the Lord's Day each week, to help the Mother Church in Jerusalem (1 Cor 16:1-4). In fact, the Jerusalem collection took place throughout the network of Churches. We know that the Churches of Galatia and Macedonia contributed generously, as well as the one in Corinth (Rom 15:26). As such, the collection indicates the mutual care and common purpose these individual, local Churches felt among themselves. Paul does not explain precisely why the Jerusalem Church is in need of special financial attention. Perhaps their hardships had resulted partly from the famine of the years 47-49. But Paul did wish to express his desire for the Gentile Churches to show solidarity with the Church in the city where the Jesus movement had first emerged within Judaism. From the Jews, the Gentiles had received great spiritual blessings. The collection expressed Gentile gratitude to the Mother Church (Rom 15:27). But Paul was only too aware that his work in helping out the Jerusalem Church was one of risk. The aid, which Paul wanted to take personally to this Church, may well be rejected. Many in that Church, whom Paul's sharp tongue calls the 'unbelievers in Judea' (Rom 15:31), saw him as an apostate from Judaism because of his lax attitude to the Jewish Law when it came to admitting Gentiles to the faith. This was the reason behind his fear that they may not accept his money. As we shall soon see, this vexed question of Jewish-Gentile relations was an issue of immense pastoral concern within this period of early Christianity.

### Slaves

Slaves would have been well represented in the early Churches. They were an everyday feature of the ancient world, usually captives from war and their offspring. People might also sell themselves into slavery to escape the insecurities of everyday life or to obtain a special job. In the Roman world they may have worked on large agricultural estates, toiled in the mines, or rowed laboriously inside the galleys. Slaves could work for the state, be assigned to the temples, work for rich families or even with those of modest income. They were thought of as little more than property but were entitled to become Roman citizens once they gained their freedom. Early Christianity lived in a world of slaves. Slavery was accepted as part of the economic and social arrangements of the time and there were no serious attempts by Christians to achieve its abolition.[29]

In keeping with his apocalyptic outlook, slavery was, for Paul, simply a present condition to be endured until the return of Christ. What is important now is union with the Lord. He writes, 'For whoever was called in the Lord as a slave is a freed person belonging to the Lord, just as whoever was free when called is a slave of Christ' (1 Cor 7:22). In his brief Letter to Philemon, Paul asked his friend to take back his slave, Onesimus, who had run away and had been staying with Paul. Slavery was of no special concern to Paul: only the way a slave ought to be treated was and that was as 'a beloved brother' (Philem 16). Paul regarded slaves as being equally one in Christ with everybody else (1 Cor 12:13; Gal 3:28). It is within this framework that Paul, a first-century Roman citizen and Jewish Christian, exercises pastoral care to a man in slavery.

## A Church Becoming Organized

As the first century progressed, the Church communities gradually became more organized. The so-called 'Pastoral Epistles' (the First and Second Letters to Timothy and the Letter to Titus) of the New Testament reflect a Church moving towards consolidation. The term 'pastoral' has been assigned to them since the eighteenth century because they deal with practical concerns of the Church: organization and ministries; ethical guidelines for different groups of people; and guidelines for dealing with false teachers. We have already seen in this literature the advice and the structures that were put in place for the care of widows. In short, these letters are about pastoral guidance and so they are of particular interest to us here.

### Leadership and Church Office

As Paul and his generation passed on and the expected return of Christ, the *parousia*, had not come about, it became increasingly necessary to formalize leadership roles within the Churches to ensure stability and organize for long-term Christian existence. Missionary expansion had now given way to the pastoral care of settled, evangelized communities. The Pastoral Letters were probably composed towards the end of the first century, a likely date being between 80 and 85.[30] Although written in the name of Paul, it is generally thought that Paul was not their author. It was not uncommon for a writer in the ancient world to use the name of some revered figure to add weight to what was being written, thus allowing the current author to stand in the tradition of the one admired. In other words, whoever wrote the Pastoral Epistles saw them as carrying on the heritage of the teachings of Paul himself.[31]

The emerging offices of leadership for the growing Churches can be found within the Pastoral Letters. Because there was a perceived lack of proper leadership in the existing communities, a group of elders known as presbyters or *presbyteroi* were to be appointed in every town (Titus 1:5-9). In this passage, and in 1 Tim 3:1-7, they appear to be identical with the *episkopoi* (the two terms appear to be interchangeable). The *episkopoi* - known also as *presbyteroi* in this text - are overseers who are not individual bishops or single leaders of particular Churches in the later sense of the term, as this office developed within the Church. We learn also that a body of elders and leaders was assisted by a group of deacons, the *diakonoi*, who were probably engaging in the tasks of practical charity on behalf of the community (1 Tim 3:8-13). It is not until Ignatius of Antioch (c.35-c.107) in the early second century that a three-fold ministry, consisting of a single monarchical bishop overseeing a group of presbyters and deacons, emerges clearly for the first time: a structure of Church ministry that was to become more solidified. Yet, there is no evidence to suggest that this structure had become the norm in all Churches by the time of Ignatius. Also, by the early second century, elders or *presbyteroi* moved from being a group sharing leadership within a Church to becoming individual leaders of smaller communities existing within a larger local Church structure.

This change, from an unstructured charismatic variety of ministries in the early Pauline Churches to a ministry of appointed leadership, evolved in different forms, according to place and time, in the early centuries of Christianity. No doubt persons perceived as being false teachers, and persecution from the Synagogue, also caused these different communities to close ranks around their community leaders, leading to a strengthening of the offices they may have held.[32]

The Jewish Synagogue had already a group of elders or *presbyteroi*, men chosen for their wisdom and often older in age. It was they who formulated Synagogue policy. Some of the early Christian communities borrowed from this Jewish model of leadership, as happened in the Jerusalem Church. Raymond Brown argues that the term *episkopos* was not only a term for secular administration, adopted by Gentile Christianity, but was found also within Jewish sectarian groups, such as the Essenes who are known to us from the Dead Sea Scrolls. There is nothing to suggest in the Pastorals, claims Brown, that these presbyter-bishops led the Eucharist or administered baptism, functions that were conferred on the single bishop or his delegate as we meet them in the writings of Ignatius of Antioch.[33] Certainly, earliest Christianity had nothing equivalent to the Jewish cultic office of priest, something that faded within Judaism itself after the Roman destruction of the Temple and its sacrificial cult in the year 70.

The Pastorals indicate that screening processes were to be used in selecting the presbyter-bishops. What was expected of these Church leaders? They were not to have been married more than once; their children had to be believers and not be a source of any kind of scandalous behavior; and they were not to be hot-tempered persons, heavy drinkers or out to make money. These leaders were expected to be devout in living holy and blameless lives (1Tim 3:1-7; Titus 1:5-9). Similar qualities were demanded of deacons (1Tim 3:8-13).

## Women

What about women? How large a place did they have in these New Testament Churches? About a quarter of the persons mentioned by name in Paul's letters are women. Many of these appear in a long list of people Paul greets at the end of his Letter to the Romans (Rom 16:1-16). They worked as missionaries, community leaders, teachers and prophets. They differed in opinion about things and some were led astray by false teaching. In all of this they were no different from men.[34]

Priscilla, and her husband Aquila, whom we have already met, supported a house church wherever they moved. Wealthy women in the first century were noted for opening their houses to different cults. House churches were at the heart of the missionary activities of early Christianity. As some women were among wealthy and prominent converts from the upper classes (Acts 17:4, 12), they opened their homes to the Church in this way. These included such women as Nympha of Laodicea (Col 4:15) and Lydia from Thyatira who engaged in the lucrative purple dye trade (Acts 16:14-15). As these house churches would have resembled clubs and associations for like-minded people that were common in first century Roman society, these well-to-do early Christian women must have developed a leadership and influence within the house churches that would have been denied them in wider society. Yet the Pastorals, at a slightly later period in time, reflect a more negative image of women. They are now unable to teach, let alone tell, a man what to do. Women, provided they live modest lives characterized by faith, love and holiness can experience salvation by having children. The wearing of jewellery and gold are to be avoided (1 Tim 2:9-15). The picture of women in the New Testament is far from being an even one. While acknowledging that we catch only glimpses of the place of women in leadership and ministry in the New Testament literature, feminist theologian Elisabeth Schüssler Fiorenza states forthrightly that these sources do show that the Christian movement in these early days '... did not espouse the love patriarchalism by which the later church adapted itself to the structures of its society.'[35]

## False Teachers

Finally, the three Pastoral Letters sound alarm at the dangers associated with the false teachers, particularly it seems with those who purvey the misleading teachings of the Jewish Circumcision party (Titus 1:10) and those engaged in what is termed 'profane chatter' (2 Tim 2:16). We shall see in the following chapter that the issue of orthodoxy will become increasingly a concern of Christianity from the second to the fourth centuries. As the infant Church became better organized, a more defined and comprehensive belief system developed. This pastoral preoccupation with right beliefs turned into a polemic, aimed at preventing harm coming to believers, for 'their talk will spread like gangrene' (2 Tim 2:17). Also to be avoided were those who proclaimed that the resurrection of the faithful had already taken place (2 Tim 2:18) and the fanatics who taught that marriage was to be forbidden (1 Tim 4:3). Teachers who mislead people in this way were thought merely to have succeeded in raising irrelevant doubts (1 Tim 1:4).

Interestingly, these three letters, in their pastoral concern for keeping their readers free from error, indicate a particular preoccupation with preserving a body of sound doctrine, 'our religion' (1 Tim 3:16). This is a phrase never found in the letters of Paul but one used widely in other religions with which Christianity was in competition as it spread throughout the ancient Mediterranean world. For Paul, on the other hand, faith meant more a relationship of trust than a body of truths.[36] It is an issue within pastoral care about which we are to hear much more in the coming centuries.

## A Church Separating from the Synagogue

Christianity began as a movement firmly within Judaism. Jesus was born into a Jewish family. He was raised within the faith of Judaism and practiced it all his life. His earliest followers before and after his death were Jews. The Christian movement, in its earliest stage of development, did not understand itself as being a new faith but saw itself more in terms of one of the many sects existing within first century Judaism: the sect of the Nazarene. Jews of the time were accustomed to tolerating a diversity of doctrinal viewpoints among themselves that formed into different groupings. Pharisees, Saducees, Zealots, Essenes all existed alongside each other. A new sect, not part of existing movements, was known by the word, *hairêsis*.[37] The earliest followers of Jesus within Judaism would have been covered by this term and allowed to debate their points of view within the synagogues. Yet the drift towards a separation came early as large numbers of Gentiles in the diaspora entered the ranks of the Church. It could be argued that the most pressing pastoral concern of first-century Christianity was whether living out belief in the risen Christ continued to be a Jewish phenomenon or whether the adherents of this movement were part of something entirely new and distinct. It took time, but not a lot of time, to sort out, as both internal and external factors came into play. Pastoral care, at this time, was very much about settling policies on the matter and then assisting Jewish and Gentile Christ believers to live in unity. The New Testament writings can be understood only against this background, one that was often a source of bitter dispute between the different parties involved within earliest Christianity.

### Stephen and the Hellenists

The story of Stephen, narrated by Luke in the seventh chapter of the book of Acts, is the first indication of a discontinuity developing between Judaism and the Jesus followers. Luke has embellished the story to suit his apologetic purpose. Stephen's speech, as we have it, is largely, no doubt, a reconstruction of the event. True, Stephen speaks as a Jew and does nothing to attack the Jewish Law. But there is a radical shift of thinking that takes place in this incident bringing Stephen into conflict with official Judaism that leads to his martyrdom, the first major persecution of the infant Church. The story illustrates well the tension between two groups of Jews in Jerusalem: the more traditional Hebrews and the Hellenist Jews from the diaspora for whom Judaism had been broadened by the influence of a foreign, Greek culture and language. Stephen belonged to the Hellenist party. Now there appears to have been disquiet among the Hellenists because so many of their members, perhaps some of their best young people, were becoming active followers of the sect of the Nazarene. Stephen was among them and had come to prominence for his youthful enthusiastic spirit of evangelism for the cause. He seems to have seized upon that element of Jesus' teaching that downplayed the importance of the Temple. For Greek-speaking Hellenist Jews from the diaspora, such talk by this young man must have been unsettling and provocative. One of the reasons why Hellenist Jews migrated to Jerusalem was to be part of the Temple cult. For most Jews living in Jerusalem at the time, the Temple was of great economic, political and religious significance in their lives. Stephen's speech was one that emphasized the rejection of the Temple as the focal point of God's presence. It is easy, then, to understand why he was quickly disposed of by stoning. We are told Paul, or Saul, as he was then known, entirely approved of Stephen's demise.

The breach between Judaism and Christianity had started. It was also the beginning of the process of translating and interpreting the gospel into Greek terms, something that would become more prominent in the doctrinal disputes concerning Jesus and the Trinity in the following two centuries leading to the formulation of the Creeds. And it is possible that, as a result of Stephen's death, a theology of Jesus' death first began to be formulated where it was seen as a sacrifice replacing the Temple sacrifices.[38] Luke does appear to have modeled his account of Stephen's death upon that of Jesus. It was in Antioch, notes Luke, where the name 'Christian' first appeared. The term distinguished this group as Jews who welcomed Gentiles and whose faith centered on Jesus as the Christ (Acts 11:26).

To assist us now in further understanding the breach which developed between Christianity and Judaism, we shall consider Judaism under four heads; these will correspond to early, first-century (CE) Judaism's four pillars, namely, monotheism, the Covenant, the Law, and the Jerusalem Temple and sacrifice. All four would lead to troubles with those Jews who followed Jesus.

### Judaism's 'Four Pillars'

### 1. Monotheism

The first pillar of first-century CE Judaism was monotheism, that is, belief in only the one God, named Yahweh. This belief separated Judaism from other religions of the Roman Empire. Polytheism characterized the life of the Greco-Roman world. It led to syncretism throughout the Roman Empire: different local or national gods could be thought of as manifestations of one and the same divine being. The Greek Zeus and the Roman Jupiter, for example, were thought of as the same god. It was a belief system that enabled the Romans to incorporate and unify defeated nations by absorbing their local gods into the syncretistic whole of the empire. It was a policy adopted earlier by Alexander the Great.[39] Judaism was special in its commitment to belief in one God who alone could be worshiped. Jews did give recognition to other immortal beings, greater in power than human beings, existing somewhere between themselves and the one true God. These were named angels, cherubim and seraphim. Yet only the one creator God could be worshiped who had shown the Jewish people special favor in their history, what would be considered an audacious claim by anybody who was not Jewish.[40]

John's Gospel, in particular, provides us with a clear picture of difficulties concerning Jewish monotheism within early Christianity. John was the last of the four Gospels to have been written, most probably in the late 80s or 90s, with editorial work done on it sometime around the year 100. Its theology of Jesus is what is often called 'high christology' stressing the divine side of Jesus' nature, much more so than the Synoptic Gospels of Matthew, Mark and Luke. Raymond Brown has provided us with a fascinating possible reconstruction of the Johannine community with whom this Gospel and the three New Testament Letters of John are associated.[41] Brown divides the Johannine literature into four phases.

The first phase, up to the 70s or 80s, precedes the writing of the Gospel but shapes its way of thinking. A fairly standard group of Jews in or near Palestine accepted Jesus as Messiah. But there was also a group of Jews who joined them with an anti-Temple bias who had been successful in making converts in Samaria (Jn 4), a Jewish region in tension with the Jerusalem Temple. These people understood Jesus as having been with God, whom he had seen and whose word he had brought down to the world. They had a pre-existent, high christology, reflected strongly in the opening Prologue of the Gospel (Jn 1:1-18). Their ideas led to conflict with Jews who saw these Christians in John's Church as virtually abandoning monotheism by making a second god out of Jesus (Jn 5:18). The leaders of this Jewish faction expelled the Johannine Christians from the synagogues (Jn 9:22, 16:2). The Gospel narrative, as we now have it, reads back into Jesus' life these later conflicts experienced by John's Church, a literary characteristic of all four Gospels. These Christian Jewish people, now thrown out of their synagogues, became most antagonistic towards 'the Jews', a term that has now taken on hostile meaning as it is used throughout the Fourth Gospel, especially within the Passion account.

In phase two of the life of this particular Church, writes Brown, John's Gospel was written. As 'the Jews' had proven themselves to be blind and unbelieving (Jn 12:37-40), the entry of Greeks into the Church was welcomed, being seen as part of God's plan of fulfillment (Jn 12:20-23). All, or just part of the community, may well have moved to the diaspora, possibly Ephesus, which, in a tradition, became associated with John and Jesus' mother, Mary. The rejection experienced by these Johannine Christians led them to view 'the Jews' and 'the world' as opposed to Jesus. Their Gospel's one-sided emphasis on Jesus' divine, pre-existent nature, shaped by their conflict with the Synagogue leaders, resulted in their need to stress the commandment of Jesus to love one another (Jn 13:14; 15:12, 17) that is such a characteristic of John's Gospel.

Brown, continuing his reconstruction, suggests that the First and Second Letters of John were written in the third phase of this Church's life (c.100). The community seems to have split in two. One faction is represented by the author of the First and Second Letters of John (another writer distinct from the evangelist) who completed the Fourth Gospel's message by balancing its view of Jesus as divine with a stress on the humanity of Jesus who came in the flesh and taught us how to live. The other group, by way of contrast, maintained an exaggerated emphasis on Jesus' divinity, to the point of questioning the importance of his humanity. This latter group were accused of believing Jesus' humanity, and their own human behavior, to be of little importance to their faith. This group was seen as the anti-Christ in the First and Second Letters of John.

In the fourth and final phase of the life of this disturbed community, the Third Letter of John was written, according to Brown's reconstruction. The fracturing of the Johannine Church led to the development of pastoral structures and resulted in the inclusion of those who were prepared to balance their belief in Christ's human nature with that of his divine nature. Those who continued to maintain the more extreme views concerning the divinity of Jesus in all probability drifted off into the heresies of Docetism (Jesus is not truly human) and Gnosticism (the world is not of God's creation). As such, the Johannine Church was able to come into closer communion with the Christian Church as a whole and preserve for it the high christology tradition of John's Gospel.

Brown has provided us with a brilliant interpretation of how elements of earliest Christianity may have come into conflict with Jewish monotheism. Christological controversy would continue to dog believers until it was resolved in the great councils of the Church, especially that of Nicaea in 325.

John's treatment of 'the Jews' also needs to be situated within the context of a changing Judaism. In the year 70, the Romans had torched Jerusalem and obliterated the Temple. The country was in ruins after the Zealots had failed in their violent resistance tactics. Around the end of the first century, John's Church - as we see it reflected in the Fourth Gospel - coincided with that period when the Rabbinic Council had gathered at Yavneh (Jamnia) under the leadership of Yohanan ben Zakkai and Gamaliel II. Their task had been to reconstruct Judaism without a Temple cult, something that had been so central to its religious life. They did this by making the Torah the central feature of Jewish religious life and increased the importance of the Synagogue where the Law could be learnt, discussed and prayed. It is highly probable that John's pejorative use of the term 'the Jews' reflects a local Jewish leadership sympathetic to the aims of the Yavnean rabbis who were in a desperate struggle to keep Judaism alive in very different and difficult circumstances.

They saw themselves as the only true and legitimate heirs to pre-70 Judaism. Dissident groups within Judaism, such as the Christians, were distrusted, opposed and persecuted. They threatened too much the fragile state of Judaism at this time. John's Church experienced at first hand this situation and hence its efforts to denounce 'the Jews', depicted as being primarily responsible for Jesus' death in the Fourth Gospel's Passion narrative. In reading John's Gospel one sees a bitter and deadly contest between the followers of Jesus and 'the Jews'.[42]

So much had circumstances changed that, by the middle of the second century, Justin was defending Jewish Christians against Gentile Christians.[43] The latter were desirous of excluding from the Church those who were still engaged in Jewish practices including circumcision, dietary rules, and observance of the Sabbath and Jewish festivals. This group of Jewish Christians, who a century earlier had sat in judgment on Gentile believers, had now become a marginalized minority and, what Henry Chadwick has called, 'bizarre deviationists'.[44]

## 2. The Covenant

The Covenant, Israel's election, was the second of the four great foundational pillars of Judaism at this time. It, too, was to contribute to 'the parting of the ways'. Judaism believed Israel to have been singled out by God. God gave this people his special care provided they worshiped God alone and obeyed God's laws. This agreement was known as the Covenant. This is what set Israel apart from other nations. Other people might show interest in becoming part of the chosen race, provided they were accepted into this community of God's people and accepted God's Law. Such sympathizers were not uncommon but there was no great evangelistic outreach on the part of Judaism in the time of the New Testament.

Once Paul and his fellow missionaries began accepting large numbers of Gentiles into the Church, a real strain was placed upon the Jewish interpretation of the Covenant election. Later Jewish thinking did develop ideas along the lines of apocalyptic universalism (Isa 66:18-24). But what Paul was doing in the diaspora Churches went far beyond this way of seeing things. Paul's answer to his critics, developed most fully in his Letter to the Romans, was simple. He did not want to merge Jew and Gentile - something impossible to do, as ethnic identity cannot be changed. In this context, James Dunn offers some insight into the significance of Paul's use of words. The terms 'Jew' and 'Judaism', in Paul's thinking, emphasize ethnic and religious distinction. Paul, to justify his apostolate to the Gentiles, switches terms and uses instead the word 'Israel'. A 'Jew' is defined primarily by relation to land, and this is ethnicity. This differentiates him or her from peoples of other lands. The term 'Israel', on the other hand, is something different. The word 'Israel' is defined primarily by relation to God. What is at stake here, claims Dunn, is the identity of Paul's Gentile Churches. The theological task is to understand who is 'Israel'. Paul does this by including Gentiles within the word 'Israel':

> For if the function of 'Israel' as a name is to identify primarily by relation to God and to God's choice, and not by differentiation from other nations and races, then the issue of whether Gentiles can be included may be resolved on quite a different basis. Strictly speaking, it is not possible to include 'Greeks' within 'Jews'; that is simply a confusion of identifiers. But it might be possible to include 'Gentiles' within 'Israel'. And this in effect is what Paul attempts to do in Romans 9-11.[45]

But, in the long run, it was not to work. Christianity, while acknowledging its Jewish roots, was to separate and move away. And, as we have seen in John's Gospel, anti-Semitism was never far from the surface. The consequences for humanity, as we so well know, would be horrific.

### 3. The Law

The third pillar of Judaism was the Law, known as the Torah, given to God's people through Moses as part of the Covenant. Obedience to God's Law, as written in the first five books of the Jewish Scriptures (the Pentateuch), was the means of living within the Covenant. A characteristic feature of the Law was circumcision that identified the male Jew. Tacitus (c.55-c.117) wrote: 'They adopted circumcision to distinguish themselves from other peoples by this difference.'[46] There was also the Sabbath observance, the holy day, a distinctively Jewish institution that was understood to be part of creation (Gen 2:2-3). And there were the dietary regulations about which Jews could be so scrupulous.

Paul was not against the Law as such. His argument, expressed so forcefully in his two Letters to the Galatians and to the Romans, was about what the Law required. His arguments are complex. For Paul, the Law had to be understood in terms of faith in Christ by which a human being relates to God. People had misused the Law, in Paul's view, and this had led to unfortunate consequences. The Law merely exposes human weakness but can do nothing about it. Instead of seeing the Law as a guide for our actions, it had become an end in itself, as a way of establishing a right standing with God. It was as if one could earn God's favor. The Law reveals human sinfulness but can really do nothing about it. It is Christ alone who can save us because he has destroyed death through his resurrection. As such, he has conquered sin. The only way out of sin, argued Paul, was by faith in the power of Christ to save us.

Paul's acceptance of Gentiles into the Church and his attitude to the Law, particularly over circumcision, came to a head at the Council of Jerusalem in the year 49. It is described well in Acts 15:1-35 and Gal 2:1-10. It was to be the first major turning point of the Church, affecting so decisively its future direction. What led to circumcision becoming a major dispute at this time in the early growth of the Christian branch within Judaism during the late 40s? In earlier years some Gentiles had been accepted into this new Jewish movement of those who followed the Nazarene called Jesus. For example, Peter accepted Cornelius into the movement without requiring him to be circumcised (Acts 10). Peter had been called to justify this action before the strict Jewish party of followers in Jerusalem who had been initially scandalized by his behavior. Peter succeeded in winning them over to his point of view (Acts 11:1-18). But uncircumcised Gentiles were being welcomed into the Church in great numbers in the diaspora, alarming the Jerusalem Church. As well, the political situation in Judea was becoming more unsettled with the forceful tactics of the occupying Romans. The Emperor Caligula (37-41) tried to have a statue of himself placed in the Jerusalem Temple, a blasphemous deed in the eyes of the Jews.[47] The pressure was building to make no concessions to any kind of innovation that threatened Jewish religious and national identity. Any relaxation on circumcision, the sign of God's Covenant with Israel, could expect opposition. The Circumcision party in Jerusalem, as they were known, feared that the Christian movement to which they belonged would become almost entirely Gentile - with only a loose relationship with mainstream Judaism - if key elements of the Torah were abandoned. The matter had to be settled and Paul, accompanied by his two staunch supporters, Barnabas and Titus, traveled to Jerusalem to put forward their case at this first major assembly of Christians.

Like any meeting attempting to resolve a dispute, politics was at work. The Circumcision party, especially those among them who were converted Pharisees for whom the Torah was so important, wanted to keep to the strict demands of the observance of the Law and insisted that the Gentile converts would have to be circumcised. On the opposing side of the debate was Paul who had been so successful in his mission to the Gentiles and who was not prepared to see this threatened by the conservative group in Jerusalem. Peter was known to be able to go either way in this dispute. By temperament, he was prone to vacillate, as demonstrated by his changing behavior in association with Gentile believers in observing the Law (Acts 10:28; 11:1-18). James, the leader of the Jerusalem Church, was the key player. His word would carry weight. After hearing all the arguments from the different interest groups, Paul's persuasiveness won the day. Circumcision was not required of Gentile converts. It was a decision, not realized by those who made it, that would result in Christianity becoming, in a short space of time, a religion separate from and alien to Judaism. But there was some compromise insofar as the observance of certain Jewish dietary laws was expected of Gentiles. But, as we know, this demand would not last.

### 4. The Jerusalem Temple and Sacrifice

The fourth and final great pillar of Judaism had been the Jerusalem Temple and the sacrificial cult that took place there. Before its destruction by the Romans in the year 70 - having been completed only seven years earlier - the Jewish Temple was an impressive structure. Its walls of stone rose to a height of a hundred feet, as tall as a modern ten-storey building. There was only one Temple and here God was believed to dwell among God's people. The Temple was divided into different courts according to who was allowed to enter them. It was the center of political power within Judaism. Especially powerful were the High Priests and their high priestly families. The Sanhedrin exercised a wide range of executive and legislative powers endorsed by the Romans. The Temple tax was imposed upon every adult, male Jew. The thousands of pilgrims drawn to the Temple at the time of the great feasts, especially Passover, ensured that the Temple remained the financial center of the nation.

It was the daily cult of sacrifice that was central to the life of the Temple. One can imagine the smell of roasting animal flesh that constantly filled the air of the holy city. In their religious role within the sacrificial cult of Jerusalem, the priests acted in their capacity of slaughtering and butchering the animals. The Temple resembled an abattoir. The altar, dripping with blood, was the place where the sacrifices were offered. Temple worship was, indeed, a bloody and messy affair.

There were different kinds of sacrifice. The holocaust was that in which the entire victim was burnt and belonged entirely to God. Nothing was given back to the priests or worshipers, except the skin of the animal. Communion sacrifices were different. In this case, the priest and the people offering the sacrifice shared in the eating of the cooked animal and, in doing so, were believed to be taking part in a meal with God. Participants in the communion sacrifices had to be in a state of ritual purity. There were also sacrifices to expiate sin. Of particular importance, in this case, was the annual feast day, the Day of Atonement. Vegetable sacrificial offerings might consist of unbaked wheaten flower mixed with olive oil. Finally, there was the sacrificial offering of incense in the Temple.[48] This elaborate and large-scale ritual all ended, never to be revived, with the destruction of the Temple by the Roman army less than forty years after the Christian movement had begun.

After the destruction of the Temple, Judaism had to reconstitute itself without a sacrificial cult that previously had been so central to its life. As we saw happen with the reforms of the rabbis at Yavneh, the Torah became the central feature of Jewish life centered upon the Synagogue. This led to the teachings of the Mishnah, published in about the year 200, which itself formed the basis of the Talmud. Judaism developed its identity without a geographic or cultic basis. As for the Christians in the Jerusalem Church, they continued to worship in the Temple after their conversion (Acts 2:46; 3:1; 5:12, 21, 42). With the destruction of the Temple, there were consequences for both the Jewish and Gentile Christians as well as for Jews themselves. This fourth pillar of ancient Judaism was given a new theological meaning within the Church.

The ritual meal of the Eucharist, as practiced by the early Christians, increasingly took on a sacrificial interpretation. Paul instructed his Church at Corinth about this matter of the Eucharist as a sacrificial ritual within the context of the abuses that had been going on there when they gathered to share the Lord's Supper (1 Cor 11:23-27). As such, the Eucharist came to be seen as providing Christians with a ritual distinct from the communion sacrifices carried out in the Temple. As Christians loosened their bonds with Judaism, Christ came to be understood, through his death on the cross, to be the one and only priest offering his life in a single sacrifice that had made an end to all other sacrifices. These sacrificial ideas about Christ are theologized most fully in the New Testament Letter to the Hebrews, perhaps written to a group of Jewish Christians who had fled into exile and who were nostalgically longing for Temple worship as it existed before the Temple was razed in the Jewish War against the Romans. These new Christian beliefs concerning a reinterpretation of the Temple and its sacrifices, as we can see, were yet a further element contributing to Christianity's gradual separation from Judaism, hastened by the historical event of the destruction of the Temple itself. Christianity was about to enter a new phase by challenging and then, remarkably, overcoming the state. Such conditions resulted in the Church having to sharpen its self-understanding by redefining its identity and beliefs. New pastoral concerns arose to meet these new circumstances.

# Chapter 2

# Martyrs, Sinners and Heretics

## Christians under Persecution

Whereas the earliest Christians faced hostility from the Synagogue when they wrestled with the issue of establishing a distinct and separate religious identity, new generations of Christians faced a far more dangerous and deadly foe in the Roman State. Judaism enjoyed the privilege of freedom of religion within the Roman Empire insofar as Jews were exempt from the requirement of having to worship the Roman gods. Christianity, once it severed its ties with Judaism, enjoyed no such privilege. The age of martyrs had begun.

Such a situation posed new and difficult challenges for pastoral care. Beginning in the latter part of the first century and continuing throughout the second, third and early fourth centuries, pastoral care was characterized by the task of assisting Christians to persevere in their faith in the midst of violent opposition and threat of death. Pastoral care, in these centuries, aimed at strengthening the faith of men and women who lived in dangerous times. And certainly it would also have been about comforting believers who had lost family and friends in the terror. And, as we shall see, there was the problem of what to do about Christians who proved weak in time of trial and succumbed to the demands of pagan worship. Should they be forgiven and welcomed back into the life of the community after a suitable penance, or should they be kept permanently apart? This latter issue was to cause bitter feelings among Christians and a pastoral response by the Church leadership had to be found. Not everyone was prepared to become a martyr.

### Christians Violating the Roman Laws

The Romans believed that the gods were the guardians of Rome, responsible for its security and well-being. Failure to give them their proper honor, through rites of worship, could bring disaster upon Rome. The safety of the empire depended upon keeping them appeased. This was best done by sacrificial offerings. Such rituals might be as simple as the pious offering of a little food or wine upon a god's shrine in the home, to an elaborate sacrificial cult, like the slaughter of great numbers of oxen upon the altar of Jupiter overlooking the Roman Forum. Belief in the gods was at the heart of the Roman State. Christians, in their refusal to recognize these gods, were seen to threaten the established political order that kept Rome together. As such, they were attacking the *pax deorum*, the peace that the gods brought to the empire. Their rejection of the gods, in favor of the Christ figure, was perceived as subversive, threatening to destabilize the order of the empire itself. Tertullian (c.160-c.225) once remarked sarcastically: 'If the Tiber rises too high or the Nile too low, the cry is "The Christians to the lion".'[1] The problem, then, was not that the Christians claimed a new god. Rome had a pantheon of gods. One more would make no difference. The difficulty was that the Christians refused to recognize any of the gods other than their own. They isolated themselves from the popular religious festivals of the state and, when the pressure came from different emperors, refused outright to participate in the pagan cults. From the Roman pagan point of view, they were atheists in regard to the state religion. Other factors were involved that led to Christians becoming a despised group throughout the empire. As their meetings were often held at night and in seclusion, all kinds of wild rumors circulated about them, such as accusations of cannibalism associated with their eucharistic meal. Separating themselves from the cults, they were regarded with suspicion.

### History of the Persecutions

The first violent persecution of Christians occurred in Rome as early as 64 when, according to Tacitus, the Emperor Nero (54-68) made them a scapegoat for the terrible fire that devastated much of the city. Christians, being a generally despised minority group, were an easy target.[2] In the first century, trouble broke out again for the Christians under Domitian (81-96) who introduced compulsory emperor worship. By the early second century Christians were becoming more widely known and loathed by much of the populace. Pliny (c.61-c.113), governor of Bithynia in Asia Minor, was unsure how to deal with them. Christianity seemed to have spread widely in his province. Meat that had been initially sacrificed to the gods had become difficult to sell later in the markets. Pliny was approached to see what he could do about this troublesome group of people who were affecting even the local economy. Apart from superstitious beliefs, he found nothing too disturbing about this new religious sect that he claimed was attracting every class of people. He sought guidance from the emperor as to how to deal with Christians. Trajan

(98-117) cautioned his governor against responding too harshly to the situation.[3] Persecution came in waves and was far worse in the eastern parts of the empire.

What seems to have surprised the Romans about the Christians was the way in which they seemed unafraid of death. Lucian (c.120-d.after 180), an educated pagan, observed: 'The poor wretches have convinced themselves, first and foremost, that they are going to be immortal and live forever, in consequence of which they despise death and even willingly give themselves over to arrest.'[4]

A particularly bloody measure against dissident Christians was meted out in Lyons in 177. Among other reasons for it, it was an attempt to cut costs in staging the public games in the arena. Gladiators had to be provided at some expense to the local nobility. To save money in having to employ such professional warriors, condemned criminals - such as Christians - began to be used in their place.[5] But systematic measures of persecution did not begin until the third century when the situation deteriorated badly and Christianity had spread widely throughout the empire.

In the year 249 things went very wrong for Christians. Emperor Decius (249-51) issued an edict ordering everyone throughout the empire, except the Jews, to make sacrifice to the gods on appointed days. People were issued with special certificates by the authorities to indicate they had done so. The Decian persecution was violent but of short duration. But, as we shall see, the certificates authenticating an individual's worship of the Roman gods would prove to be a source of great unrest in the life of many third-century Christian communities. Valerian (253-60) and Gallienus (253-68), joint emperors, had policies of persecution. But worse was to follow under Diocletian (284-305) who had the aim of exterminating Christianity entirely by a well-organized plan of persecution that was implemented in stages. Christian leaders were the first to be targeted.

But then came the long awaited turning point. Galerius (305-11) ended Christian persecution with his Edict of Toleration, proclaimed in 311. In doing so, the dying emperor asked the Christians to pray to their God on his behalf. Galerius died a week later. The privilege of toleration, given to Judaism since the first century BCE, was now extended to Christianity.

### Constantine and the Edict of Milan

Events were moving rapidly for both the empire and the growing numbers of Christians within it. Constantine (d.337) had been proclaimed emperor in 306 at York by his troops. In 312 he crossed the Alps with the intention of seizing power from his rival, Maxentius (306-12). At the Battle of the Milvian Bridge in that same year, he defeated Maxentius outside Rome and established himself as joint emperor. Constantine had a dream the night before the battle to fight under the sign of the Cross. Following his success, he attributed his military victory to the Christian God. In 313, at Nicomedia, the Edict of Milan was issued in the joint names of the two emperors, Constantine and Licinius (308-24). It proclaimed a policy of benevolence towards Christians and all other faiths. The right of Christians to freedom of worship was assured and their property handed back. The age of martyrdom was over. Not only were Christians free. Constantine embarked on a policy of uniting Christianity with the state. From being a persecuted minority, Christianity became the imperial religion that was to sweep away paganism. In the year 330, Constantine moved his capital to the East, to Constantinople, the site of the old Greek city of Byzantium where a new center of the Christian faith would coexist with imperial rule. Rome was no longer the seat of secular authority, the vacuum to be filled by the religious and temporal power of the popes. The imperial transfer of authority to the site of Constantinople, on the Bosphorus, would soon lead to religious and political tension with the western part of the empire, especially with the Roman Church.

With persecution ended, Christians came to venerate the martyrs at their tombs and, through preservation of martyrs' human remains, came the cult of martyrs. The appeal of the tomb-shrine of the martyr-saints spread rapidly around the Mediterranean world and became one of the characteristic features of Christian antiquity, taking on increasing importance in the medieval Church. Christians believed that the saint in heaven was also, in some spiritual form, present at his or her tomb and could intercede before God for the believer's salvation.[6] Christians sought pastoral care from the dead as well as from the living.

### The Martyrdom of Perpetua

During the period of persecution a pastoral literature grew up describing the Christ-like sufferings and deaths of the martyrs. Such stories had the purpose of edifying Christians in the face of their own trials and helping them interpret martyrdom as a way of participating in the sacrifice of Christ on the cross. As such, the martyr was assured of an immediate place in heaven, a 'baptism by blood'. The writer of the *Martyrdom of Polycarp* states they 'were no longer men but already angels'.[7] So the martyrs did not just die bravely for a cause. The martyrs also became identified with the redemptive power of Christ's sacrificial death on Calvary. Their loyalty, confidence and endurance, as told through heroic stories, served as a powerful pastoral aid in helping Christians live out their faith in whatever circumstances.

One of the best known of these stories of martyrdom, probably part historical, part legendary, is that of Perpetua, recorded in the *Acts of Perpetua and Felicitas*. Joyce Salisbury's translation and enthralling commentary on the text introduces us to the perilous world of the early Christian martyrs.[8] Perpetua, along with a small number of North African Christians, was martyred in the arena at Carthage on 7 March 203, during the persecution of Septimius Severus (193-211). She was twenty-two, newly married, with an infant son. Accompanying Perpetua to her death was her Christian slave girl, Felicitas; another slave, called Revocatus; two men, named Saturninus and Secundulus; and a catechumen known as Saturus. They were all young people. The story of their martyrdom was recorded by an anonymous Christian from North Africa. It is allegedly based on Perpetua's own words kept in her diary while in prison.

The story, written in a clear and engaging style, allows us to enter the terrifying world of the martyr and catch something of the fearless faith that so inspired these women and men in their willingness to die for their beliefs. As well, we are introduced to something of the nature of pastoral care in the age of the martyrs.

We are not told of the circumstances that led to the arrest of Perpetua. Her first concern was for her young son whom she passed into the care of her mother and brother. Like any mother, Perpetua yearned for the presence of her child and requested that he be allowed to remain with her in prison, and this wish was granted: 'My prison had suddenly become a palace.' Perpetua's father was greatly concerned for her welfare and did all he could to persuade her to renounce her defiant stance against the state religion but she refused, noting how her father 'left me in great sorrow'. Persecution, as we can see, brought terrible pain and division within family life.

We know from the work of Tertullian, *To the Martyrs*, that the Church offered two forms of practical, pastoral help to people in prison held on charges of refusing to engage in pagan worship. First, there were funds held on behalf of the whole community to make life more comfortable for Christians in prison. Second, individual Christians gave from their own resources to help their brothers and sisters in the Lord in such circumstances. It was part of the Church's pastoral care of almsgiving. Such pastoral assistance was given to Perpetua and her imprisoned companions by two deacons of the Carthaginian Church, Tertius and Pomponius. As was customary, they bribed the guards to allow Perpetua and the other Christians to be able to go to a better part of the prison for a few hours to refresh themselves.

The time had come for Perpetua's public trial before the proconsul, Hilarianus. Her father was distraught and made one last desperate appeal: 'Perform the sacrifice – have pity on your baby.' Perpetua called on the deacon Pomponius to assist her by going to her father and bringing her child back into the prison. Her father refused this final request of his daughter. Family ties had now been strained to the limit by Perpetua's religious intransigence. Perpetua faithfully recorded all these events in her diary. But the bulk of her account consists of her visionary dreams while in prison. Dreams had importance in antiquity as they do in much modern psychology. The dream was considered prophetic and the dreams of future martyrs were especially valued and interpreted.

Commenting upon the text describing Perpetua's martyrdom, Salisbury notes that tensions would have mounted as the time of the killing of the Christians in the arena drew near.[9] Highly superstitious Carthaginians would have been uncertain as to how much magic these Christians possessed, something that could ruin the anticipated violent spectacle of the entertainment to be staged. Realizing this, the tribune ordered their amenities within the prison restricted for fear they might escape.

Perpetua again sought to improve her situation in prison. On the night before her death she requested of the tribune that her brothers, and others, be permitted to visit her and her companions and to dine with them. Shrewdly and ironically she pleads: 'For we are the most distinguished of the condemned prisoners; seeing that we belong to the emperor, we are to fight on his very birthday. Would it not be to your credit if we are brought forth on the day in a healthier condition?' The tribune agreed.

We are then led into the conversations that took place among these Christians as to what they could expect. Saturninus bravely 'insisted that he wanted to be exposed to all the different beasts, so that his crown might be all the more glorious'. But Saturus, the catechumen, showed less bravado. He 'dreaded nothing more than a bear, and he counted on being killed by one bite of a leopard'.

Whereas bears dragged and slowly ripped apart their victims, big cats such as the leopard stunned their prey with a single blow and effectively killed them with one bite.

Carthage had a large arena for the public games, second in size to the Colosseum in Rome, which held about thirty thousand people. Before the vast mob screaming for blood and excitement, Perpetua faced her awful death. She had been sentenced to die in the games planned for birthday celebrations honoring the family of Septimius Severus. Such brutal spectacles to entertain the populace were considered religious events dedicated to the gods. Tertullian had warned Christians not to attend them because this would constitute an act of idolatry.[10] But it seems many went anyway.

The parade of condemned criminals from the prison to the arena was filled with pageantry and had all the elements of a Roman *pompa*. But the Christians, including Perpetua, provided something novel to bemuse the crowd. They marched into the amphitheater joyfully as if they were going to heaven. Part of the customary ritual was to dress the condemned in liturgical costumes of the gods. Perpetua, acting as spokesperson for the Christians about to die, announced that they refused to wear the pagan costumes of the priests of Saturn and the priestesses of Ceres, popular gods in Carthage. Again a tribune was obliging and waived the ritual on this occasion.

Perpetua and her slave girl, Felicitas, were led naked into the arena enmeshed in a net, to the sound of roars from the crowd. But even this hardened mob were shocked at seeing these young women in such a state. As a result, they were permitted to be clothed in unbelted tunics.

Animals could be unpredictable in their response within the arena. Sometimes they could refuse to attack. So they were often starved the night before the games or even especially trained to devour humans. This can be seen in a North African mosaic depicting a condemned man being wheeled in a small chariot towards a big cat with a trainer using whips to control the beast.[11]

A wild heifer was released within the arena and charged towards Perpetua and Felicitas, tossing the two women around mercilessly. Seeing her brother and other Christians in the stands witnessing the horror, she screamed out to them to remain firm in their faith. Saturus had his wish granted in being killed from a leopard's bite, but he did not die as quickly as he had hoped. He was drenched in blood with the crowd roaring in approval: 'Well washed! Well washed!' Unconscious, a gladiator cut his throat to finish him off. Amidst the bloody mayhem we are told that the martyrs kissed one another with the Christian ritual of peace. Perpetua was the last to die. Unfortunately for her, the young gladiator proved nervous and inexperienced and, while attempting to cut her throat, hit a bone instead. Screaming in pain, she grabbed his knife and guided it to her throat, interpreted subsequently as a gesture of her free embrace of death.

Not all martyrs faced their death so publicly in the amphitheater in the gladiatorial games and wild beast shows. Many met their deaths through other means, such as beheading, crucifixion, strangulation or being put to the sword. Many Christians charged for refusal to take part in the official cult of the empire simply remained imprisoned and might be lucky enough to be freed after completing their sentence.

### Martyrdom Literature

We can do no more than imagine and attempt to reconstruct the nature of pastoral care in the age of the martyrs within early Christianity. Pastoral care must surely have been very much about visiting the condemned in the prisons to ease their burdens in whatever ways possible, as the deacons Tertius and Pomponius did for Perpetua, and to comfort them and pray with them before meeting their death. But one distinctive feature of pastoral care in the age of martyrs that we do know about in some detail was the Church's use of letters, homilies and other forms of exhortation to boost the morale and faith of the martyrs and the wider Church of which they were part. The martyrdom literature within the earlier patristic period describes the ordeals suffered by martyrs, such as Perpetua and her companions, as well as theologizing on the meaning of martyrdom and instructing Christians on how they ought to respond in faith to the threat of persecution. Such literature, often in the form of letters, had a definite pastoral function. It aimed at helping Christians who were facing the threat of martyrdom to keep firm in their faith; to comfort those who had lost family and friends in the persecutions; and to assist Christian communities situate their experience of oppression within the larger plan of salvation in Christ their Savior.

Tertullian wrote an encouraging letter, *To the Martyrs*. It was addressed to imprisoned Christians in Carthage in 202. Attempting to boost their spirits, Tertullian contrasted the world 'which has the greater darkness, blinding hearts' with the seclusion of the prison. There they have greater liberty to pray, for, as the Gospels state, Christ himself sought seclusion for this purpose.

Cyprian (d.258), some fifty years later, wrote a letter, *On Facing Martyrdom*, to a later generation of North African Christians facing the Decian persecution. From this letter we learn that those imprisoned had the daily opportunity to receive the Eucharist, presumably brought to them by other members of the Christian community. As we learn from Perpetua's story, permission for entry into prison by outsiders seemed easy enough to obtain. Cyprian's letter, attempting to strengthen believers facing the prospect of martyrdom, contains some of the more common themes of pastoral advice and teaching within this kind of writing. Such themes include: remaining strong in faith despite the fear of physical torture and death; rejoicing in death; following Christ in his sufferings; interpreting martyrdom as receiving the victor's crown and assured entrance into heaven; interpreting martyrdom as an athletic contest or battlefield that allows the opportunity of victory; understanding the persecutors to be the Antichrist; and warnings to those unwilling to give their lives freely for Christ. This form of pastoral writing, arising out of a Church where great numbers of its members faced the likelihood of long imprisonment or violent death, was a bold effort to bring consolation and hope for those living in extreme times. Cyprian himself was to end his life as a martyr in 258. His death is recounted in the *Acts of Cyprian*.

Origen (*c*.185-*c*.254), another North African of the third century, was born into a Christian family in Alexandria and became a brilliant scholar. His writings attempt to interpret the teachings of Christianity in a way intelligible to thoughtful and educated pagans. He could be called a Christian Platonist. His instructions to the catechumens of Alexandria, an important feature of pastoral life in the early Church, became well known. His speculative turn of mind did not allow him to draw easy conclusions. Origen represents one of the earliest attempts at a coherent synthesis of the Christian faith.[12] Origen's views of martyrdom, prayer, and Scripture merge into a single vision of the Christian life as a movement toward perfect knowledge of God and perfect union with God through Christ.[13]

Because his own father, Leonidas, suffered martyrdom along with some of his students, Origen could write about this subject in later life in a very personal way. His *Exhortation to Martyrdom* was composed during a persecution of Maximinus (235-38). The exhortation is addressed personally to Ambrose and Protoctetus, a priest and a deacon respectively. As with other martyrdom literature, Origen's principal concern is that these two ministers of the Church remain committed to their faith, a faith being tested in difficult times. Certain 'opponents' had been claiming that it did not really matter if Christians performed the pagan sacrifices. The *Exhortation to Martyrdom* is constructed around three key themes. First, the Christian seeking perfection should imitate the example of Christ as closely as possible. Second, Christ gave himself up on the cross by means of both the holocaust of his physical body and through his inner detachment from the world. And third, the Christian follower of Christ must be prepared to imitate him in both these aspects – holocaust and inner detachment - when the occasion arises, turning away from perishable realities. Martyrdom allows for the possibility of a fuller participation in Christ. In Origen's pastoral theology, the martyr not only imitates Christ but becomes one with him in sharing in Christ's saving power. The martyr's use of his or her own body, then, has salvific possibility, by being the instrument the Christian has for self-oblation. Once the martyr has escaped from the body and this world, there arises the freedom to contemplate God.[14] In de-emphasizing the survival of the body to support the ideal of martyrdom, Origen's Platonist thinking is expressed in a clear and striking way. Origen was imprisoned and tortured in 250 and survived just a few years.

### Martyrdom or Suicide?

A pastoral problem that faced Christian leadership during this time of persecution was an over-enthusiasm on the part of some Christians to embrace death. Many of the martyrs appeared reckless in their desire to be arrested and killed for the sake of their religious beliefs. Was it fearless faith deliberately provoking the authorities, or active religious suicide? A similar issue, although in very different circumstances, exists today among more extreme elements within the Islamic faith with terrorist suicide missions in the name of religion. The apparent willingness of many Christians to rush to their deaths in the age of persecution astonished many pagans. The Stoic emperor, Marcus Aurelius (161-80), had no ethical objections to suicide but felt it must be done in a fitting way: 'not, like the Christians, in a spirit of theatricality.'[15] Some recent scholarship suggests that the common depiction of Jesus' death, in the works of the Fathers of the Church, as a freely chosen sacrifice, was a powerful influence on the imagination of early Christians that led to their actively seeking out death by martyrdom.[16] Ignatius of Antioch, condemned to death in 107, was led as a prisoner to Rome. On the way, he wrote a letter from Smyrna in Asia Minor to the Christians of Rome begging them not to prevent him being given over to the wild beasts. The letter reveals a longing for death:

> I am dying willingly for God's sake ... entice the wild beasts that they become my tomb, and leave no trace of my body ... Beseech Christ on my behalf, that I may be found a sacrifice through these instruments.[17]

To what extent some pious literature, such as this from the pen of Ignatius, who is facing imminent death, is suicidal or simply a literary device remains arguable. Nevertheless, Clement of Alexandria (c.150-c.215), Origen and Cyprian all attempted to temper the misguided sentiment of religious enthusiasts actively seeking out martyrdom.[18]

Martyrdom had become something of a real pastoral concern in the early fifth century when persecution by the state had ended. Fanatical Donatist Christians, uncompromising in their attitude to Christians who had weakened under persecution, had preferred to kill themselves in religious zealotry rather than 'convert' to the Catholic (i.e. non-Donatist) Church. They drew their inspiration from martyrs of an earlier period.[19] St Augustine (354-430), the North African bishop of Hippo and theologian whose extraordinary intellect so definitively shaped the pathway of Christian thought, directed a great proportion of his energies as a pastor and scholar towards the problem of the heretical Donatists. Augustine condemned such voluntary deaths, and others like it, in Book I of his monumental work, *The City of God*.[20] It was Augustine who gave to Christianity the first systematized condemnation of suicide as a sinful act.

### Christians Initiating New Members

Gradually, baptism came to be practiced by Christians as the culmination of a drawn-out process initiating new members into its ranks. By the late second century this procedure had become well organized and represented a significant dimension of pastoral care within early Christianity. As the Christian movement developed in its identity and became increasingly institutionalized, standards for admission became more demanding than in the earlier, apostolic period and its immediate aftermath. New members had to be nurtured and prepared for this new way of life. They required intensive pastoral care. We learn how this initiation of new members was done in the Roman Church from Hippolytus (c.170-c.236), in his work, *Apostolic Tradition*. Like most early Christian practices, preparation for baptism would have varied from one Church to another. But the basic structure described by Hippolytus appears to have been widely adopted.

There were four broad steps in incorporating new members. The first step involved persons coming forward to learn more about this new faith and to be admitted formally to the community on a provisional basis. Acceptance was not guaranteed. Those seeking admission were first introduced to the community by the person who had recruited them. They were then questioned about their motives for conversion. Certain occupations proved an obstacle for admission, including pimp, gladiator, teacher of pagan philosophies, soldier, actor and sculptor of carved images of pagan gods. People pursuing such occupations were required to quit them if they wanted to be Christians. However, such restrictions must have varied from Church to Church for we know soldiers, for example, were among the early Christians. Once accepted into the community, the convert was considered no longer a pagan but a novice Christian.

The second step was that of the catechumenate. It lasted usually for three years but this remained flexible according to circumstances. This was a period of instruction conducted more in the way of a liturgical service of the word than tuition.

In the weeks leading up to Easter the catechumen entered into the third stage of preparation for full admission into the Church. This was a time characterized by recurring public Scrutinies. The catechumen was examined as to how well he or she had been living the Christian way of life. If found acceptable, the person was set apart or 'elected'. Throughout these weeks before Easter there were frequent, public ceremonies of the laying on of hands by other members of the Church and exorcism. On the fourth Sunday of Lent the catechumen was formally presented with the four Gospels, the Creed and Lord's Prayer: the privileged knowledge of those about to be received as full members into the Christian community. At the evening Easter Vigil there were immediate preparations for full admission. They received a final exorcism and recited together the Creed, something that had been disclosed to them in the earlier, fourth Scrutiny.

The fourth and final stage of the pastoral care of new members to the Church was their baptism, presided over by the bishop. A candidate for baptism stripped off his or her clothes and descended naked into a pool of water. Here a presbyter, deacon or deaconess was waiting and engaged in a final questioning about belief in the Holy Trinity and the Church and then immersed the person three times in the water. Stepping out of the water spiritually reborn, while still naked and wet, the newly baptized was anointed with oil to signify their new dignity and then dressed in special baptismal clothing. Standing before the bishop, the baptized Christian was signed on the forehead with the oil of chrism, a gesture that signified the outpouring of the Holy Spirit. These rites were followed by an embrace of peace given by the bishop. The baptismal rites having concluded, the bishop ascended to his throne and the Mass continued with the singing of the Gloria. The newly baptized were now permitted to remain for the whole duration of the eucharistic liturgy and received Holy Communion for the first time at this Easter Mass. Following their baptism, during the weeks after Easter, the new Christians received intensive instruction in the Christian faith.[21]

As the numbers of people who were wishing to be Christians increased, the attention given to their pastoral care by way of preparation for Christian initation must have been considerable, especially since it comprised liturgical, instructional and disciplinary elements. It involved the whole Christian community in different ministries: sponsorship by a family member or friend; instruction in the Scriptures and doctrinal beliefs of the Church; disciplinary scrutiny; liturgical rites. This ancient form of welcoming new members into the Church has been revived, with modification, following the reforms of the Second Vatican Council, in the latter part of the twentieth century. And it has served as a pastoral model for catechesis and the building of Christian community in general.

## Christians Seeking Forgiveness

### Montanists

A Christian, and former pagan priest, by the name of Montanus, with the support of two women, Priscilla and Maximilla, who had left their husbands, began a revivalist movement in an Asia Minor village within Phrygia in the middle of the second century. The sectarian movement, later to be known as Montanism, was characterized by its devotees claiming ecstatic experiences and engaging in prophetic utterances. The movement was an apocalyptic phenomenon belonging to a series of movements of enthusiasts that seem to keep turning up in history. Montanists expected a speedy end to the world as they awaited the heavenly Jerusalem to descend into Phrygia. Its followers were known for their excesses and included among their number charlatans and opportunists. They had a rigorous approach to fasting and penance, forbidding members to flee from the threat of persecution. Extremists, the Montanists advocated a return to a purer form of Christian living. Stressing the importance of living directly under the guidance of the Holy Spirit,

Montanism posed a direct challenge to the developing institutions of Church leadership among bishops, presbyters and deacons. Like so many other enthusiast movements throughout history, Montanists maintained a position of exclusivism: those who failed to support it were believed to be deficient in the Holy Spirit. There were a number of bishops appalled by its divisiveness yet in the town of Thyatira the whole Church became Montanist.[22]

In the North African Church, Tertullian, in later life, was attracted to Montanism because of the movement's perfectionist approach to faith. This led him eventually to place himself outside the Catholic Church, which he condemned as being unspiritual and compromised by its worldly standards. He became opposed to the Church's forgiving grave sin, such as adultery or apostasy, committed after baptism.

### Readmitting Apostates

Montanism was indicative of a growing hardline spirit within early Christianity that was to lead to controversy about how to deal with human frailty: what sort of pastoral response was required for people who had sinned seriously after being baptized? The matter was brought to a head following the persecution under Decius in the middle of the third century, almost a century after the appearance of Montanus. In the year 249, Decius had ordered everyone within the empire to worship the Roman gods. To indicate they had done so, a certificate known as a *libellus*, was issued by special commissioners. Possession of a *libellus* ensured that a person would no longer be harassed. Many Christians, afraid of imprisonment or execution, promptly lapsed by making offerings to the gods. In Carthage, for example, there was such a crush of Christians coming forward to make the pagan sacrifices that they had to be turned away by the magistrates until the next day. Outside Carthage, entire congregations of Christians apostatized, sometimes led by their bishop.[23] Others got around the problem by bribing the officials who issued the certificates, thus providing them with the necessary documentation to ensure their safety.[24]

After the persecution had ended, the question was what to do with the *lapsi*, those who had lapsed as a result of pagan worship or had obtained a *libellus* by bribery to save themselves from harm. As well, it was the onerous task of the local bishop to issue his own certificates to those who had boldly confessed their faith by their public refusal to engage in the pagan, state cult. These *confessors*, many of whom had served prison sentences during the persecution, were held in high esteem within the Church communities. A group of sixty-five 'certified' confessors from Carthage arrived by ship in Rome. But were they all genuine? It was possible that some among them may have obtained forged certificates. But the situation was even more complicated. The custom had arisen for confessors to be able to dispense certificates of pardon for serious sins. These documents were known as *libelli pacis*, letters of peace. Confessors were granted privileges. In Carthage, they had gained control of the Church's leadership during Cyprian's absence when he went into hiding for a period of time to escape the persecution. Human nature being what it is, such certificates of pardon were sometimes given rather too freely.[25]

But, the important question was what to do with the *lapsi*. Apostasy was considered by all in the Church to be a major sin. It was a significant pastoral care issue that dominated affairs in the Church because apostasy had become so widespread and involved large numbers of Christians in the Church at the time. There were two schools of thought as to how to respond. Cyprian of Carthage, who himself was to die as a martyr in 258, at first argued that no human being had the power to remit apostasy, the matter having to be left to God's judgment alone.[26] Cyprian found guidance in the rigorist teachings of Tertullian. But Cyprian's views on the matter changed. He came around to maintaining that after a suitable period of time and penance, those who had lapsed ought to be readmitted to the Christian community upon recommendation by the bishop. It was a view that sided with a compassionate understanding of human weakness and a realistic appraisal of the situation of a significant section of the Church's membership. To avoid *lapsi* being treated severely, or leniently, according to the dispositions of individual bishops, the matter was referred to a council of North African bishops who met in Carthage in 251. Such a move was an attempt to arrive at a common pastoral policy. The power of the confessors to remit penances for the lapsed was rejected - a decision which attempted to curb their increasing power in the Church. The *libellatici* who had fraudulently obtained the *libellus* certificate (claiming they had made sacrifices to the pagan gods but had not done so) were to be subject to vigorous investigation and assigned penances according to the seriousness of their sins. The *sacrificati* (who had actually performed pagan sacrifices) were to be readmitted to the Church only on their death-beds.[27] The bishop of Rome was notified of the decision taken by this local Church.

The problem of those who had lapsed through apostasy was a divisive issue also within the Church in Rome. A Roman presbyter, named Novatian, advocated the rigorist line that pardon could not be granted to those guilty of serious sin. This applied to both those who had sacrificed to the Roman gods, the *sacrificati,* as well as to those Christians, the *libellatici,* who had falsely obtained documents claiming they had done so. Such apostates were expected, in Novatian's view, to undertake a lifetime penance but reconciliation with the Church could never be granted. God might be able to forgive such sinners but the Church was unable to do so. Otherwise, the integrity and holiness of the Church would be put into question. However, there was one concession. In their final hours before death, they could be given 'proper care and solicitude' if they showed genuine repentance.[28] Novatian's rigorist pastoral policy was opposed by Cornelius (251-53), Bishop of Rome. The situation led to schism in the Roman Church when Novatian had himself consecrated as a rival to Cornelius, the Bishop of Rome. The Novatianist Church persisted into the fifth century, and even longer in more isolated areas. The crisis of the *lapsi* was, in effect, a dispute over ecclesiology that is ever present in the Church in one way or another: is the Church an elite group of the holy, or a 'big Church' embracing both saints and sinners? The answer that is given determines the response to any number of disputed pastoral concerns: membership; admission to sacraments; styles of leadership; forms of Christian community.

### Valid Sacraments

A further controversy, following on from that of what to do about the *lapsi,* concerned the validity of sacraments administered by bishops and presbyters who had apostatized during persecution. In the North African viewpoint, led by Cyprian, they were still considered apostates and unable to administer valid baptism. Congregations should clearly separate themselves from such people. The situation became more involved when schismatic followers of Novatian baptized some new converts. The question arose as to whether they required a further baptism. Cyprian upheld the view of Carthage that anyone baptized by a heretic or schismatic would need to be rebaptized.

But the thinking upon the pastoral question of the validity of sacraments was different in Rome where a separate tradition had developed. Stephen, its bishop, taught that, provided baptism was performed in the name of the Trinity, it was valid, irrespective of the moral status of the minister performing it - a teaching that was to be accepted eventually as the orthodox position. But a tense situation had developed between the Roman and African Churches over the matter, one that was to surface again in North Africa among the Donatists in the fourth and fifth centuries.[29]

## Donatists

The Donatists provide a striking example of the ongoing conflict between those holding a rigorist policy of pastoral practice and those holding a more balanced one in the early centuries of Christianity. The Donatists were no mere fringe group in the North African Church but a widespread popular movement that struggled for supremacy alongside the mainstream, Catholic Church in that region. Donatism may well have been the larger group of the two in Augustine's time.[30] As we have already seen, Augustine was constantly in bitter dispute with the Donatists and supported the imperial policy of their repression. Donatist origins go back to their refusal to accept Caecilian as the Bishop of Carthage; he was consecrated probably in 311. The problem was that Caecilian's consecrating bishop was a *traditore*, one who had caved in under pressure during the persecution and handed over the sacred Scriptures and liturgical vessels to the authorities. Because of this, the opponents of Caecilian consecrated a rival bishop named Majorinus who was quickly succeeded by Donatus, from which the schism takes its name. The Donatists, taking the rigorist position, believed that sacraments conferred by *traditores* were invalid and even those who received the sacraments from their hands were infected with sin. The Donatists, put under pressure by coercive laws against them, saw themselves as new martyrs. Their intransigence, in their perfectionist ideas about the Church, led some Donatists to associate with wildly extremist groups called the Circumcelliones. Donatism remained a characteristic feature of African Christianity until the Muslims wiped out the Church there in the seventh and eighth centuries.

We can see, then, how the persecutions and what followed in their aftermath colored strongly the shape of pastoral practice within early Christianity, particularly as to whether a rigorist or moderate stance was to be taken towards those who had weakened under pressure. The two issues of persecution and sin were inseparably linked. Fundamental issues emerged as to who could be forgiven and under what conditions; the validity of sacraments administered by those priests and bishops considered to be in serious sin; and the minimum level of moral purity and holiness expected of believers. The answers given to these questions determined the manner in which pastoral care for individuals and communities was fashioned.

## The Order of Penitents

Within the first three centuries of the Church it was assumed that baptism was the only special rite needed for repentance. By becoming a Christian through the rite of baptism, one was expected to have turned away from sin towards Christ. The ideal was that of complete holiness. But there was also the realization that Christians were not perfect and needed forgiveness through prayer, the partaking of the Eucharist and through charitable deeds, especially almsgiving.[31] The actual specific rituals for penitential practices in the early centuries of the Church for more serious sins, as discussed in the patristic texts, are not clearly defined and do vary from region to region. But clearly the reconciliation of sinners, as we have already seen in the discussion concerning those who had weakened in faith during the persecutions, was at the heart of pastoral care ministry within these early centuries of Christian history. Yet, during this time, the ministry of reconciliation was forever a matter of dispute between the rigorist and tolerant parties within the Church. But two penitential practices do stand out. One was the public confession of faults for serious sin before the bishop and assembled community, known as the *exmologesis*; the other was the isolation of the penitent from the community.

Hermas, who was writing from Rome in the middle of the second century, alludes to the possibility of a sinner's being readmitted to the community after some form of public penance during a period of exclusion.[32] Similar ideas are expressed by Irenaeus of Lyons (*c*.130-*c*.200) in the latter half of the second century.[33]

Tertullian is the first witness among the early Church Fathers to provide us with details of a ritual for penitents seeking forgiveness of grave, postbaptismal sin.[34] The penitents were required to wear penitential clothing of sackcloth sprinkled with ashes; to abstain from fine food and drink; to engage in continual prayer; to groan publicly for their sins; to bow before the presbyters and kneel before the people, asking for their prayers; and to perform charitable actions. They were to confess their sins, the *exmologesis*, during temporary exclusion from the assembled community, in the vestibule. As David Coffey notes,[35] the word 'confession' had a broader meaning than our use of the term today. It referred primarily to a confession of faith, followed by praise of God, especially for his mercies and, only then, to a confession of one's personal sinfulness.

But what liturgical process concluded the period of penance in Tertullian's Church remains unknown to us. The process might have lasted for weeks, even years. However, public penance of this kind could not be repeated. It was a demanding experience, done only once in a lifetime: something in the ancient Church that led a great many people to postpone public penance until the end of their lives because it so disrupted everyday living. This basic outline of a public, penitential ritual became fairly uniform in the Church from the third century. Tertullian, as he moved in the direction of the extremist views of Montanism, adopted the line that sins such as adultery, murder and apostasy were reserved to God's judgment alone.[36] Sinners guilty of these offences could not be reconciled with the community through public penance. Tertullian's earlier pastoral compassion was replaced by rigidity and harshness. In the long term, the more humane position of the Church, forgiving the penitent offender in the name of God, was to prevail.[37]

Cyprian's testimony to the practice of penance for apostates, amidst the confusion of ideas and practices within the Carthaginian Church, has already been mentioned. It is the most detailed account of penitential practice within the first three centuries of the Church.[38] Penitents were viewed as a distinct group within the Church. The penitential process is attested to by Cyprian as consisting of three stages. First, the penitent was segregated from the rest of the community and engaged in works of penance. Next, there was some liturgical form of *exmologesis* in which the penitent publicly confessed his or her sin, during which time there was a laying-on of hands, probably a form of exorcism. Third, at the conclusion of the penitential period, reconciliation with the Church took place by means of another laying-on of hands by the bishop. This expressed a renewed peace with the Church and was followed by readmission to the Eucharist.[39]

From the period of the fourth to the sixth centuries a more definite Order of Penitents emerged in the Western Church, similar to the Order of Catechumens. Each local Church developed its own stages of the penitential process, its degree of rigor, and its duration. The liturgical rites of penance for serious sin after baptism were public, not private, and usually entered into only once in a lifetime, following baptism.[40] The understanding that priestly absolution was what imparted divine forgiveness did not occur until about the middle of the thirteenth century, a view taken up and developed by St Thomas Aquinas (*c.*1225-74). This view was expressed by a number of theologians and endorsed at the Council of Florence in 1439.[41]

The story of penance in the Eastern Church is somewhat different. Penitence was understood not so much as a matter of Church discipline that was regulated but as an inner spiritual journey in the quest for holiness. Spiritual guidance, rather than public ritual, was emphasized. The penitent sought out a Christian teacher noted for holiness of life rather than submitting to the discipline of the bishop and Church community. This Eastern notion of penance was to find its home in monasticism where the monk was guided through a life of penance towards greater perfection by a revered spiritual figure. In the East, direction of souls by spiritual masters became more important than disciplinary absolution by priests, as developed in the West.[42]

### Christians Caring for the Poor and Needy

Christians stood out in the Roman Empire in their generosity towards those in need. They both impressed and bewildered their pagan neighbors by the way in which they cared for one another and others outside their communities. The pagan satirist, Lucian, commended them in somewhat condescending language:

> It is incredible to see the ardor with which the people of that religion help each other in their wants. They spare nothing. Their first legislator has put it into their hearts that they are all brothers.[43]

He went on to conclude that any charlatan or trickster could get rich quickly by taking advantage of such people. A Christian homily, from the early second century, considers almsgiving to be even better than prayer and fasting.[44] Chadwick maintains that the charity shown by the early Christians was probably the most potent single cause of Christian success.[45]

Such charity was motivated not only by the belief that all were brothers and sisters in Christ. Almsgiving and other acts of human kindness were thought of, also, as a means of penance in seeking God's forgiveness for sin, something Christianity inherited from Judaism. Cyprian has a whole treatise devoted to almsgiving in which he understands charitable works as providing Christians with merit, thus providing for their heavenly reward.[46] While in hiding during the persecution, Cyprian wrote to the presbyters and deacons to ensure that they continued caring for the widows, the poor and strangers by using money he had left behind with the presbyter, Rogatianus. His pastoral solicitude is also shown in his instructions about using Church funds to redeem some Numidian Christians who had been taken captive.[47] With sarcasm, Clement of Alexandria attacked people who seemed to care more for their pet animals than they did for the poor.[48] As well, almsgiving was linked with the

Eucharist in early Christianity where gifts were brought up and offered for distribution to the poor and needy. Tertullian claimed that the *agape* meal, apparently separated from the Eucharist early in the second century, was intended for the feeding of the poor. Each month, wrote Tertullian, money would be collected at this meal to bury poor people, care for the destitute, look after those who had been shipwrecked, as well as attending to the needs of those in the mines, banished to islands and in prison.[49]

During the fifth century, an association of pious clerics in Alexandria dedicated itself to caring for the sick. The clerics were known as the *parabalani,* the reckless ones, because of their unselfish outreach to the victims of plague. It seems their charitable efforts were well known and respected in the city. At one point, their number grew to six hundred.[50]

Within the Roman Empire, from the second century BCE, the state had freely distributed grain to the poorer classes. This grain dole, known as the *frumentum,* was often appropriated by people not in need of such assistance. Like so many government officials before and since, Julius Caesar made cuts in social welfare. He reduced the number of recipients eligible for the grain dole by almost a half. The food dole was still in operation by the time of Constantine in the fourth century, although bread, rather than grain, was then given away. Under Constantine, it seems the Church took over distribution of much of the state food dole and its clerics were paid fees to do so.[51] From this time on, Christian pastoral care would be linked in various ways with state welfare.

In the Eastern Church of Constantinople of the fourth century, its eloquent bishop John Chrysostom (*c.*347-407) defended the Church against critics who attacked it over its wealth. After the Peace of Constantine, the Church had accumulated great wealth. Pagan shrines lost funds and the Church's assets became swollen, benefiting from the emperor's generosity. The Bishop of Constantinople reminded his critics that the Church dealt with hordes of poor people who were on its relief rolls.[52] Amidst the wealth and splendor of Constantinople, John Chrysostom lived a simple, ascetical life and often attacked the court and wealthy citizens for their extravagances, something that led to his falling out of favor with the empress. But the wealth of a Church now enjoying state protection brought its problems. Pope Damasus I (366-84), in Rome, was accused of living in such luxury that one of the Roman pagan senators, Praetextatus, remarked in a disparaging manner that he would be only too happy to convert to Christianity if he were made Bishop of Rome.[53]

Although Christians continued to accept slavery as part of the social and economic fabric of society, to free a slave had become a charitable thing to do. It was common practice for a Christian wishing to free a slave to state this intention solemnly in the presence of the bishop. As well as individuals, the Church community itself would sometimes set aside funds for this purpose. Slaves were considered equal within the community of Christians although one can assume that discrimination against them would have not been uncommon. Belief and practice are not necessarily identical. Several emancipated slaves did become bishops, among them Pope Callistus of Rome (c.217-22). Towards the end of the fourth century, slaves could not be ordained without their owners receiving financial compensation: a measure aimed at protecting property rights in the time when the Church had attained state recognition.[54]

### Christians Seeking Unity: The Great Church Councils

One of the defining features of fourth century Christianity, particularly within the Eastern Churches, was the acrimonious theological debate concerning the relationship of the three divine Persons in the Trinity and, following on from this, the relationship between the divine and human natures in the incarnate Jesus Christ. Out of these debates that inflamed extraordinary passion, came the great councils of the Church that defined orthodox belief as formulated in the Christian Creeds. To follow this story closely would lead us through a labyrinth of Greek philosophical concepts supporting varying theological viewpoints that leave the modern Christian bewildered. None but the trained theologian can hope to understand fully these controversies of the fourth century Church.

One may well ask why a history of pastoral care need give attention to the matter. Well, for one thing, bishops led the disputes and they had pastoral responsibilities for their Churches. The conflict of those holding opposing ideas became so intense that whole congregations and regional Churches were caught up in the mêlée. It was not just an academic debate among theologians. The different theologies, touching on the very understanding of the divine, were splitting the Church apart. Ecclesiastical leaders, as well as successive emperors anxious to keep the sprawling empire glued together, recognized the need for reaching a common understanding of the core beliefs of the Christian faith. The pastoral task of seeking unity, a problem in the Jewish and Gentile Churches of Paul's day, had again presented itself on a much larger scale within a Church that rapidly had become the official religion of the empire. The holding of a common belief among Christians has always been at the heart of genuine pastoral care. And a history of pastoral care can take interest in these early Church doctrinal controversies because they illustrate so well how Christianity borrowed from the intellectual movements of surrounding cultures to express its beliefs and practice. In a new time and setting, the Jewish gospel of Jesus was now being expressed and lived with the help of pagan Greek philosophy. In doing so, it would look forever different. Christianity, drawing upon contemporary culture and ideas, must always incarnate itself in the world of its time if its pastoral outreach is to be credible and accepted. The great Ecumenical Church Councils, and the Creeds that came from them expressed in peculiarly Greek terms, are testimony to this fact of the continuing process of the inculturation of the gospel in the life of the Church. So let us briefly take up the story.

### Athanasius v Arius: The Debate Concerning the Trinity

> If in this city you ask anyone for change, he will discuss with you whether the Son is begotten or unbegotten. If you ask about the quality of bread, you will receive the answer, that 'the Father is greater, the Son is less.' If you suggest that you require a bath, you will be told that 'there is nothing before the Son was created.'[55]

Gregory of Nyssa (c.330-c.395), brother of Basil, wryly notes above how theological debate over the nature of the Trinity in Constantinople had taken hold of everybody's mind. Even the dock workers handling the cargo from the ships, and all kinds of trades people, whistled or chanted jingles indicating what side of this disputed question they supported: like football supporters of today singing their team's theme song in the stadium.[56] It is difficult for us to imagine just how passionate ordinary Christians allowed themselves to get about religious tenets. Congregations were divided over the matter, and violence frequently erupted between opposing sides. Shabby political deals and maneuvering occurred as the parties concerned attempted to get their side of the arguments accepted.

A presbyter in Alexandria, Arius (c.250-c.336), became involved in a dispute with his bishop, Alexander, concerning the divine nature of Christ the Son and his relationship with the Father. Christ was Son of God, but what did this mean precisely? At the outbreak of the dispute, there was no official teaching on these questions concerning the Trinity. Arius was of the opinion that Christ was created in time, after his Father, and so lacked qualities that the Father had possessed eternally. As such, Christ was in some sense inferior or subordinate to the Father. Nevertheless, Christ was superior to, and different from, all other creatures since he is God's agent in the creation of everything else. Thus Christ himself is the only direct creation of the Father. Arius, excommunicated by a regional gathering of bishops, was banished from Alexandria but soon found support elsewhere with another synod backing him. He felt sufficiently supported to return to Alexandria. This move resulted in riots on the streets in the Egyptian city. Arius attracted a wide following, although his supporters and opponents were never homogenous groups, which confused matters even more.

Emperor Constantine, anxious to settle the dispute that was threatening the unity of the empire, convened a council of the Church in 325. The quarrel was as much a power struggle between bishops of important episcopal cities as a theological debate. Writing a century later, the Church historian Socrates of Constantinople (c.380-450) maintained that these theological disputes were to be treated as a mere figleaf for the drive to power and authority.[57] The council met in the comfortable surroundings of the emperor's palace at Nicaea (the modern Turkish city of Iznik), on the shores of a picturesque lake. Constantine had little understanding of the subtle theological differences being discussed. His interest was political and he was intent on getting an agreed statement of unity from his bishops. The gathering to resolve the issue was termed the First Ecumenical Council. But its membership hardly represented the whole Church. Nearly all of the more than two hundred to three hundred bishops in attendance (the exact number is unknown) were from the Eastern Church, with probably no more than about five representing the Latin-speaking Western Church which, at the time, had little interest in Greek philosophical disputes that pertained to doctrine. The Latin mind was more pragmatic when it came to matters affecting the Church.

Alexander (d.328), the bishop of Alexandria, was anxious that the council might settle matters because his Church was the one where Arius had started all the trouble. Accompanying his bishop to Nicaea was Alexander's fiery secretary and deacon, Athanasius (c.296-373), who participated in the debates. Pushed along by the emperor, a statement of agreement was reached at the council. The key to the agreement was the insertion of the word *homoousios*, meaning consubstantial, or 'of one substance', used to describe the relationship between Father and Son in the Trinity. It meant the defeat of Arius and the few supporters who remained with him: Arius was condemned, his books ordered to be burnt and he was sent into exile. Constantine breathed a sigh of relief that the matter seemed to have been settled and gave each of the bishops a departing gift by way of gratitude. The First Ecumenical Council of Nicaea had lasted just a month.

But the peace proved to be a fragile one. Within months after the council, some bishops withdrew their signature of support for the use of the term *homoousios*. Arianism was still very much alive. The up-and-coming star in this protracted controversy was the young Athanasius. In 328 he succeeded Alexander in becoming Bishop of Alexandria, something that helped him to be the outspoken voice of Nicene orthodoxy. Athanasius argued that Arius' Christ could not redeem sinful humanity because he was not fully divine; only God could save humanity. Arianism touched the very heart of Christian belief.

Arian bishops, such as the influential Eusebius of Nicomedia (d.*c*.342), returned from exile and worked immediately at undermining the Nicene party in the eyes of the emperor. Possessing an autocratic and aggressive temperament that easily made enemies, Bishop Athanasius found himself opposed by other factions, like the Meletian ascetics and other disgruntled clergy. Athanasius faced accusations of fraud, bribery, sacrilege, rape and even murder, but the charges could not be substantiated. Nevertheless, Constantine lost patience with the troublesome bishop and sent him into exile at Trier. But Athanasius was soon to return to Alexandria to reclaim his position as bishop of that unsettled diocese: Constantine died and Athanasius thought his position was now more secure. But his enemies were still strong and Athanasius was forced into hiding for three weeks before fleeing to Rome in fear for his safety. There, his strong anti-Arian views met with acceptance. At about the same time a meeting of bishops in Antioch repudiated the teachings of Arius but avoided any use of the Nicene term *homoousios*. But the troubles for Athanasius were to continue. He was exiled a total of five times throughout his life. The final victory for the orthodox faith on the disputed question of the trinitarian relationship between Father and Son came during the time of Emperor Theodosius I (379-95) at the Council of Constantinople in 381, which upheld the Nicene faith: the council was held in the midst of an acrimonious row over who was the rightful bishop of Constantinople, the imperial capital. The words of what we call today the Nicene Creed, incorporating the teaching of the First Ecumenical Council of Nicaea, were formulated at this Second Ecumenical Council in Constantinople. It taught that Father and Son are equally divine and of equal status, Christ being 'of one substance' with the Father. Athanasius, posthumously, had won the day.[58]

Arianism divided fourth century Christianity like nothing else. Despite the teaching of the councils, it was to flourish for another three centuries, especially among the Goths who had converted to Christianity. In Ravenna, which had become the capital of the Western Empire from 402, the Arian form of Christianity prospered under the Ostrogoth ruler, Theodoric (c.455-526).

### Cyril v Nestorius: The Debate Concerning the Incarnate Christ

The Arian controversy about the nature of the Trinity was to lead to another doctrinal dispute dealing with the relationship of the divine and human natures in the incarnate Christ. There were two rival schools of thought representing two cities: Antioch and Alexandria. Again, the Church was split down the middle. From a pastoral point of view, the issue had to be resolved and unity achieved on a fundamental issue of Christian belief. Otherwise the message of the gospel would continue to be drowned out by internal, factional strife. The behavior of Church leadership, in the persons of its bishops and theologians, was far from edifying and did little to model the spirit of discipleship found in gospel teachings. If the leadership had become so riddled with jealousies and scheming behaviors in the search for truth, what could one expect of its flock?

Once again there were two leading characters in the dispute. On the side of Antioch, representing the Syrian Church, was Nestorius (d.c.451) who had become Patriarch of Constantinople in 428, placing him in a strong position to advance his theological ideas. Nestorius' fanatical disposition led him to order the closing down of a neighboring chapel, secretly used by the condemned Arians, just five days after becoming patriarch of the imperial capital. Angered by Nestorius' high-handedness, the Arians set fire to the building and the flames spread throughout the entire quarter of the city. Nestorius was blamed for this misfortune.[59] He had been much influenced by the Syrian theologian, Theodore of Mopsuestia (c.350-428). Nestorius had ridiculed those who used the term Theotokos, mother or bearer of God, to describe Mary. The title had become widely accepted in both speculative theology and popular piety. He saw it as an example of loose and undisciplined thinking concerning the incarnation of Christ. Mary, he argued, was the mother of the man Jesus, not the mother of God. He worried that the title fostered popular devotion to Mary as a goddess.[60] But Nestorius' teachings seemed to deny the full humanity of Christ. Nestorius was said to have proposed that there were two separate persons in Christ – one divine and one human – in contrast to the orthodox teaching that in the incarnate Christ there is but a single Person who is at once divine and human. He was criticized for splitting Christ in two and minimizing his divinity. In more recent scholarship it is disputed whether Nestorius was heretical and to what extent his critics misrepresented his teachings.[61] We know his theological views only through the writings of his opponents. Whatever, his opinions quickly found favor in Constantinople and in major cities of the Eastern Empire.

Opposing Nestorius was Cyril (d.444), the Patriarch of Alexandria, who insisted on the essential unity of the divine and human natures in Christ. Cyril wanted to make the term *Theotokos*, used to describe Mary, a litmus test for orthodoxy, as far as the incarnation of Christ was concerned. To deny this term, in Cyril's thinking, was to deny the full divinity of Christ and hence heretical: a regional dispute between Egyptian Alexandria and Syrian Antioch threatened to spread throughout the Christian world.

The controversy grew more acrimonious. Attempting to gather damaging evidence against Nestorius, Cyril suggested an exchange of letters between them. Nestorius fell into the trap that was laid for him by his opponent. Writing in deliberately provocative language, Cyril hoped to lure his enemy into a response that could be used to condemn him. Cyril had his men in the imperial court of Emperor Theodosius II (408-50) at Constantinople to foster his interests. He also sought out the support of the monks in the city who were distrustful of Nestorius, their new Patriarch. As well, Cyril won the sympathy of Pope Celestine I (422-32) in Rome who had been annoyed by Nestorius' defense concerning hospitality he had offered to refugee followers of Pelagius (see p. 83).[62] Nestorius was well liked by Eudocia, the emperor's wife, but the emperor's sister, Pulcheria, had little time for the patriarch. As Chadwick observes, 'Theodosius had to live with two quarrelling ladies.'[63]

To hold empire and Church together, Theodosius decided to hold another great council of the Church in Ephesus in 431, the Third Ecumenical Council. The gathering was to prove to be a tempestuous one characterized by shady deals and underhand tactics on both sides. Things got off to a stormy start. Before all the bishops had arrived, Cyril, claiming to be the senior prelate present, apart from Nestorius (who was under suspicion), summoned the council to begin before everyone had arrived, despite wide protest. Heavy rain and floods had delayed many who were making their way to the council. It was a devious tactic to beat the main opposition before it had the opportunity to oppose him. Cyril, the master tactician, then managed to get the assembled delegates to condemn Nestorius on the grounds that his theology was in conflict with Nicene teaching. Nestorius had refused to appear before this gathering to face his accusers and later referred to it sarcastically as 'the Council of Cyril'. He saw him himself as a delegate, not as a defendant.

Meanwhile, the rain eased, enabling the arrival of more bishops in Ephesus, including John of Antioch (d.441) leading the Syrian contingent hostile to Cyril: a rival council was convened in the city in opposition to that of Cyril's gathering. There were now two parallel councils. The latter one pronounced Cyril deposed because of his disorderly handling of proceedings, and riots broke out in the city. The matter was referred to the emperor, assisted by his court advisers, who sided with Cyril's party. True to form, 'Cyril knew how to buy them.'[64] There was a certain amount of compromise on both sides. Nestorius was put in prison and replaced as the Bishop of Constantinople. He later died in exile in Egypt. The union of the two natures within the incarnate Christ and the term *Theotokos* were assured as orthodox teachings. Yet the faith of the Church, resulting from the council, had been formulated by means of intrigue, treachery, bribery and generally dishonorable ecclesiastical governance.

Not everybody was happy and the dispute lingered on for another twenty years, leading to the Fourth Ecumenical Council of Chalcedon in 451. This reaffirmed earlier council teachings concerning the Person of Christ and defined the limits of legitimate speculation on this matter. The Monophysite heresy came as a result of Chalcedon. It flourished among those who maintained the view of there being but a single nature in Christ - a far more strict form of the christology of the Alexandrian school of thought - a position which virtually denies the full humanity of Christ.

These theological controversies of the fourth and fifth centuries stand out as perhaps the most characteristic feature of the Church at that time, especially in the East where Christianity was strongest. Pastoral care, in all its different forms, occurred within a disturbed and divided Church but a Church that offered people a faith that paganism seemed no longer able to supply. Struggling with their own inner lives as they sought to define more precisely their beliefs, Christians were at the same time becoming increasingly concerned to reach the hearts and minds of people seeking the spiritual amidst the daily struggles of their lives. Alongside the doctrinal controversies, the writings of the early Church Fathers witness also to this spiritual tradition of pastoral care. What has become known as the 'consolation literature' stands out as testimony to this tradition.

## Christians Offering Consolation

### The Nature and Origins of the Consolation Literature

Letters of consolation are well represented within the vast body of patristic literature of early Christian times. These letters - along with homilies and treatises - were written to comfort bereaved Christians mourning the death of somebody they loved. They are filled with compassionate appreciation of the human emotions associated with loss. At the same time, they expound Christian beliefs concerning life beyond death: they are composed to strengthen faith and provide hope amidst affliction. As well as dealing with death, the consolation literature is concerned sometimes with other misfortunes, such as the threat of martyrdom, the hardships of exile or, like Cyprian's treatise, *On Mortality*, fear of the plague. The letters, within this form of early Christian literature, were more commonly addressed to individuals but were also intended to be read widely, and served as a pastoral aid: to comfort and to teach, to counsel and to catechize. This literature provides a rich source for our understanding of how one common form of pastoral care was practiced at the time.

The consolation literature has its origins in pagan classical writings, as in the works of Plutarch (c.46-d. after 119) and Cicero (106-43 BCE). The philosophy of Stoicism, particularly that of Seneca (c.4 BCE-65), influenced the early Christian literature of consolation. The Stoic tradition arose from the belief that the conditions of life beyond human control are simply to be accepted as inevitable, and it led to a certain passive indifference to pain and death. Seneca wrote a letter, *To Marcia on Consolation*. Marcia was a prominent Roman matron who was grieving the loss of her son. Seneca urged her to accept the insecurities of life. Death is but an exit from pain to an everlasting peace, he reminded her. The dead are only absent for we shall soon follow them. Had her son lived, Seneca reflects, for many years he may have been deprived of the purity that characterized his relatively short life. The boy will be raised up to the highest heaven where he will join a holy company of people, such as Scipio (236-184 BCE) and Cato (234-149 BCE). Seneca wrote a number of such letters to bereaved friends. Such thoughts as these provided by the

Stoics, as we shall see, reappear almost identically in the consolation literature of the early Church Fathers but infused with the new beliefs of the Christian faith, 'for the human soul craved more, and required more, than these could supply.'[65]

### Jerome

Jerome (c.342-420) wrote a number of consolatory letters.[66] His *Letter to Paula, concerning the death of Blesilla* provides us with a good example of this form of pastoral correspondence. Blesilla, a young and innocent girl, had died in 385, evidently as a result of excessive ascetical practices. Her death happened just three months after her conversion. Jerome wrote to her grief-stricken mother, Paula, as she struggled to make sense of the untimely demise of her daughter. Jerome begins by expressing his own deep feeling of sadness, something too great to be borne with sheer resignation. He describes how this entire letter to Paula is written in his own tears. Jerome then goes on to praise Blesilla's qualities as the reason for why he feels so distressed: her commitment to prayer; her brilliant conversation; and her outstanding intellect, especially as evident in her mastery of languages. Jerome then raises the age-old question of why God allows the innocent to suffer. How is it that godless people live to an old age, ponders Jerome. Much of the letter is peppered with illustrations from the Jewish and Christian Scriptures. Attempting to keep Blesilla's memory alive forever, Jerome tells her mother that all his labors will be dedicated to her honor: 'In my writings she will never die.' At the same time, this pastor and teacher wants to help Paula get over the death, despite the tears she naturally feels as a mother who has lost her dear daughter. Christians, Jerome reminds her, must show restraint in their grief, reflecting a Stoic belief borrowed from the pagan world. But the letter is filled with hope. Jerome concludes with a literary device of Blesilla addressing her mother from the grave with a recapitulation of his arguments.

### John Chrysostom

John Chrysostom, the fourth-century Bishop of Constantinople whom we have already met, was an outstanding preacher who held his congregation in rapt attention during his homilies in the imperial capital. Hence the name 'Chrysostom', meaning 'golden mouthed', that was later given him. His letters are equally inspiring for their eloquence and clarity of Christian teaching. The *Letter to a Young Widow*, written around 380, addresses various aspects of her suffering surrounding the death of her husband, Therasius. Her grief is especially difficult because she is so young and subject to a whole range of new problems. The death of her spouse, seemingly a wealthy man, left her feeling vulnerable as she now had to take responsibility for business affairs. As a young and widowed woman, she would miss affection through sexual intimacy, the bishop reminds her. But John, forever the ascetic, cautions her to keep her bed sacred from the touch of any other man. She should not be like the pagans, warned Chrysostom, and give into gloom, self-pity, despair and reckless indifference. John eulogized on the virtues of the deceased: affectionate, gentle, humble, sincere, understanding and devout. Her husband's death was an untimely one, John reminds her, for he never lived to achieve his goals, especially that of attaining the civic rank of prefect. Unfulfilled expectations add to the feeling of loss. In the letter, she is instructed that those who have lost their husbands are wedded to Christ: in place of Therasius, she has God. Therasius's death is not death, writes her pastor, but only a kind of emigration from the worse to the better, from the world of men and women to that of angels and archangels. Having been released from troubles, he has come to a state of greater peace and tranquility. John's letter of consolation however is tinged with unhappiness of a broader scale as it makes reference to the war their emperors, Valens (364-78) and Theodosius I (379-95), had with the Goths: this tragedy resulted in Constantinople's citizens experiencing a heightened sense of the fragility of human life. The widow's grief is situated, then, within the context of the troubled times in which she is living. Unlike the women who sent their husbands off to war and could do nothing for them when they met death in battle, this widow can be consoled insofar as she had the opportunity to care for him in his final hours. John ends his words of consolation reminding the widow that her husband would stand in heaven with God.

John Chrysostom wrote a series of consolation letters, while in exile, to the wealthy and beautiful deaconess Olympias, known as the *Letters to Olympias*. He had developed a particularly close relationship with this woman who had married at sixteen years of age and was widowed just two years later. In one piece of correspondence he told her he would write letters to her for as long as she wished. In offering comfort to the bereaved woman, it would appear John received consolation in return amidst his own discomforts and sorrows while in exile. His banishment from his beloved city was the result of having antagonized the empress and various ecclesiastical enemies. He shared with Olympias his hardships:

he was forever cold; deprived of the use of a bath; suffered insomnia; and was prone to vomiting and headaches.

> The man who, in his younger days as a priest, had juggled unthinkingly with the soiled coin of classical misogyny in order to dissuade monks and clergymen from entering into spiritual companionships with ascetic women, now depended for the survival of what little remained of his ecclesiastical program on the 'finesse' of a woman, 'sitting in a small back room,' in distant Constantinople. [67]

### Gregory of Nyssa

Following the death of their brother Basil (c.330-79), we read of a dialog between Gregory of Nyssa (c.330-c.395) and Macrina (c.327-79) in Gregory's treatise, *On the Soul and the Resurrection*. Although not in the form of a letter as such, nevertheless, it is in the style of the consolatory letters. Macrina, as a devout Christian - whom Gregory calls 'The Teacher' - rebukes her brother for the depth of his mourning over Basil's death since sorrow belongs only to those who have no hope. But Gregory reminds his sister that every human effort is directed at remaining alive. The design of houses to keep out the heat and cold; farming that produces food to keep people alive; medical treatments to help the sick; armor and defensive weapons to protect one from the enemy in war: all these aspects of human life are a result of our attempts to ward off death. So why should they not grieve their dear brother? How can the departure from this life of a loved one mean nothing? Gregory is attempting to reconcile two realities: the human emotion of grief with the faith of the Christian in the afterlife.

### Ambrose

Ambrose (339-97) was a civil official of high rank in the imperial capital of Milan. At a noisy meeting in the cathedral at which he was present, the crowd shouted, 'Let Ambrose be our bishop!'. He was not even baptized! But that did not deter his many admirers. Ten days after his baptism he was the new Bishop of Milan. He was a man of extraordinary refinement who had the strength of character to bring emperors to their knees, and an eloquence that held 'sceptical connoisseurs and ardent believers' [68] spellbound during his sermons. Ambrose was the model pastor of his diocese, making himself accessible to all who called upon him. Large numbers of pagans were presenting themselves to the Church as converts and Ambrose saw to it that they were well prepared for admission. Ambrose believed in music as a valuable aid to pastoral care and introduced congregational singing of psalms and hymns into his churches, something that was apparently quite novel in the Western Church at the time. It seems this singing broke down the strong class barriers so prevalent in the imperial capital and, by doing so, enabled the Church to be more of a religious community.[69] Augustine - as an earnest young man in search of the truth - came under his spell and was baptized by the Milanese bishop. In a time when Christianity had suddenly become fashionable and was experiencing extraordinary vitality from its new found, favored status within the Empire, Ambrose sought to bring the Church into closer association with the imperial court.

A close, brotherly bond existed between Ambrose and Satyrus. In the latter years of his life, Satyrus had served as manager for his brother's secular affairs. When Satyrus died, Ambrose was grief-stricken. He preached the sermon at Satyrus' funeral and delivered a second address a week later. As was his custom, Ambrose subsequently revised the homilies and published them. They have come down to us as *The Two Books on the Decease of His Brother Satyrus*.

In these homilies, Ambrose makes no apologies for his tears and makes the point that not all weeping is the result of unbelief or weakness. He reminds his congregation that even the Lord wept for someone (Lazarus) who was not a family member, but he, Ambrose, is weeping for his beloved brother. Amidst his sadness he has no desire to turn away his thoughts to other matters and, instead, engages in a life-review of experiences he has shared with Satyrus. As so often happens in grief, Ambrose expresses the thought that he would have been only too willing to give up his own body in death in place of Satyrus. Ambrose then proceeds to rationalize the death that makes so little sense to him: Satyrus' death meant he was spared falling into the cruel hands of the barbarian plunderers; he was saved from having to see other relatives die; he was protected from having to witness the violation of the holy virgins and widows in the Church. The virtues of Satyrus are then described, such as his simplicity and lack of attachment to material pleasures, including fine dining. Having dealt with his feelings about his brother's death, Ambrose then proceeds to situate these within his Christian beliefs of an afterlife. He draws on the Scriptures to support his teaching. As he tells his listeners and himself, death is not the end of our nature but simply the conclusion of life in this world.

Ambrose's two sermons, characteristic of the consolation literature as a whole, are an attempt to develop his Christian doctrine directly from human experience and relate this experience to sacred Scripture for the purpose of a more committed Christian life: a way of doing theology that today is known as 'practical theology'.

### Augustine

It is difficult to find a more poignant example of grief, but one accompanied by confident faith, than that where Augustine - the outstanding scholar and dedicated Bishop of Hippo - describes the death of his mother Monica (c.331-87), at which his own son, Adeotatus, is also present. The mother-son relationship had been extremely close, perhaps too much so. We can let Augustine speak for himself as he gives expression to his deep-felt sorrow in Book IX of the *Confessions*:

> I closed her eyes, and a huge sadness surged into my heart; the tears welled up, but in response to a ferocious command from my mind held the fount in check until it dried up, though the struggle was intensely painful for me. But as she breathed her last the boy Adeodatus burst out crying; he was restrained by all of us and grew quiet. By this means something boyish in myself, which was sliding towards tears, was also restrained by the man's voice of my heart, and it too grew quiet. We judged it unfitting to mark this death by plaintive protests and laments, since these are customarily employed to mourn the misery of the dying, or death as complete extinction. But she neither died in misery nor died altogether. The evidence of her virtues and her sincere faith gave us good reason to hold this as certain.

> What was it, then, that gave me such sharp inward pain? She and I had grown accustomed to living together; an exceedingly gentle and dear custom it was, and its sudden disruption was like a newly-inflicted wound. I found some solace in her commendation of me, for in that last illness she would at times respond with a caress to some little service I rendered her, calling me a devoted son, and with deep affection would declare that she had never heard from my lips any harsh or rough expression flung against her. But what is that, O my God, who have made us? What common measure is there between the respect with which I treated her and the service she did to me? Being now bereft of her comfort, so great a comfort, my soul was wounded; it was as though my life was rent apart, for there had been but one life, woven out of mine and hers.[70]

Augustine goes on to express how he held back his tears at his mother's funeral but inwardly felt oppressed with sadness, while yet calling on God to heal his pain. He mentions how he sought comfort in the public baths but found such relaxation to be of no help. But gradually he allowed his tears, for so long held back, to flow freely. Expressing his belief that God does not search our faults with rigor, Augustine prays that Monica will find a place with God: a request he believes that has already been granted. He concludes the account of his mother's death and his grief with the words, 'may she rest in peace'.

Subsequently, in 429, as Augustine himself lay dying in his beloved North African city of Hippo, the Vandals crossed the straits and laid siege to the city. The attack was to last fourteen months. Augustine died on 28 August 430, shortly before his city was torched and plundered. Augustine symbolizes the end of one of the great periods of the Church's pastoral life as the Roman Empire disintegrated in the West. In its place would emerge, in time, a stronger Church with the Bishop of Rome filling the vacuum left behind by the absence of an emperor residing in the West. It would be a time when Christianity would embrace new races of people and incorporate them into the City of God. In so doing, the Church would become itself transformed. Pastoral care had to take on new challenges and develop more novel means of engagement within this new world.

# Chapter 3

## Monks, Barbarians and Pastors

Before turning our attention to the series of invasions by barbarian tribes into the Roman Empire, and what this disturbing and often violent course of events meant for pastoral care, it is appropriate to consider first the rise of monasticism. Monks, turning their backs on the world in search of a more immediate experience of God, may seem a strange group of people with whom to associate the pastoral task of evangelizing marauding hordes of warrior peoples. Yet it was monasticism, in both its Eastern and Western forms, which shaped significantly the pattern of Christian life and manner of pastoral response during the time that is commonly referred to as the Dark Ages or the early medieval period.

### Monasticism

#### Understanding Human Nature: Origen and Augustine

Monasticism, with its harsh ascetical practices, consciously replaced martyrdom. It was understood as a martyrdom to self: for the monk, hunger, discipline and constant prayer brought about a stark confrontation with the realities of the human passions that had to be constantly subdued. By overcoming fleshly desires, one was then able to enter more freely into the world of the spiritual in the quest for the discovery of God. Evil was no longer encountered outside, as in the era of persecution, but within oneself. The monastic way of life was a highly visible struggle with sin. The monastic vocation was understood as a means of entering freely into suffering, with the intention of uniting oneself with the sacrifice of Christ on the cross.

It is crucial to appreciate the understandings of human nature that underpinned and gave inspiration to this monastic way of living out the Christian life. Otherwise, it makes little sense. But looking beyond monasticism, one can understand and assess pastoral care in general - in all its various forms and different settings - only by examining the understanding of the human person upon which each form is based. The way human nature is interpreted, one's chosen anthropology, guides and directs pastoral practice at any moment of time in the Church's long history.

Origen and Augustine, representing the Eastern and Western traditions of early Christianity, crafted, in their own distinct ways, two theological frameworks concerning human nature that influenced early monasticism in particular, as well as Christian life as a whole. But although their teachings have left a permanent imprint on theology and pastoral practice, it has not gone unchallenged. This is not to deny the importance of other early Church Fathers. Yet Origen and Augustine can be considered among the most significant in terms of their enduring influence.

We have already met Origen when discussing his theology of martyrdom in the previous chapter. Born in Alexandria, he was a man who traveled widely in his capacity as an outstanding teacher. He left a large body of writings that made him a biblical exegete, spiritual master and speculative theologian.[1] Peter Brown, in his brilliant study of the place of the body and sexuality in the earliest centuries of Christianity,[2] provides us with a study of Origen, the man, and his theology. Brown takes up the story alleging that Origen, as an idealistic young man of about twenty, had himself castrated to avoid temptation in his pastoral work of catechizing women.[3] The action was religiously motivated. But castration, while making a man infertile, is no guarantee of chastity. Brown raises the question as to whether there might be something deeply disturbing about the youthful Origen's self-prescribed mutilation. Was he choosing to opt out of being male, to belong to neither sex? Did the castrated Origen, unable to display the professional credentials of a philosopher's beard, choose to be a walking lesson of the basic indeterminacy of the human body, asks Brown. The story highlights the growing distrust of sex emerging in the early centuries of Christianity.

Origen taught that every human being had fallen away from exposure to God's love through self-satisfaction. The outcome is that all human beings, except Christ, experience a relentless sadness and frustration. For Origen, the body is above all else subject to this frustration and dissatisfaction as the human being attempts to transcend the limits of the self. The important question, then, was how to reconcile the desire for transformation with the limitations imposed by a particular human body.

> It was only by pressing against the limitations imposed by a specific material environment that the spirit would learn to recover its earliest yearning to stretch beyond itself, to open itself 'ever more fully and more warmly' to the love of God. The body posed a challenge that counteracted the numb sin of self-satisfaction.[4]

Origen, under the influence of Platonism, believed the joys of the spiritual realm were hidden by the obstruction of the body, with its accompanying physical appetites. One had to transcend the body and its needs, the limits of self, by means of renunciation so as to move towards restoring harmony between creature and God. While admitting that, for married couples, there is no sin in the sexual act, he was unprepared to say that it was holy.[5] The procreation of children, not human pleasure, is the reason for God's gift of sexual relations within marriage.[6] Sexual union keeps the married partners in the realm of the flesh and so hinders a rise to the spirit. It surely is not accidental, claimed Origen, that the only people in Scripture said to have celebrated their birthdays were Pharaoh and Herod. In Origen's view of things there is a real mistrust of the body and its urges. Jesus, he believed, may have had a body but had no experience of erotic urges.[7] Origen's ideas about human nature are developed most fully in the De Principiis (On First Principles).

In more specific terms, Origen taught that the human being is made up of a spirit (pneuma), a soul (psyche) and a body (soma). The spirit within the person is a participation in the Holy Spirit. The spirit is the teacher of the soul and the soul becomes spiritual in proportion to its assimilation to the spirit. But the more the soul surrenders to the body, the less spiritual becomes the soul. Every person's life, then, is a combat over the soul fought through a struggle with the body.

It is not difficult to see how Origen's theology was the undercurrent of the way of life of the Desert Fathers, ascetics of the East living out their monastic ideals by means of a relentless purgation of the flesh. These monks of the desert - mostly uneducated men - were driven by a religious outlook that was given sophisticated theological interpretation by Christian teachers such as Origen.

Turning now to Augustine. His theological ideas about human nature arise largely out of his involvement in the Pelagian controversy that focused on grace and sin. It was Augustine, more than anyone else, whose ideas about the nature of humanity shaped Christian thinking in the West about the human body and how Christians should live their lives within the limitations that human nature imposed. Western monasticism, with its ascetic practices, gave a perfect expression of Augustinian theology.

Augustine's theology is, above all, that of human sinfulness. Everyone is infected by original sin as a consequence of the Fall of Adam and Eve. Holiness in the Church is not so much that of its members but of Christ. The Church is made holy by Christ alone. Yet this perfection will be fully realized only at the Last Day. Augustine, as we have already seen, fought the Donatists who were desirous of a Church limited to the perfect. This idea went against Augustine's basic theological instincts.

But it was from his other great conflict, with Pelagius, a British theologian living in Rome, that Augustine developed his theology of human nature. For Pelagius, human beings possess a total freedom of the will. There is human weakness, but God asks nothing of human beings that they are not capable of doing. Otherwise, this would reflect negatively upon the goodness of God. A person is fully responsible for his or her own sins as well as good deeds. God has made humanity with total free will. God's commands, then, are capable of being obeyed and must be obeyed. God has created human nature to be free and capable of responding to him. Nothing can be claimed to be too difficult, argues Pelagius, for God knows human weakness and demands nothing that is impossible. Perfection, then, is both possible and obligatory. Pelagius understood grace to operate through the natural human faculties that have not been compromised in any way. Grace is external enlightenment by God. It informs people of their moral duties. But, for Pelagius, grace does not actually help a human being to perform these duties. Grace 'enlightens', rather than actively assists, a person to do good actions. Again, human beings are fully responsible for their sinfulness as well as their holiness.

Augustine tackled Pelagius head-on.[8] In agreement with Pelagius, Augustine affirmed human freedom. But free will, argued Augustine, has been weakened and compromised - but not destroyed - through sin. Grace is needed if freedom of will is to be restored and healed. Because of the Fall, sinfulness permeates the lives of human beings for, in some sense, the whole human race participated in Adam's fall. Original sin is a hereditary disease into which one is born: a force that holds human nature captive and causes guilt. Augustine's thinking, then, is very different from that of Pelagius for whom there is no inwardly inherent human disposition towards sin. For Pelagius, sin occurs only through free and deliberate human action. The distinction may be a subtle one but they are two very different understandings of human nature.

Grace, according to Augustine, is God's gift to heal, forgive and restore. Human nature is essentially frail and weak as a result of original sin and cannot choose good without God's assistance through grace. Human freedom is acknowledged but it is an impaired freedom. For Augustine, grace is the real and redeeming presence of Christ within the person. Every good action, then, is the result of God's grace working within human nature. Justification or salvation is the grace of God working within us.

Out of these ideas Augustine developed his notion of concupiscence, the inheritance and punishment of original sin. Concupiscence was identified, in Augustine's theology, especially with sexuality. As a result of the strong sexual drive, reason and will no longer have dominion and control over the body, as was the case before the Fall. Concupiscence, argued Augustine, is even present in legitimate sexuality within Christian marriage. Augustine understands marriage as being good because it has been given by God for filling up the number of the elect in the kingdom of heaven. Sexual relations in marriage, claimed Augustine, are for that purpose only. The idea of sex as an erotic passion, a physical and emotional experience that could be ennobling and an expression of human love, was foreign to Augustine's mode of thinking.

It is Augustine's doctrine of predestination, never accepted as orthodox teaching by the Church as a whole, that is particularly troubling. Augustine had a dark view of human nature: humanity is a *massa damnata*, a lump of sin justly deserving damnation that is saved only by the grace of Christ. Such is the consequence of original sin. But God has divided the human race into some who will be saved by the power of grace and others who will be damned. In the mind of Augustine, if all were damned, there would be no room for God's mercy; if all were saved, there would be no place for God's justice. God's mercy is entirely gratuitous so that the elect should be thankful, but the damned have no grounds for complaint. As to whom in particular God chooses to either save or damn is beyond our grasp, for the judgments of God are inscrutable. Yet the reasons for such choice on the part of God will be revealed at the Final Judgment. The elect are saved through the grace of baptism. Not every baptized person, however, will be saved, for not all will be given the free grace of God for perseverance to the end. Yet martyrdom can be as effective a cleansing from sin as the waters of baptism. Augustine is not entirely consistent in his writings about predestination, and his ideas have been interpreted in different ways.

Augustine's grand vision of humanity, more than that of any other Western theologian, has been an enduring feature affecting the Christian view of the human person that pastoral care, in its different guises, has come either to embrace or reject. Augustine's ideas on grace, salvation and predestination would be revisited over a thousand years later, amidst the doctrinal turbulence of the Protestant Reformation in the sixteenth century, whose effects last to our own day.[9]

Any study of the history and practice of pastoral care cannot avoid Augustine's massive influence upon the Church. For while Augustine's teachings about sinful human nature, uncontrollable concupiscence surrounding the body, and an elect number of Christians who had been singled out by God for salvation, undoubtedly flowed into the consciousness and subconsciousness of Western monasticism, these teachings, in turn, were passed on to the Church as a whole.

### Eastern Monasticism: The Desert Fathers

Christian monasticism has its origins in the East, particularly in Egypt, where it first flourished. It has been customary to see St Antony (251?-356) as the founder of the Christian monastic way of life. *The Life of Antony*, attributed to Athanasius, was a literary success and did much to spread the holy monk's fame. But there were others who contributed to the foundations of Eastern monasticism, including Macarios the Great (*c*.300-*c*.390).[10] But it is Antony who is the best known.

Antony's parents both died when he was young. This left him with the responsibility of caring for his younger sister. But Antony felt the call to the ascetic life. He disposed of his belongings, arranged for his sister to be taken care of and then set himself up in a hut on the outskirts of his village. We are told of Antony's encounter with the devil as he wrestled in anguish with his new style of life. But this only led him to add to his austerities. His fame for holiness spread as people sought him out for spiritual counsel. As a result, he decided to move to more remote places, among tombs in the region of his village. After about fifteen years of attempted solitude, he fled further into the Egyptian desert, to a place called Pispir, where he practiced solitary asceticism for the next twenty years. In an abandoned fort where he lived, Antony's cell was filled with visions of lions, bears, bulls, leopards, snakes and scorpions: for him they were symbols of the evils and torments he endured in his solitary battle with the devil. Hallucinatory experiences were not uncommon among such ascetics. Louis Bouyer writes:

> Solitude is a terrible trial, for it serves to crack open and burst apart the shell of our superficial realities. It opens out to us the unknown abyss that we all carry within us ... Seen in this light, which is their own, the strange devilries described by ancient monasticism should neither disconcert us nor deceive us.[11]

These monks must have aroused bewilderment in those who encountered them, with their emaciated bodies, unkempt beards, ragged clothes, and minds that must have been sometimes driven half mad by self-imposed solitude in the wilderness. They directed Christianity in an unconventional and striking pathway. The majority of them were probably illiterate – and so, unable to read the Scriptures - but they would have memorized key texts. A colony of hermits, living in their caves or huts, was called a *laura*, meaning a passage, possibly derived from a common pathway that connected their cave dwellings. Within these monastic colonies the hermit-monks would usually gather once per week for some form of common prayer. Otherwise it was a solitary existence. They did not consciously look for opportunities to care for others. Their lives were ones of silence and aloneness. But if a brother monk was in need, or if a visitor sought them out, they might pray for their guest and offer spiritual advice. It was customary for these solitaries to seek counsel from an elder monk. Some monks, no doubt, were more welcoming than others. Christ was the one they served outside of society, in the desert. 'The first Christian monks were at once an ambiguous sign, heroes, but marginal; they were not "tame".'[12]

Antony lived out his later years as a hermit by the Red Sea but people continued to come in search of him for spiritual guidance. Try as he might, Antony could not escape being the pastor of souls. Antony, and the many hermits who followed in his path, became known as *anchorites*.

A more tame, communal and institutional style of monastic life is said to have originated with Pachomius (*c*.290-346), a pagan soldier who converted to Christianity in the early fourth century. He spent seven years in solitude as an *anchorite* before setting up a collection of buildings in Tabbensi in Upper Egypt. There, he gathered some companions into a religious community under the authority of a superior. A detailed rule of life was observed. Pachomius' monastery continued to attract new members. There were times set aside for communal prayer and the diet was usually less severe than that of the solitary anchorites. Monks who followed this more communal form of asceticism and life under an established rule came to be known as *cenobites*. By the time of his death, Pachomius governed nine monasteries of men, and two of women, that were scattered along the Nile. His Rule influenced subsequent monastic movements in both the East and the West.

Monasticism was a lay movement within the Church. For the first three centuries, Christianity was very much an urban phenomenon.

Its leaders, the bishops and teachers, were generally literate men drawn from cities. The countryside remained largely pagan. But as the gospel spread into rural areas where people were less educated, large numbers of peasant farmers were drawn into its fold. The first monastic settlements were populated largely from these agrarian communities.[13] Like any human endeavor, people were attracted to this way of life for any number of reasons. There were those in search of genuine holiness. But in all probability this unconventional form of Christianity attracted its fair share of misfits, the mentally disturbed and those seeking refuge from the law or the payment of taxes.[14]

Much is made of the desert in these early Eastern monastic movements. The monks became known as the 'Desert Fathers'. It is in the desert that one confronts the demonic most forcefully, the place of temptation. The desert is a harsh and merciless environment. The isolation can attack both the body and the mind. The desert is also the place without food. Within its vast emptiness, there is less distraction. The presence of the desert motif in spiritual literature is, in some respects, more a literary device than a reality. The Pachomian monasteries were most often situated in inhabited land in cities and villages: the 'town monks'. But the desert monk became the primary image of monastic renunciation in Egypt.[15]

Can we speak of any significant pastoral function associated with these early monks who increasingly became an important feature of the Church in Egypt, Syria, Mesopotamia, Palestine and Cappadocia - a religious movement that began in the late third century? It was a common practice for a monk to seek out another more senior monk as a spiritual father to share his struggle in finding God. The spiritual father guided the monk to search deeper into his heart in pursuit of spiritual enlightenment. It was pastoral care within the monastic community. As has been already stated, monks did not necessarily live in remote regions out in the desert. They lived also in, and on the fringes of, villages, towns and cities. As such, the monks must have had a significant impact upon the community around them in terms of commerce as well as religion. People surely sought them out for spiritual guidance and the assistance of their prayers to help alleviate the usual human problems of sickness, anxiety, poverty and so on. The monk served as a powerful and visible reminder to all of the need for repentance and prayer.

At the same time, in some places the monks of the Eastern Church were innovative in organizing a variety of welfare services to serve their surrounding communities and, by doing so, helped to integrate monasticism more fully into the wider life of the Church. Basil, one of the great Fathers of the Church in the East, provides a good example of this kind of pastoral, monastic outreach.

Basil was born into a moderately wealthy aristocratic family in Cappadocia, the brother of Gregory of Nyssa, and Macrina. This family we met earlier in the consolation literature. Basil had a broad education that began in his native Caesarea and that later continued in the great cities of Constantinople and Athens. He took up life as a solitary, anchorite monk in Syria and Egypt, and remained a monk even when, later, he was made Bishop of Caesarea.

Basil went about reorganizing monastic life, as set out in his two works known as the *Longer Rules* and *Shorter Rules*. There was a balance of prayer and work in the life of the monk while avoiding excesses of asceticism. He had a firm conviction that human beings by their nature were social beings, having a natural desire to love and care for other people.[16] Basil's vision was firmly within the cenobitic tradition of monasticism rather than the solitary life of the anchorite-monk. The Basilian monasteries were placed in the towns, as well as in the countryside, for in an urban environment they were better situated to engage in charitable work. Basil brought together the pastoral role of the bishop with the ascetic life of the monk. The Basilian monastery was to welcome all guests. Basil ensured his monasteries would be places of pastoral care: in Caesarea his monastery had a whole variety of buildings attached for charitable purposes: a hospital, leper colony, center for the distribution of food, and a school for children.[17] This charitable monastic complex was called the *Basileias*. Care of the sick seems to have predominated and Basil himself was engaged in dressing people's wounds. A hospice for travelers who needed care was also provided, as these people required 'nurses, physicians, beasts for traveling and attendants'.[18] Basil saw a clear connection between spiritual asceticism and practical charity. The *Basileias*, in the words of Gregory Nazianzen (329-89), was 'the new city, a storehouse of piety, where disease is regarded in a religious light, and sympathy is put to the test'.[19] It was as much a place for religious formation as a refuge for the distressed.[20]

The spirituality of the Desert Fathers was synthesized in a work known as *The Ladder of Divine Ascent* by John Climacus (c.570-649). The thirty steps of the ladder – the number of steps corresponding to the age at which Christ was baptized - outline monastic virtues and vices in both the anchoritic and cenobitic traditions.

John Cassian (360-435), born near the Black Sea, traveled to Egypt to learn how to be a monk. By 415 he had founded two monasteries near Marseilles. His two works, the *Institutes* and the *Conferences*, provided the Western Church with a detailed knowledge of the rules and spiritual teachings of the leading Fathers of the Egyptian desert. Cassian acted as the bridge between the monastic East and West: his two works influenced Benedict's *Rule* over a century later.

## Western Monasticism: The Rule of St Benedict

Throughout the Middle Ages, monasticism dominated the life of the Western Church. Monasteries were, in a short space of time, to be found dotted everywhere across the map of Europe. The word 'monk' is derived from the Greek word *monos*, and means 'alone'. Although primarily places of contemplation achieved through withdrawal from the world, monasteries in the West did in fact provide pastoral care to those outside their walls. People turned to the monks and their abbeys for their spiritual nourishment: to listen to sermons; to be given instruction; to confess their sins; to seek the prayers of the monks for themselves and their dead; to be healed of sickness; to seek out care for orphaned children; to be given food and shelter; to be baptized and receive Holy Communion; and to bury their dead. In many instances, the monastery was the equivalent of the parish insofar as it provided pastoral care for the people living in its locality. The monk was called to the perfection of Christian living by witnessing to the combined love of God and neighbor, exemplified first of all in a common life within the monastery, which was under obedience to the abbot.

St Benedict (c.480-545) is regarded as the father of Western monasticism. What we know of Benedict's life comes from the *Dialogues* of Pope Gregory I (c.540-604), known better to us as Gregory the Great. The work is not a biography in the strict sense but a work written primarily to edify and inspire. Benedict had died when Gregory, himself to become a monk, was a young child. According to Gregory's account, Benedict was born into a respected Roman family in Nursia, in central Italy. He traveled to Rome for his education but was repelled by the loose morals of the city. This led him to live out a solitary life for three years in a cave at Subiaco. While there, Benedict acquired a great reputation for holiness and was invited by a neighboring group of monks to be their abbot. But Benedict's leadership proved far too strict for these monks who were used to a more relaxed way of life. They attempted to poison him. Benedict left the company of the disaffected monks and set about establishing a number of small houses of his own, each consisting of twelve monks. Yet Benedict met more trouble. His row with a neighboring priest, whom he believed was living an immoral life, forced him to move again. He found his way to Monte Cassino, about ninety miles south-east of Rome. Here he burnt the groves, a place of pagan worship, and took possession of a temple to Apollo and a ruined citadel on top of the mountain. Benedict had been successful in converting some local pagans. It was about the year 529 when he set up his monastery on the mountain and here Benedict was to remain for the rest of his life.

At Monte Cassino, Benedict wrote his *Rule* that was to have an extraordinary impact upon Western monasticism and, indeed, upon the life of the entire Church.[21] Had it not been for his *Rule*, Benedict would have faded from history as just another holy abbot, and not the towering figure presiding over medieval Christianity.

Benedict's *Rule* is a relatively short work of some seventy-three brief chapters and borrows from other monastic Rules circulating during his time. The guiding image of the *Rule* is that of a family house under the control of a strong father-figure known as the abbot, reflecting the structure of well-to-do Roman family households of the period. The *Rule* can be summed up as guiding the monk on a dynamic journey towards God.[22] Its appeal came from its ability to combine successfully spiritual wisdom and practical common sense. Because of its brevity, the *Rule* is flexible, open to diversity and modification, according to particular circumstances of time and place. Central to the Benedictine way of life is the daily, common prayer of the Divine Office (psalms, hymns, Scripture readings, texts from the Church Fathers and prayers) chanted seven times throughout the course of the day from as early as 2 a.m. The *Rule* sets out a balanced life for the monk consisting of prayer, manual work and spiritual study. Extremes of asceticism are avoided. The tone of the *Rule* is that of moderation. The abbot is to adapt his approach to the monks, according to each person's character, using either persuasion or rebuke, according to what is needed. A monk is to commit himself to the Benedictine *Rule* by the three vows of stability (designed to ground a monk in his own community), fidelity to the monastic way of life, and obedience to the abbot.

To what extent did the Benedictine Rule allow for monasticism to provide pastoral care? One curious feature of the medieval Benedictine tradition was to make provision for the special needs of children within the monastery. It became customary for parents to be able to offer children to the monastery, either out of piety or poverty or in circumstances where the monastery took responsibility for orphaned or abandoned children. Benedict demanded that the parents were to disinherit such children so that they would not be tempted to return to the world when they grew older. Such child-monks were carefully supervised in the monastery until about the age of fifteen when they were admitted as adult members to the community.[23]

Benedict's *Rule* makes provision for hospitality. Guests at the monastery are to be treated as if they are Christ himself. Precise procedures are laid out in the *Rule* for receiving them. These include a reverential prostration, prayers, the reading of Scripture and the kiss of peace: a ritualized procedure ensuring that guests were aware of the true nature of their surroundings. As monasteries developed, rich and high-ranking people made frequent use of the guest facilities in abbeys. At the same time, the *Rule* laid down that the poor and pilgrims were to be shown the greatest care. Medieval pilgrims were only too eager to accept the hospitality offered by monasteries as they traveled to the holy shrines. The journey could sometimes last for months, even years, and be dangerous. Monasteries were founded along the great pilgrim routes, such as the one to the shrine of Santiago de Compostella in Spain, to provide accommodation and spiritual sustenance to the traveler. The pastoral care offered was both practical and religious.

Monks, in Benedict's monastic arrangement, were expected to remain within their monasteries in an enclosed society. The monastery was to be surrounded by a wall, and entry was through only one gate: a town plan common in the medieval world where a city's inhabitants were under constant threat from outside, hostile forces. The *Rule* provided for the gate to be managed by the porter who had to develop the necessary skills in handling visitors.[24] On the other hand, in the spirit of Benedict's flexibility, the *Rule* allowed monks to journey outside the enclosure when circumstances made this necessary. Such circumstances were to become more common. As we shall see, the Benedictines passed through their monastery gates and were largely responsible, as missioners, for the conversion and renewal of much of Europe and the British Isles in the centuries of the early medieval world. Many became bishops and some even popes.

In his study of medieval monasticism, Ludo Milis takes a somewhat different angle by arguing that monasticism originated as an ideal that was concentrated on a longing for heaven and, as such, a system of charity to the wider world was largely absent from its way of life.[25] From the monk's perspective, the social order is the creation of God. If it is not working out properly then this is the result of human sinfulness. Disorder could be overcome only by self-denial and escape from the material world, not by social action. Those who chose poverty voluntarily were the 'better poor' compared to those who just found themselves poor. Spiritual poverty was of higher religious value than economic poverty. Concern for the poor, the sick and homeless, maintains Milis, was normally only ever a marginal issue for the monasteries. For example, he discusses the care of the sick within monastic life which the *Rule* of Benedict indicates was care primarily for its own members. Where monks did found hospitals, they were not normally staffed by monks but administered from afar. It was rare to find Benedictines directly involved in caring for the sick, writes Milis. An outreach form of ministry was directed towards hospitality but this was more for persons who chose temporary exile and hardship for the religious purpose of pilgrimage and less a matter of assistance to the destitute. Voluntary self-denial was more highly regarded than involuntary suffering.

However, this viewpoint that early monasticism was little interested in pastoral care for those who were not monks is open to challenge. Yet Milis does remind us of the fact that, at least in its outlook, monasticism was concerned more with the journey with Christ to heaven than the journey to Christ in the suffering and dispossessed.

At the same time, as Milis clearly acknowledges, the sick and poor did look for help from the monasteries and the monks did respond. There were precious few other agencies, apart from the Church, to carry out social welfare. We do well to remember that the monks were responsible for building roads, clearing and draining swamps, cultivating the land with crops and breeding livestock. Each monastery had a vast complex of buildings: churches, workshops, stores, dairies, barns and libraries. Monasteries, as time went by, became a significant part of the economic life of medieval Europe. As major landholders in a feudal world, the Benedictine monks had responsibility for the large numbers of people who worked their estates. Although engaged in manual labor, Benedictine monks spent a great part of their waking hours in common prayer. Workers were needed for their estates. As with their counterparts, the feudal lords, mutual obligations existed between the monastic landowner and tenant. Landowners were responsible for their tenants' welfare. One can only assume that lay people must have found material as well as spiritual help from religiously dedicated monks, whether as tenants or as vagrants.

By the time of the High Middle Ages, Benedictine monasticism had grown into a powerful movement. Monasteries developed into exceptional centers of learning and scholarship that gave new meaning to their pastoral apostolate. Particularly under the direction of the great French monastery at Cluny, Benedictine monastic life evolved into networks of faith and culture that exerted extraordinary power over medieval society. We will take up these later developments in the following chapter.

## Irish Monasticism: The Celtic Tradition

Overlooking the River Shannon, which gently winds its way through the countryside of County Offaly, are the superb stone ruins of the monastery of Clonmacnoise. Round, phallus-like towers - used once as lookouts and places of shelter and storage in time of invasion - perhaps witness to a druid past. They stand alongside distinctively ringed Irish high crosses and the remains of gravestones and churches. The monastery once lay at the crossroads of medieval trade routes linking all parts of Ireland. St Ciarán, the son of a chariot maker, is alleged to have founded the monastery in 548. Clonmacnoise had such a reputation that monks from all parts of Europe went there to study and pray. The monastery was widely known as a center for literature and art. Many kings of Tara and Connaught chose the monastery as their place of burial. The ruins of today are largely from the tenth to the twelfth centuries. The original buildings, like other early Irish monasteries, were constructed of wood, clay and wattle that have since been swallowed up by the passing of time. Unlike the well laid out monasteries elsewhere in Europe, Irish monasteries were an assortment of beehive-like small huts. Irish monks lived a cenobitical, communal style of life, but possibly some solitary anchorites lived on the fringes of the monastic settlements. The Shannon was a deadly artery for Vikings who plundered the precious silver and gold liturgical vessels of Clonmacnoise on at least eight occasions between the ninth and twelfth centuries: hence the importance of the round towers. Undefended monasteries, with their treasures, were easy targets. It was from an Irish Celtic monastery, probably on the remote island of Iona off the south-west coast of Scotland, that the magnificently illuminated Book of Kells was produced around 800. A manuscript of the four Gospels, it found its way to the monastery of Kells in County Meath for safekeeping before ending up in Trinity College, Dublin, where it can be seen today. In a country without towns, these Celtic monasteries were active centers of pastoral care serving the local people.

The Romans never conquered Ireland. The country was divided into numerous tribal units constantly at war with each other. The different tribes engaged in trade as well as making raids on Roman territory to the east, in Britain. St Patrick (c.390-460), as a youth of sixteen, was a victim of one such raid and was sold as a slave in Ireland before managing to escape some six years later. He came from a clerical family. His grandfather had been a priest and his father a deacon. Patrick was ordained a bishop and, at about the age of forty, he returned to Ireland as a missionary in 430. The Irish were the first race in the West, not part of the Roman Empire, to become Christian. Patrick's mission met with remarkable success. He organized the Irish Church along the same lines as existed in Britain and Gaul: geographic territories headed by a bishop. The system was not to last. A century after his death the Church there became very different from anywhere else in the Christian world in its pastoral structures. What was the reason for this? The Church in Ireland had to adapt itself to a tribal society in which there were no cities. The monastery and its abbot replaced the diocese with its bishop as the main pastoral unit. Such monasteries were closely linked to particular clans with the abbot usually a kinsman of the tribal chief. Bishops in Ireland at this time, had a more restricted role and certainly less power than their counterparts elsewhere in the Christian world: they were called upon to perform certain religious rites, such as the ordination of clergy, and were available to the monastic abbot when he required their special services. It was the abbot in the Irish Church who had the primary responsibility for pastoral life, as pastoral ministry in that land revolved around monasteries.[26]

However, this commonly held view of the early Irish Church, organized primarily along monastic rather than episcopal lines, is challenged by some scholars. Richard Sharpe asserts that there is no evidence that pastoral care in local communities was dependent upon monks. In eighth-century Ireland, Sharpe argues, bishops established a good deal of control over churches. Within early Christian Ireland's small kingdoms (a kingdom was known as a túath) there was usually a larger church with its bishop. A rich layman often owned the church. He had control of the church's property. Sharpe maintains that the bishop had the power to impose a levy on the owner of these churches if pastoral care was not provided. The bishop used money raised in this way to ensure pastoral ministry was available to the people of that area.[27] Both monks who were also priests (regular clergy) and priests under the direct charge of the bishop (secular clergy) provided pastoral care. Sharpe concludes:

The mother-churches were surely communities of priests and other clergy, some of whom may have been monks living under vows; the communal life may well have included regular singing of the office, but it did not exclude priests from pastoral activity. In recognizing that such churches were communities, it is all too easy to lapse into the phrase 'monastic community' and so 'monastery', but we must avoid exaggerating the distinction between regular and secular communities.[28]

Throughout their history, the Irish have been thought of as wanderers, forever in search of new places in which to live. The early Irish monks were no exception. Between the sixth and ninth centuries wandering Irish monks were a familiar sight across Europe. Just off the west coast of Ireland, lashed by the winter storms of the Atlantic Ocean, is the small and inhospitable island of Skellig Michael. It appears more a place for seagulls to make their nests on its craggy rocks than for humans to set up their dwellings. But Celtic monks did construct their simple huts there and survived in this extraordinary place for the best part of seven hundred years: Celtic monks were forever in search of unwelcoming places to engage in their penances. From many of these penitential habitats Irish monks turned their attention to pastoral outreach: they set out to convert pagans. This remarkable story will be taken up later in this chapter.

## The Mission to the Barbarians

### The Fall of the Roman Empire

From the time of Constantine the Church enjoyed peace and growth, promoted by a strong state. The invasion of a host of barbarian tribes into the empire and the havoc they wreaked shattered all that. Yet from this upheaval the Church was able to stir itself by gathering its resources and embarking upon the pastoral task of the conversion of these unfamiliar peoples. Leading the army of missioners were the monks. Monasticism took on a new role as contemplation and pastoral care went hand in hand.

This mission has to be seen in the context of the course of events that occurred during the last days of the Roman Empire. Constantine had made himself sole emperor of both the Eastern and Western sectors of the empire and ruled, no longer in Rome, but from Constantinople in the East. From 395 to 480 the rule of the empire reverted back to two emperors, one in the East and one in the West, with equal rights. Greek was the language of the East and Latin that of the West, ensuring the development of two different cultural expressions of both Church and state. Despite these arrangements, the empire was understood to be a single unit and not two empires.

Its frontiers had always been under constant threat. The Eastern frontier had more or less stabilized by 363 as the threat from the Persian enemy had subsided. In the Western provinces it was a different story. Visigothic tribes in the north, outside the empire's frontiers, began to stir. They were refugees in flight from the dreaded Huns who had pushed westwards. The Visigoths were permitted to cross the Danube in 376. Unhappy with the way their Roman officials had treated them, these people entered into conflict with the forces of the empire and won victory in 378, at Adrianople, where they killed the Emperor Valens. Like other barbarian invaders after them, they were permitted to settle within the empire as federates, bringing with them their families, animals, belongings and religion. It was not long before they were on the move again and, under their leader Alaric, sacked Rome in 410. It was the beginning of the end for the empire.

Other Germanic tribes were also on the march by the early fifth century, penetrating the empire at various points: Ostrogoths and Lombards in Italy; Vandals in North Africa; Visigoths in southern France and Spain; Franks in Gaul; Angles, Jutes and Saxons in Britain. They were followed in later times by more waves of bloodthirsty peoples, such as the Avars, Magyars and Vikings.

The last Roman Emperor of the West was an adolescent by the name of Romulus Augustulus (475-76), pushed aside by the barbarian Ostrogoth named Odoacer (c.435-93). He was succeeded by Theodoric (c.454-526). By this time the capital of the Western Empire had long moved from Rome to Milan (354) and then to Ravenna, at the beginning of the fifth century (404). Strategically situated on the Adriatic, Ravenna was far more accessible to the Eastern provinces than were Rome or Milan. The Roman Empire was now centered in the East and, in effect, had been reduced to what is called the Byzantine Empire. It survived until the final assault on Constantinople by the Muslim Turks in 1453.

Emperor Justinian (527-65) responded to the losses by a vigorous assault on the barbarians but was able to do little more than win back territory in North Africa and the coastal areas of Italy, including Rome and Ravenna. Justinian adorned Ravenna with magnificent churches and the city became the seat of the Byzantine ruler of Italy, known as the *exarch*, until the middle of the eighth century.

By way of conclusion to this story of invasions, there was the rise of Muslim rule in Arabia, inspired by the teachings of the prophet Mohammed (c.570-632). Muslims, united in their zeal for conquest by a holy war, *jihad*, overran Byzantine territories in the Balkans, captured Christian lands in the Middle East and swept across North Africa. By 711 they had crossed the straits into southern Spain where the Visigothic kingdom fell before it. Christians were forced to retreat to the north of the Iberian Peninsula. Working their way across Central Europe, the Muslims were finally defeated near Poitiers by the Frankish warrior, Charles Martel (*c.*690-741), in 732. Muslim domination in Western Europe had been averted. But vast areas of land where Christianity had once flourished, had been wiped out and replaced by the new Muslim faith.

### Arianism and the Barbarians

The barbarian tribes that descended into the Roman Empire and became absorbed into its life and institutions were not all pagans. Great numbers of these people were already Christian, but baptized into the Arian form of the Christian faith. Alaric, who had sacked Rome, was an Arian Christian, as was Odoacer, the Ostrogoth who had ousted the last emperor of the West. The orthodox faith, as we have already seen, had been agreed upon in the early Ecumenical Councils of the Church. The heretical Arian form of Christian faith became no longer acceptable within the empire. But Arian Christians continued to exist and to flourish. Among these was Ulfilas (*c.*311-383). He was a descendant of Christian captives who had lived among the Goths for a number of generations. Ordained a bishop, he and some companions went to live among Gothic Christians outside the boundaries of the empire. Here they had considerable success promoting Arian Christianity. Among those converted to the Arian Christian faith were Visigoths, Ostrogoths, Burgundians and Vandals. These people brought their distinct form of Christianity with them when they moved inside the empire. As such, these Arian Christians lived alongside Catholic Christians. The Arians, belonging to the different barbarian tribes, built their own baptisteries and churches where they settled and ruled.[29] In time they began to be assimilated further into the religion of the local Roman population and by the early seventh century Arianism had virtually died out in the West.[30]

### The Conversion of England

The date when Christianity first reached the Roman province of Britain remains obscure. But, in all probability, it was brought by traders and soldiers from the Continent in the early third century. Julius Caesar had arrived in Britain in 55 BCE but conquest of the eastern and central portion of Britain did not begin until 43 CE under the Emperor Claudius (41-54). In 410 the Roman army was withdrawn from Britain to deal with the problem of uprisings in Gaul. The army never returned and the island was left undefended. It would appear that by the fourth century the Church in Britain, organized along Roman lines, had its own bishops who attended general councils of the Church abroad.[31] Roman Christianity was all but obliterated in the late fifth and sixth centuries with invasions of diverse Germanic peoples that included the Angles, Jutes and Saxons. The country split into numerous, small kingdoms constantly at war with each other. England was in need of reconversion. We learn of what happened from the monk Bede (c.673-735) in his *Ecclesiastical History of the English People*.[32] However, in the Celtic west of the country Christianity probably continued to remain in some form.

The story of a mission to England and the rebirth of Christianity in that land begins with Pope Gregory I. Before becoming pope, he was walking one day through the slave market in Rome. A group of fair-haired young slave boys caught his eye. Gregory asked where they were from. When informed that they were Angles he responded by saying that they were more like angels! The conversion of the Angles became a task, then, dear to his heart. It's a charming story but precisely what really stimulated the future pope to organize a mission to England remains uncertain. The earliest clue is a letter dated 595 with Pope Gregory giving orders to his agent in Gaul indicating, among other instructions, that money should be used to ransom Anglo-Saxon boys aged seventeen or eighteen who were then to be placed in monasteries for the service of God. His purpose is unclear. However, a priest was to accompany them on the journey lest, as pagans, they fall seriously ill and need baptism. Were they to be trained as missionaries to their own people? The evidence is silent.[33]

Gregory, himself a monk, acted further by sending a group of monks to convert and offer pastoral care to this far-off region of the Anglo-Saxons. The leader of the mission was Augustine, a monk from the same monastery in Rome - St Andrew's on the Caelian Hill - which Gregory had founded. The party set off on their long journey. After reaching Lérins, in Gaul, they began to lose heart and Augustine returned to Rome to ask the pope for permission to abandon the whole enterprise. But the mission was too dear to Gregory's heart. He made Augustine (d.604 or 605) an abbot-bishop and ordered him to resume the task and not be disheartened by any fear-mongering talk concerning possible hardships that awaited them in Britain. Crossing the English Channel, the forty monks and small number of priests landed on the island of Thanet in 597. According to Bede's account of the mission, they sent interpreters (Frankish priests) to Ethelbert (d. *c.*616), king of Kent, to inform him of their arrival. Ethelbert, with his entourage, crossed the water to meet them in the open air where the king felt safer from the threat of any magic powers his visitors might possess. The Roman monks approached him in procession carrying a silver cross and chanting litanies, out to impress their hosts. First impressions counted for much. Now Ethelbert's wife, Bertha (d. before 616) happened to be a Christian for she was a daughter of a Frankish king, something that greatly facilitated the mission. It meant there were already contacts between Ethelbert's kingdom and the Frankish Church on the Continent. Ethelbert permitted the Italian missionaries to settle in Canterbury and allowed them to go about their business but he himself was not ready, as yet, to accept their faith. A monastery, just outside the city of Canterbury, was built to house the monks and an old church from Roman times was restored and made into a cathedral. Canterbury now had its first archbishop. It is reported that there were ten thousand people baptized on Christmas Day 597. The way of bringing new Christians into the Church had changed dramatically since the days of the catechumenate - with its rigorous standards of entry and lengthy preparation for baptism – of just a century or two earlier. Pastoral care, as it related to evangelization, now looked vastly different in the age of mass baptisms. Ethelbert eventually was baptized. In the meantime, Pope Gregory I sent out more missionaries. Augustine's Church in Canterbury was to remain strongly attached to the papacy in Rome to which it owed its immediate origins and directions.

Almost at the same time as the Roman mission to Britain, another took place by Irish missionary monks to Northumbria, the north-east region of the country. But others had been there before the Irish monks arrived. Christianity was first brought to these northern lands by the Italian, Paulinus (d.644), who was chaplain to Ethelburga (d.*c.*676), the daughter of King Ethelburt in Kent. The plan was for Paulinus to convert the region of Northumbria by gifts, including the gift of Ethelburga as a bride to its pagan leader, King Edwin (*c.*585-633). The marriage took place as planned and Edwin was baptized by Paulinus. The Italian priest, Paulinus, was made the Bishop of York, the same city where Constantine had been proclaimed as emperor by his troops a little more than three hundred years earlier. But, in the end, things did not work out well. Edwin was killed in battle and Paulinus and Ethelburga fled back to Kent by boat. Although there had been numerous Christian converts, no organized form of Church structure remained for pastoral oversight.

Iona, the site of a monastery off the north-west coast of Scotland founded by an Irish monk named Columba (c.521-97), became the source of this new mission to the Anglo-Saxons in the northern part of Britain. And it was to have lasting effect. The Celtic monk Aidan (d.651) set up a missionary abbey on the island of Lindisfarne, granted to him by King Oswald (c.605-42). From here he and his companions set out to evangelize Northumbria. Again, a monastic pattern of evangelization was undertaken, assisted by clergy. An interesting feature of monasticism in Britain was that of the 'double monasteries' for men and women: they were similar to those on the Continent. They were primarily for women, to which men were attached, and governed by saintly abbesses, such as Hilda of Whitby (614-80) and Ethelreda of Ely (d.679). These double monasteries were ruled by women largely of royal or noble birth. Ethelreda was married to King Ecgfrith but decided to become a nun, founding and building her double monastery at Ely upon her own land which had been a dowry from a previous marriage.[34] Northumbria soon became a flourishing center of Christianity. Monasteries, such as those at Jarrow and Wearmouth, became known for their amazing literary and artistic works.[35] In 995 the bishop's cathedral moved from the island of Lindisfarne to the more convenient site of Durham on the mainland.

Two traditions had thus arisen in Britain by the seventh century: the Roman tradition associated with Augustine centered on Canterbury in the south, and the Celtic tradition linked with Aidan at Lindisfarne in the north. Although united in doctrine, each Church had its distinct traditions. A dispute arose over the date for celebrating Easter with the matter finally being settled in a synod held at Whitby in 664. Here the Roman tradition prevailed, thus setting a precedent for Roman influence and custom upon the whole English Church. Bishops were often abbots and so pastoral care was strongly, but not exclusively, monastic in character. The monk served as the pastoral model for the people by living an ordered Christian life of prayer and penance: he could be both a contemplative and a missionary.

### Mission to the Franks

The Northumbrian monks also turned their attention towards the continent of Europe. In 678, Wilfrid (634-709), having been expelled as Bishop of York, set out for Rome to appeal to the pope. Upon landing in the lowlands of Frisia (the area of the Netherlands), he was received well by the King Aldgils and preached the gospel with great success during his winter sojourn. Willibrord (658-739) built upon the mission to the Frisians in 690, having previously spent some years earlier in an Irish monastery. He set up the see of Utrecht that was to prove a gateway for missionary activity elsewhere.

Winfrid, later named Boniface (680-754), is remembered not only for his efforts in bringing Christianity to the people of Frisia and the Frankish territories of Germany but also for his work of reforming the Church already in existence there. Christianity, in many places, was still closely connected with pagan ideas and practices. It seems that the Franks had never been adequately catechized: conversion usually was by peoples rather than individuals. The Franks received the Christian faith after the conversion of their king, Clovis (c.466-511), whose wife was already Christian. Like Constantine almost two centuries earlier, Clovis embraced Christianity after winning a military battle that he attributed to the intervention of the God of his Christian wife, Clotilde (474-545). Clovis and more than three thousand of his warriors submitted themselves to the waters of baptism sometime in the 490s. It was a significant moment in the history of the Church. As Clovis extended his kingdom, conquering more of Gaul, Catholic Christianity spread throughout tribes of people that formerly had been Arian. The Franks occupied the large mass of land that was the economic, military and political heart of Western Europe.

Boniface stands in the English monastic tradition of missionary activity. He came, not from Northumbria, but from Wessex in England. Like Willibrord before him, Boniface was intent upon bringing Roman traditions and papal ordering to his pastoral task of the episcopal organization of the Church in Germany. He took with him the blessing of Pope Gregory II (715-31) and set off on his mission in 719, after some earlier unsuccessful efforts to convert the Frisians. As Lawrence remarks:

> This re-exportation to Northern Europe of the Anglo-Saxon idea of Roman ecclesiastical order had momentous consequences for medieval Christendom.[36]

Boniface's pastoral methods followed a pattern: preaching, confronting pagan customs, conversions, and setting up ecclesiastical structures. In some places he founded small monastic communities. This was all accompanied by regular reports to the pope and journeys to Rome to discuss progress and to seek further advice. There is the famous incident of Boniface confronting pagans near Geismar, in Hesse. Situated there was a sacred oak tree dedicated to the god Thor. Boniface proceeded boldly to cut down the tree and, to the crowd's amazement, failed to experience any of the expected reprisals from the gods. Boniface then took the wood of Thor's oak and constructed a little chapel. The local people were suitably impressed and, after the fall of their god, requested baptism.

Central to Boniface's pastoral strategy was the reform of the Church of the Frankish people, especially its clergy. Bishops were required to assess their catechetical teaching and guard against persisting pagan customs among the clergy and people; priests were to dress simply and were forbidden to carry weapons or to hunt. But, as tends to happen with most reformers, he met stiff opposition. Frankish bishops resisted Boniface's attempt to 'clean up' the clergy, especially their tradition of nepotism, with the office of bishop being handed down from father to son, and lifestyles characterized by hunting and carousing: Bishop Milo of Trier and Reims died in a boar hunt.[37] Boniface was about establishing order, hoping to rid the Franks of their habits of compromise and laxity. Christian priests were known to make sacrifices to the god Jupiter and the slaves of Christian masters had been sold for pagan sacrifice.[38] Such abuses needed to be eradicated. His pastoral plan to achieve his goals was one of education, legislation and severity: a mission aimed at civilization.[39]

To achieve his pastoral aims, Boniface relied upon the help of the Frankish kings, first under Charles Martel and then his son Pepin (714-68). After Pepin assumed the title 'King of the Franks' in 751, it was Boniface who, as the pope's representative, crowned him. Following Pepin's death, one of his sons, Charles (c.742-814), organized much of Western Europe (contemporary France and Germany) into the Frankish kingdom. He became known as 'Charlemagne' (Charles the Great). In the year 800 Pope Leo III (795-816) crowned Charles at the Christmas Mass in St Peter's Basilica in Rome. The pope conferred upon him the title 'Holy Roman Emperor': Church and state came together.

The conversion of Germany was largely the achievement of missionaries from England. It was the monks, above all, who spread the Christian faith and tended to the pastoral needs of the people: preaching, teaching, administering sacraments and providing charitable care for those in need. Many monks, in the early medieval Church, were both evangelists and pastors while at the same time witnessing to a life characterized by asceticism and contemplative praise of God. Not all were saints but, then again, their vocation as monks was to be that of repentant sinners.

## Mission to the Slavs

Eastern Europe, populated by Slavs, attributes its reception of the Christian faith to two Greek brothers, Cyril (826-69) and Methodius (*c.*815-85). Both were monks in Bithynia. In the 800s a Slavic state known as Moravia arose. The two missionary brothers devised a Slavic alphabet (subsequently called 'Cyrillic', after Cyril) and translated the Bible and liturgical texts into this new language. Their style of pastoral care was a successful effort of enculturation of the gospel, especially by means of language. By the end of the first millennium most of the Slavs of Eastern Europe were Christian and the Church had three official liturgical languages: Greek, Latin and Slavonic. Again, the pastoral mission of evangelization was the work of monks.

## The Celtic Penitentials

The pastoral response to the reality of human weakness - sin - within the lives of individual Christians altered greatly in the early medieval Church from the 'public penance' of the patristic age. This marked change of penitential practice originated in the monasteries of the Celtic churches. It involved disclosing a list of sins in private to a confessor who imposed a penance. The confessor had access to manuals that classified sins according to their category and level of seriousness. He then matched these sins with appropriate penances to be carried out by the sinner. The manuals classifying sins and their corresponding penances were known as *penitentials*. Everything was strictly measured. Unlike the penitential practice of an earlier time, this form of pastoral care, first of all, covered all kinds of sins, not just the more serious variety such as apostasy, murder and adultery. Second, it was carried out in a private rather than a public way. Third, it did not involve being associated with a special group or distinct Order of Penitents, as previously was the custom. Fourth, this type of penance could be used frequently and not just once in a lifetime. And finally, the confessor had a more direct role in assessing guilt and in guiding a person's conscience and spiritual life. This form of penance proved far more flexible in its adaptability to the moral circumstances of different penitents. Originally designed for monks, it spread and found common usage among all ranks of people within the Church, and it developed into one of the most characteristic forms of pastoral care within the Catholic tradition. It was a big innovation in pastoral care.

Among the Celtic monks there was a characteristic severity in their search for holiness. From this arose the need for a means to monitor the extent of moral failure, and a frequent recourse to some form of penitential discipline fostered this. Manuals that opened up the whole range of possible sins, and the manner by which they could be atoned for through penances, proved ideal.

### Penitential Texts

Penitential texts were compiled widely during the sixth to the eighth centuries, especially in Ireland. There, the monastery was the main place for providing spiritual care for people in general. It was, in effect, the parish. The private confession of sin and the acceptance of a penance according to the requirements laid out in the penitential manuals, originally designed for monks, soon became a common means of religious practice for everyone. It became known as the 'tariff penance': a system of well defined penalties imposed for moral offences. These penitential manuals were written originally either in Latin or Gaelic. The list of sins set out in these books, in fact, relied upon the work of earlier writers, especially John Cassian. He had identified eight principal vices: gluttony, lust, covetousness, sorrow, anger, spiritual disgust, vanity and pride.[40] The penitentials offer no form of liturgical rite of the confession of sins. They simply list the sins and their corresponding penances.

The earliest penitential texts that are known to us come from Wales and possibly some, or all of them, made their way to Ireland. There are four principal Welsh texts: *Gildas on Penance; Synod of North Britain; Grave of Victory;* and the *Book of David.* The first two of these texts deal with the sins of monks and clerics only while the latter two are concerned with the sins of all the baptized.

There are three main Celtic penitentials that are of Irish origin: *Penitential of Finnian; Penitential of Columbanus;* and *Penitential of Cummean.* These Irish texts all date from the late sixth to the mid seventh centuries. The *Penitential of Columbanus* was used widely throughout the continent of Europe and may well have been composed outside Ireland. Columbanus (c.543-615) traveled extensively throughout Europe. His text is divided into three parts, one each for the use of monks, clergy and laity: each group has its distinct types of sins requiring their own forms of penance. Columbanus' manual provides for greater attention to each individual penitent and the role of the confessor became more demanding. The text of Cummean is the most developed of all the penitentials. Other minor Irish texts are generally decrees from a variety of Irish synods that provide for more severe forms of penance.[41]

### Religious and Secular Influences

What influences came to bear upon the Celtic penitentials that had lasting meaning for the development of sacramental confession? In ancient Irish law some form of compensation had to be given to the injured party when a crime had been committed. The principle of compensation was an integral part of *brehon* law. Compensation had to be commensurate with the extent of the injury as well as the status of the offended person. In the penitential texts certain penances that involve forfeiture of material wealth or loss of status within clerical rank may also reflect punitive practices contained within *brehon* law. It is quite possible that secular Irish *brehon* law codes may have been used as models by monks when composing their own religious penitential texts.[42]

Within Irish monasticism, provision was made for a spiritual guide known as an *anamchara*. It is a Gaelic word meaning 'soul-friend'. Such persons were highly esteemed within the community of the monastery. Each monk was expected to have his *anamchara*. This institution may possibly be traced back to the druids who respected certain figures for their wisdom as teachers and judges.[43] In the lives of the early Irish saints there is a common saying: 'Anyone without an *anamchara* is like a body without a head', a saying attributed to two sixth-century saints, Brigid (d.*c*.523) and Comgall (*c*.516-*c*.601), the latter being a teacher of Columbanus.[44]

A more direct Christian influence would have been the monks of the Eastern Church who confided in each other about the state of their spiritual lives. This practice was called *exagoreusis*, the opening of one's heart to another. The aim was to arrive at a state of *hesychia*, or peace of heart. But among them the emphasis was on spiritual healing. Within the Western *penitentials*, by way of contrast, there was more stress on judgment, with the appropriate penalties. Punishment and expiation tended to be given more prominence than inner conversion, although this was not absent.[45]

### Characteristics of Penance

The penitentials placed much emphasis upon the detailed confession of particular sins whereas in the older penitential practices, in the time of the early Church Fathers, it was generally a matter of expressing sinfulness in a more general manner. Sins were of an infinite variety: habitual drunkenness in a bishop; stealing a horse; setting fire to a church; a monk talking privately to a woman; worshiping the moon, sun or stars; homicide; and an array of sordid sexual behaviours. In the Celtic form of penance, the confessor took on the role of judge. His task was to assess both the gravity of the sin and the degree of guilt. As judge, the confessor had to ensure that the punishment, namely the penance, matched the sin. At the same time, a confessor was understood as standing in solidarity with the sinner and may even have joined with the sinner in a penance of fasting and prayer.

In the *penitentials* one can see developing a method of pastoral care that was more attuned to the specific needs of each individual, an approach that was perfected in the *Pastoral Rule* of Gregory the Great. The pastoral minister, in the person of the confessor, was required to possess skills and aptitude in discerning the roots of the penitent's sins. The latter *penitentials*, especially, provide the confessor with a range of Scriptural and patristic texts to assist him in his guidance of the penitent. The confessor was expected to be a physician of the soul who was able to diagnose the illness and prescribe the needed remedy: pastoral care had reached a new level of sophistication. In the *Penitential of Columbanus* we read:

> For as doctors of the body compound their medicines in diverse kinds; thus they heal wounds in one manner, sickness in another, boils in another, fractures in another, burns in another. So also should spiritual doctors treat with diverse kinds of cures the wounds of souls, their sicknesses (offences), pains, ailments and infirmities.[46]

Penalties tended to be heavier for clerics than laypeople. Finnian (c.495-579), for example, ordered a quarrelsome cleric to go on a diet of bread and water for half a year and abstain from meat and wine for a year. A layman got off the same offence with just a week's penance. But other factors also determined the severity and duration of a penance: age, sex, economic status, education and disposition. In many of the penitential manuals there was almost an arithmetic correspondence between offense and penalty. The manuals were designed to assist confessors to manage offences efficiently and simply.

Not only men but women, too, acted as confessors. It was reported that Brendan (484-577 or 583) confessed to Ita (d. 570 or 577) and Columbanus sought out counsel from holy women during his youth. Abbesses - as powerful leaders of monastic communities of women - and other saintly monastic women in all likelihood would have been engaged as confessors before the time when private confession of sin came to be understood in strictly sacramental terms, requiring the confessor to be in holy orders. This later understanding of penance in sacramental terms came about as late as the twelfth century.[47]

One feature of the *penitential* discipline was the provision for making payments of money or some other form of material offering as a means of reducing the severity of the penance, something also common in Frankish secular law of the time. The practice was referred to as *compositio*. Also a common practice was vicarious penance, where somebody else did the penance on one's behalf for a suitable fee. These activities affected the theological understanding of redemption: the death of Jesus came to be interpreted as paying the price on behalf of us all, a vicarious substitution of penance for sins committed. It ultimately led to the theology of indulgences and the abuses that followed.[48] Penances could be commuted, in which case their severity could be increased in order to shorten their duration. These practices became more common by the end of the tenth century as the penitential practices spread throughout Europe with the aid of new manuals. The Celtic system became widespread throughout the Western Church.[49]

### Opposition and Final Acceptance

The *penitentials*, produced then throughout the Western Church but bearing their underlying Celtic spirituality, met with stiff opposition. Ninth-century bishops denounced them because of confusing discrepancies among them and their lack of authorization by Church authorities. The Synod of Paris in 829 ordered the *penitentials* to be burned. Bishops had lost control of pastoral practice. Two centuries later Peter Damian (1007-72), the cardinal-bishop of Ostia, near Rome, sarcastically dismissed them. But there was nothing else to put in their place, especially for the less-educated clergy. Private penance had become firmly established as a means of pastoral guidance and devotional practice. In 1215 the Fourth Lateran Council officially endorsed the Celtic form of private penance as the authorized form for sacramental reconciliation and forgiveness. It was linked to the Easter reception of Holy Communion, and both sacraments were to be received at least once per year.

### Priests and Parishes

As a result of the barbarian invasions, unified authority in the West began to break down. It became the task of bishops to maintain order. Living in urban centers, the bishop assumed an increasingly secular role and often was responsible for overseeing civic tasks. The process had begun during Constantine's reign as Church and state became enmeshed. Under feudalism, bishops - like monastic abbots - became large landholders. Wealth was accompanied by responsibilities. Like lay landholders, a bishop could be called upon to provide funds from his estates to pay soldiers, for example. And, unlike the patristic age when bishops were theologians, by the early Middle Ages they had become far more caught up in material concerns of secular administration within their territories. Yet the bishop was the chief liturgist in his diocese and priests could preside over worship only with his authorization.

Churches fell into three main groups: the bishop's church or cathedral; the monastic church; and private churches owned by the nobility. As Christianity spread from cities into the countryside, new rural churches were set up and staffed by priests. However, the range of pastoral services provided by these rural churches could be limited. 'Baptismal churches', as the name implies, were the more important churches outside the city center; they were the authorized places for administering the sacrament of baptism. Lesser churches, on the other hand, did not provide baptismal services or Mass on major feast days. On these occasions, the people were required to go to their nearest baptismal church. Baptismal churches grew in autonomy and foreshadowed the later parish church.

Wealthy people endowed churches and these might become their own possession. They were known as 'proprietary churches' (from the German *Eigenkirchen*). In some respects, churches were thought of as property: the owner could trade them, leave them as an inheritance to family members, or even sell them. The system of the private ownership of churches grew out of Germanic law in an agrarian society where everything was viewed in terms of land. The owner of the church, often a wealthy landowner, had jurisdiction over the priest who was employed to provide pastoral services to the people on the estate. It was the owner who appointed the priest, laid down his duties, and who could dismiss him from office. After the eighth century, almost all churches, monasteries and even cathedrals were treated as the private possession of their owners, who may have been the local ruler, priest, abbot or bishop.

In cities, priests lived together in the bishop's house. By the ninth century these clerics were known as canons, forming the cathedral chapter. This was a legal and economic corporation that existed alongside the bishop. From this arrangement developed in other places the 'collegiate church', where a group of priests lived together and shared in the ministry of the pastoral care of the people: an early form of team ministry. They tended to attract a better-educated clergy who enjoyed a higher income.

Attached to these pastoral offices was what was known as a benefice. This grew out of the system of proprietary churches but restored episcopal control to Church property. The benefice provided a guaranteed income to the person possessing it. A rural priest, usually a simple peasant and married with a family and barely literate, was guaranteed some kind of income. The better paying benefices attached to more wealthy churches, dioceses and abbeys were eagerly sought by clerics of all ranks, a system that bred patronage, corruption and absentee pastors who might possess numerous benefices in their name. The result of all this was that religious institutions came to be viewed more for their financial rewards than as spiritual communities. Good pastoral care, as a result, was all too often sadly lacking.[50]

### The 'Pastoral Rule' of Gregory the Great

The *Pastoral Rule* of Pope Gregory I (who is remembered by history as St Gregory the Great), is a milestone in the history of Christian ministry. It describes the qualities needed in a Christian leader and the way pastoral care should be exercised. It soon became a standard text for those engaged in ministry and was one of the most widely known and read books of the medieval Church. It is probably no exaggeration to claim that it has fashioned for all time the way pastoral care is understood and practiced. Gregory's *Pastoral Rule* demonstrates a remarkable insight into different personality types and behaviors that call for individualized responses. As such, Gregory recognized that each pastoral case is to be handled differently. The pastoral leader must be one who clearly understands human nature and who is able to engage skilfully in interpersonal relationships. Yet these abilities of the pastoral leader must be founded upon a spiritual asceticism of *peritia*, by which he means virtuosity rendered socially useful. Charity and asceticism go together.[51] For Gregory, ministry is above all else an exercise of love done in a spirit of humility. He attempted to join the spiritual values of monastic contemplation with the needs of the active ministry. 'Gregory wants fervently to know and control each step of the heart: every footprint must be scrutinized, every feeling sifted through the flexible hand of discretion.'[52]

### *Gregory's Life*

Gregory was born in Rome of a noble family shortly before 540 and, by his early thirties, he had risen to the office of Urban Prefect of the city of Rome. His skills as an administrator had been quickly recognized. Rome was in decline as a result of the upheavals of the barbarian invasions. Much of the population of the city had fled and Italy was under the alien influence of Greek culture, ruled by the

Byzantine exarch in Ravenna. The old Roman world was quickly fading away but a new Christian Rome was starting to take form. Gregory felt the call to a life of contemplation and turned over his family home to the Church: it became the monastery of St Andrew, situated on Rome's Caelian Hill. As well, Gregory established six other monastic houses in Italy and Sicily from his family's extensive estates. But his life of peace and calmness on the Caelian Hill was interrupted. Gregory was sent on active service as the pope's representative to the Byzantine court in Constantinople. He returned to Rome and was elected pope.

As the Bishop of Rome, his duties were not just spiritual. In the confused times in which he lived, Pope Gregory I was also responsible for much of the civic administration of the city, even its military defense. He was virtually ruler of both the city and Church. In dealing with the emperor in Constantinople, Gregory was insistent upon the primacy of the Roman Church and its bishop. Gregory was strengthening the papacy and the Western Church as a whole. It was he, as we have already seen, who sent Augustine and his monks to Canterbury to convert the English. Gregory saw the importance of good, pastoral care that required a well-trained and spiritually motivated clergy able to exercise compassionate authority. In his first year as pope, Gregory set about writing his *Pastoral Rule*. In it he sums up his vision of pastoral office:

> No one ventures to teach any art unless he has learned it after deep thought. With what rashness, then, would the pastoral office be undertaken by the unfit, seeing that the government of souls is the art of arts.[53]

### The 'Pastoral Rule'

The *Pastoral Rule* consists of four sections. In the first, Gregory outlines the difficulties and responsibilities of the pastoral office. The second part sets out the qualities that a good pastor ought to possess; these include both inner and outer characteristics. The third section deals with the various kinds of people in need of care, and describes the methods required of the pastor to respond to their different requirements. And in the fourth section, which is just one chapter, the pastor is urged to be mindful of his own weaknesses.

Gregory is concerned to teach his readers how to become good physicians of the soul. This involves recognizing different spiritual diseases that require different pastoral treatments. The aim is to guide the soul towards spiritual health through the attainment of happiness and wholeness, towards sanctification and fulfillment.[54]

One interesting feature of the *Pastoral Rule* is the avoidance of specific terminology associated with holy orders in identifying pastoral ministers (bishop, priest/presbyter, deacon). Instead, the language used is of a more general nature, such as teacher, preacher, ruler, rector. The wording is fluid. In avoiding the more formal usage of specific terms, Gregory is showing that his interest is more that of function than office. While Gregory certainly had a hierarchical view of the Church, his mind in the *Pastoral Rule* is more attuned to pastoral conduct.[55]

In the first part of the *Pastoral Rule* Gregory describes the character of a good pastoral leader. The leader must be intent upon a spiritual life, having overcome the passions of the flesh. Pastoral leaders must be able to sympathize with the frailties of others and be given to prayer. Self-assessment is essential. Those who lack contemplation in their lives, who are burdened by earthly cares, unable to make good judgments or who are avaricious, are warned about taking upon themselves pastoral responsibilities. Gregory cautions against various forms of self-deception concerning whether one's motivation is honorable or dishonorable in responding to the call to ministry.

Gregory, in the second part of his text, concerns himself with the way of life of a pastoral leader. The leader must be pure in thought and exemplary in conduct. Discretion in speech needs to include the courage to speak out when required. The pastoral ruler should be able to win the trust of people so that they are unafraid of disclosing their hidden secrets. Discipline and correction are needed as much as compassion, 'lest discipline be too rigid, or loving-kindness too lax'. Gregory exhorts the pastoral leader to be astute enough to determine when vices masquerade as virtues. And prudence is required as to what should be confronted and what should not, 'for wounds are more inflamed by untimely incisions'. Gregory is aware that harsh correction can do more harm than good 'for the hearts of sinners fall into dejection and despair'. Those who preach must never depart from the reading of sacred Scripture if they are constantly to be prepared for their task.

The balanced wisdom of Gregory's methods of pastoral care is superbly explored through his 'case studies' concerning persons in different situations. Ministry has to be tailored and adjusted to individual circumstances. His advice illustrates how pastoral care is, indeed, both an art and a science. The eternal and unified truth of the gospel is one thing but how it is applied to the particular circumstances within the lives of individual persons is something else. The case studies he examines are many and varied. They include ministering to: the poor and the rich; the joyful and the sad; the humble and the haughty; the obstinate and the fickle; and the married and the celibate. He offers pastoral guidance to those who do evil secretly and good openly, and those who act the other way round. Pastoral care needs to be different towards those who sin impulsively and those whose wrong is calculated. The case studies, as one moves through them, become more subtle and complex. But the common thread is that of the pastoral minister respecting the individuality of each person.

Gregory is a realist. In the final part of the *Pastoral Rule* he observes that excellence in the way of providing pastoral care does not rid the pastoral leader of imperfections. Competence can never be separated from humility. One may penetrate sublime things and achieve much but, as Gregory cautions, one is still a mere human being. This is wise advice from an experienced pastor. Let us hear Gregory speak for himself in the final words of his text:

> See my good friend, compelled by the urgency of your remonstrances with me, I have tried to show what a pastor should be like. I, miserable painter that I am, have painted the portrait of an ideal man; and here I have been directing others to the shore of perfection, I, who am still tossed about on the waves of sin. But in the shipwreck of this life, sustain me, I beseech you, with the plank of your prayers, so that, as my weight is sinking me down, you may uplift me with your meritorious hand.[56]

This chapter has explored the rise of pastoral care in the period of the early medieval Church. Developments in Church organization and pastoral ministry that began to develop in these centuries would solidify and lead to a closer identification of Church and state, what we know as 'Christendom'. This is the time of the High Middle Ages. Charlemagne's court in Aachen, and the increasing power of the papacy in Rome, led the Western Church in new directions of ministry: the greater blending of throne and altar.

# Chapter 4

# Friars, Pilgrims and the Diseased

As Christians moved into a second millennium their appetite for building new and more imposing places of worship was unrestrained. This was the great age of cathedral building. Amiens Cathedral, for example, could have accommodated the entire city population of ten thousand people. The same was true for most of the other larger medieval cathedrals, such as those at York and Chartres. To gather the whole population of a city into one building is a function that no contemporary sports stadium could perform.[1] The cathedrals' great height symbolized the human reaching up to the divine. The medieval cathedral could be of two varieties. The 'secular' cathedrals were staffed by diocesan priest-canons, while the 'regular' cathedrals were those to which a monastic community was attached. Cathedrals became the focus of pastoral care. In these immense structures took place a ceaseless round of services of worship. Pilgrims came from near and far to pray at the shrines of the saints within them to seek healing and forgiveness. The cathedral was, and remains, the administrative and spiritual home of the bishop. The medieval cathedrals sponsored schools and gave relief to the poor. Their colorful stained glass, stone sculptures and ornate woodcarvings performed a catechetical function: they provided a rich resource for learning the biblical stories and more localized Christian heritage in an age when most people were illiterate. Cathedral building boomed between the eleventh and fourteenth centuries.

The rise of the great cathedrals coincides with urban development in Western Europe. The cathedral was the urban center for pastoral care. The growth of towns and cities, with their concentration of people, demanded new and improved forms of pastoral care that an older, rural model of ministry could not provide. Medieval towns were centers for trade and commerce and this gave rise to systems of banking. This was the new world of money, capital and credit. Urban life - with a rapidly developing merchant class - brought greater sophistication and the demand for better preaching, improved means of welfare and wider opportunities for education. Unlike more conservative and conformist patterns within rural society, town life engendered a more critical and individualistic outlook. The friars responded to these demands. Unlike monasteries that were typically in the country and enclosed, the friars took to the streets of the new urban centers to provide innovative methods of pastoral care. Yet popular piety, often extreme and extravagant, continued to flourish in towns and villages that lead us to think of medieval Christianity as being prone to forms of pastoral care characterized by superstition and corruption.

The beginning of the second millennium was also the time when the Eastern and Western Churches finally and sadly split apart in the year 1054, the fundamental difficulty being over the authority of the papacy. Eastern Christians also had not forgotten the savage attack upon their city of Constantinople by the Western crusaders. Christianity was torn apart into Roman Catholic and Orthodox Churches. Constantinople finally fell to the Muslim Turks in 1453, marking the end of the Byzantine Empire.

## Mendicant Friars

### New Religious Movements: Waldensians and Cathars

The Franciscan and Dominican religious orders, dedicated to a spirit of poverty and given to preaching, brought about one of the great reform movements within the history of pastoral care. However, they were not unique and must be seen as part of a wider movement within medieval Christianity of the late twelfth and early thirteenth centuries. At that time, there were any number of unconventional groups of piously motivated people wandering about and refusing to adopt more traditional patterns of monastic life. Largely nomadic, they moved from town to town and preached to anyone who would listen to them. Such groups often ran into trouble with the Church authorities over preaching, something which canon law restricted to clerics. They were pro-poverty groups. Many survived on alms alone. They did not fit easily into institutional structures of religious life under a rule, and Church authorities often attempted to suppress them. Some just disappeared over time or, of more worry to the authorities, moved in directions that led to heresy, thus placing themselves outside the official Church.

Among such people were the 'Poor Men of Lyons', commonly referred to as the Waldensians. They were followers of Peter Waldo (d.1216) who had been a wealthy cloth merchant from Lyons. Waldo gave away all his possessions and supported himself by begging. He and his followers engaged in preaching and followed a life of poverty.

The movement was critical of the failings of the clergy, and rejected sacraments and popular religious practices. They held pacifist views. It does not seem that Waldo himself held unorthodox beliefs as such. The main problem was that he and his followers continued to preach without authorization. The radical element in the movement propagated more extremist views and came to dominate it. The Waldensians were condemned as heretics by Pope Lucius III (1181-85). The sect spread throughout southern France and northern Italy.

An even more extreme and disturbing movement for the official Church was that of the Cathars (*katharos*, meaning 'pure'). It emerged out of several heretical sects, particularly the Bogabil movement in the Balkans. In France, the Cathars were known as the Albigenses, a name derived from the southern French town of Albi. The Cathars were dualists. The material world, for them, was bad. Because of their distrust of matter, Christ was believed to be an angel with a phantom human body. They denied belief in the resurrection of the body and rejected much of the teaching of the Church about the sacraments. There were two levels of membership within the Cathars: the 'perfect' were those who had been initiated through a special rite known as the *consolamentum*, while the 'believers' were ordinary members who did not live in full compliance with strict Cathar standards. Cathars were vegetarians and practiced fasting. Members belonging to the 'perfect' were required to reject marriage and shun material possessions. Theirs was a life of extreme moral rigor as they attempted to restore what they interpreted as the purity of the early Church. Pope Innocent III (1198-1216) launched the Albigensian crusade in 1209, resulting in a brutal and bloody repression that was to last for twenty years. A papal inquisition was begun against them in 1223, torturing and burning unrepentant Cathars. Remnants of the movement survived into the late fifteenth century.

As Lawrence notes, heresy is not a symptom of apathy but of religious fervor.[2] Whether orthodox or heretical, there appeared to be a spiritual awakening in the late twelfth and thirteenth centuries that spawned any number of pious groups of people committed to poverty, preaching and general religious fervor. It is within this broad religious landscape that the movements begun by St Francis of Assisi (c.1181-1226) and St Dominic (1170-1221) must be located.

### Franciscans

No other saint has charmed the world more than Francis. His simplicity, disregard for material possessions, love of animals and nature, gentle disposition and unlimited kindness have inspired people of all faiths as well as those without any religious beliefs. Visitors to his native Assisi inevitably come away moved by the beauty of the place and the spiritual ethos that Francis bestowed upon it.

Francis was the son of a successful cloth merchant in Assisi. In his time, Italian cities were constantly at war with each other. Francis decided to become a soldier in the war against the rival town of Perugia, during which time he was taken prisoner. After his release, Francis began to demonstrate his unconventional approach to life. With all the idealism of the young, he sold some of his father's cloth and gave the proceeds to the poor. His enraged father had him thrown into prison for such folly. But Francis' commitment to poverty was demonstrated even more dramatically one day when, in the town square in full view of everyone, he stripped off his clothes and stood naked. It was a striking gesture symbolizing destitution for Christ. The bishop, keen to maintain propriety, rushed forward to cover the lad.

Attracted to a life of simplicity and kindness, Francis helped lepers and repaired dilapidated churches in the vicinity of Assisi. He lived in caves and begged for food. One can only imagine the disappointment of his family in seeing him live what appeared to be an aimless existence. By the time he had reached his late twenties, Francis had attracted a small body of men who called themselves 'little brothers' (*fraters minores*), the group which came to be known as the 'friars minor'. In one respect they were nothing special. They resembled many such pious groups of poor laymen who were wandering around central Italy preaching a message of peace and repentance. They were vagrants, witnessing to poverty in a time when wealth was highly valued and sought after by the merchant class in the emerging economies of the new Italian city-states.

Yet Francis was distinctive in that he had a more radical commitment to poverty. Francis interpreted this as a literal imitation of the life of Christ. He and his followers were to possess nothing at all. They were mendicants – meaning 'without income' - relying on begging to stay alive.

In 1209 Francis and his eleven companions walked to Rome to seek recognition of their movement and permission to preach. Unlike the poverty movement of the Waldensians, Francis accepted the sacraments and was entirely loyal to the demands of Church authority in seeking approval to preach. Francis and his group of enthusiasts requested to see Innocent III. A greater contrast of personalities cannot be imagined: Francis and his ragged, semiliterate group of followers petitioning a pope of cultivated tastes - from a Roman aristocratic family - who had studied theology in Paris and canon law in Bologna. Yet something about Francis attracted the shrewd eye of this pope. He gave his blessing to the group and approved of their preaching, but with some conditions. They could engage in moral exhortations only and not speak of doctrinal matters that might be open to false teaching. The little brothers set off on their mission, wearing their rough clothes tied with rope. Not long after, a rule of living was created and approved by Innocent. Francis was more a dreamer than an organizer and administrative control of the order was taken over by others. At some point in his life Francis was ordained a deacon but he never became a priest. The Franciscans began as a lay movement within the Church. In the spirit of the times, Francis set out to convert the Muslims in Eastern Europe and Egypt, his mission being a 'spiritual crusade'. He was treated with courtesy by the sultan who listened to his simple message.

St Clare (1194-1253), a close friend of Francis, set up a cloistered community of women in 1212 in accordance with the Franciscan ideal of poverty and under the direction of the friars. This became known as the Second Order. Meanwhile, lay sympathizers who remained living in the world according to the Franciscan spirit became members of the Third Order.

The Franciscan Order expanded rapidly across Europe. Popes of the early thirteenth century promoted the Franciscan friars in an attempt to prevent the spread of freewheeling heretical groups dedicated to poverty and preaching. It was a policy aimed at containing enthusiasts. Within a century of Francis' death, the Franciscans had an astonishing membership of 28,000 friars.[3]

In the longer term, Francis' ideal of absolute poverty proved unworkable as the friars grew in number. Institutionalization led to the need for churches and residences. City officials and wealthy individuals were only too willing to give them land and money. Some in the order became bitter at what they interpreted to be a sell-out of Francis' vision for the friars. A bitter internal dispute dragged on between those who recognized the need to adapt while keeping a simple and humble lifestyle (the Conventuals), and those who were uncompromising and wished to retain the original stance of absolute poverty (the Spirituals).

The friars were something new in vowed religious life. They belonged to their order as a whole, unlike monks who belonged to a particular monastery. This enabled the Franciscans to be more mobile in serving the needs of the Church in different places. They established themselves in towns and cities, not in the countryside. And they engaged in a ministry of preaching - in churches and in the streets - at a time when this was neglected or of poor quality. They were noted for their practical charity and living in poverty. Their mission was decidedly pastoral and it struck a chord among people long accustomed to pastoral neglect by their own clergy.

## Dominicans

As mendicant friars carrying out a pastoral mission in the world, the Dominicans were similar to their Franciscan counterparts, but they developed something of a different style. The founders of the two orders, themselves, were dissimilar in temperament, background and outlook. Dominic de Guzman was Spanish, probably of aristocratic birth, and a priest-canon in the cathedral at Osma. While accompanying his bishop on a diplomatic mission to the court of Denmark, Dominic encountered the Cathar heresy in the person of an innkeeper in Toulouse, where he was staying. Dominic, a man of passionate temperament, spent the night in argument with him. Three years later, in 1206, returning from a second journey to the Danish court with his bishop, Dominic met up with a small group of Cistercians in Montpellier who told him of their failure to combat the Cathar heresy in southern France.

Dominic came to the conclusion that the only way to overcome the Cathars, the *perfecti,* was to form a brotherhood of men dedicated to mendicant poverty and holiness of life. In this, his ideas were similar to the Franciscan friars. However, Dominic's ideas about poverty were less romantic. For him, poverty was a means rather than an end in itself. What was distinctive, in Dominic's vision, was the need for educated men trained in preaching and evangelization, living a simple life of poverty through mendicancy. His friars were to be highly skilled in theology at the service of preaching. Study was also meant to nurture prayer in the life of his friars. Unlike Francis who was more of a dreamer, Dominic possessed superb skills of organization and was far more hard-headed.

Pope Honorius III (1216-27) approved the order in 1216, following Dominic's request to the Fourth Lateran Council the year before. The bishops of this council had taken a decision that no new orders were to be founded: existing rules of religious life had to be followed. This was an attempt to arrest the proliferation of new religious experiments. Dominic and his followers got around the problem by adopting the existing Rule of St Augustine, to which Dominic was already vowed as a canon. The Dominicans became known officially as the Order of Preachers.

Like the Franciscans, Dominican friars belonged to their order as a whole and not to any particular religious house. They were granted extraterritorial status free from local episcopal control and so they were answerable only to the pope. This gave them extraordinary flexibility and freedom to engage in pastoral activities they considered important. At the same time, it was a shrewd move to strengthen the authority and power of the papacy over the local Church, a development that had begun much earlier under Pope Gregory VII (1073-85) who had also sought to free the Church from secular control.

After 1217, the special emphasis Dominic had given to the conversion of the Cathars in the Languedoc region was abandoned. His mission there had not been successful. Dominic's small band of followers, concentrated in Toulouse, took the decision to disperse and set up new houses: they went to Paris, Bologna, Madrid and Rome. Dominic founded a number of convents for women. The earliest was at Prouille, a refuge for female converts won over from Catharism. These women were to live austere lives to match the Cathar *perfecti*.

It is generally agreed that Dominic and his followers did not engage personally in the violence and massacres associated with the crusade against the Cathar Albigensians but, instead, used peaceful means of persuasion and prayer. To what extent Dominic himself supported bloody tactics against heresy by others remains a matter of debate. However, the Dominicans were later to be involved directly in repression through the Inquisition that was created in 1231, after the war against the Albigensians had ended. The Inquisition became more widespread in the following centuries, its task being to hunt down and put to death other groups of heretics. Tomás Torquemada (1420-98), a Dominican, was the much-feared Spanish Grand Inquisitor. Such activity, in this period of their history, casts a dark shadow over Dominican achievements.

### Other Orders

The Austin Friars were another group among the new religious movements of friars that emerged in the thirteenth century. They grew out of a group of hermits living in Tuscany who moved to the towns and took up pastoral care. In 1247, Pope Innocent IV (1243-54) gave them the Rule of St Augustine upon which to base their lives, and they became known officially as the Order of Friars Hermits of St Augustine.

The Carmelites trace their origins to hermits living at Mt Carmel in the Holy Land who had gone there initially as pilgrims or crusaders. After the Latin kingdom of Jerusalem collapsed, they dispersed. One of their number, an Englishman named St Simon Stock (c.1165-1265), gained approval from Innocent IV for a modified rule of life. The Carmelites, too, became part of this renewal movement of urban pastoral ministry within the Church of the thirteenth century. There were other smaller Orders belonging to the so-called poverty movement of the time, such as the Crutched Friars and the Brothers of the Sack.

## Towns

Florence welcomed the friars. It was home to powerful, rich banking and business families, such as the Medici, Peruzzi and the Bardi. These business people were well disposed to sharing their wealth with the friars by, for example, endowing churches and charitable institutions, such as the Foundling Home for abandoned infants. Florence's impressive cathedral, with its mighty red cupola, dominates the city to this day. But no tourist misses visiting the Franciscan Church of Santa Croce in the south-east district of the city, and the Dominican Church of Santa Maria Novella in the western area by the central railway station. Both churches are of a great size and filled with Renaissance frescoes paid for by wealthy patrons. Perhaps more than any other city, Florence illustrates, through its churches, the impact the mendicant friars made upon the medieval Church. Like other towns throughout Europe, it had expanded greatly. Florence's population increased five-fold in the two centuries after 1100.[4] Such urbanization demanded the new forms of pastoral care that the friars were able to provide.

The friars generally settled in places lying outside or in close proximity to the town walls – in the suburbs or *borgo* areas of Italian cities - as happened in Florence. Across the River Arno, in the working class Oltrano district, the Carmelites and Austin friars built churches. Land was cheaper to acquire in these locations. Away from the city center with its cathedral, friary churches on the outskirts were also in closer proximity to the trades-people and artisans crammed into the narrow streets of medieval towns and cities.[5]

People in these urban areas were in need of pastoral care that the majority of diocesan clergy seemed ill equipped to meet. Few priests, apart from the elite who staffed the Church's bureaucracy and cathedral schools, were theologically literate. Traditionally, most of the clergy who ministered in parish churches or their equivalent had been recruited from the peasantry. City life demanded something different and the friars stepped in to fill the gap. They were a new kind of clergy. They lived in communities and provided a group style of pastoral practice in contrast to the more individualistic style of ministry conducted by diocesan priests. They were highly trained for the tasks of instructing, preaching and guiding people's consciences in the sacrament of penance. Their life of voluntary poverty won them respect and enabled them to identify more easily with the poor. This was an age in which people sought a more personal expression of religion than that which the older monastic spirituality seemed able to provide. Friars, living among the people, were better equipped than the older monastic orders to lead the faithful in prayer and devotion in the midst of the world. Their city churches, fostering devotion and crammed with religious art, drew the crowds as these men encouraged a renewed spiritual life for the laity.

> The ministry of the friars to the towns of Europe achieved great success because they brought new and better pastoral skills to the task and because they offered lay people a fulfillment of their religious aspirations that seemed to be denied them by the traditional assumptions of monastic theology. But however welcome their message may have been, the impact it made owed much to the idealism of the messengers. The voluntary poverty and self-imposed destitution that identified the early Mendicants with the humblest and most deprived sections of the population, in loud contrast to the careerism and ostentation of the secular clergy and corporate wealth and exclusiveness of the monasteries, moved the conscience and touched the generosity of commercial communities.[6]

## Universities

The other great contribution of the friars to pastoral life was their educational role in the new universities of medieval Europe. But first we need to situate the friars' role in education within the context of medieval systems of learning.

Prior to the establishment of universities, most formal education took place in monastic and cathedral schools. Until the latter part of the twelfth century, the majority of literate people were clerics and it was they who performed most of the bureaucratic functions of both Church and government. Monastic schools were primarily for educating monks but they also performed a role in training some of the diocesan clergy for higher positions within the Church and state. As well, in some places, they provided an education for the sons of wealthy families. The curriculum had mostly religious objectives: Scripture, study of the Church Fathers, liturgy, canon law. These subjects were supplemented by a study of Latin classical literature. Grammar, rhetoric and dialectic - known in Carolingian times as the *trivium* - equipped students to read, write, think and debate in Latin. In the medieval world, Latin was the language of the Church, government and law.[7]

Whereas monastic schools tended to be cloistered and rural, the schools attached to the cathedrals were normally in towns and populated by teachers and students from all parts of Europe. Latin was the common language of learning. The larger cathedral schools were truly international. Usually they were more open to debate concerning theological issues than were the more conservative, monastic schools. Peter Abelard (1079-1142), noted not only for his celebrated affair with Heloise but also for his academic brilliance, taught logic and theology at the Cathedral of Notre Dame in Paris. By the middle of the twelfth century, monastic schools were increasingly limited to educating monks, so that cathedral schools came to attract a wide range of students. Cathedral schools educated a minority of the clergy, mainly those from upper-class families who were destined for higher positions in the ecclesiastical world. Most diocesan priests were uneducated and received whatever formal training they may have got for their pastoral ministry through a system of apprenticeship. In terms of access to formal education, then, these clergy were little different from the peasantry to whom they ministered.[8]

By the late twelfth century and into the thirteenth century, universities were overtaking the cathedral schools as centers of excellence in learning, and they were far more independent of ecclesiastical authority. Universities developed the curriculum of study beyond that of the monastery and cathedral schools. Medieval universities generally had four faculties: arts, medicine, law and theology. At this time the university in Paris was leading the way in theological education, while in Bologna the university there was renowned for its school of civil and canon law. The earliest universities began as voluntary groups, much like the trade guilds of the time, designed to protect members' interests. In Bologna and Padua, students elected their own rector and professors to govern them and so these universities began their lives as a guild of students. In Paris and Oxford, the university - by way of contrast - was a guild of teachers. The university at Cambridge owes its origins to a strike in Oxford: some masters moved from there to Cambridge, never to return. Later, as universities became more widespread, they were founded by political and Church leaders as well as by wealthy donors.

The rise of universities coincided with the appearance of the friars. The mendicant orders were exceedingly successful in recruiting new members among the students and masters of the new universities. St Bonaventure (*c.*1217-74), an academic and sometime General of the Franciscans, led them in the direction of scholarly pursuits, but for the Dominicans, learning was a goal from their foundation. The friars became the outstanding theologians in the universities. Most notable of all was the Italian Dominican friar, St Thomas Aquinas (c.1225-74), who taught at the University of Paris.

Theology in the universities at this time became known as 'scholasticism', named after the 'schoolmen' who practiced it. The term refers to a method of doing theology rather than to any specific content. By the end of the twelfth century, translated works of ancient Greek and Arabic science and philosophy were becoming well known in Europe. Aristotle's works - and the commentaries upon them by Arabic scholars, such as Avicenna and Averroes - were studied by the friar-theologians. The pagan thought of antiquity was considered a useful tool for interpreting the Christian faith: divine revelation aided by secular thought. Scholastic theology gave emphasis to a rational and systematic presentation of Christian beliefs. It made use of fine distinctions. Using formal reasoning, breaking ideas up into small logical divisions, theological inquiry aimed at logical exactness and objectivity. In doing so, theology lost something of its scriptural foundations. Theology became a science, using ideas from ancient Greek philosophy especially, to explain Christian doctrines.[9]

Just as the friars had an immense pastoral influence by means of their street ministries and town churches, so also they seized the opportunity to make a significant pastoral contribution through their presence in town universities. Largely through their scholarship and teaching, friars were responsible for theology becoming a recognized component of advanced study within higher learning and, as such, having a more widespread presence and influence within the society that was Christendom. Medieval Christianity was, in many respects, characterized by superstition yet it 'witnessed one of the most remarkable "rationalizations" of faith in the history of religions'.[10] The friars, through their pursuit of theology in the universities, shaped pastoral practice. For example, the Dominicans produced a whole series of compendiums for confessors. These were learned theological treatises that went beyond the earlier mechanical and legalistic 'penitentials'. They offered theological expositions on all matters pertaining to the sacrament of penance.[11] Admittedly, scholastic theology was more speculative in nature and method than a practical aid to ministry. This caused concern to many medieval spiritual writers, such as Thomas à Kempis (c.1380-1471), as well as Martin Luther (1483-1546) and the Reformers. Yet, from a pastoral care perspective, it was the friars in the Church of the high medieval period who were largely responsible for educating the more privileged group of clerics destined for leadership in the Church. Their impact was immense.

## Popular Piety

### The Medieval View of Nature and the Divine

Many Christians today experience some unease in praying to God for tangible requests, such as the sending of rain or for a safe journey. Outcomes, such as these, are understood today more to result from natural forces or human activity than from immediate, divine intervention. For the medieval Christian there was no such problem concerning calling on God for help for whatever crisis might arise. It was an age that possessed little scientific understanding of the natural world and people had precious few means to control the forces of disease and the elements of nature that continually threatened their lives. Medieval women and men believed in direct and perpetual interaction between this world and the world of the divine. God was understood to control a chaotic and fearful world on a moment-by-moment basis. Miraculous expectations and explanations characterized daily life. The world was thought of as populated by unseen powers of good and evil. Devils were real beings lurking in the dark and saints dwelt in specified holy places that had to be visited. Especially after the Great Plague of the fourteenth century that wiped out perhaps a quarter of the population of Western Europe, death came to dominate the religious outlook. Death was accompanied by fear. Increasingly, fear of death became associated with fear of damnation, so that life became a continuous round of pious activities aimed at helping one get to heaven. Merit was stored up for this purpose in quantifiable sums. Salvation was considered neither to be easy nor assured. It was not only a matter of attending to one's own salvation. One had to do all one could to assist in the salvation of those who had gone before onself - the dead. Their welfare was largely dependent on the living offering Masses for them and doing good works on their behalf so as to reduce their sentence in purgatory. Superstition intermingled with genuine faith and this opened the door for exploitation. It all 'gave a desperate, almost frenzied quality to the religious life of the later middle ages'.[12] Pastoral care in the medieval Church can be understood only in the context of this pervading religious outlook of the time.

## Saints, Pilgrims and Relics

The public veneration of saints can be traced back to the second century. By about the year 200 the remains of St Peter were venerated on a shrine on the Vatican Hill.[13] The earliest Christian saints were martyrs. Their powers of intercession were guaranteed because the martyrs were assured of salvation. The cult of saints, which began with the veneration of martyrs, developed to include all kinds of Christians noted for their holiness. The saint was believed to be in some sense present at his or her tomb and could intercede for the pilgrim before God. Quite early on, miracles were regarded as a proof of sanctity.

The relics of a saint (body parts or items, such as clothing, associated with the saint) were considered to be a source of healing. The practice of the veneration of relics allowed for the power of the saint to be present in as many locations as were his or her relics, thus ensuring greater accessibility. Collectors acquired relics in great quantities. Commercial forces operated as connoisseurs vied with each other for their purchase. A shrine housing a popular relic provided a handsome income from pilgrims. Relics guaranteed prestige to political or religious figures who had them in their possession. The story is told of an eleventh century abbot named Aelfsige, from Peterborough, who was living in France during a particularly bad famine. The monks of St Florentin de Bonneval, near Chartres, had sold all they could to purchase food. All they had left was a relic, the body of their patron saint, St Florentin. Realizing the opportunity for a good investment, Aelfsige brought back to Peterborough the remains of the saint, minus the head.[14] The Byzantine emperors were particularly successful in amassing relics. When the Fourth Crusade sacked Constantinople in 1204, the relics of the imperial capital were a prized booty. St Mark's Basilica in Venice did particularly well out of the plunder. Charlemagne accumulated vast numbers of relics at Aachen, as did Philip II of Spain (1527-98) for his beloved monastery-palace of El Escorial near Madrid. Sainte Chapelle in Paris, with its exquisite stained glass, became the most celebrated reliquary ever built.[15]

What counted most in the popular mind was the power of the saint to heal, rather than a saintly reputation as a virgin, martyr or charitable person. Any saint that failed to deliver miracles would soon be forgotten. Records of miracles were scrupulously maintained at the site of a shrine.[16] The cult of saints, in one respect, was localized.

Every city, region, occupation and religious order had its saints and their fame was accompanied by legends. Some saints were more widely known and venerated, particularly the Virgin Mary. Many of the saints became specialists in different types of healing: Roche and Sebastian were called upon in time of plague; Apollonia, for relieving toothaches; and Barbara, in childbirth. In time, a process of canonization came to be established and by the beginning of the thirteenth century a full judicial investigation was required. This process was reserved to the papacy but it did not prevent unauthorized cults arising.

A healing ministry, then, was an important aspect of pastoral care in the Middle Ages through the cult of saints. Priests promoted the veneration of relics and authenticated miracles. Pilgrimages had other pastoral purposes apart from seeking healing. They could also be for the doing of penance. Ecclesiastical authority imposed penitential pilgrimages for the satisfaction of sins. They became part of the penitential system of the Church, an extension of the sacrament of penance. To make a pilgrimage was like undergoing a second baptism, starting anew the Christian life. Pilgrimages could be self-imposed as a penitential exercise. There was no better preparation for death than to go on a pilgrimage, and to die on the journey meant almost certain salvation. Or a pilgrimage could be imposed as a penalty by the civil law. Judicial pilgrimage was a form of punishment in medieval civil and criminal codes and can be understood as a form of forced exile.[17] The Inquisition, amidst its legal machinery, imposed pilgrimages for offences of heresy.[18]

During the twelfth century the granting of indulgences to pilgrims to visit specific shrines became commonplace. In 1300, to celebrate the jubilee year, Pope Boniface VIII (1294-1303) offered a plenary indulgence to those who visited Rome and took part in the prescribed prayers and visits to designated churches within the city.[19] It was a great success. One of the bridges across the Tiber, the Ponte Sant' Angelo, was frequently jammed with pilgrims that year. Pilgrimages, then, could assist in speeding up one's own passage to heaven or the spiritual benefits gained could be applied to the souls in purgatory.

It was not only at the shrines where pastoral care became involved with pilgrimages. Before setting out on such holy journeys there were many things to be done. A will had to be made. This was not only a legal document, as it is today. The medieval will was also a religious document and the Church offered pastoral guidance as to how it should be made. The manner in which one bequeathed one's property had a bearing on eternal salvation. Sometimes a testator would even arrange for somebody to make the pilgrimage on his or her behalf, to a specific place, in return for a fee. The sum would be paid to the surrogate pilgrim upon his or her return after a certificate or guarantee was produced, having been made out by the clergy at the shrine that had been visited.[20] There were other pre-pilgrimage tasks: to make amends to anybody one had wronged and perhaps to make a private agreement with one's spouse regarding the length of time before re-marrying if the pilgrim failed to return. Finally, a blessing in the manner of a spiritual initiation into the state of a pilgrim was sought from the Church. A feeling arose that the pilgrim belonged to a special order of the Church. Distinctive clothing was worn on the journey to highlight this fact. The journey could be a long one, taking many months, even several years, especially if one was going on the extended journey to Jerusalem. The danger of being attacked by bandits or national enemies was ever present. The pilgrim, then, needed to be fortified for what was often an arduous journey.

Pastoral care for pilgrims extended along the pilgrim routes. The Benedictine Rule required monasteries to offer hospitality. Monastic generosity, as one would expect, varied from house to house. The hospitality provided at the monastery of Maria Laach, outside Bonn, was described around the year 1225 as 'unequalled'.[21] On busier pilgrimage routes monasteries were unable to carry the whole load, so large guest halls - known as hospices - were built. These places also cared for sick pilgrims. In a medieval guide for pilgrims making the journey to Santiago de Compostela in Spain, certain hospices located in the Alps and Pyrenees are described:

> They are holy places, houses of God himself, ordained for the comfort of pilgrims, the restitution of the needy, the consolation of the sick, the assistance of the living, and the salvation of the dead.[22]

At the shrines, priests would be kept busy in providing an endless round of religious services. The churches would have been packed. On important feast days there were all-night vigils in the churches with the more pious attending to their prayers, while the less devout were singing aloud or shouting abuse in a night of drinking and carousing. Some sanctuaries, such as that of Cuthbert's tomb in Durham Cathedral, employed burly men to keep order. Pastoral care involved the saying of Masses, hearing of confessions, displaying the relics, authenticating claims to miracles, issuing certificates of attendance, and simply providing for the physical needs of the sick and elderly. Sumption describes, in colorful language, what it must have been like when one arrived at a holy site like Canterbury, Compostela or Rome. He captures something of the noise and vulgarity that accompanied medieval journeys of faith:

> The pilgrim was greeted at his destination by a scene of raucous tumult. On the feast day of the patron saint a noisy crowd gathered in front of the church. Pilgrims mingled with jugglers and conjurers, souvenir sellers and pickpockets. Hawkers shouted their wares and rickety food stalls were surrounded by mobs of hungry travelers. Pilgrims hobbling on crutches or carried on stretchers tried to force their way through the crush at the steps of the church. Cries of panic were drowned by bursts of hysterical laughter from nearby taverns, while beggars played on horns, zithers, and tambourines.[23]

### Indulgences and the Dead

To put it simply, authorized indulgences were understood as a means to build up credit for lessening time in purgatory. Medieval Catholics looked to the Church to provide them with pastoral protection from punishment for their sins after they died. This could be anticipated and provided for by indulgences. In this sense, strange as it may seem to us today, the Church's granting of indulgences was understood as a form of pastoral care. Indulgences rested on the belief in the 'treasury' of the Church. Because of the solidarity of all Christians as the communion of saints, whether living or dead, the Church was believed to possess a treasury of merit. This is made up of the infinite merits of Christ, together with those of the Virgin Mary, the saints and the good deeds of the living. As a result, the Church had within its power to dispense these merits in response to prayers and pious acts undertaken in a spirit of faith and charity. This dispersion of merit was granted through indulgences. Indulgences could be applied to the living, in the expectation that one's time in purgatory would be reduced, as well as to the dead already in purgatory. An indulgence freed the sinner from a certain amount of punishment due to sin by the dispersion of an equal amount of satisfaction from the treasury of the Church.

Indulgences reflected the economic order of medieval society and its system of benefices. It was important for a medieval ruler to grant benefits as well as dispense justice. Such benefits, or benefices, were a means of gaining loyalty from one's subjects, especially in time of war. Henry III of England (1216-72) had a piece of political wisdom inscribed on the wall of his castle as well as on the border of his chess board: 'He who does not give what he has will not get what he wants.' The ability to give is the first law of political life, as any politician knows.

An important function of the papacy in medieval times was to grant such benefices to ensure loyalty to Rome. They included, for example, grants of immunity from excommunication; declarations concerning the invalidity of a marriage; being awarded a bishopric, with its guaranteed revenues; the mitigation of debts; permissions for illegitimate males to receive holy orders; and dispensations of one kind or another. Indulgences were but one example of this granting of benefices.

To have the power to grant benefices to the living was one thing. But once benefices were able to transcend earthly limits and reach into the next world by means of indulgences – benefices on behalf of the dead – what a new and intoxicating power the Church now possessed. The dead, as well as the living, came increasingly under its control and care. Belief in purgatory facilitated the granting of indulgences. Although the idea of purgatory can be traced back to Augustine, it was the scholastic theologians who first used the term on a frequent basis in theological writings. Innocent IV defined purgatory as a doctrine of the Church in 1254. It was reaffirmed at the Council of Ferrara-Florence in 1438-39 against the Greeks and later, against the Protestants, at the Council of Trent in 1563.[24] As a result, a three-fold system of purgatory, heaven and hell became firmly established in Christian thinking and piety. The preaching of the friars about purgatory exploited the fears of people, utilizing terrifying images that played on the emotions of their listeners.

The medieval Church saw as one of its chief functions of pastoral care the supervision of Masses, prayers, alms, pilgrimages and all the different kinds of offerings made by the living to provide for the well-being of the dead and for the living who would one day face death. The arranging of Masses for the dead was considered the best means of providing such pastoral care for the Mass was believed to re-enact Christ's atoning death on the cross for sinners. Ordinarily a fee was established for arranging Masses for the dead. Such Masses commonly occurred on the day of burial, a month after burial, and on the annual anniversary. People made provision in their wills for Masses for the dead to be said for themselves and family members. One could never be sure just how much prayer was enough for ensuring passage out of purgatory. Bulk purchases were common for those who could afford it. One testator left provision for a perpetual endowment for Masses and founded a chapel for the purpose. Two priests were to say or arrange to have Masses said every day for the deceased members of the family. Another person in a will requested a hundred masses to be offered in two churches on the day of death or the following day.

Endowment tablets were publicly positioned in churches that provided details of the gifts made by donors and the listing of prayers and Masses that were to be offered in return. This was to remind the clergy to carry out their pastoral duties to the dead.[25] Another common practice, known from the content of wills, was to recruit the poor and offer them alms to participate in a funeral procession. Orphaned children in charitable institutions were especially singled out for this task. Making provision for the presence of the poor at one's funeral was the last great opportunity for a person to engage in an act of charity.[26] It was common practice in medieval England for the bellman to go round a parish before the burial rites to call the poor to a funeral to receive doles in return for their prayers for the deceased. Satirists, such as St Thomas More (1478-1535), ridiculed 'honorable burying' with 'so many torches, so many tapers, so many black gowns, so many merry mourners laughing under black hodes.'[27]

To accommodate the proliferation of Masses for the dead, special altars and chapels had to be built in the monastic abbeys, cathedrals and churches. The chapels used for Masses for the dead were known as chantries and might be reserved exclusively for Masses on behalf of the family of the donor.[28] A special class of clerics arose to meet this need, known as chantry priests. Their primary pastoral task was to offer Masses for the dead. These priests were generally poorly educated and often not noted for their piety or morals. Some might have had an auxiliary role in assisting parish priests in their pastoral round of duties. In Germany a form of pastoral care for the dead was the *Seelhaus* (Soul House). These were houses for women whose primary responsibility was to pray for the dead. They kept vigil over graves and attended Masses for the dead and were paid for their services.[29]

The obsession with Masses on behalf of the dead, and the stipends to support the practice, illustrates a shift in the understanding of the Mass. From an expression of community worship it had come to be interpreted as a privileged mode for seeking divine favors. This was closely linked in the medieval Church with the growth in popularity of the idea of equating ordination with accession to hierarchical power. Access to God had become the privilege of a special class within the Church.

With the Mass stipend system went a decline in participation by the laity in the celebration of the Eucharist. The Mass became more and more a privatized ritual.[30] This went hand in hand with a high doctrine of the priesthood: the priest alone had special powers and privileged access to the divine. Lay people were reduced to being spectators and engaged in private devotions during the Mass. What became important was gazing at the host immediately after the prayers of consecration rather than receiving the sacrament in Holy Communion. Masses were celebrated simultaneously at the many altars within a church so, at the sound of the warning bell during Mass, people would rush from one altar to the next to see the priest elevate the consecrated host. The sacrament of the Eucharist, then, was more to be seen than eaten. The Fourth Lateran Council in 1215 insisted that every person was to receive Holy Communion at least once per year, at Easter. Annual Communion probably sufficed for most of the laity. Staring at the host was extended outside the celebration of the Mass itself as the sacrament came to be displayed in monstrances for adoration.

The obsession with dying, which so preoccupied pastoral care in the Middle Ages, intensified with the appearance of the horrors of the Black Death that first swept across Europe in the period 1347-50.[31] Frequent epidemic outbreaks followed. Human mortality was experienced as never before recorded as the Plague relentlessly snatched away its victims, the grim reaper on his deadly mission. Death took on terrifying proportions as a continent was carried into grief. People sought to limit the effects of divine retribution in death. The fears unleashed by the Black Death undoubtedly stimulated belief in purgatory and prayers for the dead which provided for some human control in the face of mass death.

The literary form of the *ars moriendi* (art of dying) makes its appearance at about this same time. These books were meant to prepare the dying spiritually. With the invention of the printing press they gained wide circulation. Lurid woodcut pictures depicted those who die unreconciled with the Church. Supernatural beings invade the bedroom of the dying person. On one side of the room there is the court of heaven while on the other side stands Satan and his fearsome army of demons.[32] The priest at the bedside of the dying was there not only to palliate but also to interrogate. He was to ensure that the dying man or woman had recognized his or her sins and had truly repented and truly desired to die in the faith of the Church. Pastoral care, in these circumstances, was to be comforting but tough. It was the pastoral duty of all connected to the terminally ill to ensure they were given proper warning of approaching death. This was to allow sufficient time for them to complete their religious duties, among which was making a will. For the medieval Christian the will, as we have already seen, was a religious document. Measured against standards of justice and charity, the disposal of property following one's death related to one's eternal salvation. The testator was to ensure almsgiving and the provision of prayers for his or her soul following the completion of life on this earth. Deathbed pastoral care, through the *ars moriendi,* was one of the more important ministries of the late medieval Church.

Another pastoral method to help people to prepare for death, common at this time, was the art of the macabre. The human body was depicted in the process of decomposition in all its gruesome physicality - a *transi* - or it might be seen in the bones of a skeleton. It was meant to teach about the fragility of earthly life and the vanity of wealth, power and physical beauty. Sometimes the corpse might be shown as a figure of derision by the wearing of a crown, as can be seen on the walls in the lower church at Assisi. Common in this kind of iconography is the 'dance of death'. Here rotting corpses dance with various ranks of living persons. Its purpose was to serve as a reminder of the uncertainty as to when death might strike and the fate of everyone through death.[33]

## Confraternities

Late medieval religious life was characterized by the rise of devotional groups of lay people dedicated to practical charity, particularly among their own members. Many were noted for their services to the dead through prayers for the dying and deceased and the organization of funeral services. These confraternities took a variety of forms and functions. Florence had at least a hundred of them in the late fifteenth century.[34]

The *Humiliati* (humble ones) are one of the better known of the earlier confraternities that were active in northern Italy at the same time as the founding of the friars. They, too, were part of the poverty movement. While they did not wander or beg, they were committed to preaching to their own members. Some of the Humiliati dwelt within their private houses and worked while others lived a more communal form of existence. They received papal approval from Innocent III, after having earlier been declared to be heretics. While some were submissive to Church authorities, others remained on the fringes of orthodoxy or outside it.[35]

Other groups included the *Laudesi* (those who sang praise). They were noted for their public demonstrations of singing, especially to the Virgin Mary and the saints.[36] And there were the *Disciplinati,* penitential associations that had a special devotion to the passion of

Christ and included self-flagellation among their exercises of piety. The more extreme among the penitential associations were the *Flagellanti*. They engaged in hysterical behaviors involving public flagellations on the streets. Their half-naked and bleeding bodies attracted great curiosity. Devotees saw themselves as a peace movement amidst the warring city-states of Italy. The movement later spread to France and Germany. The Flagellanti began in Perugia in 1260 through the efforts of a layman named Ranieri Fasani, a member of one of the penitential associations.[37]

The *Beguines* were groups of pious laywomen that originated in the Low Countries and spread to the western parts of Germany and France from towards the end of the twelfth century. It is possible they were named after Lambert le Bègue (d.1177), although this remains uncertain. Their male counterparts were known as *Beghards*. The members adopted a common life of simplicity and prayer but were not a vowed religious order as such. They supported themselves by working in different crafts and trades. As a voluntary lay association, members were free to leave and marry after a period of time spent in the Beguinage. For a time the Beguines and Beghards were condemned as heretics because of association with extremist groups. They engaged in charitable activities and Beguines, in small numbers, have survived into modern times.[38]

Centered upon the Netherlands and northern Germany, the *Devotio Moderna* movement emerged under the inspiration of Geert Groote (1340-84). It was characterized by inward, personal conversion and contemplation and attracted both clergy and laity. It opposed the pilgrimages, veneration of relics and other external ritual practices of the period. Followers lived in group houses and without the formality of vows or special religious clothing. The men were known as the Brethren of the Common Life and the women as the Sisters of the Common Life. Its form of spirituality stressed an emotional attachment to the sufferings of Christ. The Devotio Moderna was influenced by the mystical literature of Jan van Ruysbroeck (1293-1381). The movement became popularized through a treatise of Thomas à Kempis (c.1380-1471), known as *The Imitation of Christ*. This work stressed that the following of Christ demanded that one take up the cross and live a life of asceticism. Its attention to faith through the individual person's inner life resulted in a distrust of theological learning that was interpreted as worthless and damaging to the spiritual life. Yet Groote's main concerns were pastoral. He preached widely and had an interest in educating young boys for future Church leadership. His intention was that they would be educated in a manner that gave more importance to spiritual matters than theological speculation for, he believed, true understanding came from God alone.[39]

The Devotio Moderna was part of a movement of mysticism that was widespread in the Church of the late Middle Ages. Mystics, such as Julian of Norwich (*c*.1342-after 1413) in England and Meister Eckhart (*c*.1260-1327) in Germany, emphasized personal apprehension of God. By doing so they downplayed the boundaries of orthodoxy and clerical control of devotional and sacramental life. This is not to say they were unorthodox. But the individual's personal spiritual experience was what mattered. It was fertile ground preparing the way for the Protestant Reformation's affirmation of the subjective certainty of God experienced through the individual believer's surrender in faith, something that would soon change dramatically the appearance of pastoral care throughout much of the Christian world.

## Healing Ministries

Miraculous healing at the shrines of the saints, as we have already seen, was one of the principal means of treating sickness for someone who was a medieval Christian. There was little more than the most basic medical treatment for the diseased, blind, lame, injured, mentally ill and for those with any of the other bodily afflictions that affect human beings. People relied primarily on the care of their families or neighbors for help. And, of course, the poor suffered most. But there were some forms of pastoral care offered to the sick apart from good will and the miraculous: hospitals and sacramental anointing. It is to these two forms of care that we now turn our attention.

### Hospitals

Christian institutions that cared for the sick had emerged in the Eastern Church as early as the fourth century, for example, Basil's hospital in Caesarea. In Eastern Christianity, which led the way in the development of hospitals, they were known as a *xenodichium* (from the Greek word for 'stranger'). They performed many functions, such as the sheltering of pilgrims and travelers, but their care of the sick gradually took precedence. The Emperor Constantine made provision for institutions that were to care for the sick. By the early Middle Ages in the West, institutions that looked after the sick were common but could also double as places of shelter for the poor and for pilgrims. They were known as hospices, and functioned as almshouses. Medical functions within such institutions, then, were part of a broader social service to those in need. Monasteries were particularly involved in this task. In time, institutions developed that became more specialized in the care of the sick. The eleventh and twelfth centuries, with the growth of towns, saw a great expansion of hospitals. They were often to be found in locations convenient to travelers: 'roadside' hospitals, 'bridge' hospitals, 'valley' hospitals and 'port' hospitals.[40] A rapidly developing urban market had emerged for a diverse range of medical services that drew upon the medical knowledge of the ancient Greeks, such as that contained in the writings of Galen and Arabic works of the Islamic world. Translations of these works into Latin became standard texts in the medical curriculum of the medieval universities.

The men and women who staffed many of the Christian hospitals of the time were members of religious orders living under a rule. They wore a religious habit and provided both medical and spiritual help to the inmates. Patients were expected to perform spiritual exercises. One of the best known of the religious orders dedicated to caring for the sick in the later period of the Middle Ages were the Antonines. Hospital Sisters of St Catherine were also prominent in providing medical care. The Order of the Holy Spirit had hospitals in every important town in Europe by the middle of the thirteenth century. St Bartholomew's hospital in London began its life as both a monastery and a hospital.[41]

Leper houses were a distinctive feature of the pastoral care of the sick. Once a person was diagnosed as leprous (i.e., as having Hansen's Disease) he or she was removed from common society. This might even mean separation by order of law. Rites of separation and claustration could limit the ability of these unfortunate people to engage in business or even own property. In their dependent state, the leprous relied on charity. Some of them lived in squalid settlements. Others dwelt in endowed houses for the diseased and were required to live a kind of monastic life spent in prayer and celibacy. Donors expected something in return for their generosity. The usual pattern was a group of small houses clustered around a chapel. From the twelfth century, leper hospitals were a common sight and usually were found outside the city walls with their alms boxes posted outside. In France alone, at this time, there were some two thousand leper houses. The great leper hospital of Saint-Lazare in Paris was dependent on the bishop while local authorities took responsibility for some of the smaller institutions.[42]

A curious feature of hospital care in the Middle Ages was those establishments run by military religious orders at the time of the

Crusades. At the Council of Clermont in 1095, Pope Urban II (1088-99) proclaimed a holy war against the infidel by launching the First Crusade to redeem Jerusalem from the Muslims: the battle of the cross against the crescent began in earnest. He toured France for a year, whipping up support for the venture. Salvation was promised to those who enlisted through the granting of a full plenary indulgence. St Bernard of Clairvaux (1090-1153) backed the venture and spoke out strongly of its religious value. Between the 1140s and 1270 there were five more crusades by Latin Europe against the Muslims, with territory won and lost. In 1291 the last Christian stronghold of the port city of Acre fell to the Arabs and the Christians finally left the region.

The Knights Templar were a religious order of fighting men that protected pilgrims visiting the holy places in Jerusalem, which had opened up at the time of the Crusades, from Muslim attack. As such, the Templars considered themselves to be both soldiers and monks. As well, they engaged in some charitable activities. Founded in 1119 by Hughes de Payens, the Templars were given quarters by the Latin king within the royal palace that was attached to the Jerusalem Temple, hence the name of the order. One of their functions was to garrison castles. These formed a defensive network across the Middle East. Although the idea of religious monks dedicated to military force was widely accepted at the time, some people did have misgivings about the venture. During the thirteenth century the Knights Templar may have had as many as seven thousand members throughout the Middle East and Europe.[43] Recruits took normal religious vows of poverty, chastity and obedience and lived a community life that included the prayer of the Divine Office.[44] Military orders spread their activity from the Holy Land to other parts of Western Christendom. This included Spain, where they were involved in the reconquest against the Muslims.

Other military religious orders followed the Templars, many developing from already existing religious orders. Among these were the Hospitaller Knights of St John of Jerusalem who, alongside their significant military functions, directed their attention to institutions caring for the sick. Their great hospital in Jerusalem, dedicated to St John the Baptist, cared for up to two thousand sick men and women at a time, according to the account of one traveler.[45] They had another great hospital complex at Acre and a number of lesser hospitals scattered around the East. By the standards of the time, the Hospitallers provided excellent care. Statutes of the order state that the sergeant-nurses had to gently wash the feet of inmates, change the sheets and make the beds. A detailed level of care was set out for every sick person in the hospital: inmates were to be provided with a sheepskin cloak and woolen cap and boots for going to the latrine. Cradles for the babies of female pilgrims were to be placed by the beds. Three days per week patients were to be given a diet of meat. Four doctors were to be employed in the Jerusalem hospital to diagnose diseases and prescribe appropriate medication. Abandoned children were to be cared for.[46]

Nursing care was combined with spiritual assistance. Upon being admitted to the hospital, a patient would make his or her confession and receive Holy Communion. Each day the wards were blessed with holy water. As well, the Hospitallers provided practical charity outside the hospital, such as feeding the hungry at the door and distributing clothing among poor mothers.[47] The order resembled the Templars: membership was divided into knights, sergeants, clerics, and serving brothers. The Hospitallers wore a distinctive white cross on their coat, corresponding to the red cross of the Templars.[48] The order admitted women, who lived in separate quarters. Women members assisted with the care of the sick but took no part in military activities.

Following the defeat of the Latin kingdom in the East, the military orders transferred their operations elsewhere. The Hospitallers, while maintaining their military operations, continued to run hospitals, as they did in Rhodes. The orders had accumulated great wealth over time. For example, the Templars had a subsidiary role in international banking. In London, off the Strand, they erected the New Temple. Today, the name remains and the site houses the courts of law in the city. Amidst much intrigue, the Templars were dissolved in 1312 by the French king, Philip IV (1268-1314). But the Hospitallers survived and continued their nursing activities, transferring to Rhodes, and later to Cyprus and then to Malta. They remain to this day as a charitable organization, with headquarters in Rome.

### Anointing with Oil

Rubbing oil on the body has long been associated with imparting strength and healing. Athletes in ancient times prepared themselves in this way before participating in sporting activities. Oil in lamps was one of the main means of lighting and took on a symbolic meaning of human illumination. Olive oil was the most common variety in the Meditteranean world. The Bible provides us with many examples of the use of oil in association with the body. In dry climates, it was used to:

complete bathing for purposes of refreshment
(2 Sam 12:20; Ruth 3:3);
signify respect for welcoming guests (Mt 26:7; Lk 7:46);
perfume the body (Am 6:6; Esth 2:12);
strengthen the limbs (Ezek 16:9);
heal wounds (Isa 1:6; Lk 10:34);
treat the sick (Jas 5:14; Mk 6:13); and
embalm a corpse (Mk 16:1; Lk 23:56-24:1).

As well, oil was used in liturgical rites to anoint kings (1 Sam 10:1; 16:1; 2 Kings 9:3; 11:12), priests (Lev 8:30) and prophets (Isa 61:1), consecrating them or setting them apart, for God's service. Early Christianity took up oil anointing in the initiation of new Christians to symbolize that they were strengthened against evil and consecrated to God. Interestingly, anointing with oil is still part of the English coronation ceremony.

In the New Testament Letter of James 5:14-16, we read of the practice of calling the elders of the Church to attend the sick so that they may anoint them with oil and pray over them:

> Are any among you sick? They should call for the elders of the church and have them pray over them, anointing them with oil in the name of the Lord. The prayer of faith will save the sick, and the Lord will raise them up; and anyone who has committed sins will be forgiven. Therefore confess your sins to one another, and pray for one another, so that you may be healed. The prayer of the righteous is powerful and effective.

Some commentators interpret this biblical text as referring primarily to a restoration to physical health, with only a secondary emphasis on the forgiveness of sins.[49] Others believe, on the other hand, the effects of this prayer and anointing are about a more holistic way of understanding the entire religious situation of the sick person: a future, eschatological healing through forgiveness of sin, and strength to overcome powerlessness and weakness of faith, as well as bodily healing.[50] This text of James, associated with a ritual of anointing by designated Church leaders, appears to have only slowly entered into Western Christian pastoral care of the sick. Charismatic healing, on the other hand, remained the more common means of attending to the seriously ill.

By the beginning of the fifth century, numerous documents attest to an oil anointing of the sick that was not simply charismatic. It was the bishop who always blessed the oil used for this purpose, in prescribed liturgical rites. But it was normally the laity, not the ordained, who drank or applied the blessed oil either to themselves or to others who were ill. However, presbyteral anointing was also administered. It was only from the Carolingian reforms of the ninth century that the priest became the proper minister of anointing the sick. Prior to that time, the blessing of the oil was the more important liturgical rite, rather than any specific rite for the actual anointing of the sick. It was not until the ninth century that the Roman liturgy had a special rite for administering the already blessed oil.

In the period between the ninth and eleventh centuries an important change in pastoral practice occurred concerning anointing with oil that, by then, was understood as sacramental. It was the dying, rather than the ill, to which anointing was now directed and it was aimed less at physical healing than the forgiveness of sins. This theological understanding resulted largely from the scholastic theology of the universities that understood sacraments as being primarily about the giving of grace. Hence the spiritual effects of the sacrament of anointing came to be recognized as primary. Soul, mind and body were understood by the scholastic theologians to be ordered hierarchically. Sacramental anointing became associated with deathbed penance. From now on, anointing was associated with pastoral care in the giving of the 'last rites' and was called 'extreme unction', a term first used by Peter Lombard (*c*.1100-60). It was no longer a sacrament of the sick but of the dying. Because of the increased association of anointing with the forgiveness of sins, the written sources of the period attest that only priests could anoint. Lay anointing, with oil blessed by the bishop, disappears from the pastoral care of the sick. The original order in administering the sacraments was penance, anointing and eucharistic viaticum for the dying. After the twelfth century the order changed to that of penance, viaticum and anointing. As a result, anointing rather than viaticum came to be understood as the primary sacrament for the dying.[51] Thus there were three significant changes concerning oil anointing: a change in the stress given to the various effects of the sacrament, with the forgiveness of sin given more prominence than bodily healing; a change in the position of the sacrament within the last rites; and a change in access to the sacrament, with its being restricted to pastoral care offered by the clergy.[52]

Looking ahead in time, little was to change concerning theological understanding and pastoral practice surrounding the sacrament of anointing within the Catholic Church until the reforms resulting from the Second Vatican Council (1962-65). The Council of Trent, against the claim of the Protestant Reformers in the sixteenth century, affirmed the divine origin of anointing as one of the seven sacraments of the Church. Trent taught that the sacrament of anointing was to be administered to sick persons, especially those persons who were dangerously ill and who appeared close to death. The Council made mention that only ordained priests could administer this sacrament. The revised rite of the *Pastoral Care of the Sick*,[53] following Vatican II, upheld the practice that only priests could anoint. However, an important change of pastoral practice did result from the revised rites in modern times. Anointing is no longer to be understood as primarily a sacrament for the dying but one for the sick as a whole. This change removed the sacrament's association with the 'last rites' given to the dying. As well, it balanced the different effects that could be obtained by a sick person in receiving the sacrament: spiritual strength to face the suffering and temptations to despair that come with anxieties associated with sickness; the possibility of bodily healing; and, where necessary, the forgiveness of sins. Care of the sick, through sacramental anointing with oil, was restored to pastoral practice.

Following the Reformation, anointing of the sick was removed from the 1552 Anglican *Book of Common Prayer*. Today, in most member Churches of the Anglican Communion, anointing with oil is practiced within healing services as in some Protestant Churches throughout the world.[54]

Pastoral care in the medieval Church was innovative but also prone to superstition and exploitation. The arrival of the Reformation saw an unprecedented challenge to existing pastoral care practices within the Church. It is to that story that we now turn our attention.

# Chapter 5

## Protesters and Reformers

### The Protestant Reformation on the Continent

#### Martin Luther and Indulgences

Wittenberg is a tranquil little market town situated on the banks of the River Elbe, just sixty miles south-west of the bustling metropolis of Berlin. For much of the twentieth century it was ruled by the Communist regime of East Germany. Settled as a trading post as early as 1174, by the beginning of the sixteenth century it had acquired a degree of prestige with the founding of a university there in 1502. It then had a permanent population of about two and a half thousand residents with about the same number again of university students, swelling the town's population during term time. The *Schlosskirche* (castle church) was noted for its fine collection of relics that pilgrims came to venerate, especially on 1 November, the church's patronal feast of All Saints. The relics had been acquired by the Elector of Saxony, Frederick the Wise (1463-1525). The academic community of the town used the *Schlosskirche* as the venue for ceremonial occasions and its north door functioned as a bulletin board for notices of Wittenberg's university.

Sixteenth century Wittenberg was a small but lively place where academic debate characterized community life. But compared to other university and commercial centers in Europe of the time, it was a town of little importance or interest. Yet from this relatively obscure region of Saxony was unleashed a movement that was to shake European politics and Christianity to its very foundations and occupy the attention of both emperor and pope. Pastoral care in communities and parishes, because of events in Wittenberg, would alter dramatically throughout much of the Western Church, leading ordinary Christian women and men to re-experience their faith in hitherto unimagined ways. The means by which much of the Church was to go about its ministry and interpret its beliefs would forever be different. The man who set in motion this process of change, a change that was to get beyond his control, was a young Augustinian friar. He was a man obsessed by religious scruples as a result of his perceived unworthiness before God. His name was Martin Luther (1483-1546). Brother Martin lectured on the Bible to students in Wittenberg's university.

On the eve of the feast of All Saints in 1517, as the pilgrims were beginning to stream in to pray before the relics in the *Schlosskirche*, Luther posted his ninety-five theses concerning the Church's practice of granting indulgences on the church's door, as points for theological debate. The university teacher was just thirty-four years of age. Theological disputations, such as this, were a regular feature of university life. Few of the devout pilgrims to the church would have taken any notice of the theological points on the university noticeboard as they had more pressing concerns on their minds while they went about their devotions. The ninety-five theses, for those who cared to read them, were nothing more than discussion points for consideration within the academic community of the university.[1] None of the pilgrims that day could have understood their importance. Little did they realize how much their devotional life and experience of pastoral care from the clergy would be dramatically altered in the immediate future as they hurried through the church door to get to the relics inside. But some more thoughtful people did realize their extraordinary challenge to traditional beliefs and pastoral practices. In Nuremberg, Luther's theses were soon translated from Latin into German and widely circulated. The Protestant Reformation was under way. Along with Paul's decision to take the gospel beyond Judaism to the Gentiles, Constantine's conversion resulting in Christianity becoming the state religion, and the split between the distinct traditions of the Eastern and Western Churches in the eleventh century, the Protestant Reformation marks one of the defining moments in the two thousand year history of pastoral care within the Church.

As we have already seen in the previous chapter, indulgences were attached to the veneration of certain relics. There was no more successful preacher of indulgences than the Dominican friar, Johann Tetzel (c.1465-1519). The man was a showman of the first order. He would arrive in a town, with his entourage, to the sound of bells and the carrying of banners. Flamboyant in style, he preached the indulgence from a church pulpit or, weather permitting, within the town square. Tetzel's visits to places had something of the feel of a carnival about them. The Medici Pope Leo X (1513-21), in debt and urgently needing money to rebuild St Peter's in Rome, approved the indulgence fundraising campaign. On a more local level, Archbishop Albert of Mainz and Magdeburg (1490-1545), in whose jurisdiction lay Wittenberg, needed money to pay his own mounting debts to the banking house of Fugger in Augsburg. Tetzel proved to be one of the most successful of the preachers of indulgences. If the penitent went to confession, said a few prayers, visited a church or two and placed an offering in the indulgence box, a plenary indulgence was assured. Well known was the jingle of the time: 'As soon as the coin in the coffer rings, the soul from purgatory springs.'

The circus-like antics of Tetzel shocked and angered the young and pious Wittenberg friar. Theologians might distinguish the giving of alms, associated with the indulgence, from their sale, but such theological abstractions went unappreciated by most of the people. Who could be blamed for thinking that one was 'buying' both forgiveness for sins and a passport out of purgatory for oneself and the dead? The indulgence, in Luther's view, blinded people to their need for faith and genuine repentance. It was faith alone that had the power to save, not pious good works. Luther believed it absurd to think that accumulated merit could bring about God's salvation (justification) for the individual. Practices, such as the seeking of merit through indulgences, were nothing more than superstition and a distortion of the meaning of faith, thought Luther. For this friar, faith was simply the supreme trust in God's pardoning of one's sins, God's power to save us through Christ's atoning sufferings and death on the cross. God's love is freely given to those with such faith. It cannot be earned through storing up merit from doing good works. Medieval piety was dealt a mortal blow. Arising from this fundamental theological position, Luther and subsequent Protestant teaching was to go on to reject the cult of saints, the veneration of relics, purgatory, Masses for the dead and papal authority. The whole structure, upon which much of the medieval Church's means of pastoral care had come to rest, was to change. Protestants would reject the medieval piety and the pastoral care associated with it, while Catholics would seek to correct the abuses.

Luther's ninety-five theses made no explicit mention of the doctrine of justification by faith. That would come shortly after. But his assault on indulgences in 1517 arose from his understanding of Paul's teaching on grace, as outlined in the Epistle to the Romans, particularly chapter 8, which Luther lectured upon in Wittenberg. Albert, Luther's archbishop, was so incensed that Luther's teachings were becoming widely known and hindering the flow of income from the indulgences that he reported the matter to the pope. The pope responded by simply telling the leader of the Augustinians to keep his friars under control. What threat could there be to the Church's supreme authority from an obscure German friar?

Events were to prove otherwise. Luther's fame quickly spread and won him support. His aim was not to undermine the Church by revolution, let alone found a new Church, but simply to purify the existing Church.[2] After debating the formidable Johann Ecke (1486-1543) at Leipzig in 1519, Luther became more radicalized and polemical, directing his hostilities towards the papacy. His attacks on the avarice and pomp of the pope and his court became more virulent and obscene as the years went by. Luther was now perceived as a major threat to established Catholicism. The papal bull of Leo X of 1520, *Exsurge Domine* - written largely by Ecke - condemned forty-one propositions of Luther and decreed that his books were to be burnt. The Augustinian friar was given two months to recant or face excommunication. He responded by burning the papal bull in a theatrical display of contempt. In a new papal bull of 1521, *Decet Romanum pontificem,* Luther was formally excommunicated and any city that dared offer him sanctuary was to be placed under papal interdict. Emperor Charles V (1500-58), anxious to preserve political and religious unity, allowed Luther a final chance to reverse matters at the Diet of Worms, less than a month after his formal excommunication. Luther's support was by now growing and threatening political stability among the German princes. While Luther traveled to Worms, a crowd looted the houses of the priest-canons in Erfurt following a sermon he had preached there. Civil disturbance was becoming widespread. At Worms, Luther once again faced his old enemy, Johann Ecke. Luther maintained his position and this resulted in his being declared an outlaw by the emperor.

Things had, indeed, moved rapidly from the seemingly harmless display of some points of academic debate upon the university church noticeboard, on the eve of All Saints less than four years previously. As a result of changed political circumstances, after a period of hiding in the fortress of the *Wartburg* at Eisenach, Luther re-emerged into public life the following year and taught freely his ideas. Forsaking his religious beliefs and earlier held ideas concerning religious life, he married a former nun by the name of Catherine von Bora (c.1499-c.1552) and lived with her and their children in the former house of the Augustinian friars in Wittenberg. Luther had now been rejected by his Augustinian Order, by the emperor and by the pope. In his often quoted statement at Worms, 'Here I stand, God help me, Amen', Luther expressed his conviction that God was on his side and it was this alone that sustained him. Luther never even thought of himself as a reformer of the Church. That task belonged only to God.[3] He was merely swept along by God's grace. As his biographer, Oberman, writes:

> Luther did not see himself as a man going his own way but as a man forsaken; that is how he experienced and understood the beginnings of the history of the Reformation – lonely but not alone.[4]

Luther had divided Germany. At the Diet of Speyer in 1529, a minority of the princes favorably disposed to the principles of Luther's reform 'protested' against the proceedings of the emperor and Catholic princes. It was from this protest that the word 'Protestant' came about to describe the Reformed Churches.

## Lutheran Changes to Congregational Life

Upon his return to Wittenberg in 1522, after his isolation in the *Wartburg*, Luther was no longer just the academic theologian, a hounded heretic, calling for a new theology. Luther embarked on a program of practical reform within the life of the Church. New ideas were to be put into the service of the parish congregations of Germany, bringing about a complete change in the ways of pastoral practice. How did pastoral care look as a result of Lutheran teaching?

Luther taught a doctrine of the priesthood of all the baptized, as founded in the New Testament (1 Pet 2:9). For Luther, every baptized Christian is a priest and so in no need of ecclesiastical mediators for contact with the grace of Christ. But he did not deny the importance of an ordained ministry that he saw as necessary for Church order. In his terminology, Luther used the word *sacerdotium* to describe the priesthood of all believers, while reserving the term *ministerium* for ordained ministry. As Luther expressed in *Concerning the Ministry*, 'One is born a priest, one becomes a minister.'[5] He denied ordination to be a sacrament because he believed it lacked any visible sign (such as water as in baptism, or bread and wine, in the Eucharist). Yet Luther did continue to insist that Christ himself commissioned the Church to preach the word and administer the two sacraments of baptism and Holy Communion. He also upheld the traditional understanding of ordination as conferring the gift of the Holy Spirit to enable the pastor to exercise ministry.[6]

Luther wanted, then, to distance himself from any notion of an ordained priesthood that brought with it special 'powers'. As a result, pastoral ministry was characterized by more participative forms of worship, rather than relying on a priesthood that did it all for others. Latin was abolished and all Protestant Church services began using the common language of the people. The *pastor* now led worship by facing the people, no longer with his back to them, praying on their behalf, as had been the custom. Luther encouraged congregational singing through the use of rousing German hymns. The Bible was translated into German to be heard and read by all. God, in Luther's framework, spoke to the individual person through the word conveyed by the Holy Spirit. Reading and listening to the words of the Bible were understood to bring faith to birth and nourish it. Only what was clearly expressed in the Bible could be regarded as truth; all else was irrelevant or false: the principle of *sola Scriptura* (Scripture alone). On this basis, Luther rejected the authority of the pope and taught that general councils of the Church could err. Yet Luther was anxious to steer clear of the 'illuminism' of the more radical reformers, something he thought could be all too easily misleading.[7] As well, Luther did not propose any biblical literalism for he believed any given passage had to be interpreted in relation to Scripture as a whole.[8] Preaching assumed a central place in the life of every congregation. No longer understood as a man possessing special 'powers', the Lutheran male pastor, above all, was one who proclaimed the word of God. Herein lay the essential and most important function of pastoral care.

The Reformation's push to translate the Bible and liturgical prayers from Latin into the common language of the people had a profound effect on the ordinary man and woman. Helped by the invention of the printing press that allowed for widespread distribution of books, more and more people now were encouraged to learn to read and write. Reading God's word in the Scriptures became essential for the saving of one's soul. The Reformation had a decisive role, therefore, in fostering literacy, with all its accompanying benefits for human advancement. This was one of the great pastoral achievements of Protestant Christianity.

Part of the difficulty in following Luther's teachings is that he is often inconsistent. Luther did not engage in any systematized theology, as did his disciple at Wittenberg, Philip Melanchthon (1497-1560).[9] Rather, he outlined his ideas in pamphlets and booklets in response to controversies as they arose. Luther had the temperament and style of a polemicist. He was often impulsive, volatile and extreme in his use of language. What were his views on the sacraments that had played such an important part in pastoral care in the medieval Church?[10] He accepted baptism as being the primary sacrament and as one of the two sacraments of the Church – the other being the Eucharist. Luther retained the tradition of infant baptism, believing grace truly to be given to the child by means of the proclamation of the word accompanied by the conscious faith of the sponsors who bring the child to be baptized. It was left to other Protestant reformers to restrict the reception of baptism to adults.

On the eve of the Reformation, the Mass was commonly understood in sacrificial terms whereby Christ is offered sacrificially, within the sacrament, to propitiate God for human sin and so bring merit to those for whom the priest offered it. As we have already seen in the piety characteristic of the medieval Church, pastoral care, as the offer of comfort and assurance, was heavily associated with this understanding of the Mass. People sought relief by having Masses said that would gain merit and thus reduce their time in purgatory. Luther rejected outright any idea of the Mass as a sacrifice. In Luther's understanding, we cannot offer Christ sacrificially for it is Christ who offers us.[11] There was only one sacrifice in Lutheran teaching: that which was made by Christ upon Calvary. Hence he rejected any idea of a sacrificial priesthood within the Church's ministry. Through faith alone, the Christian can receive the grace of Christ in the Eucharist for Christ is truly present in the bread and wine. Luther, unlike many of the later Protestant reformers, did not reject a true presence of Christ in the Eucharist but he did repudiate the Catholic doctrine of transubstantiation, developed by the scholastic theologians, to explain this presence. And Luther insisted that it was not through any special 'powers' of ordained ministry that brought about this presence. Rather, it is the result of the divine promise to bring about Christ's presence in the eucharistic celebration of the believing community.[12] Luther restored the custom of the laity drinking from the eucharistic cup and not receiving only the bread, as had been the custom. By doing so, he stressed the unity between pastor and people in the eucharistic rite. Even more significantly, lay reception of Holy Communion was no longer to be a rare event but common practice at each celebration. Reception of Holy Communion was an integral part of the Eucharist, rather than divorced from it. The move from a mere gazing at the consecrated bread to sharing in it meant a remarkable change of understanding from the medieval experience. This shift in theological understanding, resulting in changed pastoral eucharistic practice, made it clear that the Mass was not an action being done by another for oneself (having a Mass said for one's intention) but a communal act of worship. At first glance it may seem a small point but it made a tremendous difference for pastoral care as to the way the Christian experienced the Eucharist.

### Faith and Justification

Throughout our survey of pastoral care we have seen the importance given to penitential sorrow, forgiveness and reconciliation within the ministry of the Church. Luther, again wanting to avoid any idea of a special priestly power to forgive sins, abolished the sacrament of penance. Forgiveness of sins came directly through Christ alone. All that was needed was repentance in responding to the word of God in the Bible. Pastoral care had the task of encouraging a person to read or listen to the words of Scripture and repent in faith. The pastor was to introduce the person to God's word, not pronounce forgiveness. Here, Luther's ideas concerning justification become most apparent and here is to be found the key to understanding the Protestant Reform.

When Luther taught that the sinner is justified by faith he did not mean that a person is saved because of that faith. This would make faith a human work. It is God, Luther claimed, who justifies the sinner. All that the sinner need do is to embrace God's action in faith. But even faith is a gift of God. Luther was greatly influenced by Augustine's teachings but differs from him as to where such righteousness is located. Augustine taught that it was to be found inside the person whereas Luther understood it to be external. McGrath summarizes Luther's teaching on the matter:

> For Augustine, God bestows justifying righteousness upon the sinner, in such a way that it becomes part of his or her person. As a result, this righteousness, although originating outside the sinner, becomes part of his or her person. For Luther, the righteousness in question remains outside the sinner: it is an 'alien righteousness' (*justitia aliena*) … God shields our sin through his righteousness. This righteousness is like a protective covering, under which we may battle with our sin … Luther thus declares, in a famous phrase, that a believer is 'at one and the same time righteous and a sinner' (*simul iustus et peccator*).[13]

Melanchthon developed Luther's thought and, in doing so, differentiated more sharply between Protestant and Catholic understandings of what it means to be forgiven.

> Where Augustine taught that the sinner is made righteous in justification, Melanchthon taught that he is counted as righteous or pronounced to be righteous. For Augustine, 'justifying righteousness' is imparted; for Melanchthon, it is imputed. Melanchthon drew a sharp distinction between the event of being declared righteous and the process of being made righteous, designating the former 'justification' and the latter 'sanctification' or 'regeneration.'[14]

These theological differences may appear to us today to be splitting hairs but they had a profound influence on understanding the nature of the human person in the sight of God, something crucial for pastoral care. As we shall see, the Council of Trent opposed the Lutheran view and insisted, with Augustine, that justification is a process of regeneration and renewal within human nature that brings about a change in both the outer status and the inner nature of the sinner. The Lutheran view, by contrast, stresses the utter sinfulness of the person within the very core of human nature - calling for repentance and conversion, a theme that would become characteristic of Protestant evangelism.

The Lutheran tradition gave a very different feel to what it meant to be a Christian from the medieval tradition. No longer was it a matter of trying to perfect oneself and build up merit before God. Rather, salvation was to be experienced primarily as a gift. Christ is less an example for us to imitate, more a gift to be received. For Luther, there can be no saints. It is in the knowledge of our sinfulness that we repent and turn to God. Whereas Catholics had sought relief from their apprehension of damnation through pious acts aimed at gaining indulgences, Luther and the Protestant Reformers found solace in God's absolute free gift of grace. Yet both groups, living in the world of the sixteenth century, were in search of essentially the same thing: relief from fear and dread. As a result, Lutheranism did away with religious life in the monasteries as a special means of striving for perfection.

> For Luther what characterizes a Christian is a freedom from self-preoccupation. When one recognizes these things it is difficult to say that any amount of reform of Catholicism's practices could have averted the split which Luther's reading of the scripture precipitated.[15]

To help people grasp the Reformation teachings, Luther wrote his two catechisms, both of which were published in 1529. They remain one of the outstanding pastoral achievements of the Lutheran reforms. The *Great Catechism* resulted from Luther's visitation of Saxon parishes where he noted an ignorance concerning matters of Christian faith. It was designed especially for pastors to instruct their congregations. The *Little Catechism* was an abbreviated and simplified version for the general reader. It also contained devotional exercises for the family.

Luther's marriage to the former Cistercian nun, Catherine von Bora, paved the way for a pastoral ministry set firmly within family life. Protestantism did away with exalting virginity and celibacy, ceasing to uphold the ideal of a celibate clergy set apart from other Christians, free of all sexuality and children. Luther opened the way for domesticity in pastoral care. Priests, a caste of men different from the rest of the Christian community, along with vowed religious monks and nuns - such people had no place in Luther's vision of pastoral care.

Martin Luther was a complex man. Often extremely coarse in speech and displaying virulent hostility towards his perceived enemies, he was totally consumed in believing the power of God to be at work in the human heart. His colleagues and friends gathered at his table to listen to him and to argue. They recorded what they heard in the *Table Talk*, leaving us a vivid picture of the man who changed the course of pastoral care, the Church and human history. Europe was now set to face its bloody religious wars between Catholic and Protestant.

## Ulrich Zwingli and Changing Styles of Worship

In 1522 a group of Christian men in Zurich, drawn to the new movements of reform sweeping across the Church, engaged in a provocative act by eating a meal of sausages, in defiance of the traditional laws of fasting. Their action was defended by Ulrich Zwingli (1484-1531), the principal preacher at the Grossmünster, the main city church in Zurich.[16] Zwingli, a man of tall stature, took his preaching seriously. His voice thundered against a wide range of traditional beliefs and practices that included monastic vows, indulgences, the cult of saints, clerical celibacy, superstitious devotions and traditional understandings of the Mass. So persuasive and forthright were Zwingli's attacks on traditional religion that his code of reform was adopted as the official religion of both his city and canton. Zwingli's reforms brought about the first State Church of the Protestant Reformation.

Extremism characterized Zwingli's approach to everything. Half-measures were not his style. He ordered church buildings to be stripped of all ornamentation. Religious paintings, crucifixes, stained glass windows, holy water fonts, reliquaries, and statues: these all were destroyed. Churches began to look much more bare than they did in northern Germany as a result of the more moderate Lutheran reforms. Religious houses were transformed into schools and hospitals. For Zwingli, the Bible was what characterized true religion and whatever could not be found in its pages had no further place in the life of the Church. Zwingli believed there were only two sacraments: baptism and Eucharist. He saw them to be no more than symbols, tokens of allegiance. In no sense was Christ in any way present in the Eucharist, as Luther believed. It is in his work of 1525, *On the True and False Religion*, that Zwingli presented most fully his theological program of reform.

Central to Zwingli's ideas was a belief in predestination, based upon his doctrine of divine sovereignty, something that John Calvin was to take up and develop. Zwingli's view of human nature was dualistic. For him there was a sharp distinction between the spiritual capacity within human nature and the animality of the physical. He believed that Adam's sin had all but obliterated the divine image within the human person who, as a result, was worthy only of destruction. Yet, God, in his mercy, elected some to eternal life, achieved through the mediation of his Son Jesus Christ. The rest were doomed to destruction. Election precedes faith, which is something that is normally the sign of election, but not always.[17]

Zwingli's program of pastoral care was supported by the state for it forced his moral agenda upon the lives of its citizens. Beginning with moral reform, Zwingli quickly turned his attention to new theological understandings, especially about the Eucharist. No longer was Christ understood to be in any sense present in this sacrament and, as a result, it assumed less importance in pastoral ministry. The pulpit replaced the altar - now a simple wooden table - as the distinctive feature inside Zurich churches. The biblical sermon became the central act of pastoral ministry. It was a pastoral care nourishing faith by words rather than by sacraments or visual symbols. And it steered pastoral ministry in a direction that looked upon human beings as creatures of darkness, a select few of whom were fortunate enough to be rescued from damnation by an all powerful and sovereign God. It was a grim message.

### Martin Bucer and Church Order

In tracing the history of pastoral care within the period of the Protestant Reformation, the reforms of Martin Bucer (1491-1551) concerning Church order are of importance. Bucer, a former Dominican friar, believed that pastoral care was a matter of establishing a unified order of ministry, a matter of public policy supported by the state. He wrote about this in his work, *On True Pastoral Care*, in 1538 and set about putting his vision of things into practice in Strasbourg. No innovation in ministry was allowed to happen without the permission of the ruling *Council*. Elders played a leading role in ecclesiastical affairs in Strasbourg. Their task was primarily one of ensuring that correct beliefs and behaviors were observed by the city's population. Any form of religious unrest was to be dealt with swiftly and decisively. Elders functioned as the religious police in enforcing Bucer's Church order, one that strove for a unified civic religion.

To bring about his work of reform, Bucer valued good instruction of the people and this meant having educated pastors. The gospel was to be preached, heard and believed. Teaching and the surveillance of moral behavior along scriptural lines were what particularly interested him. For this purpose Bucer founded a seminary to educate the pastors of Strasbourg for their ministry.[18]

The task of pastoral care, for Bucer, consisted of five elements: to call to the Church those not in it because of fleshly arrogance or false doctrine; to recall those once in the Church but who had left it; to exhort to improvement of life those who were in the Church but had sinned seriously; to strengthen those in the Church weak in faith; and to protect from anguish and error those in the Church but who did not sin flagrantly.[19]

A pastoral innovation that was to cause much controversy and division in Bucer's Church was what was known as the 'core Church movement'. By fostering an inner circle of more dedicated believers, it resembled many such movements within today's Church. In attempting to recreate a Christian community along the lines of the New Testament Church, Bucer endorsed the setting up of small groups of highly committed Christians within the broader parish structure. These groups met weekly for mutual instruction and discipline. Not all the city pastors were happy with such elite groups within their congregations. It would prove to be a pastoral strategy that would lead to discord. Here was an attempt to create a two-fold ecclesiology and it failed. It survived less than two years for:

> ... there was always an ambivalence between this aspect of openness and the no less indispensable aspect of a church better structured and more energetic as a community.[20]

Bucer was less extreme than Zwingli. He desired to bring the different reformist groups into greater unity as well as maintaining links with Catholics over the issue of justification by faith. Some of Bucer's ideas had a certain compromise about them, especially his attempt to reconcile Luther's teaching on the presence of Christ in the Eucharist with that of Zwingli's notion of 'memorialism'. In Bucer's theology, Christ is given in an indissoluble conjunction *with* the bread and wine, the doctrine that became known as 'receptionism'.[21]

### John Calvin and Moral Reform

The city of Geneva became a haven for the French Huguenot Protestants fleeing Catholic persecution. Among them was John Calvin (1509-64) who was persuaded to take over the leadership in reforming the Church of this Swiss city, after having been earlier banished from it. Calvin's goal was to set about establishing an ordered and disciplined Christian community. Moral reform of the people he saw to be at the heart of this project. Calvin was a stern, austere man with apparently little personal charm. His personality was such that, unlike Bucer in Strasbourg, he had no stomach for any sort of compromise. His tidy mind drove him towards orderliness in systematizing his theology and pastoral structures in a way that Luther was never able to achieve. He sought to reproduce patterns of ministry within the early Church, as found in the New Testament. Calvin expressed his ideas in a small work he published in 1536, known as the *Institutes of the Christian Religion*. Over the years he expanded its contents so that it developed into a comprehensive compendium of biblical theology, some eighty chapters spread over four books in the final edition of 1559.

Calvin's Church was one that exercised power over the life of its people. It was a Church characterized by control.[22] There were four offices within the Church. Along with the *pastors* who had overall responsibility for pastoral care, Calvin's Church had a body of twelve *elders*. They were to cooperate with the pastors in discharging discipline. The elders were to admonish those members not living according to the required standards. As such, they were in charge of ensuring proper behavioral standards. The *doctors* had the important role of teaching, especially teaching how to interpret Scripture. And there were the *deacons* who had entrusted to them the task of the pastoral care of the sick and poor.[23] Begging, so characteristic of the mendicant friars, was strictly forbidden.

The overall ruling body of the Church was the *Consistory*, comprising six pastors and twelve elders. It met on Thursdays and functioned like a court. It had wide powers and there was little in the life of Geneva's citizens that escaped its attention. People were brought before it to be questioned and given penalties. Its role included the education of public conscience. The Consistory showed little mercy to offenders. At the same time it sought to protect the most vulnerable within the city, such as widows, orphans and children.

The Consistory had the power to pronounce a citizen excommunicated. To be unable to share in the Lord's Supper was considered a shocking humiliation.[24] Excommunication from the Church was understood by Calvin to serve a number of purposes: it safeguarded God's honor; protected other Church members from corruption; provided opportunity and incentive for offenders to repent, because of the public shame; and it ensured the Lord's Supper would not be profaned by having unworthy members share in the sacred meal.[25]

Offences that came before the Consistory were varied, examples including: the case of a woman who attempted to cure her husband by tying a walnut and spider charm around his neck; a member of the Church caught dancing; and a person who possessed a book on the lives of the saints.[26] Fraud, cruelty, sexual improprieties and cursing all received attention in the attempt to maintain religious and moral purity. Few disorders escaped the attention of the elders as they sought out offenders to bring before the Consistory.

Unlike Luther, it was Calvin's view that ministry was not a function of the priesthood of all the baptized but a recognized order in itself. Like everything else in Calvin's scheme of things, ministry had to be controlled - not that he considered ministry to be a sacrament bringing with it special powers: it was a function. But it did not belong to everyone.[27]

Preaching upon God's word in Scripture assumed a position of utmost prominence in Calvin's understanding of pastoral ministry. As Bernard Cottret interprets Calvin, preaching for him 'was the very essence of the Reformation'.[28] In Calvin's Church, preaching is the prime form of pastoral guidance, for it allows God to speak to the individual. Pastoral care is now given from the pulpit.[29] Alongside the sermon in Geneva, another important function of pastoral care was that of the 'congregations'. These were weekly conferences given over to the discussion of Scripture and led by the pastor. Bible study groups, that have become so much a feature of Protestant Churches, probably originate in Calvin's 'congregations' in Geneva.

The Reformed minister, then, had a dual ministry of pastoral care: to preach the word and oversee the moral life of the community. Pastors were encouraged to visit homes, but only if accompanied by an elder. This was to be done at least once a year to ensure households were observing the rules of the Church.[30]

Despite his preoccupation with correct moral living, Calvin upheld the doctrine of justification by faith: such faith is never devoid of good works and proper behavior. But Calvin went far beyond Luther with his disturbing doctrine of predestination. Salvation, he claimed, stands not on faith, let alone good works, but on election,[31] and salvation, in Calvin's theology, implies a free offer by God to some while others, who are denied it, are damned. Predestination was meant to emphasize God's election of human beings without reference to their foreseen merits or achievements. Calvin's purpose was to stress God's sovereignty, God having no other motive for his actions other than his glory. The concern was to downplay any human merit in the process of justification.[32]

Calvin's influence led the Churches that followed his teachings to a strictly Bible-based faith. Although Calvin preferred a weekly celebration of the Lord's Supper, pressure was brought to bear to have it celebrated just four times a year. Calvinism evokes images of austere worship devoid of visual beauty. Calvinist churches were stripped of ornamentation, with the pulpit replacing the altar as the focal point in church architecture. A simple table replaced the altar, for the latter symbolized the Eucharist as a sacrifice. The style of pastoral care was one that emphasized the spoken word of Scripture and moral uprightness of life. Calvin's contribution to Church life has been summed up as follows:

> ...what distinguishes Calvin is that he was not simply a thinker, however perspicuous and resourceful, but a religious leader of such astonishing practical ability as to place him among the most influential of the world's men of action ... In short he was a dedicated doctrinaire.[33]

### Anabaptists and Other Radical Reformers

Hanging high from the tower of St Lambert's Church in Münster to this day are several iron cages. They have been there since 1536. For three hundred years, for everyone in Münster to gaze up at, the cages contained the decomposed corpses of John of Leyden (*c*.1509-36) and two of his friends who were savagely tortured to death by red-hot tongs. Now the cages are empty. The story behind these cages marks one of the most bizarre episodes of the Protestant Reformation. John, a Dutch former innkeeper, arrived in Münster with the intention of transforming the city into an apocalyptic New Jerusalem. He was only in his twenties and assumed to himself the title of King of Zion. Mentally deranged, he secured the help of twelve elders in setting about creating his new religious kingdom in Münster. Women were forbidden to remain virgins and polygamy was fostered. John, himself, had sixteen wives to ensure a plentiful supply of new Israelites. Finally, the city was recaptured and life returned to normal. Meanwhile, in Amsterdam and throughout the Netherlands, there emerged another religious sect known as Adamism, because of its practice of nudity. Earlier, a former Franciscan friar by the name of Thomas Müntzer (c.1490-1525) and initially a follower of Luther, was preaching fanatical sermons in the Saxon town of Zwickau. His message included forecasting the destruction of the Roman Church and the common ownership of all property. He rejected the practice of infant baptism and insisted upon a second, adult baptism. The movement for exclusively adult baptism gained adherents and its members came to be known as the Anabaptists. The sect initially was centered on the city of Zurich. But Anabaptism quickly spread to the Netherlands, northern Germany, Austria, Moravia and Poland.

Anabaptist groups, and other sectarian movements originating in the sixteenth century, were diverse religious communities. Jacob Hutter (d.1536) founded the Hutterite Brothers in Moravia. Characteristic of this movement was the custom of several families living together in the same *Bruderhof* (brother house), with members holding their goods in common. Mennonites trace their beginnings to the Dutch Anabaptist leader Menno Simons (1496-1561) who held pacifist views and believed in the complete separation of Church and state. His followers refused to serve the state in any way. Hence Mennonites tended to live outside the general community, seeing the world as corrupt. The Spiritualists emphasized inward religious experience and understood Scripture to mirror and articulate personal spiritual experience rather than creating and defining it. Pastoral care among the Spiritualists steered clear of institutional Church structures. The Socinians held anti-trinitarian beliefs and stressed the humanity of Christ to the near elimination of his divinity. Driven out of Poland, they found a leader in an Italian named Lellio Sozzini (1525-62) from whom they derive their name. Sozzini emphasized the ethical dimensions of Christianity. The Unitarian Church traces its roots to this movement.

Evangelical Anabaptists were known for their community spirit. Unlike the unstable and wild John of Leyden, most were quiet, peaceful and hardworking people. The apocalyptic views of the Anabaptists led them to be suspicious of, or opposed to, secular rule, so provoking prince rulers and city governments to react with hostility. Many Anabaptists were persecuted and executed, being seen as a threat to religious and civil order. Pastoral care in Anabaptist communities was characterized by stern discipline, mutual support, often a sharing of all material goods in common, and hard work.

The value of hard work was a feature of evangelical Protestantism.[34] Luther attacked begging and said that mendicant friars should be put out to work if they wanted to eat. Linked to Luther's doctrine of the priesthood of all believers, Protestant teaching rejected the earlier dichotomy between the active and contemplative forms of life. Secular work was no longer understood as being inferior to the religious life of the monks, nuns and friars. Nor was work any longer considered an ascetic or penitential discipline, as it was for elements of the Christian monastic tradition. The poor no longer possessed any special sanctity in the way that inspired the 'poor man' religious movements of the late twelfth and thirteenth centuries, such as that of Francis of Assisi. In the Protestant world, the poor were as much sinners as the wealthy.[35] As a result, pastoral care in regard to the issue of poverty began to look very different in the various Churches that emerged out of the teachings of the friar of Wittenberg.

## The Protestant Reformation in England

### Henry VIII and His Marriages

Portraits of King Henry VIII of England (1491-1547), particularly those by Hans Holbein (1497-1543), show him to be a monarch of commanding presence. A man of immense bulk, he appears confident, intelligent and formidable: a majestic figure who arouses awe and fear. The Protestant Reformation in England began under Henry's reign not so much out of a desire for religious change but for political reasons of national independence. Henry had been faithful to the Catholic religion and had little sympathy for the new doctrinal changes and religious practices happening on the Continent. Yet he desperately wanted his marriage to Catherine of Aragon (1485-1536), a Spaniard, to be declared invalid by the papacy. Offspring of the marriage had either been stillborn or died in infancy. There was one daughter, Mary Tudor (1516-58), who survived and who was to become queen. But Henry's desire was for a male heir and this became an obsession. Infatuated with Anne Boleyn (c.1509-36), the king wanted to marry her with the hope of a son being born of the union. Pope Clement VII (1523-34), despite the wily Cardinal Thomas Wolsey's (c.1474-1530) best efforts on Henry's behalf, refused to grant an annulment. But this was only partly because Clement believed the marriage to be valid. The king argued that Catherine had previously been married to his deceased elder brother, Arthur, and the dispensation for Catherine and Henry to marry under these circumstances had been invalid. Clement however was reluctant to grant Henry's request on other grounds. The pope had no intention of risking the wrath of the Spanish-born emperor, Charles V. His troops had sacked Rome in 1527, the year Henry began seeking to have his marriage annulled. Frustrated in his efforts, in 1529 the English king got rid of his Lord Chancellor, Wolsey, for failing to obtain an annulment for him, and married Anne in 1533. Thomas

Cranmer (1489-1556), already holding strong Protestant views, was appointed Archbishop of Canterbury and declared Henry's marriage to his new queen to be valid. Unfortunately for Anne, she was later to be beheaded. Four more wives were to follow in Henry's increasingly desperate efforts to have a male heir.

In the space of three years between 1532 and 1534, through a series of Acts of Parliament, a complete constitutional revolution had taken place in England whereby ecclesiastical power was united with civil power under the king's own supreme authority. Those who refused to take the Oath of Supremacy, recognizing the monarch as the Supreme Head of the Church in England, were considered to have committed treason and risked imprisonment or death. Thomas More, who had resigned as Lord Chancellor, and John Fisher (1469-1535), the Bishop of Rochester, were among those beheaded in the Tower of London. Both later were to be declared martyred saints. Many other 'traitors' went to their deaths in the Tower or at the Tyburn gallows.

Henry, to the end of his life, remained attached to the traditional Catholic doctrine and forms of worship. Nevertheless, religious change was afoot. Desperate for revenue, the king entrusted Thomas Cromwell (c.1485-1540) to dissolve the monasteries throughout the realm. Almost a thousand-year tradition came to a tragic end in England. The monasteries had been at the heart of Western civilization. Their missionary work, education, spirituality, literary output and artistic achievement had been immense. The vast number of religious houses in England, with both their land and the treasures they contained, yielded a fortune to the Crown. While the English people had relied on pastoral care from the parish clergy, they also received much inspiration, spiritual guidance, and practical charitable assistance from the monks and nuns of the religious orders. Their rapid and forced disappearance from the English landscape by 1540 altered the shape of pastoral care in that country.[36] Chapters of priest-canons replaced monks to offer worship and pastoral services in those cathedrals throughout the country that previously had monasteries attached to them. These included Canterbury, Durham, Winchester, Ely and Norwich – cathedral churches that were once abbeys housing monastic communities.

Reformed religion in England can be traced back to regular gatherings of a small group of Cambridge scholars who regularly discussed the new Lutheran theology in a Cambridge pub, the White Horse Inn. The group acquired the name 'Little Germany' and included Thomas Bilney (*c.*1495-1531) and Hugh Latimer (*c.*1485-1555), important figures in the English Reformation. Reformed ideas had been boosted in the country with the appearance of William Tyndale's (*c.*1494-1536) English translation of the New Testament in 1526. Miles Coverdale's (1488-1568) English edition of the complete Bible was published in 1535. Once the new Protestant ideas had been launched in England, orders went out for a copy of the English Bible to be placed in every church of the realm so that all could read it.

### Edward VI and Religious Change

With the death of Henry and the reign of his young son Edward VI (1537-53), who came to the throne at the age of nine, Protestant sympathizers went about the task of implementing religious change more strenuously. Reformers from the Continent were welcomed into England, including Martin Bucer from Strasbourg. Many of the Lutheran reforms were implemented in England: images were removed from churches; Masses for the dead in chantries forbidden; Holy Communion was given to the laity from the chalice; biblical texts and prayers were read in English during religious services; and clergy were permitted to marry. Cranmer's thinking had developed along the lines of strictly Reformist theology. He had come to accept justification by faith alone; he rejected Catholic understanding of the real presence of Christ in the Eucharist and repudiated any idea of the Mass as a sacrifice. Above all else, Cranmer's contribution to the reformation of the English Church was that of a liturgist. The 1549 Prayer Book begins to reflect the new theology. Bucer, however, wrote a critique of the 1549 Prayer Book on the grounds of its conservatism. In this work, later to be given the title of the *Censura,* he objected to the provision of kneeling, the wearing of vestments, anointing with oil, and clothing with a white garment at baptism, and exorcism.[37] Cranmer's 1552 Prayer Book was modified from the earlier 1549 edition and has remained the standard book of ritual for Anglican worship. It provided for the introduction of Mattins and Evensong to which the laity were invited. These two services of morning and evening prayer replaced the seven monastic offices recited throughout the day. The frequent Masses may have disappeared and the ritual drastically simplified but a new style of worship had been introduced: 'The bells were indeed tolled, and the laity began arriving at their newly whitewashed churches.'[38] It is Thomas Cranmer's 1552 Prayer Book, above all else, that has come to characterize the faith and daily worship pattern of the Anglican Church.

In the story of pastoral care during the period of the English Reformation, a most important measure arose out of Edward's first Parliament, which transferred to the Crown all chantries, free chapels, colleges, hospitals, alms houses, fraternities, guilds and similar institutions. In effect, they were secularized. The move completed Henry's work of taking over the religious houses. A.G. Dickens writes that the loss of these institutions from the Church, which had been so central to its ministry of pastoral care, impinged directly upon the social and spiritual life of the English people:

> ...the sordid competition of all classes for a share in ecclesiastical spoils impugned the credit both of the government and of the religious principles which that government was claiming to promote by destroying 'superstitious' institutions.[39]

### Mary Tudor and the Catholic Revival

Protestant ways received a major reverse when the daughter of Catherine of Aragon, Mary Tudor became queen. Mary was most assuredly Catholic in her religion. She married the widowed Philip II of Spain, the son of Charles V, in Winchester Cathedral, but Philip was to spend little time in England. Mary immediately set about restoring Catholic practices. The old forms of religious worship were reintroduced and bishops sympathetic to Reformed principles were removed from their sees. The new queen began restoring relations with Rome. The English cardinal, Reginald Pole (1500-58), returned to his homeland as papal legate and was appointed Archbishop of Canterbury, succeeding the deposed and imprisoned Thomas Cranmer. Stephen Gardiner (c.1490-1555) was made new Lord Chancellor. Foreign refugees, supporting Protestant ways, were ordered to leave the country. Amidst these changes, Mary began her policy of the persecution of Protestants, resulting in her being remembered in history as 'Bloody Mary'. Five bishops were among those burned, including Cranmer himself. Their stories of martyrdom are told in the *Acts and Monuments* of John Foxe (1516-87), commonly known as 'Foxe's Book of Martyrs'.[40] It was no longer safe to adhere to the Reformist teachings.

### Elizabeth I and Religious Settlement

Upon Mary's death, England's new queen set about dismantling the Catholic religion. It was the third major religious change in England in twelve years. Elizabeth I (1533-1603), daughter of Anne Boleyn, came to the throne in 1558 to rule over a people divided about matters of religion. At the time of her becoming queen it is reputed she believed in the doctrine of the real presence, while Mass continued to be said in the royal chapel. The story is told that at her coronation Elizabeth went to Westminster Abbey and was greeted at the door with clergymen holding candles. 'Away with those torches! We see very well', she exclaimed.[41] Elizabeth was not in the same mould as her Catholic predecessor yet the coronation ceremony took place in the traditional Latin rite.[42] But Elizabethan England was set to become more Protestant. The Act of Supremacy of 1559 re-established the monarch as 'Supreme Governor' of the Church and the state. All officials, including ecclesiastics, were required to take the Oath of Supremacy. Some changes were made to the 1552 Prayer Book that removed all offensive references to the pope and softened eucharistic doctrine by opening the way for belief in a real presence falling short of transubstantiation. The 1559 *Act of Uniformity* ensured only services within the new Prayer Book were permitted.

The Thirty-nine Articles, summarizing the beliefs of the Church of England, were drawn up in 1563. Among the Articles, 'Romish' doctrines of purgatory, pardons, image worship and invocation of saints were outlawed. Clerics were permitted to marry and worship was forbidden to occur in 'a tongue not understanded of the people'. In England, bishops remained within the ministry of holy orders, thus distinguishing the English Church from many of its Continental Protestant cousins. In Elizabeth's reign the Church of England had been given a distinctive form that was decidedly Protestant but shared in a structure of Church order that kept certain Catholic characteristics. As such, Elizabethan Anglicanism was distinctive within the wider Protestant Reform of the sixteenth century.

More recent scholarship has raised the question as to how willing the majority of English people were to submit to the religious reforms of the sixteenth century. Green maintains that in England 'the majority of men and women neither wanted nor greeted the Reformation', for they cherished their traditional religious practices within the parishes that were swept away by force.[43] Duffy, in *The Stripping of the Altars: Traditional Religion in England c.1400-c.1580*, has argued at length that no substantial gulf existed between the clergy and educated elite in relation to the great majority of people concerning devotional life in the earlier part of the sixteenth century. He writes:

> ... late medieval Catholicism exerted an enormously strong, diverse, and vigorous hold over the imagination and the loyalty of the people up to the very moment of the Reformation. Traditional religion had about it no

particular marks of exhaustion or decay, and indeed in a whole host of ways, from the multiplication of vernacular religious books to adaptation within the national and regional cult of saints, was showing itself well able to meet new needs and new conditions.[44]

Whatever the truth, the Protestant Reformation had definitely come to England but in its own special colors. It was distinct from Protestant reform elsewhere, especially in its retention of the order of bishops.

### John Knox and Presbyterianism in Scotland

Meanwhile, in Scotland, John Knox (c.1513-72) set about reorganizing the Church according to Calvinist teachings, having earlier served as a minister in Geneva. Knox was an inspired preacher, popular in the *Kirk* of St Giles in Edinburgh. Virulently anti-Catholic, the Scottish reformer organized the parishes there on a system of government by elders (presbyters). The *Scottish Confession*, the *Book of Discipline* and the *Book of Common Order* were all composed under Knox's guiding hand and transformed the pastoral practice of the Church in Scotland along lines similar to that in Calvin's Geneva. It was to become known as *Presbyterianism*.

### Catholic Resistance and Persecution

During the reign of Elizabeth I, the picture of the Catholic faith within England was one of 'safe houses' for undercover priests and hidden chapels in homes where the Mass and other sacraments were celebrated. Adherents to the old, Catholic ways quickly became an alternative Church as religious change took hold and transformed English Christianity. In the eyes of the authorities they were considered traitors and risked fines, imprisonment or death. Pastoral care, according to Catholic ways, had become an act of treason. Because of the dangerous situation that had now arisen in the country, some English Catholics asked Rome if they could attend Protestant services while privately continuing in their loyalty to the Catholic religion. Their request was refused. The best that Pius V (1566-72) was prepared to do for them was to appoint priests with the authority to absolve those who had weakened and were guilty of schism. There was to be no compromise. The situation between the English queen and the Roman papacy hardened when Pius issued the bull of 1570, *Regnans in Excelsis*, excommunicating Elizabeth. His action was intended to free those who maintained loyalty to the Catholic faith from obedience to her laws. But, by his action, the pope had made their situation far more perilous.

There were a number of factors that made Elizabeth nervous of her subjects who remained loyal to Catholic teachings. There had been a Catholic-inspired rebellion in 1569, led by northern earls, to topple her and put her Catholic cousin, Mary, Queen of Scots (1542-87), on the throne. As well, there was fear of an alliance with Spain and threat of invasion to oppose Protestant reforms. By 1574 Catholics had been forced to organize into a separate Church outside the established Church of England. The defeat of the Spanish Armada by England in 1588 worsened the feelings which the queen and her government had towards Catholics.

Pastoral care of the English Catholics - they were known as 'recusants' - relied on English priests returning to their country after seminary training on the Continent. In 1568 William Allen (1532-94), formerly principal of St Mary's Hall, Oxford, and in exile on the Continent, founded a college for educating English priests at Douai in France. Over four hundred priests from Douai College worked as missionary priests in England between 1574 and 1603. Seeing the threat they posed, Elizabeth enacted a statute making it treason for any Catholic priest to enter England who had been ordained abroad or for anyone to provide them with aid or shelter. About a quarter of these priests were executed under Elizabeth.[45] They went about pastoral care by hearing confessions, saying Masses, baptizing children and generally encouraging and sustaining Catholics in their position as a persecuted minority within English society. Many of these priests were members of the new religious order of the Jesuits. Among them was St Edmund Campion (1540-81), a brilliant academic of humanist leanings who turned Catholic. And there was St Robert Southwell (c.1561-95), noted for his poetry. Both were canonized in 1970. Such recusant priests were typically recruited from the landed gentry and from within the universities of Oxford and Cambridge. It was a deliberate pastoral strategy to put in place a Catholic ruling order ready to restore the Catholic faith when the political situation became more favorable.[46] This led, from the late sixteenth century, to English Catholicism's being characterized by a special affinity with some elements of the upper classes. They were in a position to afford better protection than lower-class Catholics and to assist priests who were seeking a base from which to conduct their ministry. Yet the policy resulted in many Catholic sympathizers, outside the enclaves of the upper classes, lacking adequate pastoral care to sustain their loyalties. Consequently, they simply abandoned their religion to fit in with Protestant ways, which became increasingly identified with nationhood.[47]

Deprived of sufficient numbers of clergy to provide worship, instruction and spiritual nourishment, English Catholics came to rely more and more on printed material from abroad. English Catholic women, in search of contemplative life, left their country to join convents in Europe. Catholic life in England became increasingly different from the reforms of pastoral care on the Continent resulting from the Council of Trent, so that:

> The Counter-Reformation entered England not in the guise of reforming bishops, diocesan synods, and a strengthened sacramental life centered around the parish, but rather as an intensely individual spirituality.[48]

Not until 1850 – well after the Reformation - was there to be a Catholic hierarchy of bishops in England.[49]

## Catholic Reform: The Council of Trent

### The Work of the Council of Trent

The Council of Trent (1545-63) was the Catholic Church's response to the turmoil and religious divisions that had resulted from the Protestant teachings, initiating what has come to be called the period of the 'Counter-Reformation' or 'Catholic Reformation'.[50] It had become increasingly obvious that Catholicism had to reform itself. Pastoral care needed to be freed of its many deficiencies and abuses, while doctrines had to be more clearly articulated. *Laetare Jerusalem*, the papal bull that opened the Council, listed three goals: to eradicate religious schism; to reform and bring peace among Christians; and to reclaim the holy sites in Palestine for Christians. Spread over many sessions, the Council was destined to last for eighteen years, by the end of which time many of the original delegates had died.

Trent, the conciliar city, was chosen because it was a predominantly Italian city while yet belonging to the Holy Roman Empire of the German nation. Strategically located at the foot of the Alps on the Brenner Pass, it was the divide between Latin and Germanic Europe and so symbolized the divisions resulting from the Reformation. The Southern Italian bishops, housed in the Palazzo Prato, thought the place far too cold and complained of the choice of the site while other prelates made do by ordering fur coats from Venice.[51] Trent was the location for all sessions of the Council, except for two sessions held in Bologna in 1547. The Council, in its alpine setting, proved to be a watershed in the history of pastoral care.

Justification by faith alone, as we have seen, was the central platform of the Protestant reformers. Trent tackled the issue head-on in its sixth session. Agreeing with Luther, it affirmed a human being's incapacity to be justified by his or her own works apart from the assistance of the grace offered through Jesus Christ. But good works, influenced by grace, can contribute to an increase of justifying grace. Trent's teaching differed from Reformers, such as Melanchthon and Calvin, by asserting that justification is the process of both forgiveness and regeneration within human nature through the free acceptance of divine grace. As such, justification through Christ brings about a change in both the outer status as well as the inner nature of the sinner.[52] While holding on to Augustine's teaching that concupiscence remains after baptism, Trent views the effects of sin more to be debilitating rather than radically destructive.

Disputes concerning the doctrine of justification - technical issues for debate among theologians - appear abstruse to the modern mind. Yet the need to clarify the doctrine persists and, in today's more ecumenical climate, continues to be examined and reassessed on all sides in order to reach more common ground.[53] But it is a doctrinal point that does have important implications for pastoral care. A continuing theme throughout this book has been the claim that pastoral care is greatly influenced in practice by one's view of human nature. Whether one chooses to emphasize the dark side of human nature or its more optimistic characteristics, or whether one focuses on how these two sides of the person are interrelated, one's approach will determine what is in need of healing and change and how it should happen. Pastoral care, for example, looks very different in strictly Lutheran evangelical theology, which emphasizes the corruption of human nature, from the way it looks among those who stress a view of socially oppressed humankind in liberation theology, and from within Eastern Orthodoxy's view of the 'divinization' of the believing Christian through the grace of the Holy Spirit. The connections between human sin, freedom and God's grace are foundational to a Christian anthropology out of which pastoral care emerges.

As for the sacraments, Trent taught that baptism, confirmation and holy orders imprint a permanent 'character' upon the soul and, as such, they cannot be repeated. The 'whole Christ' was affirmed to be present in the sacrament of the Eucharist, 'truly, really, and substantially under the forms of things sensible'. This presence of Christ within the Eucharist was defined more precisely by means of the theology of 'transubstantiation'. The sacrifice of the Mass and that of Christ on Calvary were taught to be one and the same. Hence, the Mass is not an addition to the sacrifice of Christ on the cross but makes present its benefits. Trent understood penance as one of the seven sacraments, consisting of three elements in obtaining divine forgiveness: contrition, confession of sin and satisfaction by means of an imposed penance.[54] The emphasis in Trent's teachings on the cultic identity of ordained priesthood, with accompanying special 'powers', was intensified in reaction to Protestant teachings. The council's approach to the sacrament of holy orders brought about no real change in the sharp distinction between 'agents' and 'those acted upon' within the Catholic approach to ministry.[55] The effect was to contain ministry within holy orders.

Of a more practical nature, Trent introduced reforms that had a direct bearing on the manner of pastoral care. The council, in its fifth session, discussed the Bible: it recognized the importance of Catholics' being clear about the teachings of their faith through proper teaching and preaching. It gave to the pope the task of seeing that a catechism be produced incorporating the teachings of the council. In this, it was following Luther's lead. The *Catechism of the Council of Trent* appeared in 1556 under Pius V and was intended as a textbook for parish priests to use in instructing their people. As for preaching, the friars, especially, were noted for this task. But in many instances their preaching had degenerated into rhetorical techniques that gave more attention to popular devotions and vulgar salesmanship in the promotion of indulgences. Greater importance was to be given to the Scriptures in preaching as a result of Trent's reforms. To help to ensure this was carried out, the clergy were to be instructed in the Bible so as to promote a higher standard of Sunday preaching.

In the medieval Church it was common for bishops and priests not to reside in their dioceses or parishes but to administer them through resident delegates. This system came about as a result of benefices. Cathedrals, churches, monasteries and other religious establishments had attached to them a benefice that provided a flow of income to those who held office over them. More enterprising clerics would accumulate a number of benefices associated with more profitable religious institutions, and dispensations could be gained for non-residence or multiple benefices. Financial greed and careerism led to a widespread system of absentee bishops and priests. As a result, pastoral care became sadly lacking. The Roman Curia, in particular, filled up with absentee bishops and cardinals who rarely visited the dioceses for which they were responsible. As Hubert Jedin notes, it was an understood dictum among those who championed reform at the Council of Trent that the bishops' neglect of residence and pastoral duties 'was one of the most grievous abuses that had to be removed'.[56] Trent affirmed that in the sphere of Church offices and holy orders the requirements of pastoral ministry have a prior claim over personal gain. What had been common practice - the accumulation of dioceses by an individual bishop - was now forbidden. The decrees of the council tightened the obligation for bishops to be resident in their dioceses and to be actively engaged in pastoral duties within them. As such, the Council of Trent reforms marked a giant leap in pastoral care. Jedin remarks:

> Many a curial official must have perused the new regulations with deep concern. Gone were the care-free days of the Renaissance Popes, when a humanist or mere parasite, could without scruple take his place at the richly decked table of the Church and with the revenues of his benefices enjoy, maybe, an *otium litterarum*, while his life had no apostolic character at all.[57]

Another of the decisive pastoral reforms to emerge from Trent was the creation of seminaries, under episcopal supervision, for the education of the diocesan clergy. For, until Trent, many priests had been theologically illiterate, especially in rural areas. Trent placed upon every diocese the obligation either to erect a seminary for the training of local clergy or to combine with other dioceses in erecting a regional seminary. Preferably, a seminary was to be located near the cathedral church. As such, it was something of a return to the days of the medieval cathedral schools for educating clergy that had all but disappeared with the breakdown of feudalism and the rise of universities.[58] But such clergy education was meant for all, not simply the privileged few. This policy of setting up seminaries took time to implement but by the early decades of the seventeenth century the quality of education, piety, moral behavior and pastoral zeal of diocesan priests had improved greatly. Many of the seminaries relied on religious orders, such as the Jesuits, to staff them. The French Order of the Company of Saint Sulpice, founded in Paris by Jean Jacques Olier (1608-57) in the middle of the seventeenth century, was dedicated to the seminary apostolate for training priests, as was also the Society of the Sacred Heart, founded by John Eudes (1601-80). Their work will be discussed in the following chapter. As well as the study of theology, the new seminaries gave special attention to a round of spiritual exercises and instilled in candidates for priestly ministry a sense of dutiful obedience. What emerged in the post-Tridentine Church was the development of an educated, spiritually minded and celibate priest with pastoral zeal for those placed under his charge. At the same time the new Tridentine seminaries produced a more clericalized and standardized type of professional priest, distanced in lifestyle from the people to whom he ministered in the parishes.

### Charles Borromeo: A Tridentine Bishop

The perfect model of the new style bishop who resided, preached and organized pastoral care within his diocese must surely be St Charles Borromeo (1538-84), Archbishop of Milan. He was the first archbishop to reside there in eighty years. From a noble family, and having received clerical tonsure at the age of seven, to secure income from a benefice, he was made a cardinal at the age of twenty-two and was to go on to a clerical career in the Roman Curia. During the Council of Trent he served as a middleman between the papal legates and the pope. Ordained a priest, he took Trent's reforms of Catholic renewal to heart when he entered Milan as its archbishop in 1565. He transformed himself from being a Renaissance prelate into an assiduous pastor of the Catholic Reform.

Charles Borromeo has been described as 'an austere, dedicated, humorless, and uncompromising personality',[59] who believed strongly in the central role of the bishop within the pastoral life of the diocese. His pastoral zeal was combined with an exceptional gift for administration in rebuilding the organization of the diocese of Milan. He set about a thorough reform of the clergy. He built three new seminaries in Milan to prepare priests for serving the city and rural parishes, and for missionary activity in Switzerland. Believing in the value of a core, inner group of strong and dedicated priests, Borromeo founded the Oblates of St Ambrose to lead his work of reform. A strict code of discipline was enforced among the priests of Milan. This even prompted a friar, who resented the new restrictions, to attempt to assassinate him. This plot on the archbishop's life only ensured the strengthening of his reputation for holiness among his people. Borromeo took care to visit the parishes and religious houses of his diocese and called together numerous provincial councils and synods to implement Catholic reform. He used the technology of the printing press to disseminate a new Office book of prayer, missal and catechism. Like the Protestant Reformers, he believed in the importance of preaching.[60] Borromeo was afflicted with a speech impediment but this did not stop the Milanese flocking to his cathedral to hear him proclaiming the word of God. Like his predecessor a millennium earlier - the great Ambrose - Charles Borromeo was a gifted and zealous pastor who made the Church in Milan an example of pastoral innovation and evangelism. Borromeo's archdiocese became a model for the rest of the Church during the time of the Catholic Reformation.

The Council of Trent aimed at changing the public face of the Church and was successful in providing Catholicism with renewed confidence. The vigor of the post-Tridentine Church expressed itself visually and musically in the art of the Baroque. It was an attempt to assert Catholicism's strength, power and beauty against the Protestant world of the time. But it was the rise of the new religious orders, particularly the Jesuits, which enabled Trent's vision of the Church to become a reality. It was these new bodies of men and women who provided pastoral care with energy and direction and who led the Church's mission beyond Europe to the 'New World'.

# Chapter 6

## Spiritual Enthusiasts

In the year 1667 it must have been an extremely satisfying feeling for Gian Lorenzo Bernini (1598-1680), as he stood under the blue Roman sky in St Peter's Piazza, to gaze upon the masterpiece he had created. After eleven years of supervising this vast engineering project, work on the piazza was now complete. Two great semi-circular white colonnades, supported by 284 columns, had been designed and built to sweep out from either side of the new St Peter's Basilica which towered above this vast, urban space. Above the colonnades had been placed ninety-six statues of saints and martyrs, representing the spiritual heritage of the Church. Architecture had been utilized in an extraordinary manner to portray the Church of the Popes reaching out to embrace the entire Christian world. Holiness and secularity were now to work more closely together towards a common good: crushing heresy and nurturing the true Catholic faith. The Baroque had arrived and was to triumph in the post-Tridentine Church.

In the late sixteenth and seventeenth centuries a great rebuilding program had got underway in Rome. The ancient, pagan temples and public buildings were looted for their Travertine marble, to build the new baroque churches. Papal Rome would take on the new Protestant Christianity and work to win over and nurture adherents to the Catholic religion through the beauty of art. The aim was simple: impress, convert and uplift. The British art historian, Kenneth Clark, observed that papal Rome of the seventeenth century was 'the most grandiose piece of town planning ever attempted'.[1] The Jesuit Church of the Gesù became the prototype of the baroque church that would be imitated around the world. Such churches were designed to overwhelm through their flamboyant magnificence. No expense was spared. Gold, precious stones, stucco angels and cherubs – all of this had the purpose of transporting the worshiper into another world. The Church of the Gesù: here one could stare up into the illusion of a painted ceiling that seemed open to the outside sky, a crowded scene of saints and sinners. The saints are in rapture, surrounded by clouds and the brilliant light of heaven. The damned, with their wretched faces, look as though they are about to tumble down on those below in the church. These baroque churches throughout Italy and Catholic Europe, of immense proportion, to hold the crowds who came to hear celebrated preachers expound the biblical message as interpreted within the teachings of Trent, were deliberate showpieces. The Catholic celebration of the sacraments, so emphasized by the Council of Trent, was held in settings of religious theater, supplemented by the glory of the music of such composers as Pierluigi da Palestrina (1525-94) and Claudio Monteverdi (1567-1643), and the full pomp of liturgical celebration. But Protestants - like the Cistercian monks who had begun earlier - dispensed with images and turned religious sentiment entirely inward. Pastoral care among Protestants, aimed at fostering faith, was primarily through the spoken word founded on the written text of the Bible. Catholics, on the other hand, set about nurturing faith through the sublimity of art and the outward, tangible symbols of the sacraments. The Baroque symbolized this difference above all else.

Despite these different emphases in the way of pastoral outreach, Catholics and Protestants in the sixteenth, seventeenth and eighteenth centuries shared a common preoccupation: a quest for a different kind of spirituality and one that inspired extraordinary efforts to implant the gospel message in the New World. This, beyond everything else, is what most characterizes pastoral life in this period of Christian history.

## The Jesuits and the New Religious Orders

### Ignatius of Loyola and the Jesuits

St Ignatius of Loyola (1491-1556) - the founder of the Society of Jesus (the Jesuits) - was a military man. Soldiering rather than praying had been more his lifestyle. But that was all to change. More than any other group of people, it was the Jesuits who characterized the new and energetic spirit of the post-Tridentine Church. Ignatius' life can be fully appreciated only within the context of the *Reconquista*, the reconquest of Spain from the Muslim Moors whose last kingdom at Granada fell to the Catholic monarchs, Ferdinand and Isabella, in 1492. This momentous event for Spain occurred only a few months after Ignatius' birth in the castle of Loyola, situated just south of the Pyrenees. Ignatius' world of Spain was one of a militant Catholicism that was characterized by intolerance, fierce loyalty, and total service. As a young man, in a military campaign to take Pamplona from the French in 1521, Ignatius was wounded in the right leg. During the boredom of a forced convalescence, the young soldier read a book on the life of Christ and *The Golden Legend*, a collection of writings on the lives of the saints. That was it. He would now be a soldier of Christ! Filled with zeal, Ignatius set off on a pilgrimage to reach Jerusalem in a journey that took him across Spain. He visited the shrine of the Virgin Mary in Montserrat, near Barcelona, and then retired to nearby Manresa where he stayed a year, living a life of extreme asceticism. Here Ignatius had visions - so characteristic of Spanish spirituality of the time - that may well have been hallucinatory experiences arising from the physical deprivations he had imposed upon himself. Such compulsive penitential practices led to his experiencing religious scruples and depression. With the help of some kind people in Manresa, he recovered from his disturbed mental and spiritual condition and made his way to Rome, before traveling on to Jerusalem. Later, on returning to Spain, Ignatius' one desire was to be a priest. He undertook studies in Barcelona, Alcalá, and Salamanca. He was imprisoned a couple of times by the Inquisition for suspected 'illuminism', a doctrine that emphasized a more interior type of spirituality, free of ecclesiastical supervision. It was later, while studying at the University of Paris, that he attracted a small group of companions who were to become the nucleus of the Society of Jesus. In 1537 they went off to Italy where Ignatius and others were ordained as priests and their little group took the name of the Society of Jesus. They had hoped to journey to Jerusalem to convert the Turkish Muslims but failed to get beyond Venice. Pope Paul III (1534-1549), in 1540, formally authorized this new religious body of men within the Catholic Church.

The Society of Jesus expanded rapidly. By the time of Ignatius' death in 1556 there were a thousand members. This number had swelled to five thousand by the end of the sixteenth century and to twenty-two thousand in 1640.[2] Numerical growth went hand in hand with geographical expansion across Europe and to the New World. The order that Ignatius had founded was characterized by a spirit of unquestioning obedience, as well as by a high degree of organization and a military structure. The Jesuits were foot soldiers for Christ. The 'fourth vow' of the Society was that of total obedience to the pope. In fact, Paul III had exempted the Society from the authority of local bishops. This allowed Jesuits to preach and administer sacraments without the authorization of local parish priests and bishops. Indeed, they were 'the pope's men' in a new and self-confident Church.

The Jesuits were first and foremost pastoral in their outlook. The Society offered its members an intensely active form of spirituality. Two pastoral roles stood out: those of teachers and missioners. For such tasks they were well educated and schooled in holiness. The early Jesuits sought to identify with the values, and to seek the support, of the upper levels of society, for their Constitutions taught that the greater good was achieved by influencing those in positions to influence others. At the same time, they were to shun personal comfort.[3]

The *Spiritual Exercises* of Ignatius Loyola remain to this day one of the outstanding means of growth and perfection in the spiritual life. They have served as a pastoral guide to countless people in helping to shift the mind, heart and will from this world to that of Christ. Ignatius began formulating them at Manresa but they were not to be completed until 1548, by which time he was in his late fifties. The *Exercises*, a journey in faith over four weeks, give emphasis to the imagination as the person is invited to picture different scenes in the mind. A guide, consisting of rules and advice concerning the Christian life, accompanies the meditations. The first week of the *Exercises* feature a series of purifying meditations on the destructiveness of sin, which causes a deviation from one's true purpose in the world, and the sufferings of hell that may be incurred from committing sin. The kingdom and person of Christ become the central focus of the *Exercises* for the remaining three weeks: Jesus' life and ministry, passion, and resurrection.

The Jesuits, from the beginning, committed themselves to education. Jesuit education was aimed not only at the improvement of the individual. It was directed to inculcating a Christian ethos in the wider society through an educated elite who would wield power and influence. It was the adoption of a new kind of social responsibility. For this purpose, Jesuit schools emphasized rhetoric, which dealt with the art of public persuasion.[4] Much of the work of the Catholic Reformation was achieved through Jesuit education by means of their widespread network of schools in Europe, and their schools that were to spread rapidly from Macau in southern China to Lima in Peru. It was the largest international network of schools ever to have been seen. Jesuit schools went beyond the traditional learning of philosophy and theology to include the physical sciences.

> With independence of judgment he (Ignatius) envisaged an educational structure for which he took the stones from the ancient world of the classical authors, the medieval world of the great universities, and his contemporary world of Renaissance passion for humanism.[5]

The education of priests in seminaries, as envisaged by the Council of Trent for the purpose of ensuring an improved spiritual life and pastoral zeal, was put largely into the hands of the Jesuits. Education was at the heart of the much-needed pastoral reforms following Trent and Ignatius saw to it that Jesuits took the lead.

As we have already seen, confraternities were a common feature in the medieval Church to foster devotion and charitable works among the laity. Jesuit schools promoted such confraternities, adapting them for their young students and placing them under the patronage of the Virgin Mary. This was a strategy to counteract the Protestant move to de-emphasize the Virgin Mary in Christian life. These congregations for lay Christians became known by the title of the Sodality of Our Lady, distinctively Jesuit, just as the mendicant friars had their Third Orders for encouraging greater lay piety. They were soon extended beyond the schools to include adults in the wider community.[6]

The pastoral care of the poor and marginalized received the attention of the new Jesuit Order. They visited the city jails, bringing food, teaching the catechism and hearing confessions. Ignatius's followers begged alms to pay for the release of prisoners convicted of debt and to ransom prisoners taken captive by the Muslim Turks. As well, Jesuits sought to remedy the unsanitary conditions found in the prisons by arranging for those who were sick to be transferred to hospitals. A young Belgian Jesuit scholastic, named Julian, went to the effort of building small huts near the Palermo prison for sick inmates. Impressed by his charity, the civic authorities ordered more shelters of this kind to be constructed. Jesuits ran hospitals and a significant number among them were doctors. This situation led Pope Gregory XIII (1572-85) to promulgate a general exemption for Jesuits from the Church's law that forbade clerics and religious from practicing medicine, but only under the condition that no other doctor was available. When plague broke out in Rome in 1556, Jesuits were assigned specific streets within the city to care for the victims. No doubt many died from the disease as a result.[7]

One form of pastoral care that began among the Jesuits in sixteenth century Italy was that of caring for prostitutes. At this time in Italy the courtesan enjoyed an acceptable social status among the upper levels of society. But there were also many poor women driven into the profession. Among them were pious women who visited the churches and came under the care of the clergy. In fact, the civic authorities of the time – in Italy and beyond – issued regulations requiring prostitutes to attend church on certain days to listen to sermons directed especially at them. This happened in Seville, for example, where the brothels were ordered to close on Sundays and the prostitutes had to attend Mass. In Rome, San Agostino was their preferred church, where Lenten sermons were preached especially for them. Many of these women chose to be buried in San Agostino. In a letter to Lorenzo de' Medici one such courtesan stated: 'I went to confession and gave the priest two golden ducats, gold I say. I now regret it to the bottom of my heart.'[8]

Ignatius founded the Casa Santa Marta in Rome in 1542, under the patronage of St Martha, where as many as sixty women could find temporary refuge, and spiritual guidance aimed at changing their way of life. There were similar Jesuit institutions in other cities. As well, Jesuits cared for the children of such prostitutes. Girls, no younger than ten or twelve, were provided with a basic education for about five or six years and then given dowries so they could marry or enter convents. Such children were sometimes taken in without the consent of their mothers.

The Jesuits, and other clergy ministering to prostitutes, sought to help them change their ways by urging them to marry, or to work as servants in wealthy households, or to enter a special kind of convent for former prostitutes known as a *Conversae*. Here former prostitutes would live under strict cloistered conditions and practice a life of penance. These convents were usually under the patronage of St Mary Magdalene and were widespread throughout Europe in the sixteenth century.[9]

### Philip Neri and the Oratorians

St Philip Neri (1515-95) is remembered by the expression 'the Apostle of Rome'. Having had some kind of mystical experience while spending nights in prayer at the Roman catacombs, he was ordained some years later in 1551 and lived with a community of priests. Philip became popular, especially because of his kindness and wise advice in the hearing of confessions. He took great interest in ministering to boys and men and held regular spiritual conferences for them. His pastoral zeal and attractive personality drew many more priests to his community and there emerged the Congregation of the Oratory, probably named after the room in San Girolamo where they held their meetings. It was a new kind of organization for priests, a confraternity rather than a vowed religious order. The growth of the movement saw the establishment of new houses, each of which was autonomous. The Oratorians believed that excellence of worship was what was needed to bring people to the churches and they employed Palestrina to compose music for their liturgies. Preaching was made an important ministry and usually four sermons each day were delivered in the churches of the Oratory. Philip Neri was greatly loved in Rome and many sought his guidance, including several popes.[10]

### Other New Religious Orders for Men

The Theatines were one of the earliest of the new religious orders of the sixteenth century. Like the Jesuits, they offered their unswerving loyalty to the papacy in the highly centralized Church arising from the Council of Trent. The Theatines were founded at Rome in 1524 by Gaetano di Thiene (1480-1547). The order was an austere one and dedicated to social welfare. This led to the Theatines establishing a number of hospitals. Another concern was their commitment to the reform of the clergy as a whole. Most Theatines were drawn from the nobility and this gave something of an aristocratic air to the order. Their pastoral work focused on city churches where preaching was given priority.[11]

The Somaschi were another religious order of priests established a few years after the Theatines, at Somasca, in the north of Italy, by Jerome Emiliani. Like the Theatines, they offered pastoral care to the sick, and shared with the Jesuits a ministry to prostitutes. Their work in education was primarily among poor children and orphans.[12]

Named after their Church of St Barnabas in Milan, the Barnabites set about the task of the Catholic Reformation in striving to improve the spiritual life of both the laity and clergy. They were founded by Antonio Maria Zaccaria in 1530. Charles Borromeo enlisted their support in his efforts for reform within his diocese of Milan. The order engaged in the usual pastoral concerns of preaching, confessions, care of the poor, visiting the sick and those in prison. As well, the Barnabites were known for their outdoor religious gatherings, like the Protestant Methodists at a later time. Such evangelism had about it a theatrical quality that made the Barnabites popular among the people.[13]

Better known today are the Capuchins. The order traces its foundation to a Franciscan friar named Matteo da Bascio (c.1495-1552) who was dissatisfied with the lax observance of St Francis' Rule in his monastery at Montefalcone. Accompanied by a few sympathizers, he fled to remote regions of Italy. Sometimes this small band of men would appear in the towns to beg and preach their message of repentance. They got the name of *scapuccini* - the hooded men - with their distinctive pointed cowls covering their heads. Opposed strongly by the Observant Franciscans, they obtained papal recognition as a religious order in 1528. Something of a scandal was later to break out among them when in 1542 their General, Fra Bernadino Ochino, sought refuge in Protestant Geneva following a papal summons to Rome on suspicion of heresy. The Capuchins won widespread support for their work among the sick during epidemics. Innovative pastoral initiatives of the Capuchins at this period included the setting up of *botteghe di Cristo* (shops of Christ) to sell cheap food in times of famine and to provide banking services in the form of interest-free loans. The order directed its pastoral care to many of Italy's poorer, rural areas. These alternate Franciscans were greatly loved for their simplicity and kindness.[14]

### New Women's Religious Orders

Women had something of an invisible role in the life of the Catholic Church during the time of the Catholic Reformation. In a male-dominated Church that was preoccupied with extolling the virtues of priestly celibacy, women counted for little in pastoral ministry. It was consecrated virginity rather than any form of pastoral involvement that was upheld as the form of a dedicated life for women. The alternative was marriage and the raising of children within the privacy of family life. Vowed religious life among women was restricted mainly to a life of prayer hidden behind the walls of cloistered convents. Reflecting the wider society of the time, there was deep suspicion within the leadership of the Church of any form of female religious undertakings in pastoral care. A few courageous and gifted women attempted to break the mould. Among them was Angela Merici (1474-1540), founder of the Ursulines, and the Englishwoman, Mary Ward (1585-1645), who set up schools on the Continent, especially for English girls unable to get a Catholic education in their now Protestant homeland.

Who were the women who entered the cloistered life of convents at this time? Of course, there were many who felt a genuine call to the contemplative life. Becoming members of such institutions was nothing unusual in an age when religion permeated everyday life. But convents were also heavily populated with widows. These women had to be able to afford to pay a dowry as they sought out the security that religious houses provided. In a highly structured class society, with its system of arranged marriages, particularly among the more wealthy, family tactics often determined whether daughters would marry or enter a convent. And, in a time when so many young men died in warfare, there were inevitably more young women than men looking for partners, and convent life was considered to offer a suitable alternative to marriage. Large families were the norm and it was common for at least some of the children within a family to enter religious life in monasteries and convents.

St Angela Merici's Ursuline Order is generally considered the oldest among all the teaching orders of women; it is named after their patron, St Ursula. Angela had gathered about her a group of northern Italian middle-class women in Brescia. It was a lay organization comprised of single and married women, along with widows. As well as gathering for prayer to grow in their own spiritual lives, these women engaged in many different kinds of charitable work that included staffing hospitals, orphanages, and hostels for prostitutes and homeless women. Of particular interest to them was the offering of religious instruction to girls. These Ursuline women lived in their own homes. In 1544 community life and simple vows were introduced that changed their ethos and way of life. What emerged – a semi-contemplative, monastic form of life out of which Ursulines managed their schools – went against the spirit of their founder, Angela Merici.[15] There developed within the Ursulines, as happened in other orders, a certain contradiction: a desire for an active pastoral ministry but within the limitations imposed by the confines of convent enclosure. The order became particularly successful in France. In Paris, especially, it became something of an aristocratic organization where it fell under the patronage of two noble widows.[16] But the initial goal of having laywomen teach and involved in charitable work, while continuing to live within the wider community, was doomed to failure in a Church where celibate men made the final pastoral decisions and aristocratic patronage imposed its own ideals.

This move from an unenclosed to an enclosed order can be seen also among the Angelics of San Paolo, the female equivalent order to the male Barnabites, founded in Milan in 1535. They were initially under the leadership of Paola Antonia Negri (1508-55). They were a familiar sight on the streets of Milan, tending to the poor and needy. These women closely associated themselves with the Barnabites in religious activities. So much was this the case that Mother Paola, a woman with a seemingly commanding presence, was able to exercise a form of religious leadership over these men. But it was not to last. The 'spiritual mother' came to the attention of the Inquisition, ever vigilant to stamp out any form of religious thinking and practice that deviated from established ways. Mother Paola was imprisoned. Her Angelics were put under enclosure and the 'spiritual mother' was replaced, as leader, by a man. So much for pastoral and religious innovation in the Tridentine Church when it involved women.

Mary Ward is another example of this period, thwarted in her efforts to get women involved in pastoral care. Her background is that of the English Catholics following the Protestant Reformation - 'recusants', a minority persecuted for their religious beliefs. Deeply influenced by the Jesuits and their way of life, her intention was to set up on the Continent a religious institute for women that was not enclosed (she could not do so in England because of the Protestant religious climate), and whose members would be engaged in teaching girls, while not wearing distinctive religious dress. Her schools were intended to reflect the Jesuit emphasis of a humanist tradition of education that, alongside religious studies, gave attention to a study of the classics and drew upon the new learning of the Renaissance.[17] Her plan was to make her schools the female equivalent to the Jesuit schools for males. Her intended order was novel for her sisters who, like the Jesuits, were to live outside enclosed religious houses and be free of local, episcopal jurisdiction. Mary Ward's Institute of the Blessed Virgin Mary, popularly known as the 'English Sisters', set up convents in different parts of the Continent. But male opposition, which included Jesuit suspicion of her intentions in using the Society's Constitutions to regulate an active pastoral life among women, and an earlier law of Pius V for solemn vows and strict enclosure on all religious houses of women, led to the suppression of her institute in 1630. Mary herself was accused of heresy and schism, and imprisoned for a time in a convent of the Poor Clares in Munich. She managed to clear her name and was able to open new houses for her sisters along slightly different lines. She returned to England in 1637 where she was to live out the remaining years of her life.

## Jansenism and the New Morality

### Port-Royal and the Jansenists

Port-Royal was a Cistercian convent located just a few miles outside Paris. Like so many religious houses of the seventeenth century, its inhabitants had fallen into a relaxed way of life. But the seventeenth century was to become a time of reform for such institutions. At Port-Royal this reform went to extremes under the influence of the bleak, austere and despairing doctrine of Jansenism.[18] The pessimistic spirit of Jansenism was felt far beyond the cloistered walls of religious houses like Port-Royal, especially throughout France. It affected Catholic life as a whole in the seventeenth and eighteenth centuries. Its powerful and lasting appeal was to result in the general suppression for a time of the all-powerful Jesuit Order that so vigorously opposed the movement.[19] Jansenism is of interest in the history of pastoral care because of its influence on the way large numbers of Catholic Christians came to view human nature, something that we have already seen to be so fundamental in determining the way the Church goes about its pastoral response to material and spiritual needs.

Jansenism has its origins in the writings of Cornelius Jansen (1585-1638), Bishop of Ypres, who emphasized the weakness of the human will and the irresistible power of God's grace, and who, like Augustine and Calvin before him, stressed the corruption of human nature. According to Jansenist thought, original sin had resulted in humans' total loss of any sense of the moral and religious value of their actions. The will, then, is always sinful in its attractions and choice of conduct. Echoing the predestination theologies of old, human beings are abandoned and at the mercy of an arbitrary election by God: predestination to salvation. Once given, God's grace is irresistible: Jansen's theology, then, leads to a form of determinism. For Jansen, there is the sharpest of contrasts between human corruption and redemption. It is a dualism that affects the way that life is to be lived out.[20] Jansenism stresses the dark side of human nature and the need for strict asceticism and moral perfectionism. It deprives life of its warmth and joy. Cardinal Jules Mazarin (1602-61), who ruled France as prime minister and who was far from being an ascetic himself, once described Jansenism as 'reheated Calvinism'.[21]

Under the influence of Jean Duvergier de Hauranne, better known as 'Saint-Cyran' (1581-1643), Abbot of the monastery of Saint-Cyran and chaplain to Port-Royal, the nuns of Port-Royal enthusiastically adopted Jansenist thinking in their efforts to reform. Angélique Arnauld (1591-1661), who had become Abbess of Port-Royal as a mere child at the age of ten, was totally devoted to Saint-Cyran and obediently followed his commands as she began her reforms when she was sixteen or seventeen. Saint-Cyran encouraged some of his male penitents to set up hermitages near the devout women at Port-Royal in imitation of the ascetic lifestyle of the Desert Fathers of old.

Because of Saint-Cyran's growing power, which was considered a threat to the religious stability of France, he was imprisoned for a time. After his death, the movement passed into the hands of Antoine

Arnauld (1612-94), a prominent figure within the intellectual society of Paris and a brother of Angélique. He is remembered best for his work, *De la fréquent communion*, published in 1643. Its influence upon pastoral practice concerning the reception of Holy Communion was long-lasting. The book immediately caused great controversy in its demand for moral perfection before a person could consider partaking of Holy Communion. Consequently, the attitude arose that Communion should be received on only rare occasions. Arnauld's propositions fostered an excessive and scrupulous reverence for this sacrament. Such ideas ran contrary to Jesuit teachings that recommended a frequent reception.

The rift between Jansenist notions and that of the Jesuits was further widened over pastoral practice in the confessional. Jesuit casuistry taught the moral theology of 'probabilism'. This position held that if there was reasonable doubt as to the rightness or wrongness of an action, one was free to follow a solidly probable opinion even when the opposing opinion might seem to favor the law. Arnauld and his Jansenist supporters would have none of that and insisted on complete certainty before an action could be performed, the position of 'rigorism'.[22] The issue reached beyond academic debate to the way individual priests went about their ministry in preaching, catechesis, pastoral guidance, and especially within the sacrament of penance. This difference of pastoral approach is still evident in our own times.

Blaise Pascal (1623-62) was the most brilliant commentator in support of the Jansenist movement and in his denunciation of the Jesuits, especially after the condemnation of Antoine Arnauld by the academic community of the Sorbonne in 1655. A frequent visitor to Port-Royal, Pascal used his literary talents to promote an austerity in religious practice. The theme of human 'vileness' recurs in Pascal's *Pensées*.[23] As has already been stated, pastoral practice rests squarely upon the shoulders of one's understanding of human nature. Jansenism is a clear illustration of this point with its puritan program of moral renewal. The convent of Port-Royal was eventually suppressed and destroyed in the early years of the eighteenth century. In 1713, Jansenism was formally condemned in the papal bull of Clement XI (1700-1721), *Unigenitus*. Ronald Knox (1888-1957) has summed up Jansenist thinking and its impact, perhaps better than anyone, in his book, *Enthusiasm*, in which he wrote:

> Overlooked in its cradle by the mournful faces of Saint-Cyran and Mother Angélique, Jansenism never learned to smile. Its adherents forget, after all, to believe in grace, so hag-ridden are they by their sense of need for it. Everything in the world is wicked.[24]

## Alphonsus Liguori

The sacrament of penance had a place of central importance within Catholic life following the reforms of the Council of Trent. One of the most characteristic features of the life of the priest, resulting from the Council, was his pastoral task of urging people to a sense of contrition, to examine their conscience, and to confess their sins regularly within the sacrament. Compact wooden cabins or small rooms characterized the inside appearance of Catholic churches in their provision of a special space for the 'hearing of confessions'. In assisting the clergy to deal with particular problems of conscience that might arise with penitents, a system known as 'casuistry' was developed. The Jesuits took the leading role in this work of moral theology. Endless case studies of moral dilemmas were thought up and solved. As we have seen above, the Jesuits favored a school of thought known as 'probabilism'. Following the suppression of the Jesuits, this work was taken up by St Alphonsus Liguori (1696-1787) and by the religious order he was to found in 1732, the Congregation of the Most Holy Redeemer. The order became known as the Redemptorists.

Alphonsus had studied and practiced law in the courts of Naples before deciding to become a priest. He had, then, a lawyer's mind. As a pastor and theologian, his concern was for young priests in their task of offering sound moral guidance in the confessional. Alphonsus' moral theology was always motivated by pastoral concerns, a theology shaped by daily life, yet Alphonsus lived in a time when many priests were under the influence of Jansenism. Such confessors frequently refused absolution to penitents or deferred it for considerable lengths of time. By way of reaction, other confessors took a rather lax view of sin and repentance. Both positions were a source of distress to Alphonsus and he sought to develop a system of moral theology that would steer a middle path between these two extremes of pastoral practice.

One common practice Alphonsus encountered in his ministry among the less sophisticated people in the rural areas around Naples, especially among men, was that of cursing the dead. It was a way of expressing anger, a seemingly common habit among Latin peoples. Alphonsus thought that such language was not really blasphemous, if a sin at all. He believed it to be nothing much more than a cultural manifestation among unlettered people. He distributed his moderate moral analysis for comment among theologians. Most accepted his thinking on the matter. But there was one Dominican, a friar from Bari, who attacked Alphonsus bitterly. He wrote his critique under a pseudonym. In his view, Alphonsus' analysis was 'ignorant', 'stupid', and 'rash'. Alphonus felt the need to defend himself and his reply became the prelude to his first major work in moral theology, the *Adnotationes*, published in 1749.[25]

More than forty-four different works were to follow. But opposition to his ideas from Jansenist sympathizers grew in strength. Chief among these was the 'anti-probabilist', Giovanni Bottari, director of the Vatican Library in Rome. In Lisbon, Alphonsus' books were publicly burnt on top of Jesuit publications. His work, *Moral Theology*, reflected his deep pastoral care for his only purpose, as he stated forthrightly in this book, was that it should help priests in their work of the 'salvation of souls'.[26] Like Gregory the Great's *Pastoral Rule* of the late sixth century, Alphonsus offered detailed guidelines for the pastoral care of specific types of individuals; these included peasants, the dying, children, adolescents, those experiencing scruples, and the deaf and dumb. At the same time, Alphonsus reflected the prejudices of his age. For example, he was opposed to male hairdressers for women because this presented an approximate occasion of sin![27] The *Practica* served as an appendix to the two-volume *Moral Theology* in which he outlined what he considered to be the ideals of a confessor. Apart from books on moral guidance, Alphonsus produced works of popular devotion to counteract what he saw as the harm being done by the cold and rigorous agenda of Jansenism. With reluctance, Alphonsus became a bishop.

## Guidance in the Spiritual Life

### Teresa of Ávila and John of the Cross

Sixteenth-century Spain was characterized by excess. In terms of wealth, there were unlimited quantities of gold pouring into the country from the galleons sailing back from the Spanish colonies in the newly discovered Americas. A passion arose to purify the country of foreign elements, so that Muslims and Jews were required either to convert to the Christian faith or emigrate or, otherwise, face slaughter. Spain was sealed off from Protestant influences at work to the north where it was engaged in warfare against its Protestant-controlled territories in the Netherlands that were seeking political and religious independence. Strict conformity characterized life in the Iberian Peninsula of the sixteenth century. This was expressed first and foremost through the ruthless repression and terror of the

Inquisition, 'deemed a department of the cure of souls'.[28] In the mind of a sadistic cleric like the Dominican Grand Inquisitor, Tómas de Torquemada (1420-98), the Inquisition was thought of, by its exponents, as pastoral care designed to preserve the purity of faith by requiring heretics to repent in order to save their souls. It offered the choice of public repentance or torture and imprisonment. It was as much an instrument of the Spanish Crown as of the Church.[29] A cruel intolerance characterized much of the spirit of Spanish Catholicism. Yet it was also a land of learning. Francisco Ximénez de Cisneros (1436-1517), while Archbishop of Toledo, had founded the University of Alcalá in 1508, largely out of his own private income. Here he promoted Renaissance learning within the study of theology. This resulted in its becoming a center for Catholic humanism to which he attracted scholars from the universities in Paris, Bologna and Salamanca. Religion in Spain had a mystic fervor and intensity unlike anywhere else. It is from within this Spanish world of Tridentine Catholicism that the spirituality of St Teresa of Ávila (1515-82) and St John of the Cross (1542-91) came forward.

Teresa's family was one of mixed Jewish and Christian blood. In 1535, as a young woman of twenty, she entered the Carmelite convent of the Incarnation, in Ávila. The ladies in the convent combined their hours of prayer with a fairly relaxed way of life. Women with means would retire to such convents for a life of tranquility and security. Visitors were welcomed, to relieve the monotony of an enclosed institution. But in later life, Teresa sought more than what had sustained her in the past. She set out on a way of perfection. Her life filled increasingly with visions and periods of religious ecstasy. In an age of reform, Teresa set about establishing a Carmelite convent that would return to the more strict way of life, reviving the primitive rules of the Carmelite Order with intense practices of poverty, fasting, prayer, silence and strict enclosure. Now in her late forties, she founded in Ávila the convent of St Joseph where this way of life could be properly observed. It was in this convent that Teresa wrote *The Way of Perfection* for the instruction of her Carmelite sisters, having earlier completed the *Life*, a spiritual autobiography. These works, along with *The Interior Castle* and a number of smaller books on the spiritual life, describe the life of prayer: from prayerful meditation to what is called mystical marriage. Much of the later years of her life were given to traveling back and forth across Spain, in her covered wagon, founding reformed Carmelite convents whose sisters were known as 'Discalced' (without shoes) Carmelites. In this work she was assisted by John of the Cross, who performed the same task among male, Carmelite friars. Teresa's life is an extraordinary combination of activity and mysticism. Like so many mystics before her, Teresa often used explicitly erotic, sexual imagery to describe her religious experiences.[30] The legacy she has left us in her writings – intended primarily for her own Carmelite sisters - has provided a rich source of spiritual guidance in the life of prayer. Her books have become classics in Christian spirituality, something that led to her being declared, in 1970, a Doctor of the Church. It is because of this outstanding contribution to spiritual guidance that Teresa, like John of the Cross, occupies an important place in the history of pastoral care.

John of the Cross, as we have seen, was closely associated with Teresa in reforming the Carmelite Order. It was no easy task for there was much resistance to change. In fact, there was so much resistance that John was flogged and imprisoned for nine months in a monastery in Toledo after failed attempts to persuade him to abandon reform of the order. A final separation between the Calced and Discalced Carmelites came about in 1579-80. Unlike Teresa, John was a true poet and trained theologian. His writings on the mystical life are largely commentaries upon his own poems. His four great prose works were written shortly after one another, within the space of couple of years after his escape from prison: *The Ascent of Mount Carmel, The Dark Night of the Soul, The Spiritual Canticle,* and *The Living Flame of Love.* Central to John's mystical theology is the insight that the spiritual journey is a process of absorption into God. Such union can come about only by means of a life of total detachment. His writings offer a detailed and comprehensive account of the successive stages of the journey of the soul to God: purgation, illumination and union. Such a journey consists of going out from God-given light into a black and unknown darkness, before reaching the goal of total union with God. Deification or divinization, for John, is the goal of human life. This calls for the union of the two extremes that appear infinitely distant: God and the human person. Negatively, this is the elimination of all that is contrary to God; positively, it is a sort of divine substitution for what has been discarded.[31]

Unlike the *Spiritual Exercises* of Ignatius, the mystical writings of Teresa and John do not set out any prescribed format of spiritual activities. Rather, they simply describe the pathway of spiritual development and offer counsel for following it. Like Teresa of Ávila, John of the Cross remains one of the great spiritual guides of the soul. Both their writings are a rich mine for pastoral guidance in a mystical tradition that takes us beyond the rational to far deeper levels of the religious psyche.

### The French School of Spirituality

It was a summer's day in July 1593 when Henry IV (1553-1610) knelt humbly before the Archbishop of Bourges upon the steps of the abbey church of St Denis, on the outskirts of Paris. The church was the traditional burial place of the kings of France. The French king renounced his Protestant upbringing and expressed a desire to be reconciled with the Catholic faith. To explain his conversion, legend has it that he made the famous remark, 'Paris is well worth a Mass!'. Under the Bourbon monarchy, France was destined to become a strong nation, united in its Catholicism. The seventeenth century would see a renewed and vigorous Church emerge in France, nourished by a deep spirituality.

Whereas mysticism reached a peak in Spain in the sixteenth century, it was in the seventeenth century that it flowered in France. This French school of spirituality was a restorationist assault upon the humanism of the Renaissance as well as an attempt to counteract Protestantism and foster the ideals of the Council of Trent's spirit of renewal.[32] Most of those involved in the movement were engaged actively in a pastoral role as spiritual directors; it was at this time that this ministry reached its peak. Its appeal was to the heart in which religious sentiment was interiorized. It found its spiritual founder in Pierre de Bérulle (1575-1629) who introduced both Teresa's reformed Carmelites to France and Philip Neri's Oratory. For Bérulle, the principal task of a human being is the worship and adoration of God. It is the incarnate Word and the mysteries associated with the historical person of Jesus to whom this reverence is directed. As Michael Cox remarks, he was obsessed with God as man.[33] At the same time, Bérulle gave attention to human nothingness and depravity. His best-remembered work, among his spiritual writings, is the *Grandeurs de Jésus*.

In the great Church of Saint-Sulpice in Paris stands a monument to Jean-Jacques Olier who became pastor there in 1642. The parish, it seems, was rather run down and his intention was to revitalize it. To assist in this task, he founded there the Society and Seminary of Saint-Sulpice for preparing a well-educated and spiritually formed diocesan clergy, filled with pastoral zeal. His seminarians studied at the nearby Sorbonne. During Olier's time as pastor, nearly fifty priests served on the parish staff of Saint-Sulpice.[34] Sulpician seminaries were to spread quickly throughout France. Olier established catechetical centers to oppose Calvinism and Jansenism and was active in alleviating the hardships of the poor. He was admired as a brilliant preacher, fostered eucharistic devotions and provided spiritual direction for the people of the parish and beyond. Fired with missionary zeal, Olier was responsible for organizing a mission to the French colony of Montreal, in Canada, for the purpose of evangelizing the indigenous people. Olier's natural, pastoral bent was to have widespread effect. Strongly influenced by Bérulle, he popularized his form of spirituality, seeking to apply it in his pastoral role as a spiritual director and in his many devotional writings. Like Ignatius Loyola and many other spiritually gifted persons, as a young man in his early thirties, Jean-Jacques Olier suffered a depressive illness accompanied by excessive feelings of guilt. And like them, he attributed his recovery to the work of the Holy Spirit. This experience affected profoundly his spiritual outlook.[35]

St John Eudes combined an active pastoral ministry with writing on the spiritual life. A priest of the Oratory, he founded in Caen the Congregation of Jesus and Mary, known as the Eudists, dedicated to the work of seminaries and missionary activity. As we have already seen with religious orders in Italy beforehand, John Eudes took an active interest in the moral and spiritual rehabilitation of prostitutes. For this task, he founded the Institute of Our Lady of Charity that would develop much later into the Order of Our Lady of Charity of the Good Shepherd, under the direction of Mary Euphrasia Pelletier (1798-1868). John Eudes, along with Margaret Mary Alacoque (1647-90), is best remembered for having introduced devotion to the Sacred Heart of Jesus, which came to characterize French spirituality. But John was to give more attention to devotion to the Immaculate Heart of Mary than to the Heart of Jesus in his spiritual writings, especially in his work, *The Admirable Heart of the Most Sacred Mother of God*. The devotion, giving attention to the physical heart, reflected a new kind of personalism and a 'high Mariology'. It was a spirituality of redemptive love that Jansenist sympathizers criticized as being insufficiently rigorous.

In the silent world of her Visitandine convent at Paray-le-Monial, St Margaret Mary Alacoque claimed to have had private revelations of Jesus that gave direction to a devotion to his Sacred Heart. Initially, many regarded her claims as delusional, but with the help of some Jesuits, especially Claude de la Colombière, the devotion to the Sacred Heart of Jesus became popular. It was founded on a spirituality of reparation for the sins of humanity. Active pastoral efforts were undertaken, especially from the beginning of the nineteenth century, to promote the devotion with the help of a sentimental, religious art in which the heart was depicted with a wound, surrounded by a crown of thorns, with a small cross above and light radiating out.[36] The devotion was to win much support around the world after it was made a feast day of the whole Church by Pius IX (1846-78) in 1856 and again reinforced in the encyclical, *Haurietis aquas* of Pius XII (1939-58) in 1956.

The Bérulle spiritual tradition found expression in the educational endeavors of St John Baptist de la Salle (1651-1719). Having studied for the priesthood in the seminary of Saint-Sulpice, de la Salle directed his attention to the needs of the lower classes within French society of his time. He founded a group of brothers - laymen living in community – to offer free education for boys, without the usual requirement of their needing Latin for the beginners' classes. It was formally set up as an institute, with a rule and vows, in 1694. John Baptist de la Salle's spiritual writings furnished the inspiration for his Brothers of the Christian Schools, especially as outlined in his work *Meditations for Time of Retreat*.[37] In time, the brothers moved somewhat away from the poor towards the education of the bourgeois who preferred the more practical, vernacular curriculum they offered rather than the traditional classicism of French Catholic teaching of the eighteenth century found especially within Jesuit schools.[38]

Another graduate of the seminary of Saint-Sulpice was St Louis-Marie Grignion de Montfort (1673-1716). His spirituality was filled with a devotion to the Virgin Mary that he imparted to the simple and humble, and which he developed in his *Treatise on True Devotion to the Blessed Virgin Mary*. In the tradition of the French school initiated by Bérulle, the spirituality of de Montfort was that of self-annihilation and human depravity that was not unlike that of Protestant revivalism that would follow. His own revivalist activities included the lighting of bonfires of irreligious books beneath the effigy of the devil, dressed as a woman of high society.[39] He founded a society for both missionary priests and religious sisters.

Among the many notable spiritual directors in seventeenth-century France were Jacques Bénigne Bossuet (1627-1704) and François de Salignac de la Mothe Fénelon (1651-1715). Bossuet's brilliance as an orator led him to preach in the French court where he secured the duty of tutor to the Dauphin. He was virulent in his opposition to French Protestants. Fénelon, too, was active at the French court where he offered spiritual direction to Madame de Maintenon (1635-1719), who secretly married Louis XIV (1638-1715) in 1685. Like so many other clergy emerging from the seminary of Saint-Sulpice, Fénelon was greatly interested in the spiritual life and published a series of articles on true and false mysticism. These were attacked ferociously by Bossuet who was instrumental in having some of Fénelon's ideas on spirituality condemned by the Holy See in Rome. Nevertheless, like the writings of Bossuet, Fénelon's letters on mystical spirituality were widely read and influenced French Catholic life.

But it is the writings of St Francis de Sales (1567-1622) that have withstood best the test of time among the spiritual guides of the French school of spirituality. The reason for Francis de Sales' continuing popularity can be glimpsed in the Preface of his best known work, *Introduction to the Devout Life*, arising out of his many letters of spiritual direction.

> I want to teach people who live in crowded cities within their families, in the middle of domestic cares at home or in the press of public affairs in their professional life ... It's a mistake, even a heresy, to want to banish the devout life from the soldier's camp, the manual worker's workshop, the court of princes, the homes of married people.[40]

The devout life, then, is not just for a privileged group: it is for all. The appeal of Francis de Sales can be found in his positive outlook upon human nature. Instead of emphasizing corruption, his writings stress the beauty of human nature, something that draws us towards the love of God. Francis directed the widowed St Jane Francis de Chantal (1572-1641) in the spiritual life for the best part of twenty years and, together, they founded the Order of Visitation of Holy Mary, the Visitandines, which was less strict than most other religious orders for women of that time.

St Vincent de Paul (c.1580-1660) entered the priesthood for personal ambition, after having been taken captive by pirates and sent to Tunisia as a slave for two years, earlier in his life: at least that is the legend surrounding his life. His overriding desire was to get himself a benefice that would guarantee him a handsome income to provide for his needs and those of his peasant-stock family. Nine years after his ordination he went to Paris, where Pierre de Bérulle was his spiritual director. He managed to obtain a rather lucrative position as chaplain to the wealthy Gondi family. Count de Gondi was General of the Galleys and it was among the prisoners in these ships that Vincent began acts of charitable service that came to characterize his life. At the same time, he was struck by the spiritual neglect of the peasants on the Gondi estates, perhaps reminding him of his own humble family origins. By way of response, Vincent founded the Congregation of the Mission, commonly called the Lazarists or Vincentians, which had the preaching of missions to poorer people in rural areas as one of its main goals. The large priory of St Lazare, in Paris, was donated to the congregation for its work. Each day vast numbers of the poor of Paris went there to be fed. Here Vincent de Paul set up his Tuesday conferences to foster high ideals as well as mutual support among the clergy of the city. Vincent de Paul was one of the most outspoken opponents of Jansenism.[41]

Spiritual direction had become prominent as a means of pastoral care in seventeenth-century France. It was through this ministry that Vincent de Paul met St Louise de Marillac (1591-1660). They were to remain lifelong friends. Louise was a sophisticated woman who was well educated and from a family of upper rank. She and Vincent established lay confraternities among wealthy women to attend to the needs of the dispossessed. At this time in France there was a vast increase in the number of women in religious life. Louise de Marillac was part of this movement in founding, under Vincent's direction, the Daughters of Charity, with their large and distinctive white headdress like that worn by Breton peasant women: these women became a well-recognized feature of the religious landscape in France and elsewhere. Those who joined her order were mainly peasant girls who worked alongside the upper-class women of the Ladies of Charity confraternities in serving the poor. Class distinctions were to be put aside in bringing relief to the poor and in offering comfort to the sick. The Daughters ran hospitals and took in abandoned children, something that developed into a program of foster care that was considered novel for the times. In the tough, port city of Marseilles these women attended to the needs of the galley prisoners and, on the battlefield, they nursed wounded soldiers. It was not easy or pleasant work. In another pioneering move, Louise's Daughters of Charity introduced craft workshops among the elderly in special homes for the aged that foreshadowed modern occupational therapy. Between them, Vincent and Louise developed a charitable system - founded upon the spiritual ideals of the French school of spirituality - that was outstanding in its range of social services within French society at the time.[42]

### Eastern Orthodoxy and the 'Philokalia'

Meanwhile, in the Eastern Orthodox Church, a new spiritual movement spread in the late eighteenth century with the publication of the *Philokalia* ('Love of [Spiritual] Beauty') in 1782.[43] It represents a wide collection of spiritual texts from the fourth to the fifteenth centuries. These deal with the hesychastic (solitary) life, asceticism, prayer and mystical union. The *Philokalia* has helped the spread of the continuous repetition of the 'Jesus Prayer' among Orthodox Christians. The prayer, 'Lord Jesus Christ, Son of God, have mercy on me', is at the heart of Orthodox spirituality. The theme of *theosis* (deification) is prominent in the early Eastern Fathers of the Church, such as Basil and Athanasius. It refers to the indwelling of the human person in the trinitarian God: God dwelling within us through the Holy Spirit. The Orthodox theology of deification and union, of humanity being transformed into the divine likeness, is not to be confused with any notion of pantheism.[44] The *Philokalia* was read by both monks and laity and remains a central text in Orthodox mysticism.

## The New World

In 1493, the year after Christopher Columbus (1451-1506) set foot upon the coral island of San Salvador in the Bahamas (the discovery of the Americas), the notorious Borgia pope, Alexander VI (1492-1503), divided the New World into two. Drawing a line down the length of the Atlantic Ocean, all lands to the west of the Azores were allotted to Spain while the Azores and the lands to their east were allotted to Portugal. The two Catholic kings, for purposes of evangelization, were given wide powers over the Church in these vast, new lands. Four years after this papal carving up of the world between the two maritime superpowers, Vasco da Gama (c.1469-1524) reached India, preparing the way for the emergence of a Portuguese trading empire in the East. It was assumed that all conquered peoples converted to the Christian faith would become Spanish or Portuguese in their ways. Nestorian Christians had reached China as early as the eighth century and Christian Franciscan missionaries had been making their way there overland during the late thirteenth and fourteenth centuries, until they were expelled by the Ming dynasty in 1368.

### Jesuit Missions in the Far East

The Portuguese established Goa as the capital of their trading empire in the East. An associate of Ignatius of Loyola, and among the founding members of the Society of Jesus, St Francis Xavier (1506-52) went as a missionary to Goa in 1542. His earlier days in the East were spent attempting to evangelize the Tamil pearl-fishers along the Fishery Coast. He had little respect for India's Hindu religion and authorized house to house searches for Hindu statues. A Basque Spaniard, Francis shared his country's obsession with racial purity.

His racial prejudice led him to favor the Japanese over the dark-skinned Tamils of southern India.[45] Growing restlessness, a trait of all adventurers, led Francis to set his sights on the Moluccas, islands providing a lucrative spice trade for the Portuguese in what is now known as Indonesia. It was a four thousand mile sea journey from Goa. After spending time in these islands, he returned to Goa, and, from there, he was to set out for Japan, the land of his true dreams. Xavier landed at Kagoshima, capital of Japan's southern-most kingdom, where he remained for nearly three years. Ever in search of new places, the Jesuit missionary traveled north and reached the religious center of Miyako (Kyoto). Presenting himself as a Portuguese ambassador, Francis presented the daiymo of Yamaguchi with gifts. It worked. Francis was granted permission to speak publicly about the Christian faith and was even given a disused Buddhist temple for accommodation. Some Japanese were baptized and the Church in Japan grew. Realizing that the Japanese saw in China the source of their philosophy and religion, Francis believed his best chance of evangelizing the Japanese was to first establish his presence and influence in China.[46] Despite being denied diplomatic status by Portuguese authorities to enter China, he persuaded Chinese merchants to help him make the dangerous move of going into China through Canton. But he was not destined to get there, dying in the cold on the island of Chang-Chuen-Shan. The best the Jesuit missionaries were able to accomplish was to set up a base at Macau, a Portuguese trading post in the Canton estuary.

Some thirty years after the death of Francis Xavier, a young Italian Jesuit missionary - with shaved head and dressed in the attire of a Buddhist monk – arrived in Macau. The year was 1582. His journey had been a long one. He was fascinated with Chinese culture and moved to open the minds of the people of Asia to the truth of the Christian gospel. For this zealous and highly intelligent missionary, Christian teachings could be as much Chinese as they were Italian or Portuguese. His missionary theology was far more advanced than that of Francis Xavier, his predecessor, whose fame rests in opening up much of the Far East to Christian missionaries. But the brilliance and foresight of this latest missionary troubled a Church in the West that thought of itself as European, with the God-given task of 'bringing civilization' to 'inferior' peoples. But the young Jesuit pressed ahead, no doubt filled with the humanistic spirit of the Italian Renaissance, which sought to bring culture into greater harmony with the Christian faith. Quickly, the young man transformed himself into a Confucian philosopher, mastering the local language and attracting the curiosity and respect of the educated classes. He spoke of ethics rather than original sin and kept the crucifix well out of sight, realizing it could be an unsuitable symbol within the Chinese culture in which he had immersed himself.[47] His name was Matteo Ricci (1552-1610).

It was Ricci's intention, true to Jesuit thinking of the age, to convert the elite of Chinese society who were in a position to influence the wider society. Imbued with humanism, Ricci impressed his Chinese hosts with his knowledge of the natural sciences. Clocks, prisms, mathematical instruments, maps of the world and other artifacts, Ricci showed to the Chinese: things that appealed to the inherent curiosity of this people he was trying to convert. His efforts could be described as pre-evangelization, designed to impress and win over their confidence. Yet Ricci went further. He observed carefully Chinese ritual ceremonies and permitted new Chinese Catholics to continue to participate in them after their baptism. He sought to express Christian doctrines in Chinese thought. Ricci, and other Jesuits who were in China with him, lived and behaved as Chinese literati. Opening a house in Bejing in 1601, Ricci and his fellow Jesuits gained the respect of the emperor. On one occasion they presented the emperor with a statue of the Virgin Mary and a clock that struck the hours. The clock remained a prized possession of the emperor but the statue of Mary he sent off to his mother![48] Conversions to Christianity were not great in number. Yet by 1620 there were approximately five thousand Catholics in China.[49] Ricci is remembered for his extraordinary efforts at inculturation, a method of pastoral care that respects and incorporates local culture into the beliefs and life of the Christian religion.

A similar story unfolded in India where another Italian Jesuit, Roberto de Nobili (1577-1656), became a *sanyassi*, an Indian holy man. He arrived in India at the age of twenty-eight. Dressing in the red-ochre clothing of a holy man, and with the characteristic marking on his forehead, and eating a diet restricted to rice, fruit and herbs, de Nobili studied Indian philosophy and mastered the Tamil, Telugu and Sanskrit languages. Encountering the rigid caste system of India, Roberto appreciated the importance of converting the highest - ranking Brahman caste and of appointing missionaries for the differing Indian castes. Roberto, coming from an Italian noble family, decided he was able to give himself the revered title of an Indian rajah to assist in earning him respect among the local people.[50]

The Jesuit, Alessandro Valignano (1539-1606), first reached Japan in 1579. He was of the firm opinion that the only way for the Church to make real headway in Japan and China was in its becoming thoroughly Japanese and Chinese. For him, these cultures were sophisticated societies, equal to European cultures. Yet he believed this was in no way true of some of the other cultures where Jesuit missions had been established, such as in India and the Moluccas. In this, he shared the prejudices of the majority of Western people of his age.[51] His policy of inculturation of the gospel was a selective one.

It was among the Italian Jesuits that a pastoral strategy of adapting the Church to local conditions found acceptance in the New World of the East. But these enlightened Jesuit missionaries had their opponents, even within their own ranks. The controversy intensified as opponents of cultural accommodation believed it was a pastoral practice that diluted and falsified Christian teachings. Seeking to justify their policies, some Jesuits took heart from words of the Vatican Congregation of the Propagation of the Faith, a body set up in 1622 to ensure that the Church's missionary activity had greater independence from the Spanish and Portuguese Crowns. Its enlightened Secretary, Francesco Ingli, wrote in 1659:

> Do not regard it as your task and do not bring any pressure on the peoples, to change their manners, customs and uses, unless they are evidently contrary to religion and sound morals. What could be more absurd than to transport France, Spain, Italy or some other European country to China? Do not introduce all that to them, but only the faith which does not despise or destroy the manners and customs of any people ... Do not draw invidious contrasts between the customs of the peoples and those of Europe; do your utmost to adapt yourselves to them.[52]

But the official Church hardened its stance against such innovation and the Jesuit style of pastoral care was condemned, a final decision being taken by Clement XI in 1704 and 1715. In his comprehensive analysis of the 'Chinese Rites' controversy, Andrew Ross makes the following observation on the condemnation:

> As a result of this, Christianity, in a tragically short time, went from being a respected possible option for Chinese of all ranks to being a fringe sect for people on the margins of society ... because the eighteenth-century Church could not shake itself free of Europeanism.[53]

In Asia, Christianity declined. The exception was in the Philippines and in Vietnam, where Spanish and French missionary activity was strong.

### Spanish Mission in the Americas

In the newly discovered Americas, rich in natural resources that brought immense wealth to Spain and Portugal, the conversion of native peoples was carried out with zeal. The stated ideal was that this should happen without force. The reality was often otherwise. Mass baptisms were common, with indigenous men and women having but minimal understanding of their new faith. While native Indians were frequently employed as catechists, there was little enthusiasm to educate and ordain local people. In fact, this did not become possible until 1772, following a Church council in Lima, when a ban on ordaining native Indians was removed.[54] In Latin America, the Church was implanted in the context of the 'conquistadors' - of young men armed with swords, in search of adventure and riches: the land was to be plundered, with the local people serving the needs of their privileged and powerful European rulers. Within just fifty years of Columbus' arrival, the taking of Central and South America was complete. It was an evangelization through conquest that included the transfer of religion, with the support of the state, to a new culture. There was a moral duty to baptize the native peoples for outside the Church, it was believed, there was no salvation.

Within the United States, in the second half of the sixteenth century, Florida was chosen as the site of the first permanent settlement of the Spanish - a strategy designed to help protect Spanish ships from French pirates off the Florida coastline. The first missionaries in Florida were Jesuits, but they were soon to be replaced by Franciscans who subsequently established a number of mission stations along the Atlantic coastline as far north as Georgia. But as British colonies developed along the eastern seaboard, the Franciscan missions collapsed. More successful were the eighteenth-century Spanish missions along the Californian coast, including those of San Diego and San Gabriel (Los Angeles). The Franciscan friars ran the missions in what were self-contained colonies. Once baptized, native Indians were not permitted to leave a mission. Floggings and other harsh forms of punishment were common.[55] In return for being housed, fed and clothed, Indians worked the mission farms – which included orchards, vineyards, and paddocks for cattle - in what Jay Dolan describes as a 'cultural conquest'.[56] Disease, infant mortality and hard labor took their toll on the Indian population. In fact, the Indian death rate was double that of the black slaves on the other side of the country.[57] The system reached its high point in the early nineteenth century but came to an end as a result of Mexican independence in 1821. Afterwards, the missions were secularized. The discovery of gold in California left what was once a tightly controlled system in disarray.

## The French Mission to Canada

The French, too, pursued the 'pastoral care' of native American Indians, being drawn to the coast of Newfoundland because of fishing and the fur trade. In 1608 Samuel de Champlain (1567-1635) founded Québec and, from there, French traders and missioners penetrated into the Great Lakes. France bestowed upon the Jesuits the task of converting the inhabitants of Canada, where Church and state were closely intertwined. Other orders were to follow, especially after the suppression of the Society of Jesus in 1773. The French view of the Indians was mixed: they were either regarded as an inferior race to be civilized or they were seen in the light of Jean-Jacque Rousseau's (1712-78) romantic notion of the 'noble savage'. Unlike the Spanish and English, the French generally had a more positive view of the human nature of the native people among whom they lived. They adopted a policy of greater assimilation, despite persisting racial prejudice.[58]

## Spiritual Revivalism

### The Enlightenment

To appreciate the vitality of Protestant revivalism, it is necessary to situate it within the context of the 'Enlightenment' that happened in France. The Enlightenment movement is associated with the work of the *philosophes*, intellectuals such as Montesquieu (1689-1755), Voltaire (1694-1778), and Diderot (1713-84), although it is generally agreed now that the movement first arose in England.[59] The English philosopher, John Locke (1632-1704), maintained that all knowledge is based upon observation and experience. The Enlightenment marks one of the great turning points in the history of Western civilization as reason and science replaced religion as the criteria for arriving at truth. The aim was to rid people of religious superstition and replace the authority of religion with that of reason. Truth derived not from the weight of an authority that made pronouncements but from the reasonableness of rational argument and what could be verified by means of scientific analysis. The aim of the French *philosophes* was not the destruction of religion, but the articulation of a more rational form of religion - something of a 'natural religion'. Enlightenment thinking launched most decisively the secularization of Western thought.[60] The Enlightenment found political expression in the French Revolution and, across the Atlantic, in the American *Declaration of Independence* and *Constitution* formulated by the founding fathers of the United States. Men such as Benjamin Franklin (1706-90) and Thomas Jefferson (1743-1826) sought to foster Enlightenment ideals of religious tolerance, intellectual freedom, liberty, equality and human rights in what was predominantly a Protestant society with Puritan origins. This is something of a paradox, for American revivalist religious movements from the eighteenth century onward are, in many respects, a reaction against Enlightenment ideals. Revivalism, with its stress on the emotions, personal experience, soothing biblical assurances and lack of cerebral, theological analysis, stands in contrast to the rational, ordered, scientific agenda of the Enlightenment. Revivalism is a religion of the heart far more than of the head. Revivalism was the Protestant answer to Catholic mysticism.

### The Methodism of John and Charles Wesley

Oxford University, center of brilliance and invention, was the nest out of which the Methodist Church was hatched. The Oxford 'Holy Club' was a small group of pious, Christian students who held regular meetings for Bible study and prayer, young men in search of a deeper spirituality. It was founded by Charles Wesley (1707-88) but the leadership passed on to his older brother, John Wesley (1703-91), who was ordained a priest in the Church of England in 1728. Often ridiculed by their peers, they were given the names 'Bible Moths' and 'Methodists'. They saw their Christian faith as calling them to social concern. This led them to visit the sick, the poor and the imprisoned, to whom they offered free legal advice. Full of idealism, John and Charles set off across the Atlantic for Georgia to evangelize the Indians and English colonists. Charles secured a job there as secretary to the governor while John took up preaching and condemning the slave trade and the evils of gin. Things did not work out well in Georgia for the Wesley brothers. After a disastrous romantic affair with a woman, Sophia Hopkey, John was forced to flee Savannah in order to escape legal action; he went back to England. Charles had already quit the American colony by this time and had returned home.

Back in England, John came in contact with the Moravians and in 1738 decided to go to Germany to visit their leader, Nikolaus von Zinzendorf (1700-60). Strongly opposed to the prevailing spirit of rationalism, the Moravians stressed a felt experience of faith, a quietism that left everything to God. But despite his admiration for the Moravians, Wesley was troubled by their apparent lack of interest in social concerns.[61] In 1738, at a meeting in Aldersgate Street in London, John Wesley had a profound conversion experience during a reading of Luther's *Preface to the Epistle to the Romans*. He described what happened:

I felt my heart strangely warmed. I felt I did trust in Christ, Christ alone for salvation; and an assurance was given me that he had taken away my sins, even mine, and saved me from the law of sin and death.[62]

Deputizing for a close associate who had gone to America, the revivalist preacher George Whitefield (1714-70), John went to Bristol for a ministry of open-air preaching in which Whitefield had previously been outstandingly successful. Wesley's evangelism in Bristol is thought of as the beginning of the Methodist movement.

Particularly in the north of England, new towns were growing rapidly and the people who lived in them were offered little in the way of pastoral care. The Church of England, in the eighteenth century, seemed to lack the organization and spirituality needed for widespread evangelism in these new industrial centers.[63] Methodism filled the gap. John Wesley introduced a system of local, lay preachers to continue the task of evangelism on his departure from a particular community. They were often men of lower social origin and limited education, a social group to whom Methodism held special appeal. Lay preachers were often given responsibility for a number of Methodist communities, moving from one to another, a pastoral structure known as the 'circuit' in Methodism. John Wesley traveled incessantly on horseback throughout the British Isles for his revivalist meetings that were often outdoors when the weather permitted. Wesley fostered a strict moralism: this included abstinence from alcohol, gambling, and the theater. Yet it was accompanied by a strong stance against social injustice. For example, John Wesley opposed slavery and persuaded the American Methodist Conference of 1780 to declare it as being against the laws of God. Meanwhile, it was Charles Wesley who provided the music for Methodist revivalism through which it expressed its spirituality and characteristic form of hymn-singing during worship. He is said to have composed over five thousand hymns. Like Francis de Sales, John and Charles Wesley believed that a deeper spiritual life of sanctity was a possibility for everyone, not just for the chosen few. Christ's atoning death for sin was definitely emphasized in their preaching and hymns but this was accompanied by the belief in God's perfect love for all his people. John Wesley was quite opposed to Calvinistic ideas about predestination to damnation. It was something that was to lead to his split with George Whitefield in 1741.

While Charles Wesley remained firmly within the Church of England, John became more and more independent of it. Yet it was only after the death of the Wesley brothers that Methodism became a Church separate in identity from the Church of England. Within the Church of England itself, it was the Evangelical wing of the Church that emphasized inward, personal conversion but this was within the parish system that the Wesley brothers had largely abandoned. In America, Methodism flourished and by 1855 it was the largest Protestant group in the United States.[64]

## The Great Awakenings

George Whitefield, an Englishman born in Gloucester, could attract as many as thirty thousand people to his open-air revivalist gatherings in Boston Common.[65] His preaching must have been electrifying. He had begun outdoor evangelism in Britain but made frequent visits to the United States where his evangelistic tours had an enormous impact. Whitefield, Methodist associate of John and Charles Wesley, is the most prominent figure of the eighteenth-century Protestant revivalist movement in North America known as 'The Great Awakening'. Whitefield had restored hell in his preaching. He worked his sinful congregations to fever pitch, offering them one last chance to repent. The Great Awakening was to leave a permanent imprint on the style of religious life in the United States, despite its being a short-lived movement. The Baptist Churches of the South, especially Georgia, where Whitefield had close associations, were probably those that benefited most from it.[66] Billy Graham (b.1918) and a plethora of American television evangelists are its offspring, in a tradition that reaches back to the English Puritans who had first arrived on American shores in 1620 aboard the *Mayflower*. In Canada, The Great Awakening was felt in the passionate words of Henry Alline (1748-84), which brought many Protestant Canadians to a new relationship with their God.

The 'Second Great Awakening' occurred in the United States in the early nineteenth century, especially among Congregational Churches in New England. Yale University became a focal point. The university's President - Timothy Dwight (1752-1817) - attempted to discourage students from adopting skeptical, Enlightenment ideas. His desire was to move them towards an experience of Christian conversion. Lyman Beecher (1775-1863) was another figure in this evangelical revival. It helped the spread of the American Methodist and Baptist Churches. By the 1840s there were more Methodist churches than federal post offices in the United States![67]

Early Methodism held particular appeal to the poor and marginalized in American life, including slaves. With its emphasis on piety rather than property, in the latter years of the eighteenth century, Methodism was often seen as a threat to the established social order in the southern states. Black slaves became preachers who were able to instill racial pride within their people and 'testified to Wesleyan beliefs in the distinction between God's and humanity's rankings.'[68] White preachers might preach obedience and docility in this world and the bliss of salvation in the next. But once black slaves received Christianity, it provided a tool for survival, self-pride and hope for freedom. American black Christianity, especially strong in the Baptist and Methodist Churches, came to be characterized by an intense, spiritual fervor. Drawing upon their African roots, black American slaves developed a form of Christianity that was 'passionate, deep in spirituality, earthed in music, dance, and shouting'.[69] Among many black congregations today in the United States, the spirit of the Great Awakenings is clearly evident.

This surge in Catholic and Protestant spirituality, with its stress on felt religious experience, has to be seen as partially a reaction to Enlightenment thinking that sought to emphasize the rational and scientific, a movement that came to a head in the turmoil and bloodshed of the French Revolution.

# Chapter 7

## Liberals, Workers and Missionaries

### The French Revolution and Civil Liberties

Nôtre-Dame Cathedral in Paris has witnessed many spectacular festivities amidst its Gothic masonry and colored medieval glass. Yet, in its long history over eight centuries, no event has been as extraordinary as the Festival of Reason that took place there during the height of the French Revolution. At the time, the Paris Opera was performing the production, *Homage to Liberty*, by Gossec. The sets were moved from there across the city to decorate Nôtre-Dame. A cast of dancers, singers and musicians enthusiastically made a grand entrance into the cathedral on the festival day itself, accompanied by members of the National Assembly. Into this church that so symbolizes France, dedicated to the Virgin Mary, an attractive young opera star was carried on a chair, dressed in a white tunic and blue cloak, with the red cap of liberty covering her long, flowing hair. Bowing to the flame of Reason burning in the sanctuary, she seated herself on a bed of flowers and plants before a large papier-mâche mountain surmounted by a pagan temple. There was a stirring rendition of the *Marseillaise* and a number of impassioned speeches as uniformed soldiers marched about the aisles carrying busts of Jean-Paul Marat (1743-93) and other martyrs of the Revolution. A similar ceremony was held across Paris in the Church of Saint-Sulpice and throughout France some two thousand churches were renamed as Temples of Reason.[1]

The French Revolution marks the beginning of the modern world: a massive social, economic, religious and political upheaval that brought to fruition the principles of the Enlightenment with its philosophy of liberalism. The Revolution's slogan of *Liberté, Égalité* and *Fraternité* meant the end of the old ways, the *ancien régime*, as freedom and democracy gave to the people a new vision of themselves and how life was to be ordered. In many respects the Church represented the old order of hierarchy and unquestioned authority and it now found itself in a hostile world. As has been mentioned before, the work of pastoral care always rests upon assumptions about human nature and the old assumptions were now under serious question as people experienced themselves as free and equal, possessing human rights. The Church had to accommodate itself to the new conditions. But as the nineteenth century progressed, the Catholic Church, in particular, while recognizing the need for new understandings and forms of pastoral leadership, dug in its heels over the issue of civil liberties. It withdrew more and more into itself by turning its back on, and resisting, many key aspects of modernity.

The French Revolution, traditionally understood as beginning with the storming of the Bastille in 1789, was initially accepting of the Church while it recognized the need for its reform. The Church was seen to control too much of the nation's wealth. Bishops had been chosen almost exclusively from the nobility. In October 1789 the National Assembly took over all Church property to place it at the disposal of the nation. Clergy were to be paid by the state that now saw itself as responsible for social welfare and the maintenance of public worship. The following year the Assembly decreed that the vows of all those in contemplative religious orders were to be suspended as these people were seen to have no useful social function. Monasteries across the country were rapidly closed. Those religious in teaching and charitable orders were allowed to continue. In July 1790 the *Civil Constitution of the Clergy* was introduced: it brought about a complete restructuring of the French Church, free of papal control. All bishops and parish priests, now requiring to be elected like other civic authorities, were obliged to swear an act of allegiance to the Constitution of the French State as the Church became thoroughly subjected to the civil authority.[2] Many of the clergy followed the orders of Pius VI (1775-99) by refusing to take the oath of allegiance, and suffered the consequences. But the Constitutionalists among the clergy, who did take the oath, remained secure.

Things got worse for the Church in France as the Constitutional Church began to weaken and the process of de-Christianization accelerated during the period of the *Terror*, which began in 1792 and lasted until Maximilien Robespierre's (b. 1758) death in July 1794. It was during this time that Louis XVI (1754-93) and Marie-Antoinette (1755-93) went to the guillotine. Thousands of others suffered a similar fate. Joseph Fouché (1758-1820), a former priest of the Oratory, became a dedicated member of the revolutionary Jacobin party, initiating a vigorous program of de-Christianization in Nièvre. He fostered a cult of the Republic that saw him solemnly unveiling a bust of Brutus in one of the churches, identifying the Revolution with the republican sentiments of ancient, pagan Rome. Clergy of the area were ordered to renounce their vows of celibacy and either marry, adopt a child or look after an elderly person.[3] Fouché ended up as Minister of Police.

During the period of the Directory (1795-99), the Church in France began to make something of a recovery but it was a shadow of its former self. Pius VI resisted the reforms that he interpreted as a challenge to the authority of the papacy. At the age of eighty-two he was taken prisoner by the French for refusing to renounce his temporal power. A frail and disillusioned old man, he died in exile at Valence in 1799 where his name was recorded in the local register as 'Jean Ange Braschi, exercising the profession of a pontiff.'[4]

Napoleon Bonaparte (1769-1821), a pragmatist who was aware of the importance of religion for keeping people happy and fostering nationalism, negotiated a concordat in 1801 with Pope Pius VII (1800-23). Its purpose was to govern Church-state relations and it acknowledged Catholicism as the religion of the majority of French citizens. Bishops, representative of all social classes, were appointed to dioceses. Among them were former Constitutionalists while others were bishops of the *ancien régime*. But the majority of them were new. Napoleon, in his quest for grandeur, invited Pius VII to Paris to crown him emperor in the cathedral of Nôtre Dame, on a cold December morning in 1804. But as the pope was about to take the crown from the altar, Napoleon grabbed it and placed it upon his own head. The significance of the gesture was not lost on the congregation.[5] The tension between France and Rome reached a climax five years later when Pius excommunicated Napoleon for his incorporation of the Papal States into the French Empire. By way of retaliation, the emperor arrested the pope. Like his predecessor, Pius VII was taken by a waiting coach into exile. Following Napoleon's exile in St Helena, Pius returned to his home in the Quirinal Palace in Rome some six years later. This humiliating ordeal of the papacy soured relations between the Roman Church and the secular powers of a new Europe.

## Liberalism and the Papacy

The changes that had come over the Church in France during this time were the result of the forces of liberalism, something that cannot be neatly defined. Political liberalism worked to shift power from the Church and nobility to the secular state as rationalism replaced religious authority and privilege. Democracy, freedom of thought and civil rights were understood as giving power to the people. But the movement was not confined to France. Napoleon's troops carried with them the new French ideas, and revolution broke out all across Europe with nationalist movements emerging to challenge the status of the Church. In Germany, Otto von Bismarck's (1815-98) attempts to curb the power of the Church became known as *Kulturkampf* (culture struggle).

In France, as the Church rapidly lost its power and privilege during the Revolution, pastoral ministry came under increasing threat as religion was curtailed and its practitioners often persecuted. Pastoral care had to be reconstructed in a Church that now stood in a new relationship to the state. Indeed, this is just what happened as antireligious sentiment began to decrease. Seminaries re-opened in France and in the period 1800-15 some six thousand priests were ordained.[6] The post-Napoleonic era saw a bursting forth of new religious orders of women and men, the like of which had never been seen in the Church. France led the way but it happened all over Catholic Europe. Ireland, for example, saw the creation of many new orders as Catholicism became increasingly invigorated as it freed itself of English Protestant restrictions, when emancipation was achieved in 1829 through the political struggles of Daniel O'Connell (1775-1847) and his Catholic Association. These orders were highly visible in the community and mainly given to apostolic work, especially teaching, nursing and the care of children in orphanages. Women religious were now freed from convent enclosure that had been imposed upon them by the Council of Trent. As we shall see later, the orders followed the emigrants and sent many of their members to the New World: to such countries as the United States, Canada, Australia and New Zealand. Some orders took on a more missionary apostolate, sending priests, sisters and brothers to Africa, Asia, Latin America and the Pacific Islands.

In its economic form, liberalism was a doctrine of *laissez-faire*: free trade and commercial activity without constraints. This variant of liberalism was also to shake the Church for, as we shall see, it moved pastoral care from being just charity to the promotion of justice on behalf of workers vulnerable to exploitation and oppression in the new age of the industrial revolution. Catholicism responded cautiously, even defiantly, in the nineteenth century to both political and economic liberalism. But the forces for change by way of pastoral responses to modernity were there.

Félicité Robert de Lamennais (1782-1854) represents the nineteenth-century attempt to harmonize liberalism with Catholicism. He believed in a free society, free speech, the separation of Church and state, and a democratically elected government. But Lamennais wished to combine his liberalism with being an Ultramontane ('beyond the mountains'), a believer in the absolute powers of the pope who resided across the Alps in Rome. He envisaged the pope as the religious figure who could draw society together by intervening directly in worldly affairs. He believed it was the pastoral task of the Church, especially through the office of the Bishop of Rome, to ensure the defense of democracy and the rights of the poor. In other words, the Church's magisterium was to reach into the heart of social and political life.

It was Lamennais' desire to free education from the control of the state and, for this purpose, he founded the Congregation de St Pierre, but it was to have a short life. With the fall of the restored Bourbon French monarchy in 1830, Lamennais joined company with a couple of brilliant young thinkers who included Pére Lacordaire (1802-61), who was to become a renowned Dominican preacher, and the layman Charles Montalambert (1810-70), who was in later life to take a seat in the French Chamber of Deputies where he continued to espouse Catholic social principles. For a brief period of time these three men published the journal *L'Avenir*, to help spread the new Catholic liberalism with its defense of religious liberty amidst an increasingly anticlerical state. *L'Avenir* carried as its heading 'God and Liberty'. As Ultramontanes, these Catholic enthusiasts saw the papacy as the religious institution to lead and defend this quest for freedom. The call to freedom and respect for human rights would become central to the concept of pastoral care in the modern world.

*L'Avenir* looked beyond France by supporting the Poles, who were trying to free themselves from control by the Russians. As well, it sided with O'Connell's Irish independence movement and the Italian nationalist patriots of the *Risorgimento*. The paper stood for a socially involved Church in the cause of liberty. This included support for an International Workers' Association, a form of pastoral care exercised in the political arena. But warnings against the Church's aligning itself with the forces of liberalism came from a number of quarters. Many of the bishops were wary of supporting liberal causes; they had already shaken the Church so badly. For example, *L'Avenir* was banned from the diocese of Chartres and the paper was soon forced to suspend publication because of nervous shareholders.[7]

Worried about the growing opposition to his ideas, Lamennais decided to get the matter settled in Rome and made his way there with Lacordaire and Montalambert. As Ultramontanes, they looked to the pope for guidance and support. But Gregory XVI (1831-46) was in no mood to look kindly upon any liberal ideas when he was fighting Italian democratic, nationalist movements aimed at eliminating the temporal power of the pope within the Papal States. The three young Frenchmen were kept waiting for weeks before Pope Gregory would grant them an audience which lasted a mere fifteen minutes. The pontiff was cool but polite, seemingly more interested in talking about the art of Michelangelo, while taking pinches of snuff, than in discussing the agenda of L'Avenir. This would be dealt with in due time. The young men were sent on their way with medals and rosaries.[8]

Disappointing news did not take long to come out of Rome. While staying in Munich on the return journey to Paris, Lamennais received a copy of Gregory's encyclical, Mirari vos (1832). It was clearly a direct repudiation of the liberalism of L'Avenir, although Lamennais himself was not specifically named. After all, as a keen Ultramontane, he had done so much to support the papacy. The separation of Church and state, and religious liberty, were rejected in principle, although it was acknowledged they might be tolerated in practice. And there could be no support given to liberal revolutionaries. Lamennais, along with Lacordaire and Montalambert, humbly offered a written submission to the encyclical's teachings, but they were clearly disappointed. It was a victory for the opposition.

However, Lamennais soon became bitter, especially when Gregory sold out to the Russians by advising Polish Catholics to give up their rebellion and submit to the Czar whom they were told would show them every kindness. This advice was given in his brief, Superiori anno (1832), and led to widespread anguish and anger across Catholic Europe towards Rome. With political rebellion continuing to grow in Italy, the pope backed away from showing support for any struggle involving political and civil liberties. It would take a Polish pope in the following century to reverse such matters. Lamennais continued to write in support of liberty in his book, Payroles d'un Croyant. He was still functioning as a priest. A response to his work soon came in another encyclical, Singulari nos (1834). It was a reactionary document that rejected any idea that sovereignty lay with the people. In the pope's eyes, such ideas threatened the monarchies of Europe and his own position as temporal ruler of the vast Papal States within Italy. Gregory, with his characteristic rigidity, had set the Catholic Church in a direction firmly opposed to liberal ideas that were reshaping the modern world. Disillusioned by his Church's apparent disinterest in a pastoral stance that stressed social and political reform in the name of freedom, Lamennais abandoned the Catholic Church. His work has been described as having had 'a profound impact on the dissident tendency within European Catholicism, where a critical mind was no obstacle to profound belief'.[9]

Ultramontanism, but in a form separated from liberalism, became a growing force within nineteenth century Catholicism and led to the isolation of the Catholic Church from mainstream currents of secular thinking and political movements. The Church was adopting an increasingly reactionary position. In Pope Pius IX (1846-78), popularly known as Pio Nono, the trend reached a climax. Originally perceived as a liberal, this pope remained firmly enclosed within a Church hostile to contemporary social and political developments in the wider world. Like his predecessors, he, too, was unable to separate in his mind the temporal and spiritual dimensions of the Church and remained firmly opposed to the Church's surrendering the Papal States. But Montalambert was continuing his cry for a 'free Church in a free state'. In Germany, Johann Von Döllinger (1799-1890), a Church historian, called for a German Church free of state control and hit out at the temporal power of the papacy. In 1863 he was a key figure behind the Congress of Munich where a liberal Catholicism was defended in opposition to the Roman policy of the time. Meanwhile, in England in 1845, John Henry Newman (1801-90) was received into the Catholic Church. He published his *Grammar of Assent* in 1870: it included a thorough investigation of the place of a free conscience in the life of a Christian.

Pius IX issued *Quanta Cura* and the *Syllabus of Errors* in 1864. It was a full frontal attack on modernity. The *Syllabus* consisted of eighty propositions gathered from earlier papal statements but taken out of their original context. It was meant as a clear assertion of the Church's authority against perceived forms of contemporary rationalism, modern philosophy and religious liberalism. Yet Pius's thinking has to be seen within the context of his world, especially the anticlerical legislation of the Piedmontese government, which he interpreted as threatening the sovereignty of the Church. Without a formal consultation with other bishops – hence, on his own authority – Pius IX proclaimed the doctrine of the Immaculate Conception of Mary, in 1854. It was a clear move to strengthen the power of the papacy at a time when it was under threat from the outside forces of Italian politics. Ultramontanism reached its heights at the First Vatican Council in 1870, with its teaching of papal infallibility under certain defined conditions, as set out in the Council's document, *Pastor*

*Aeternus.* The doctrine that so strengthened papal spiritual powers was issued as Italian nationalist forces were poised to invade the Papal States, including Rome itself, under Victor Emmanuel (1820-78). Just days after the proclamation of the infallibility decree, Napoleon III (1808-73) ordered French troops to vacate Rome to engage in the Franco-Prussian War that had just broken out. The pope was without military protection. The Papal States, ruled over by the popes, had been a territory within Italy of sixteen thousand square miles, with three million inhabitants. Pius IX saw it reduced to a few acres of the Vatican under the new laws of 1871. The pope, forced to move out of his old home of the Quirinal, which had become King Victor Emmanuel's Palace, now was the 'Prisoner of the Vatican'.

## The Industrial Revolution

As the Church was attempting to come to grips with civil liberties that had arisen out of the French Revolution, it also confronted the new world created by factories and machinery resulting from the industrial revolution. In what manner should the Church offer a pastoral response to economic liberalism that left workers at the mercy of their employers? There were few laws to protect them. The only factor that seemed to matter in the new industrial economies was the creation of wealth by means of capitalism. The industrial revolution came about as a result of mechanized farming, mobile labor, steam power, machines, metallurgy, factories, towns, improved transport, finance and changing demographics.[10] People left the countryside to live in the new urban towns and cities, with their factories disgorging thick, black smoke, polluting the rivers and forcing their workers to spend their bleak lives in rows of ugly tenements. England led the way in the creation of these new manufacturing towns: places such as Manchester, Leeds and Birmingham. Queen Victoria (1819-1901), accustomed to living in the comfortable surroundings of Windsor Castle, was appalled upon seeing the living and working conditions of her subjects when making a tour around her realm. Under the patronage of her husband, Prince Albert (1819-61), the Great Exhibition was held in London in the specially constructed Crystal Palace, a homage to science and technology, which attracted over six million visitors from all parts of the world.[11] Charles Dickens (1812-70) attempted to awaken the conscience of the nation in his novels, which described the squalor and economic hardships of industrial England. As the industrial revolution spread and made headway on the Continent, especially in France and Germany, the Church found itself with a new constituency: vast numbers of urban workers that were in need of new forms of pastoral care that would respond to their hardships.

In 1848, with the publication of the *Communist Manifesto* by Friedrich Engels (1820-95) and Karl Marx (1818-83), workers of all countries of the world were called to unite. It was the age of universal theories. Charles Darwin (1809-82) had attempted to explain the evolution of all life in his *Origin of Species* (1859). Marx created a universal theory for human society in *Das Kapital* (1867-94), with his description of the class struggle, where workers, through revolutionary means, would create a communist society characterized by economic and social equality. In Marx's messianic vision for humanity there was no place for God. It was pure materialism.

## The Social Gospel

### The Beginnings of the Social Gospel: France

Was there a Christian view that could be formulated to ensure the dignity and rights of workers and that could serve as an alternative to atheistic communism? Pastoral care was in urgent need of teachings and practices to meet the new social conditions brought about by the economic liberalism associated with industrialization. A characteristic feature of Catholic thinking upon social matters in the nineteenth century was the conviction that the social evils of the new industrialized world could be resolved only by social and political change that rested upon the principles of a Christian society. The social agenda had to move beyond charity to the fostering of workers' rights. Yet a pastoral concern of this kind remained something of a fringe movement within Catholicism throughout the nineteenth century, until it received endorsement in Pope Leo XIII's (1878-1903) groundbreaking encyclical, *Rerum Novarum*, in 1891. The encyclical set Catholic teaching in a new direction and represented what has been described as 'a kind of *magna carta* for modern social Catholicism'.[12]

Catholic social movements throughout the nineteenth century can be seen as falling into three different schools: the conservative, the liberal Catholic, and the utopian socialist.[13] The conservative emphasis looked back to a Christian past in which the Church, supported by the state, held society together. It was a paternalistic vision in which the landed classes had responsibility for those less well off. The French nobleman, Alban de Villeneuve-Bargemont (1784-1850), represented this school of thinking. He was a stern critic of industrialization and nostalgically fostered the notion of a return of much of the urban working class back to the land, in agricultural colonies, through state assistance. For those who remained in industry, Villeneuve-Bargemont proposed a system whereby workers would look after their own needs by organizing benefit associations for obtaining loans and by accessing welfare assistance. While workers should seek to make themselves more secure financially in this way, factory owners were not to forget their obligations to care for their struggling employees through a generosity based upon Christian principles of care. Social reform of this kind would depend, in the conservative approach, on a sound moral and religious education for all classes within society and the state's legislating for better working conditions.

Armand de Melun (1807-77), a member of the French aristocracy, held similar opinions. A sense of responsibility towards the poor was accompanied by a conservative fear of revolution among the working class and unemployed. Like Villeneuve-Bargemont, he favored mutual aid societies, especially for young workers, in which parish clergy were to be involved: they were known as *patronages d'apprentis*. The idea behind this pastoral strategy was to ensure that younger workers did not drift away from the Church in a country in which the working class was becoming increasingly anticlerical, especially in larger cities such as Lyons and Paris.[14] As well, de Melun drafted proposals for the French Parliament in an attempt to seek greater humanitarian legislation for workers. Such social ideas were firmly based upon Christian principles. Albert de Mun (1841-1914) and René de la Tour du Pin (1834-1925), also of the French aristocracy, founded working men's clubs within parishes that were both religious and charitable in aim. They also sought greater protection for workers relating to such matters as better working conditions, old age, and unemployment. The plight of French workers came to a head in the uprising at the barricades in the revolutionary year of 1848.

Also falling within the conservative model of social reform in France was Leon Joseph Harmel (1829-1915). His plan, too, was of a paternalistic kind. He wanted to assist workers economically and religiously through the Christian Factory Project. The owner of a wool mill, Harmel set about making his industrial plant the ideal Christian workplace in which both he and his workers would benefit. A variety of social welfare measures were introduced into the factory: a sick fund, a savings club, a store selling cheaply priced food, and a wage supplement for workers with large families. At the same time, the workers were to be involved in the running of the factory through participation in a factory council. This was meant to foster a sense of ownership, pride and loyalty within their place of work. As such, an environment was created which would positively dispose the workers towards the strong ethos of the Catholic faith within the factory itself. This form of lay pastoral care was organized in such a way that Harmel made sure that there were a few committed Catholics within each age group of the workforce. These leaders would organize religious associations, such as the St Joseph Society, to draw in other workers. Harmel believed Catholicism among the working class would flourish if their economic and social needs were attended to in the workplace. In 1889 Harmel led a pilgrimage of ten thousand French workers to Rome. Social reform and evangelization had been blended in a business environment.

In Switzerland, the Christian factory movement was set up by a priest, Theodosius Florentini (1808-65). He bought several textile factories to provide jobs for unemployed young mountain people in a work environment that was meant to be truly Christian. Usually only Christians were offered jobs. In one of his factories in Bohemia he had nuns run the business, the 'factory convent' as it came to be called. Humane working conditions in Florentini's factories were meant to go beyond the mere making of profit to the implementation of Christian charity and justice: this was pastoral care of a new kind in the industrial age. However, Florentini's factories were to end in financial ruin, and it was left to the sisters to face the burden of liquidation.[15]

By way of contrast to the conservative emphasis in the Catholic social movement of nineteenth-century France examined above, the liberal approach recognized the irreversible changes that had come about as a result of the French Revolution. Freedom and equality were understood as essentially Christian values that must be woven into all social relationships. Charles de Coux (1787-1864) was a liberal French Catholic who had been influenced by democratic principles during his time spent in the United States as a child. His articles in the liberal Catholic journals, *L'Avenir* (1830-31) and *Ère nouvelle* (1848-49), set forth a clear blueprint for social reform. He saw industrialization as reducing the worker to being little more than a cost factor to be contained as much as possible. The result was exploitation. For de Coux, the answer was in giving the worker the right to vote. He was an early advocate of universal suffrage and one of the first voices making known the exploitation of the working class by capitalists.[16]

Philippe Buchez (1796-1865) is representative of the third approach to Catholic social activism during this period, a movement that Karl Marx once named derisively as 'utopian socialism'. It aimed at a Christian democratic vision of the world of work, founded upon socialist principles. Buchez was of the firm belief that the Revolution had brought liberty but not equality. The Revolution had to be reinterpreted according to Christian ideals but many Catholics feared such views because of the civil unrest they might unleash.[17] For Buchez, Christian philanthropy was totally inadequate. Nonviolent revolution was what was needed to overcome the entrepreneur whom he saw as 'a parasitical being living at the expense of those whom he exploits.'[18] Unlike Marx, who believed the existence of the classes was a necessary stage towards the classless society, Buchez maintained that the differences in class were an unfortunate and unnecessary development from which society must free itself. Workers must become their own employers and acquire collectively both capital and tools. In 1840, Buchez founded a monthly paper, named L'Atelier, written and run entirely by workers. It was to remain in publication for eleven years. Although his beliefs were characterized by atheistic materialism for a period of time, Buchez came to the realization that his socialist ideas could be properly formulated only within Christianity's ideals of equality and justice.

It is Frédéric Ozanam (1813-53) who is best remembered among all the Catholic social activists in France of the nineteenth century because of his enduring legacy around the world: the St Vincent de Paul Society, which he founded in Paris in 1833. It was named after the saintly priest of Paris who lived some two hundred years earlier and whom we have already met in chapter 6. As a law student and a man who embodied French refinement at its best, Ozanam gathered about him a group of young men to assist the poor practically, especially by providing food and clothing. He had been moved by the impoverished conditions of families in a poorer district of Paris through which he had walked on the way to lectures at the university. The group aimed at breaking down class barriers by means of direct contact between these middle- to upper-class young students and poverty-stricken people in the emerging industrial world. As well, Ozanam's efforts were aimed towards developing a deeper spirituality within the membership of this group of lay people eager to enter into pastoral care. The movement spread rapidly throughout France and beyond. By 1846 it had reached the United States and the first Australian conference was founded in Melbourne in 1854. Ozanam's group was, indeed, more concerned with practical charity rather than with a program of social reform to alleviate the sources of poverty. However, Ozanam himself was progressive in his political outlook. He denounced economic liberalism and called upon workers to organize themselves to obtain better conditions and press for more government intervention concerning industrial matters.[19] Certainly, it would have been far more difficult to heighten social consciousness among middle- and upper-class Catholics of the time if there had not been the large network of St Vincent de Paul conferences offering the most basic kind of material relief.[20]

Drawing inspiration from the St Vincent de Paul Society, there was a pastoral plan active in France to bring workers' families together in small groups within the parishes, harmoniously united with each other in the bond of their common faith, for prayers and mutual support. A popular priest named François Ledreuille, with the encouragement of Paris's Archbishop, Denis Affre (1793-1848), set up a Workers' House in 1844 to offer practical assistance, such as helping people find employment.[21]

Amidst the revolutionary fervor that swept across much of Europe in 1848, a group of insurgents had set up barricades in Paris by the Place de la Bastille. Encouraged by a few socially minded Catholics to bring a halt to the violence – Ozanam was among them – Archbishop Affre went to the barricades in an attempt to calm the situation. A number of the rebels cheered him but, in the tense atmosphere, someone suddenly fired a gun and killed the archbishop. Public opinion quickly turned against any form of civil unrest connected with nationalist and socialist causes and the Catholic Church became strongly associated with reactionary forces. Archbishop Gousset (1792-1866) of Rheims, for example, remarked that, 'Democracy is the heresy of our time, more dangerous and more difficult to overcome than Jansenism.'[22] Catholicism began to turn its back on the struggles of workers for better conditions and, by doing so, became largely responsible for the loss of the working class from the Church in France. But in the twentieth century, the most important pastoral priority within the life of French Catholicism came to be that of winning back the Church's lost members and re-evangelizing them.

### Social Catholicism in Germany

In 1848, Wilhelm Ketteler (1811-77) delivered a series of powerful Advent sermons in the cathedral of Mainz dealing with what he saw as the great social problems of his age. His critics denounced them as socialist. In the same year, this priest was elected to the parliament in Frankfurt, so influential had he become in addressing matters of social concern that were of particular interest to German workers. Two years later he became the Bishop of Mainz. Ketteler was indeed influenced by the thinking of the prominent socialist leader of the time, Ferdinand La Salle (1825-64) whose organization, the German Workers' Association, was to combine with other socialist movements to form the Socialist Workers Party of Germany. Associations with socialist movements of this kind were to cause Ketteler considerable problems after Pius IX issued his *Syllabus of Errors* in 1864.[23] Yet Ketteler was no opponent of capitalism; he opposed merely its greed and exploitation. Initially, Ketteler limited his social activism to theoretical concepts, based upon natural law, without going into detail as to their practical application. In 1864 he published what was to be his most important book, *Christianity and the Labor Question*. His ideas attempted to walk the middle ground between liberal individualism and state-controlled socialism. He came to recognize that the state must be involved in social reform concerning the economy and conditions affecting labor. Workers should not be left to the mercy of market forces alone. At the same time, this had to be balanced by respecting the need for the different groups within society (individuals, families, workers' associations) to exercise control over their own rights and duties. Ketteler endorsed trade unions and the right of workers to strike when other avenues for seeking just demands fail.[24]

Ketteler was in no doubt that, in its duty of pastoral care, the Church must involve itself in social matters concerning the rights of workers in the emerging industrial economy of Germany. He encouraged bishops to designate some priests to be specially trained for an industrial mission among factory workers and to designate other priests to be educated in economics and the social sciences, while providing for all seminarians to be given some instruction in social issues. It was what he called 'social deaconry'.[25]

Similar to the working men's clubs in France, Adolph Kolping (1813-65) set up groups for young, unmarried trades workers in Germany. These clubs, organized by priests in parishes, offered educational and social activities for their members within the environment of the Church. From a pastoral point of view, the result was a close bond between many priests and young workers that would help keep working-class families closely associated with their Church throughout their lives.

During the *Kulturkampf*, under Bismarck in the 1870s, anti-Catholic legislation put the brakes on social Catholicism in Germany. The 'May Laws', introduced in May 1873, placed the Catholic Church firmly under state control. But few of the German bishops at the time were willing to link social reforms with that of faith. Ketteler was more the exception than the rule. Bismarck was strongly opposed to any form of social democracy. However, through a concordat he made with the Vatican, Bismarck changed tactics in the hope of winning over the Catholic Church. Indeed, the *Kulturkampf* had served to strengthen the hold of the Catholic Church upon the German people.

Meanwhile, in Italy, during the latter part of the nineteenth century, the *Opera dei Congressi* brought together many different types of organizations, including banks, cooperatives, rural workers and labor unions, to form a variety of clubs and societies aimed at improving the condition of workers, within a Catholic ethos. Founded by Giuseppe Toniolo (1845-1918), a professor of economics and law, the *Opera* was a significant example of lay leadership in pastoral care within Italian life at that time.[26]

## Social Catholicism: United States, England and Australia

Edward McGlynn (1837-1900) was one of those priests forever immersed in controversy. As a pastor in the city of New York, he identified himself strongly with the working-class poor, herded together in the crowded and unsanitary tenements of a rapidly growing metropolis. Immigrants from Europe, such as the Irish, Italians and Poles, found work there in such places as clothing factories, the docks and building sites. A few entrepreneurs made fortunes but most of the new immigrants worked for low wages under terrible conditions. McGlynn, too, believed charitable assistance alone was an inadequate response to the plight of workers. What was needed was an effort to get to the cause of the urban poverty that arose with the new age of industrialization. Only in this way could Americans live in a just and more humane society.

McGlynn was influenced greatly by Henry George (1839-97), an economist, who believed that the answer to such a problem lay in a single tax. He wrote and spoke in a style that was simple and clear and was able to generate extraordinary enthusiasm among his followers. George's ideas won widespread support, and Single Tax Leagues were to be found all over the country. But he had his opponents, including New York's Archbishop and powerful figures in the Vatican, who feared any hint of socialist thinking. McGlynn came under suspicion by Church authorities, especially when he publicly endorsed George's campaign to become Mayor of New York City. Having no stomach for compromise or simple obedience when this meant violating his beliefs, McGlynn found himself excommunicated by Pope Leo XIII in 1887 for a period of five years; during this time he served on the executive of the United Labor Party of the State of New York.[27] In a speech he delivered in the year he was excommunicated, the fiery New York priest said:

> ... and I repeat, and I shall never tire of repeating, that I find justification for loving every social cause, every economic cause, every political cause, whose object is the diminution - rather let us say the abolition – of poverty, for the diffusion of knowledge, for the refinement and the civilization of these images of God all around us.[28]

Meanwhile, the Knights of Labor, founded in the United States in 1869, became a powerful instrument in the cause of improving the lot of workers. As it gained in strength, this organization aroused much unease in some Church circles. It had spread across the border into Canada where the Archbishop of Quebec, Cardinal Elzéar Tascherau (1820-98), excommunicated members. He claimed that it was a secret society with links to Freemasonry and he sought papal support for his actions. But Cardinal James Gibbons (1834-1921) in Baltimore was of the strong opinion that any Vatican condemnation of the Knights would be unwise. He pointed out to his Roman superiors that about half of the membership of the organization was made up of Catholics. He also advised the Vatican against any condemnation of Henry George who Gibbons claimed was neither a socialist nor a communist. The Archbishop of Baltimore was successful in seeking the support of the Archbishop of Westminster (England), Cardinal Henry Manning (1808-92), in attempting to restrain the Vatican from condemning the Labor movement in the United States. It worked and Leo XIII refused to condemn the Knights of Labor and lifted Tascherau's excommunication in Canada.[29]

In England, Manning saw his role as a pastor to be one that was on the side of the struggles of working people. Manning had been a convert from Anglicanism. A great number of Catholics in England were of Irish background and generally poor. His social thinking was first articulated in public in a speech he gave to the Mechanics Institute at Leeds in 1874, subsequently published as *The Dignity and Rights of Labour*. His main thesis was that the state had the duty to intervene when workers were unable to defend their rights before their employers. In Manning's time, children were still put to work, enduring long hours with little pay. And he believed women were being exploited in the workplace, something he saw as a threat to family life. During the great dock strike of 1890, Manning intervened on behalf of the strikers in an attempt to bring the dispute to an end. The dock workers were so grateful to the cardinal that they raised one hundred and sixty pounds to endow a bed in a London hospital in his memory.[30] In Manning's view, it was better for the Church to take the lead in supporting and guiding labor rather than having it taken over by revolutionary and communist forces.[31]

Meanwhile, in Australia, the Cardinal Archbishop of Sydney, Patrick Moran (1830-1911) - an Irishman - attempted something similar to Manning by mediating in a maritime strike the same year as the London dock strike. The strikers failed to win their demands but Moran's support was much appreciated. In Australia, and the rest of the English-speaking world, there was no struggle to reconcile democracy and Catholicism, as there had been in Europe in the nineteenth century. In these countries the Catholic Church had not been associated with an oppressive social order, unlike the situation in like France, Italy and Germany. Pastoral care among working-class people had been strong and so there was little of the anticlerical feeling that might be found elsewhere.[32] As a result, Moran immersed himself in Australian public life and stood as a candidate for the National Convention in 1897 to formulate a plan for the federation of the different states into one nation. When he received the full text of Leo XIII's encyclical on social matters, *Rerum Novarum*, Moran gave a public lecture entitled *The Rights and Duties of Labour*, in Sydney's Masonic Hall, before a crowded audience representing all the major political parties of the day.[33] The Archbishop was warmly and enthusiastically applauded.[34]

## Rerum Novarum

In 1891, when Pope Leo XIII issued his encyclical letter, *Rerum Novarum*, the Catholic Church reached a turning point. Social matters were now placed firmly within the Church's mission of teaching and pastoral care. Yet it was a reformist, rather than a radical, document. Recognizing that he could no longer afford to allow the Church to remain out of step with social developments, Leo's encyclical sought a re-Christianization of society. It took into account the new economic and social realities of capitalist economies in societies based upon democratic, liberal principles. *Rerum Novarum* attempted to walk the middle ground in its condemnation of both socialism and laissez-faire capitalism. It endorsed the right to private property. Only the Church could reconcile the classes, based upon Christian principles of social order. It recognized the rights of workers to a fair wage and to organize labor to ensure just working conditions. The state had the responsibility to ensure just working conditions and economic policies for the alleviation of poverty. The pastoral responsibility of the Church was one of ensuring just conditions for all in the workplace. Leo had set the Church in the direction of supporting trade unions and social reform, within the capitalist system.[35]

It is often pointed out that *Rerum Novarum* was a document of the ultramontane Church. When it came to members of the Church pressing for better social conditions, such efforts were to be firmly under clerical control. Following the encyclical's release, Leo continually stressed that social action was to be directed by the hierarchy and not left to independent action by lay persons. Pastoral care in the social sphere was to be strictly supervised under episcopal leadership.

> Indeed the entire text reads as an analysis of and prescription for society from the point of view of the institutional church. Winning workers to the church is as important as defending their rights.[36]

Leo had brought together the reformist ideas of nineteenth-century Catholic social thinking that we have been examining. The teaching in the encyclical stressed the organic unity of society based on cooperation, shared values and a respect for authority. The Church remained, in Leo's scheme of things, as the guiding and corrective voice on social issues. The earlier rejection of liberal principles of modernity by nineteenth-century popes, such as Gregory XVI and Pius IX, had been turned around considerably, but not entirely. While endorsing much within the movements calling for social reform, Catholicism would hold out against many of the social and scientific advances of the world as it moved into the twentieth century. Pope Pius X (1903-14) would go on to condemn what he called 'Modernism',[37] a move that created a climate of suspicion and fear of anything new. But the direction set by Leo XIII in *Rerum Novarum* clearly set the foundation for the future, inextricably linking pastoral care and social justice.

## The Salvation Army

Pastoral care of the poor, which emerged out of the industrial revolution, took a very different style in Victorian England with the mission of the Salvation Army, founded by William Booth (1829-1912) and his wife, Catherine (1829-90). The Booths began their ministry as a team effort, evangelical preachers within the Methodist tradition: their organization was first known as the Christian Mission before it developed into its more military style of the Salvation Army.

Catherine was a strong advocate of women's leadership in the Church, critical of the ethos of male dominance she saw operative in Christian organizations. The Booths did not preoccupy themselves with the concerns of workers for social and industrial reform: what mattered was the saving of souls. But they did devote themselves wholeheartedly to organizing charitable relief in deprived urban areas, such as London's East End, for they believed that poverty was the devil's weapon. Soup kitchens, cheap food stores, women's refuges and workmen's shelters were among some of the charitable facilities that the Booths and their organization provided and staffed. Poverty drove people to drink and led to other social evils, such as prostitution. Hence, they believed poor people were born and bred at risk of eternal damnation. It was a view that has been described, by a recent biographer of the Booths, as being a sort of economic determinism, but one owing more to Marx than to Wesley.[38]

By 1878 the Christian Mission had been transformed into the Salvation Army, with William Booth as its first General. The Army, like the Mission that led to it, characteristically involved the poor in recruiting the poor for Christ. Reformed sinners would lead the unredeemed to salvation, especially through their testimony, using a language and style with which the poor could identify. Revivalist meetings were not usually held in churches but in secular places such as hotels and disused music halls. But the venues for religious gatherings of the Salvation Army were eventually to be called citadels, since they offered security from God's enemies. William Booth was firmly on the side of uncomplicated belief, free of theological scholarship. There was to be no room for doubt. It was the eccentric George Scott Railton (1849-1913), especially through his pamphlets, who provided the Booths with a more thought-out basis for their movement. Railton's ideas were strongly evangelical and his language somewhat wild.[39] William Booth's sermons were highly charged emotional experiences that moved the crowds and attracted the ridicule of gangs of young hooligans or brewery owners worried about Booth's call to temperance. The Army, as its name suggests, adopted military imagery: flags, uniforms, brass bands, the motto 'Blood and Fire', a magazine called 'The War Cry', and titles of rank, such as officers. William Booth admired greatly the British Army for its organization and efficiency. In temperament and leadership style, William Booth was highly autocratic. Popular within the Salvation Army were the Hallelujah Lasses, young girls who supported the evangelists with their shrieks of joy and singing of hymns to the accompaniment of banjos and tambourines. The poor loved it.

The Salvation Army was a populist movement that spread quickly. Kate, a daughter of the Booths, took it to France. A group of English emigrants to North America, led by Amos and Eliza Shirley, founded a branch of the Salvation Army in the Old Chair Factory of Philadelphia in 1879. Another group followed them from England shortly after and unfurled their flags in New York's Battery Park. In Australia, a former Bradford butcher, whom people nicknamed the 'Happy Milkman', formed an Australian corps of the Salvation Army. By 1882 the Salvation Army could be found in all five continents of the world.[40]

While the Salvation Army did much in the way of easing the burden of the poor through material relief, it was not until his older age that William Booth turned his attention to a theoretical analysis, tackling the nature and cause of poverty in his book, *In Darkest England and the Way Out*, which was published in 1890, just a year before *Rerum Novarum*. Booth's work was forthright in tone, using language of a class struggle. His concern for the poor was deep-seated. He proposed, among other things, farm colonies at home, and abroad, to remove people from the grime and impoverished conditions of industrial cities. However, the book's significance lay more in drawing attention to poverty than in any solutions it proposed.[41] The debilitating effects of alcohol, especially among the poor, has remained a principal concern of the Salvation Army. In this it has similarities with the temperance movement in Ireland, founded in Cork in 1838 by Father Theobald Matthew (1790-1856).[42] A statue of this revered priest is to be seen in one of Cork's main shopping streets to this day. His call for people to take the pledge spread quickly and could be heard in any country of the world where Irish Catholics had made their home. The Salvation Army, along with its Catholic counterpart, the St Vincent de Paul Society, were to become the best known and most respected organizations in Christianity's pastoral concern for the poor and marginalized in the modern world.

### The Age of Colonization and Mission

The nineteenth century was the great period of European expansion through colonization. It was a common saying that the sun never set in the British Empire of Queen Victoria since its vast number of colonies stretched around the globe. Missionaries followed merchants and civil servants in the hope of 'civilizing' the people of these newly discovered lands where untold riches were there for the taking. The missionaries could be relied upon for providing education, health services, and instruction in agriculture: colonial powers welcomed their assistance. While the United States was not involved in this chase for colonies, it had its own form of imperialism. This was a sense of obligation to spread the American way of life of democratic freedom, capitalism and progress, and that involved missionaries: American obligation and Christian evangelization were understood as fundamentally harmonious.[43] In the age of colonial expansion it was no longer religion that divided people but ethnicity or race. The spread of Christianity was seen as an effort to better the lives of 'uncivilized savages' so that they could resemble their white masters and benefactors. Evangelization was understood as the equivalent of human progress. As well, there was the common theological belief, held by most Christians, that salvation was not possible without baptism. There was an urgency to make as many people Christian as possible. Pastoral care was about improving the material conditions of people who were racially different so that they might better be disposed to hearing the good news of the gospel and be saved. From the point of view of the recipients, acceptance of Christianity went hand in hand with access to power and material benefits possessed by Western people. Everybody stood to benefit from such an arrangement. It was on the continent of Africa that mission activity was to have its greatest success in the nineteenth century.

## New Missionary Religious Orders and Societies

As the Church in France recovered from the Revolution and gained renewed strength following changes brought about under Napoleon, new religious orders and congregations arose with a specifically missionary focus. These included the Sisters of St Joseph of Cluny, founded in 1807 by Anne-Marie Javoukey (1779-1857), who sent missionaries to the island of Réunion in the Indian Ocean and soon after to Senegal in 1819; and the Marist fathers, founded in 1824 by Jean Claude Courveille (1787-1866) and Jean Claude Marie Colin (1790-1875), and who were particularly active in the Pacific Islands. Here Pierre Chanel (1803-41) was killed by Islanders in Futuna, the first martyr of Oceania. The re-establishment of the Jesuits by Pius VII in 1814 did much to assist Catholic missionary efforts.

Pope Gregory XVI busied himself in fostering missionary activity that until then had been largely under the control of Spain and Portugal. He appointed large numbers of vicars apostolic to oversee missionary operations in different regions of the world. Rome had now begun to take more direct control through the Congregation for the Propagation of the Faith. Gregory issued a papal encyclical on missions, *Probe Nostis* (1840). Mission areas were delineated by national colonial groupings and assigned to particular religious orders and congregations.[44] Missionary societies prospered. In Lyons, Marie-Pauline Jaricot (1799-1862) founded the Society for the Propagation of the Faith in 1822 to raise funds for missionary activity. Although its work was initially focused upon France, it soon became international in scope. In Germany, Austria and elsewhere, new missionary organizations were established.

Within Protestantism, missionary and Bible societies flourished as a result of the Evangelical Awakening. One of the earliest was the Baptist Missionary Society founded by William Carey (1761-1834) in 1792. Carey went to India the following year as a missionary. There, among his many labors, he translated the Bible into numerous languages and dialects. His lobbying was largely responsible for the abolition of the ancient custom of suttee, in which a widow is put to death at her husband's funeral.[45] In 1795 the London Missionary Society was founded as a non-denominational organization to spread Christianity. An evangelical Anglican, John Venn (1759-1813), was instrumental in founding the Church Missionary Society. Well known is the British and Foreign Bible Society, an interdenominational body for printing the Bible in many languages and distributing it worldwide; it was founded in London in 1804 and remains a strong supporter of Protestant missionary activity. The Evangelical Alliance was formed after a conference in London in 1846 at which there were some eight hundred missionary delegates in attendance, representing fifty-two denominations. Missions provided one of the main catalysts for the beginnings of ecumenism at a pastoral level in the nineteenth century.[46] David Livingstone (1813-73), the English missioner and explorer, published a book called *Missionary Travels and Researches in South Africa* (1857), a work that generated much enthusiasm for missionary activity in the heart of Africa.

Missionaries from Europe, the British Isles, the United States and Canada went to many different regions in the nineteenth century in their efforts to bring pastoral care to the whole world. In Central and South America, the United States was active in missionary work where Christianity had already taken firm root in earlier centuries under the Spanish and Portuguese.

The Manchu dynasty sought to keep China closed to foreigners but treaties negotiated in 1860 and 1884 allowed for the influx of Christian missionaries in large numbers.[47] In Japan, Christian missionaries re-entered the country after 1859, following Commodore

Matthew Perry's success in drawing up an agreement with the Japanese authorities in 1853-54 that allowed foreigners to reside there. Subsequently, thousands of Japanese Christians were found: the faith had been secretly handed on over the preceding two hundred years, during which the country had been closed to the West. The Meiji Constitution of 1889 provided a permanent guarantee of religious freedom in Japan.

In nineteenth-century India, the 'jewel in the crown' of the British Empire, the Portuguese presence within Catholicism waned. Tensions arose between Portuguese bishops and vicars apostolic appointed by the Vatican. These disputes were settled when an episcopal hierarchy was established for all of India and Ceylon in 1886. By 1905 there were one and a half million Catholics in India.[48]

Catholicism came to the Philippines as early as 1521, when Spain claimed the territory, and continued its presence until 1898, when the Philippines came under American control following the Spanish-American War. In the nineteenth century tensions grew between native, nationalist Filipino priests and the Spanish; a number of the indigenous clergy were executed. As in many Latin American countries, pre-Christian beliefs and customs were not entirely eradicated in Filipino culture, making for a distinctive folk Catholicism. The Philippines remains the only country in Asia where Christianity is dominant, although South Korea saw a strong rise in Christianity after 1883 when the Korean peninsula opened up to foreigners and freedom of religion was granted.

The Pacific islands drew French Catholic missionaries, to places such as Tahiti and Noumea, but perhaps the most famous missionary in this region was the Belgian priest, Joseph de Veuster (1840-89). Better known as Father Damien, he gave his life in ministering to the physical and spiritual needs of social outcasts in the leper colony on the Hawaiian Island of Molokai. In Tonga and Fiji, Wesleyan Methodists were prominent in missionary work.

### Cardinal Lavigerie and the White Fathers in Africa

Africa was teeming with foreign missionaries in the nineteenth century. The most revered of them all was Cardinal Charles Lavigerie (1825-92), the French Archbishop of Algiers, who founded the missionary Order of the White Fathers. The new order's novitiate opened its doors in 1868; it was followed later by the Order of the White Sisters. Lavigerie had taught Church history at the Sorbonne in Paris before becoming a bishop in the French diocese of Nancy.

But it was to be in Africa where he was to achieve fame. In North Africa he took charge of the diocese of Oran and the ancient diocese of Carthage in Tunisia, the latter being restored as the primatial see of Africa. Lavigerie's pastoral responsibilities, however, were not restricted to North Africa alone. He was also appointed Vicar Apostolic for the vast regions of the Sudan and Sahara, along with Equatorial Africa. The idea was eventually to open up the interior of the continent to Catholic Christianity. Algeria was but the launching pad of this ambitious enterprise. Lavigerie was a man of extraordinary vision.

In many respects Lavigerie's pastoral methods were well ahead of his times. He insisted upon his missionaries learning about, and respecting, local cultures as they went about their task of evangelization. His way was that of the inculturation of the gospel: to weave Christian doctrine and practice into the traditional way of life of the African. To assist in this task he fostered a spirit of inquiry whereby missioners were to learn about the legends, history and religious beliefs of the different tribes and then carefully to record this knowledge. As well, he encouraged his priests to engage in patristic studies to familiarize themselves with the vitality of early Christianity in North Africa. To identify more closely with the Muslim Arabs of North Africa, Lavigerie insisted his White Fathers wear a modified form of Arab dress as their official religious habit. It is from the wearing of such a habit that these priests derive their name.[49]

Lavigerie had a scientific bent to his character. He wanted European missioners to engage in archeological research, to collect and classify local flora and fauna, to map the land and indicate the trade routes, and to initiate linguistic research. The Archbishop was keen to share this knowledge with learned individuals and professional societies back home in the cause of the advancement of French scholarship and cultural achievement.[50] Pastoral care and learning went hand in hand.

Lavigerie shared the enthusiasm of most Christians of that time to convert as many people as possible. But he insisted that missionaries should not go about proselytizing Muslims in North Africa. His instinct was one of prudence, for he appreciated how entrenched the Muslim religion was in the lives of these people. He did not want to antagonize them and so create difficulties for a Christian presence within this society. Lavigerie was of the opinion that Christians were there for the long term and so should avoid the temptation to gain quick results. But black Africans, given to tribal religions, were a different matter, for they had no historical bias against the Christian faith as did the Muslims.[51] Lavigerie restored the practice of early Christianity of gradual conversion by means of the catechumenate, something the wider Church did only after Vatican II, a century later. The first step of the conversion was entry into the level of 'postulants', during which converts would learn the fundamental truths of the Christian faith. Polygamy, widely practiced among Africans at this time, was tolerated until the prospective Christian was ready to give up old ways. Next followed the lengthy period of the catechumenate, before baptism was administered. The whole period of preparation usually took about four years.[52] Lavigerie was keen that the faith of the African Christians should be deep rather than merely touching the surface of their lives. The pastoral care of converts required a sustained effort. As a result of such efforts, Lavigerie believed it was the Africans themselves who would have to implant the Church fully in their land: the missionary phase of foreigners was but a temporary one, although he appreciated the process would probably be lengthy. He wanted an African clergy to bring about the 'Africanization' of the Church.[53]

Finally, Africa's famous cardinal is remembered for his tireless campaign to rid Africa of the slave trade. He took time to travel around Europe, preaching about the horrors of this trade in human beings. He described in graphic terms how slave traders would come to villages, burn the huts, round up the black Africans and chain them together into gangs to be then inspected and haggled over like animals by buyers in the slave markets.[54] It was a message that was heard and it helped to bring an end to this evil. It was but part of the nineteenth century's concern in pastoral care for human rights that touched political, social, and economic freedom. These concerns were also taken to the New World by Catholic migrants, to places such as the United States, Australia, and New Zealand, as well as by Irish migrants to more nearby England. Pastoral care now faced a different kind of challenge and opportunity away from its more familiar settings.

# Chapter 8

# Migrants, Teachers and Nurses

## A Church of Migrants

The mighty sailing ships, riding the blue waves of the great oceans, must have made a majestic sight in the nineteenth century. Yet, for the earlier generations of poor European migrants crossing the Atlantic to North America or those making the far longer journey to the British colonies in the South Seas, it must have been a daunting experience. Most of them had never before been on a ship at sea: they were either city workers used to urban slums or farmers from the gentle world of the countryside. Crammed into smelly, unsanitary and airless quarters beneath deck and surviving on a diet of rancid food and perhaps cheap rum, the early migrants frequently must have had second thoughts about the wisdom of their decision to go the New World. Storms and disease took their grim toll on human life aboard such ships. However, conditions for life at sea began to improve greatly. The *Archimedes*, launched in 1840, was the first seagoing vessel with a screw propeller, and that meant faster ships. By the late 1850s steam ships were supplanting sailing ships. Iron and then steel replaced wood in the construction of ships, allowing conditions on board ocean-going vessels to be more spacious and comfortable. A highly competitive passenger industry aboard steam ships developed by the late nineteenth century, drawing much of its profits from migrants who had been encouraged by improved sea transportation to migrate in much larger numbers.

Ellis Island, in New York Harbor, was the place where most immigrants first set foot on the United States after their long and arduous journey from European port cities such as Genoa, Hamburg, Odessa or Cork. They were processed there each month in their thousands, undergoing rudimentary health checks, and then sent on their way, whether to the vastly overcrowded district of Manhattan's Lower East Side, to the mining towns in Pennsylvania and West Virginia, the industrial centers of Chicago and Milwaukee, or the vast farming plains of Oklahoma and Nebraska. Most of them were young and in search of a new life that promised greater opportunity. Many found it but others remained in conditions characterized by squalor and poverty.

The invention of the steam locomotive in Britain opened the way for transporting people and materials at rapid speed across great distances on land. In 1831 the South Carolina Company began the first scheduled steam railway service in North America for passengers and freight, using an American-made locomotive named *The Best Friend of Charleston*. The world's first transcontinental railway was completed in the United States in 1869 while, across the border, the Canadian Pacific company had begun operating a scheduled railway service from Montreal to British Columbia in 1886.[1] Steam power, which first used wood and then coal, was one of the great features of the industrial revolution. Steam opened up the vast tracts of land of North America to migrants.

In the New World - in places such as the United States, Canada, Australia and New Zealand - priests and religious accompanied migrants to provide pastoral care. They came primarily for people of their own nationalities who were attempting to adapt to conditions vastly different from those that they had left behind. In these countries, just as in the missionary territories of Africa and Asia, the nineteenth-century Church of migrants was redefining its self-understanding and ways of doing things. Pastoral care in these new lands could no longer be simply taken from a European blueprint. It required novel ways of shepherding the flock.

### The Church in the United States

Within the first sixty years of the nineteenth century the population of the United States went from five to thirty-one million people. As the century progressed, migrants kept coming in greater numbers. Within the last two decades of the nineteenth century more than two million Catholics entered the country.[2] Catholics came from many different cultures but it was the Irish who came to dominate American Catholicism following the Civil War.

The Potato Famine of the late 1840s provoked many people to emigrate from Ireland, especially from the poorer regions in the west of the country. Like most emigrants, they were mainly young. Population growth and land laws contributed also to Irish emigration. By mid century many Irish Americans, especially in the big cities such as New York and Boston, had succeeded in business and politics. They had the advantage of speaking English and were politically astute, having learnt political dexterity in their long struggle against their English overlords back home. Their Catholicism and Irishness were one and the same. By 1850 the Irish made up a quarter of the population of these two eastern seaboard cities.[3] Many Irish were drawn to the Californian gold fields and made up a significant proportion of the population of San Francisco as that city developed. In 1900, two-thirds of the country's bishops were of Irish background.[4] The Irish migrants, unlike the Germans among whom lay initiative was more pronounced, were dependent on their priests for building churches. These they attended with regularity.[5] Irish Catholicism, as it was imported into America and into other Irish settlements around the globe, was strongly Jansenist in flavor, with a heavy emphasis upon sin and guilt. The Irish priests were generally close to their people and attentive to their needs but their style of pastoral care fostered clerical dependency. In the New World, the Irish priest generally found status and income of a kind that surpassed anything that he might have found in his homeland.

Over three and a half million Germans settled in the United States between 1860 and 1900, almost a third of them Catholic.[6] It seems most of the Germans came in family groups rather than as young single men and women. Generally they were in better financial circumstances than the Irish migrants. Many among them who were Catholic had fled religious oppression during the period of Bismarck's *Kulturkampf* of the 1870s, including large numbers of priests and nuns who had to leave Germany. A lot of these people joined the march westward and in doing so opened up new farming lands. German Catholicism was concentrated especially in what became known as the 'German triangle', that part of the country from Cincinnati to St Louis and Milwaukee.[7]

Polish immigrants, like the Irish, were mainly Catholic. The majority of the Poles who had migrated to America arrived after 1880. Their homeland had suffered from partition imposed by Prussia, Austria and Russia: in the late eighteenth century, these three countries had been responsible for the carving up of the old Polish kingdom. For the most part, Polish immigrants were single, poor, illiterate and happy to take low-paying jobs, something that was often resented by other national groups. Polish Catholics were viewed by their fellow Catholics as being more in need of material assistance and spiritual care than as having the capacity for pastoral leadership within American Catholicism. The Poles, more so than other Catholic migrant groups, clung on to their old religious traditions and style of pastoral care as they attempted to preserve their distinctive form of Catholic living in their strange new surroundings.[8]

The Italians brought to America a colorful and festive Catholicism intermingled with local cultural customs. Religious practice was more a matter for the women and children and there was often an anticlericalism resulting from nationalist feelings hostile to the Church in Italy. Like the Poles, who also did not begin emigrating across the Atlantic in great numbers until the 1880s, men outnumbered the women three to one; married men would send for their wives after they had got themselves settled in their new homeland.[9]

Large numbers of Eastern European Catholics, some of them belonging to Eastern Rites, brought with them to the United States religious customs unknown to other national groups: their exotic Byzantine liturgies and unusual church architecture created a distinctive religious presence that usually was achieved only after much struggle against Latin Catholics who found these other kinds of Catholics strange and alien. Among those who came from Eastern Europe were Ukrainians, Lithuanians, Czechs and Slovaks.

In the second half of the nineteenth century, some three hundred thousand French Canadians from Quebec moved to the United States. They were outspoken in their demands to bishops whom they saw as reluctant to provide them with their own priests and churches.

In the south-west of the country, especially, many Catholics were of Mexican background. The Mexican-American War (1846-48) resulted in the incorporation of a large part of Mexico into the United States. Lacking priests, these communities built their own private chapels and organized religious communities over which Church authorities exercised little control.

Finally, the vast numbers of black slaves and their descendants were among those who traveled to America, not by choice, but by cruel coercion. Slavery has had a long history in the American Church. Spanish Catholics transported slaves to Florida in the sixteenth century; English Catholics imported slaves to work their plantations in Maryland in the seventeenth century; and French Catholics used slaves in Louisiana in the eighteenth century. Throughout the South, Catholic families – like everyone else – had slaves work for them. By and large, the American Catholic bishops remained silent during the period of the abolitionist movement of the 1830s and 1840s, believing that it was much too divisive an issue in which to get involved. In the American Catholic mind of the time, talk of abolition was associated closely with the liberal and political upheavals going on within Europe from which most Catholics, as we have already seen, preferred to distance themselves.[10] It would take a Civil War to resolve the matter. Yet an adequate resolution did not happen. It seems the best the American bishops could do was to encourage religious congregations from Europe to come to evangelize the emancipated African-American population: this decision was taken at the Second Plenary Council in Baltimore in 1866. The Mill Hill Fathers from England were the first to respond to this invitation. Segregation remained the norm in Catholic institutions: one form of pastoral care for white Catholics and a different one for black Catholics. African-American Catholics found themselves a second class group within the Church.[11]

Things improved a little following the Third Plenary Council of 1884. It instituted an annual collection for Indians and African Americans and prescribed that seminarians be encouraged to work among black Americans and that lay catechists be formed for this task as well. Katharine Drexel (1858-1955), a wealthy woman from Philadelphia, was inspired, in 1891, to establish a religious congregation known as the Sisters of the Blessed Sacrament for Indians and Colored People.

The first three African American priests in the United States were all brothers, born in Georgia. Their mother, Mary Eliza, was a slave and mistress to an Irishman named Michael Healy. One of their sons, Patrick Healy (1834-1910), became President of the Jesuit Georgetown University in Washington but concealed his African-American origins for much of his illustrious career. Alexander Healy (1836-75) was a priest of the Boston Archdiocese. And James Healy (1830-1900) became the Bishop of Portland in Maine and the first black Catholic bishop in the United States.[12] But the first priest to be recognized as fully black was Augustus Tolon (1854-97), a former slave from Missouri, who worked in parishes in Illinois and who always felt himself to be something of a curiosity in a segregated society.[13]

The most prominent black Catholic layman in nineteenth-century America was Daniel Rudd (1854-1933) who tirelessly sought justice and better pastoral care from the Church for his people. The newspaper he founded in 1886, the *American Catholic Tribune*, and a series of black Catholic national congresses sought to improve the condition of black American Catholics. The first of these congresses, all of which were socially, politically and religiously motivated, took place in the parish of St Augustine in Washington D.C., one of the oldest black churches in the country. Rudd strongly opposed segregation and fervently believed that Catholicism had the power to break the color barrier in America. Rudd's congresses called for setting up parishes and special industrial schools for blacks. As a result of damage upon blacks caused by the effects of alcohol, appeals were made for temperance. The congresses recognized the need for the Church to establish charitable institutions for blacks: orphanages, hospitals, and mental health institutions. And they demanded equal employment opportunities for black Americans and that all trade unions and other labor organizations admit black workers. Further, they called for non-discriminatory rental practices concerning housing.[14] In the absence of a black clergy, pastoral care and leadership among African-American Catholics in the nineteenth century was carried out, strongly and effectively, by lay Catholics.

Pastoral care in the migrant Church of America fostered a strong devotionalism: it was characterized by a plethora of symbolic activities and pious practices. Catholic life was a continuous round of activity, including devotion to the Sacred Heart, recurring novenas, the Rosary and Benediction of the Blessed Sacrament. There were sentimental holy cards depicting saints and First Communion images, devotional prayer books, gaudy religious paintings and statues, and festive processions among the different ethnic groups. Medals and scapulars were worn to assure heavenly protection and salvation. Catholics were enrolled in confraternities for men or for women. Revivalist style parish missions were popular, with itinerant preachers from the different orders wearing their eye-catching religious habits that contrasted with the more plain attire of the regular parish clergy. Few Catholics read the Bible and they 'heard' Mass in the esoteric, Latin language. It all reinforced Protestant perceptions of Catholicism as mechanical and given to outward form, rather than inward disposition. But such devotionalism united diverse Catholic migrants into a kind of tribalism against the dominant society that was white, Anglo and Protestant, a society often experienced as culturally strange, even hostile. Catholic migrants, despite their varying ethnic religious traditions, felt a common bond that helped them adjust to their new surroundings.

One of the pastoral issues that caused concern within the nineteenth-century American Church was the practice known as 'trusteeism'. It arose at a time when priests were few, resulting in the ownership and administration of local Church property and revenues being in the hands of lay, congregational trustees. It was they who initially had taken responsibility for building churches and setting up parishes. As well as exercising financial control, trustees might take it upon themselves to hire and fire clergy and engage in other demonstrations of strength against the power of bishops within dioceses. Among German American congregations, in particular, trusteeism of this kind was common. John England (1786-1842), when Bishop of Charleston, South Carolina, encouraged a modified form of lay trusteeism that he saw as being in keeping with American democratic values. His idea was for each parish to elect a board of trustees, with the local pastor taking on the role of president of the board. Finances were to be the principal concern of these parish boards, allowing a certain amount of authority to be shared between the pastor and his parishioners. Women were not eligible for membership.[15]

But many bishops and clergy fought vigorously against the trustee system, which they interpreted as undermining their authority. The First Provincial Council in Baltimore (1829) legislated against trusteeism in an attempt to assert episcopal authority, but it was not entirely successful. The system continued in different places and did not come fully to an end until the Third Plenary Council of Baltimore (1884), although popularly elected parish committees were allowed to continue but with limited authority. Ownership of Church property and the appointment of clergy to parishes were now firmly in the hands of the bishops.

In the closing two decades of the nineteenth century, a divisive debate took hold of American Catholicism that struck at the very heart of the way the Church went about its pastoral care. Should the Church adopt a pastoral practice that accepted the dominant values and ways of doing things of the new country so as to make the faith of the migrant better fit conditions in the United States? Or should it continue fostering the old, ethnic traditions, to maintain a style of faith familiar to, and long cherished by, the migrant? It was a controversy that became known as 'Americanization'. The bishops had already set up a dual system of parishes in the United States. Some were territorial, to which people belonged according to the geographic area in which they lived, while others were national parishes, which catered for the different ethnic groups by using their own language and customs in liturgical celebrations.

Those who believed faith could flourish only if the Church accommodated itself to the modern age embodied in American culture belonged to the Americanist party, led by Archbishop John Ireland (1838-1918) of St Paul, Cardinal James Gibbons (1834-1921) of Baltimore, Bishop John Keane (1839-1918) of the Catholic University of America, and Dennis O'Connell (1849-1927) of the

North American College in Rome. For them, Catholic life in America could be sustained only if it embraced democratic principles, separation of Church and state, religious freedom, and a willingness to cooperate with other religions in civic and social causes. They believed such American values were able to be harmonized with the essential beliefs and forms of ecclesiastical government of the universal Catholic Church. For example, members of this party strongly supported George McGlynn, who campaigned in the political forum for economic reform on behalf of American workers.

Fiercely opposed to such a stand were those who maintained that it was only by hanging on as long as possible to the language and traditional forms of Catholic life - which migrants brought to America from their country of origin - that their faith could survive in America. In this view, an ethnic Catholicism – whether German, Irish, Italian, Polish or whatever – was the best means of holding together the Catholic community in multicultural America. Migrants who had been uprooted from all that was familiar needed to gather in parishes to worship and socialize with people of their own kind. It was a far more inward looking idea of Church. The party belonging to this school of thought was led by American-born Archbishop Michael Corrigan (1839-1902) of New York.[16]

The Americanist party received a setback with Leo XIII's encyclical, *Testem Benevolentiae* (1899). While praising the achievements of the Catholic Church in the United States, Leo singled out three issues for criticism: excessive accommodation to the prevailing culture, a spirit of religious subjectivism, and a new kind of ecclesiastical nationalism. Was this a fear of a revived form of Gallicanism across the Atlantic, the assertion of a certain independence from Rome, as had happened earlier in France?[17] The Americanists did not take kindly to the Pope's observations and felt that the condemnations did not match the reality of the American Church. But they were courteous enough to thank him. Corrigan, with perhaps mixed feelings over such negative observations about his own Church, wrote a submissive response to Leo. While acknowledging he was proud of his American nationality, Corrigan went on to write: 'in the matter of religion, doctrine, discipline, morals, and Christian perfection, we glory in thoroughly following the Holy See'.[18]

In that spirit of energy and practical accomplishment that so characterizes the American way of life, the nineteenth-century migrant Church threw itself into two major pastoral concerns alongside that of church building, namely, education and health care. But the story about all this will be taken up later in this chapter.

## The Church in Australia and New Zealand

Like the United States, Australia today is a multicultural country made up of migrants from all regions of the world. But the histories of these two nations differ vastly and, as a result, the Church in each of these lands tells a very different story about itself. Unlike the Pilgrim Fathers who went on their knees in a prayer of thanksgiving upon arriving on American soil at Plymouth, Australia's first European settlers knelt down to be flogged by the shores of Sydney Cove. They were convicts sent to a faraway British colony in the South Pacific, in a journey that took eight to nine months. As a result of the American War of Independence, Britain was no longer able to ship its unwanted felons to places such as Georgia. European settlement in Australia, then, has a direct link with events in America. The first of the convicts and their jailers arrived in Australia in 1788. They found themselves confronted by a vast continent, approximately equal in landmass to the United States, inhabited by strange animals and a human population made up entirely of black, aboriginal people. Although the coastal fringe of the continent was fertile, most of this enormous island was a dry desert. Free settlers from the British Isles were soon to follow the convicts, but the nation's penal origins remain deeply ingrained in the national psyche. Transportation of convicts to Australia was to continue until 1853.

Migrants came almost exclusively from the British Isles until Australia embarked on a migration program that involved people from other national groupings. This happened in only the middle of the twentieth century, after the Second World War. Most of the migrants who came at first under the new immigration scheme were of European or Middle Eastern background because of the infamous White Australia Policy that was operating at the time. But things were to change and the country today is ethnically diverse, built on Western European traditions but set geographically on the edge of South-East Asia.

In the nineteenth century, almost all of the Catholics in Australia were of Irish origin, making the Catholic Church in Australia unlike the more ethnically diverse Catholic Church of the United States at that time. Very few free Irish settlers came to Australia as a result of the Famine. It was too far away for destitute Irish. The great age of Irish emigration to Australia was from the 1850s to the 1880s, as settlers came in search of a fortune to be made from gold or the land. It was a Church of migrants: convicts, former prisoners now emancipated or having served their sentences, and free settlers, but nearly all belonged to the same national grouping. By 1803 Governor Philip King (1758-1808) estimated that almost a quarter of the inhabitants of New South Wales were Catholic.

The Irish convicts, much to their dislike, were obliged to attend Church of England services. Three Irish Catholic priests, convicted of political offences, had arrived as convicts in 1798 and one of them, James Dixon (1758-1840), was permitted to celebrate a public Mass. But this privilege was quickly withdrawn following an uprising in which Irish convicts were involved. Many among the English establishment in the young colony identified Irish Catholicism with rebellion, such as the Anglican chaplain Samuel Marsden (1764-1838), who doubled as a magistrate. This clergyman acquired the nickname of the 'flogging parson' for his cruelty in ordering punishment for disorderly offenders. Especially in Sydney, there remains to this day a deep distrust and a certain antagonism towards clerics who moralize in the public forum.

It was not until 1820, more than thirty years after the colony had been established, that two priests, John Therry (1790-1864) and Philip Conolly (1786-1839) were allowed to exercise pastoral care among all Catholics.[19] But the two men quarreled and Conolly went to Tasmania, where, subsequently, he was implicated in some shady property deals that resulted in his priestly faculties being withdrawn for a time. Therry carried on in Sydney, performing the basic pastoral duties of administering the sacraments, caring for the sick and attending to the spiritual needs of the Irish Catholic community. Much of his time was given to the convicts, visiting the prisons and preparing those condemned to death on the scaffold. For a time he went to Tasmania, where Conolly's pastorate had deteriorated. Therry was a cantankerous character but was able to speak his people's language, one that was about money and cattle.[20] As Patrick O'Farrell notes, Therry's ministry was, more than anything else, a ministry given to practical morality, to redeeming humanity from criminal behavior in the depraved moral climate of colonial Australia.[21]

Within this small outpost of Irish Catholicism in Sydney came an English Benedictine monk to be Australia's first bishop, in 1835. His name was John Bede Polding (1794-1877) and he brought with him a small group of monks from his old home of Downside Abbey in

England. The Archbishop's dream was that of a colonial Church founded upon and drawing its inspiration and strength from monastic life: a Benedictine monastic spirituality providing a clear light for the building up of an Australian Catholicism. It was an attempt to re-ignite the medieval idea of monastic culture taming the forces of barbarism. But Polding's dream was doomed from the outset. For a start, the majority of those in his charge were not English but Irish. As well, Polding found it difficult to persuade English Benedictines to leave the tranquility of Downside for a distant and uncultivated colony in Australia. As more priests arrived from Ireland, the Benedictine dream began quickly to evaporate. About two thousand priests came to Australia in the nineteenth century. They were practically all Irish and the bishops among them came almost exclusively from the Irish College in Rome.[22] It was in Cardinal Patrick Moran, who became Archbishop of Sydney in 1884, that an Irish Church, but one with a distinctively Australian flavor, would reach its apotheosis.

Yet Polding was no monk living in seclusion from the outside world. He was a pastoral bishop engaged in a life of constant travel on horseback around his vast diocese. He would often be away for weeks at a time, visiting the Irish Catholics, living in small and remote communities around the countryside. He encouraged his clergy to do the same. In Sydney, he was able to gain permission to greet newly arriving ships with their cargo of convicts. He would take the Catholics among them and then, for a few days, he and his priests would give them religious instruction and the opportunity to repent of their sins in sacramental confession. By 1841, just six years after Polding's arrival as Archbishop, as many as seven thousand convicts had passed through this form of spiritual initiation into his struggling diocese.[23]

As well, Polding took a special interest in the welfare of Aboriginal people and expressed views as to their situation that were well ahead of his time. Tensions between white settlers and Aboriginal people over the use of land, along with racial prejudice, resulted in frequent slaughter of the native people whose spears were no match for the muskets of the Europeans. In Tasmania they were systematically hunted down, either killed or shipped off to nearby islands in Bass Strait. By 1863 only seven Aborigines remained in Britain's island colony of Tasmania, south of the mainland.[24] In Western Australia, where another Benedictine monastery existed at New Norcia, the Spanish monk Dom Rudesindus Salvado (1814-1900) attempted to familiarize himself with Aboriginal culture and language and so to reach out to Aboriginal people. But this was not typical of the nineteenth-century Australian Church.[25] It would not be until the following century that a mission to the Aboriginal people would become more organized, especially through the setting up of mission stations in more remote areas known as the 'outback'. They served Aboriginal people in providing education and health care within the context of evangelization. But these were generally paternalistic institutions, isolating those living within them from their own cultural traditions.

Australia in the early part of the nineteenth century was, to a large extent, a frontier society. The early explorers, as they moved into the unknown interior of the country, paved the way for opening up new lands to farm crops and graze sheep and cattle. Young women made their way to this new country as migrants from England and Scotland, Wales and Ireland, in search of a better life and a husband. Few probably realized the challenges that awaited them. Understanding the vulnerability of these young women and the risk that they ran of falling into prostitution was Caroline Chisholm (1808-77), the wife of an officer within the British Army in India. The pair arrived in Sydney in 1838 while he was on leave from Madras. Caroline had been raised as an Evangelical Anglican in which Christianity and social concern were bound together. She became a Catholic but her social conscience, acquired in her Anglican days, never left her. She remained in Australia and threw herself into caring for young migrant women, irrespective of their religion. She would arrange for them to be met at the docks, see to their temporary accommodation and assist some of them in finding jobs in the city. In large groups of as many as fifty or sixty women, Caroline would escort them into the countryside - or the 'bush' as rural Australia is called - to find them placements as housemaids. Her wagons, filled with young women, became a familiar sight along the dusty roads of New South Wales. She was confident her female migrants would soon meet the right man among the sons of Australian farmers.

But her efforts were not to stop there. With six children of her own, she believed that stable family life was the foundation needed for a new country such as Australia. Chisholm campaigned in London and succeeded in establishing the Family Colonization Loan Scheme to assist the economically disadvantaged to migrate as a family unit.[26] As well, she was able to persuade the British Government to provide free passage to Australia for the wives and children of convicts whose sentences had been served. Chisholm's own words sum up her convictions:

All the clergy you can dispatch, all the school-masters you can appoint, all the churches you can build and all the books you can export, will never do much without God's police – wives and little children.[27]

Caroline Chisholm's strong passion for the special needs of migrants led to her advocacy for the improvement of conditions on board the ships that brought them to their new homeland. In the 1850s this remarkable woman went to the Victorian gold fields to do what she could amidst the social upheavals that characterized such places. But upon a return visit home to England, she fell into poverty and died. Caroline Chisholm is remembered as a Catholic laywoman who made an outstanding and unique contribution to the life of Australia in the care she provided amidst the circumstances of a pioneering society, a care that came out of her Catholic faith.[28]

Unlike Australia, New Zealand was not settled by convicts. Until well into the twentieth century, the majority of those who migrated there came from the British Isles. Many Scots settled in the South Island of the country. In the earlier part of the nineteenth century New Zealand fell within Rome's designation of the Pacific region: a missionary responsibility of the French. The country's first bishop was Jean-Baptiste Pompallier (1801-71) who arrived in 1838. But by 1872, with New Zealand being an English-speaking country, the two French bishops had departed and the country found itself with two Irish bishops. Most of the Catholics were Irish free settlers who increased greatly in numbers following the gold rushes and a government-sponsored immigration program in the 1870s. As happened in Australia, New Zealand Catholicism was of an Irish flavor. But New Zealand was a more Protestant country, by proportion of population, and Catholicism had a weaker presence than its neighbor across the Tasman Sea. The indigenous Maori people fared much better in New Zealand than did the Aborigines in Australia and the Church turned much of its pastoral attention to serving their needs.[29]

### English Catholicism

In nineteenth-century England, like today, Catholicism was made up of three distinct groups, of which migrants were one. And most of the Catholic migrants were Irish who congregated in the larger cities such as Liverpool, London and Manchester. There, the Irish migrants found jobs after their short crossing of the Irish Sea. By 1850 the Irish made up eighty per cent of the Catholic Church in England.[30] Most came from a farming background and adjustment to city life was often difficult. Many of the English Catholics looked down upon the Irish, seeing them as belonging to a lower social class in which their religion was inseparable from political agitation against England's rule over Ireland.

The second group of Catholics in nineteenth-century England was made up of the 'old' Catholic families, those who had preserved their Catholic faith throughout the upheavals of the English Reformation. Many of these people came from upper-class society and were deeply attached to their faith, which drew its inspiration and identity from the memory of the English Catholic martyrs. They were particularly strong in the north of England and saw themselves as a socially oppressed group within English society. These Catholics attempted to make themselves as distinct as possible from Anglicans, especially in their style of Catholic worship.

The third group among English Catholics were those who converted from Anglicanism, especially in the aftermath of the Oxford Movement, which sought to bring more Catholic doctrine and devotional practices into the life of the Church of England.[31] John Henry Newman (1801-90) was the most famous of these converts. He was an academic from Balliol College in Oxford and was received into the Catholic Church in 1845. He introduced the Oratorians of St Philip Neri into England in 1848. The following year Newman opened the Oratory house at Alcester Street in Birmingham, a place that he described as a 'gloomy gin distillery of which we have taken a lease, fitting up a large room for a Chapel'.[32] Newman intended the Birmingham house to be a base from which to evangelize workers in the large industrial towns of the Midlands. The Birmingham Oratory, with a parish attached, thrived and was a source of many converts to Catholicism from the working class. But Rome had other ideas. It desired the English Oratorians to exercise an apostolate among the better educated and upper classes, as was to happen at the London Oratory that opened in 1849. It was an effort to raise the tone of English Catholicism and make it more respectable in a country where the Catholic Church was in the minority and looked down upon by the powerbrokers of the land who belonged to the established Church of England. Newman provided the intellectual basis for a renewed Catholicism through his many publications. In 1879, in his old age, he was made a cardinal.

Earlier, it was only in 1829 that English Catholics came to enjoy full rights as citizens, including eligibility to enter Parliament, but certain restrictions persisted concerning the exercise of Catholic practices in public. In 1850 the Catholic hierarchy was re-established in England, with Cardinal Nicholas Wiseman (1802-65) as the first Archbishop of Westminster. It was Wiseman's pastoral challenge as leader of the English Church, as also that of Henry Manning (1808-92) who followed him, to bring together the three potentially divisive groups that made up the Catholic population. Unlike what happened in the United States and Australia in the nineteenth century, most of the Catholic bishops in England were not Irish but English, drawn from the 'old' Catholic families and Catholics who had converted from Anglicanism.

Wiseman loved Rome and everything Roman. He had lived there for twenty-two years, after having gone to the English College in that city as a sixteen year old adolescent. He was fond of dressing up in the resplendent, scarlet robes of a cardinal. Ostentation came naturally to him. The Oratorian priest, Frederick Faber (1814-63), himself not backward in adopting pomp and ceremony in the cause of the gospel, once quipped about Wiseman that 'when in full tog he looked like some Japanese God'.[33] Wiseman, and then Manning, championed ultramontanism. They molded English Catholicism, so long cut off from direct Roman influence, into a Church fiercely loyal to the papacy. They saw a 'Roman' stamp as fundamental if the Catholic Church was to be an effective instrument of pastoral ministry within a predominantly Protestant society existing in England. Catholicism had to look different and appear as part of a larger and more powerful institution that was universal.

English ultramontanes favored building churches in the neoclassical style of the Italianate Baroque whereas the 'old' English Catholics leant more towards the neo-Gothic revival made popular by Augustus Pugin (1812-52). He had become a Catholic in 1834, a decade before the Oxford Movement led to a flow of converts from Anglicanism. Pugin firmly believed that the way to redeem the casualties of Christianity resulting from the bleak world of nineteenth-century industrialism was through the art and spirit of the Gothic Middle Ages. For Pugin, the Gothic and Catholicism were synonymous.[34]

Manning, also a convert from Anglicanism, was one of the principal figures in the movement to promote the doctrine of papal infallibility, so desired by Pius IX, at the First Vatican Council. Ultramontanism found strong support in England. William Ward (1812-82), another convert to Catholicism and extreme in his support of ultramontane principles, is said to have remarked that nothing would please him more than a new papal infallible statement on his breakfast table every morning accompanying *The Times*.[35] But there were those who were less enthusiastic about such a policy, notably Newman, believing it to be harmful to the fostering of a distinctive English form of Catholicism acceptable to the wider society in Britain. For Catholics such as Newman and John Acton (1834-1902), ultramontanism ran the risk of making Catholicism an alien element within English life. Manning wrote critically in 1866:

> I see much damage of an English Catholicism, of which Newman is the highest type. It is an old Anglican, patristic, literary, Oxford tone translated into the Church.[36]

Yet Manning mixed freely with members of other Churches. He involved himself in many social causes that saw him drawn into the wider community. These interests included penal reform, education, improved housing, and trade union disputes. His pastoral involvement reached deep into the life of Britain in the cause of social reform.

Father Frederick Faber's style of Catholic evangelism contributed to another characteristic form of pastoral care in the nineteenth-century English Church, namely, emotionally charged piety. He, too, was a convert from Anglicanism and belonged to the English Oratory, like Newman. Yet in temperament and theological outlook the two men could not have been more different. There was considerable tension between the Birmingham Oratory, led by Newman, and Faber's London Oratory, which moved from its original site to the current one in Brompton. Faber's approach promoted sentimental, popular prayers that included devotions to Jesus and Mary of the most saccharine kind. A celebrated preacher who drew great crowds, Faber employed a florid rhetoric that used vivid images. By doing so, he could arouse strong emotions in his congregation. The Father Faber spirituality was that salvation was never easy and human beings were under the constant threat of eternal punishment. He composed many hymns that became so familiar a sound in Catholic churches. Faber's method of a devotional style of pastoral care was extremely popular in Victorian England and his hymns and books were known widely throughout the English-speaking Catholic world.

Finally, mention should be made of two Italian priests involved in pastoral activities in England at this same time and who had great impact. First, there was Luigi Gentili (1801-48), a member of the Rosminian Fathers. He was a popular preacher among the working-class poor of the large industrial cities. His general appeal resulted in large numbers of converts that included dissenters, such as Methodists and Baptists. Dominic Barberi (1792-1849), whom Newman once described as a man whose 'very look had about it something holy',[37] conducted missions that breathed fresh life into the Catholic people. Under the influence of priests such as Faber, Gentili and Barberi, a popular style of Catholicism flourished in England.

## Catholic Education

### American Catholic Schools

It was not until the nineteenth century that education became widely available for all classes of people in Western countries. Schooling came to be assumed to be the responsibility of government since education was seen as a basic human right according to the liberal values of free and democratic societies. It was in the state of Massachusetts in 1852 that education was first made compulsory for children eight to fourteen years of age. By 1918 compulsory education had extended to every state in the Union.[38] However, the Catholic Church in the United States came to interpret public education as a threat to its own value system in a predominantly Protestant land. And so, in the American immigrant Church, the widespread provision of independent Catholic schools, staffed by religious sisters and brothers, became an urgent pastoral priority.

Important for understanding the beginning of the Catholic school system in the United States is locating its origins in the context of the Public School Society of the early nineteenth century. This organization, under the direction of evangelical Protestant gentlemen, was responsible for running schools in New York with the aid of government funding. Because of the Protestant ethos that the Public School Society fostered in the schools, many Catholics grew to resent what they saw as religious intrusion and discrimination in the education of their children. As a result, Catholics requested public funding to run their own schools or exemption from the taxes they were paying into the common educational fund. The Irish-born bishop of New York, John Hughes (1779-1864) led this campaign over a two-year period. It failed. The debate had been a bitter one. The result was that no public money was to be made available to any school that taught religious sectarian doctrines.[39] Hughes became a leading advocate for Catholics who were setting up their own schools throughout the country.

Horace Mann (1796-1859), a Unitarian, opposed sectarian religious dogma of any kind. As Secretary of the Massachusetts Board of Education from 1837, Mann was behind the drive for public schools that had become part of everyday life in America by the 1850s.[40]

Public schools were meant to be secular in nature. Church-sponsored Sunday schools were to provide religious instruction.[41] Nevertheless, Public schools were seen to endorse the dominant Protestant values of the day that were the basis of American culture. Catholics saw this as an imposition of Protestant ideology and became more strongly committed to setting up a separate Catholic school system for the education of their children. Catholic schools were also seen to assist in strengthening the ethnic traditions among the different groups of immigrants, many of whom felt alienated from a secularized system of education.

While the Catholic school system developed, the Vatican issued an instruction to the American bishops in 1876 that spoke out against public schools and endorsed the policy, set at the First Plenary Council of Baltimore (1852), of setting up Catholic schools throughout the country. Exercising its muscle, Rome ordered that parents who refused to send their children to Church schools should be denied the sacraments. While such a pastoral policy was implemented widely throughout the American Church, some bishops spoke out against it.[42]

Catholic schools received a boost through decisions reached in the Third Plenary Council of Baltimore (1884). The Council obliged pastors to ensure that a parochial school, where it did not already exist, was in place within their parishes within two years. Parents were ordered to support Catholic schools financially and to send their children to them. Encouragement was also offered for the building of Catholic high schools but it was only in the twentieth century that these became widespread, although colleges for men were founded in different parts of the country during the nineteenth century. These included Manhattan College (1852) and Boston College (1863).[43] Catholic women's colleges did not become established until towards the end of the nineteenth century, for example, Trinity College in Washington D.C., founded in 1897. Bernard McQuaid (1823-1909), the Bishop of Rochester, was a strong voice in support of Catholic schools. But not all the bishops favored a separate Catholic schooling system. These bishops believed Catholic schools segregated American Catholics from the overall community as well as acting as a financial drain on Church resources that could be put to better pastoral uses. A spokesperson for this viewpoint was Edward Fitzgerald (1833-1907), Bishop of Little Rock, Arkansas, who was also, incidentally, one of only seven bishops to vote against the doctrine of papal infallibility at the First Vatican Council. Fitzgerald once remarked that bishops 'were ordained to teach catechism not to teach school'.[44] But the Bishop of Little Rock was a minority voice. Catholic schools, as well as colleges and universities, became, and have remained, a central feature of pastoral ministry within American Catholicism.

To staff such a vast enterprise as the country's Catholic schools, bishops recruited from abroad and founded religious orders and congregations within America; these orders also swelled the numbers of religious sisters and brothers throughout the Church in the nineteenth century. A vocation to religious life now became a profession of teaching or nursing. The Sisters of Mercy, for example, founded by Catherine McAuley (1778-1841) in Dublin, embarked on a worldwide mission of pastoral care in education and health. Pastoral ministry, such as education, was the public face of Catholicism that touched families first-hand, especially in immigrant countries like the United States. These religious women and men followed migrants to staff the schools and provided a cheap source of labor. Far too often they were exploited by bishops and pastors.

Among the religious were the Irish Christian Brothers founded by Edmund Ignatius Rice (1762-1844); he opened a boys' school in Waterford in 1803 and formed his religious society in 1809. In the French city of Lyons, the Marist Brothers of the Schools was founded by St Marcellin Champagnat (1789-1840) in 1817. In the United States, the Marist Brothers began staffing schools from 1886. Not only were sisters and brothers recruited in vast numbers from Europe, they were also drawn from the many new religious foundations born within the immigrant Church of America.

Elizabeth Seton (1774-1821), the first American-born saint, canonized in 1975, was a wealthy widow from an Episcopalian family whose husband had died in Italy. She was received into the Catholic Church in New York in 1805. At the invitation of the Sulpicians, she founded a school for girls in Baltimore. She later moved to Emmitsburg, Pennsylvania where she immersed herself in the growing Catholic school system and founded the Sisters of Charity of St Joseph, sisters especially dedicated to the education of poor children. She sent sisters to care for the dispossessed in Philadelphia and New York. Among her special concerns were black Americans for whom she provided much needed material and spiritual care. Her religious community grew rapidly to number sixteeen hundred members by 1900.[45]

### Australian Catholic Schools

The emergence of Catholic schools in Australia followed a remarkably similar pattern to that in the United States. Catholics in both countries found themselves living in a predominantly Protestant environment in which sectarian feelings ran high. Immigrant Catholics in both places wanted to preserve their Catholic identity in what many of them perceived to be an environment hostile to their faith. As well, nineteenth-century public education was founded upon the principles of liberalism and Catholics saw this as promoting secular values antagonistic to their religion. And, in the different English colonies within Australia where most Catholics were of Irish background, the Irish political question of home rule was inseparable from Irish Catholicism. Catholics did not want their children indoctrinated in state-controlled schools where the Irish position would be drowned from consciousness. A public education system that was free, compulsory but secular held as little appeal for immigrant Catholics in Australia as it did in America. In both places the pastoral plan was for an alternative system that consumed both their money and energy. Catholic schools, like churches, were built on the pennies of struggling Catholic workers. As such, they comprised an amazing achievement. Catholic pastoral care in both countries became strongly identified with Catholic schools.

Until about 1848 schools in Australia were left in the hands of the various Churches and assisted by small government grants. From the late 1840s governments in the different Australian colonies began to set up denominational boards of education, composed entirely of lay staffs, and supplemented by small educational boards at the local level. Accordingly, there was a range of boards to oversee state-run schools and the different denominational schools. Denominational schools continued to receive funding. As a result, from 1848, Catholic schools increased four-fold to number some two hundred schools in 1858.[46] But the good times were not to last. State funding for denominational schools began to diminish greatly as governments sought more control over education. Some bishops, most notably James Goold (1812-86) in Melbourne, believed government-controlled education was a sinister attempt to annihilate the Catholic faith. But the state's aim was to raise standards of education within the country. The question then arose as to how far the Church was prepared to compromise its style of schooling for purposes of obtaining school grants from governments.

Things came to a head with the New South Wales *Public Schools Act* of 1866, introduced by Henry Parkes (1815-96), a public figure who would later be influential in leading the independent states into federation as a single Australian nation in 1901. Parkes was no friend to Catholics and was known for his cry of 'No Popery', which helped to serve his political ambitions. Parkes' Act abolished denominational school boards and placed all schools under a Council of Education. It now became apparent that government-supported schools would be neither Protestant nor Catholic. They would be neutral. Catholic parents saw this as an infringement on their right to educate their children in the way they wanted. And Church leaders believed they had an obligation to ensure that a Christian education would be available to children. A form of schooling that overlooked religious doctrine was seen as a grave deficiency.[47]

Archbishop Polding in Sydney, by way of response, established a Catholic Association in 1867 to lobby for better government aid to denominational schools. In the ecclesiastical background to this debate was the formal condemnation of purely secular schools run by governments that Pius IX had issued in his *Syllabus of Errors* of 1864. Protestants saw this condemnation as influencing Catholics into becoming enemies of Australian values and nationality, something that Catholic leaders were quick to reject. It was the Americanization debate of the nineteenth century replicated in a different cultural setting.

In 1869, the Provincial Council of the Catholic Church in Australia laid out a clear blueprint for the future of Catholic schools. Catholic schools received the full go-ahead to be institutions that would create a clear Catholic ethos through both their doctrinal syllabus and their overall religious atmosphere. The bishops stated forthrightly that no government had the right to enforce attendance at schools where religious teachings had no place. Pastoral care demanded that parents themselves accept the responsibility to educate their children in the Catholic faith by supporting Church-sponsored schools. Archbishop Roger Vaughan (1834-83), also an English Benedictine monk from Downside Abbey like Archbishop Polding, and who had succeeded him as Archbishop of Sydney, placed the education issue to the forefront of his pastoral priorities in the 1870s and 1880s. Vaughan was academically inclined and naturally drawn to the issue of education. Government aid to Church schools in Australia came to an end in 1880 with the *Public Instruction Act*. But the Catholic school system continued and expanded, on its own, without financial assistance.[48] So much emphasis did Vaughan give to Catholic education that he was able to write in 1880:

> I look upon the crisis we have gone through as resulting in the salvation of the Catholic religion in this colony. Nothing less would have done it.[49]

Vaughan was also very much interested in higher education. He founded, and became Rector of, St John's College for young men within the University of Sydney, an institution modeled in architecture and spirit upon the colleges of Oxford and Cambridge. He intended to create an educated lay and clerical elite to lead the Catholic Church into a respected and influential place within Australian society.

As had happened in the United States, an army of religious orders and congregations were imported from Europe to staff Catholic schools. In the Irish Church of Australia, the bishops looked principally to Ireland to supply religious sisters and brothers, and they went there on recruiting campaigns. Many young people, often just adolescents, responded and went to Australia to teach in schools in cities and in remote rural areas. Most never saw their families again. These pioneers relied more on faith and goodwill than upon any kind of adequate training for teaching. Often they found themselves living in conditions that were both physically and emotionally demanding.

Mary MacKillop (1842-1909), a young teacher in her twenties, lived in the small town of Penola in the state of South Australia. Here she met an English priest, a man in his thirties with an interest in geology: Julian Tenison Woods (1832-89). He combined his priestly duties with being in charge of education within the diocese. Their personalities were very different. She was practical, decisive and clear sighted. He was a volatile and restless dreamer with such a presence that, as his biographer Margaret Press observes, 'people did not easily ignore him or forget him'.[50] At Woods' suggestion, Mary opened a small school in the town in what had once been a horse stable.

At a time when the education issue had become so central in Catholic life in Australia, MacKillop and Woods went about setting up a new religious congregation of women with a pastoral mission of teaching the poor. Despite a series of setbacks and disappointments – which included Mary's being excommunicated, for a short time, on the charge of insubordination, by the authoritarian Franciscan Bishop Lawrence Sheil (1815-72) of Adelaide - large numbers of women joined the Congregation of the Sisters of St Joseph. By 1871 the Josephites were in charge of thirty-five schools in the Adelaide diocese.[51] However, Woods, with his difficult temperament, was to break off his friendship with Mary, something that caused her much pain.

The Josephites, committed as they were to reaching out to the poor, took on schools in places that other religious sisters were reluctant to accept: small country towns and city slums. A condescending parish pastor in Townsville thought of them as 'ignorant servant girls'.[52] Mary MacKillop became the first Australian to be beatified, in 1995. Without the Sisters of St Joseph, Catholic education in Australia probably could never have achieved what it did: the pastoral care of so great a number of young Australians whose minds and hearts were opened to learning and to God.[53]

### Catholic Schools in England

The development of a Catholic school system in England followed a similar pattern to that in Australia and the United States. By the 1850s, in all three of these countries, Catholic bishops had begun to push seriously for Church-sponsored schools that would provide education resting upon Catholic principles. Catholic schools would exist alongside schools run by governments, the latter being seen as based upon entirely secular foundations. Things came to a head in England with the passing of the 1870 *Education Act* that brought in a unified system of national education in which religion was explicitly excluded from government-sponsored schools. The bishops responded rapidly by issuing a joint pastoral letter of condemnation in 1871. In it they criticized any notion of education from which religion was excluded seeing it as 'not even instruction'.[54] Catholic schools continued to be eligible for public funding but opinion was divided among the Catholic bishops about whether to accept this money. Many feared the lack of Church control when schools received government aid. By the end of the nineteenth century, a little less than a half of Catholic elementary schools were being given government aid.[55] Cardinal Manning led the way in England for promoting Catholic schools in the latter part of the nineteenth century.

Catholic secondary schools also grew in number since many boys from Catholic families no longer sought an education on the Continent. This was because of the upheavals of the French Revolution as well as the easing of anti-Catholic legislation in England itself. The Benedictines set up secondary schools in Downside and Ampleforth, and the Jesuits in Stonyhurst. Secondary schools such as these, which catered to the more wealthy class of Catholics, expanded in number in the second half of the nineteenth century.

As elsewhere in the Catholic world, large numbers of religious congregations and orders moved into schooling in England, seeing this as an emerging field for pastoral care. Long established orders such as the Dominicans, Franciscans and Augustinians became involved in education along with brothers who had a specialized teaching apostolate, such as the De La Salle Brothers. Among women religious, Mary Ward's Sisters, the Ursulines and the Sisters of Charity were prominent. New English orders were founded, such as the Sisters of the Holy Child and the Sisters of the Infant Jesus.[56] Especially through its network of schools, Catholic pastoral care in England became more and more visible.

## Nursing

Modern methods of nursing are generally ascribed to the innovations of Florence Nightingale (1820-1910) in her care for the sick. It was she who turned nursing into a recognized profession. By the middle of the nineteenth century hospital conditions had improved greatly with better sanitation. Hospitals took on the character of curing people, something that became more possible as a result of the scientific advances which were being made within medicine. No longer were hospitals almshouses where people simply lingered in forbidding conditions, waiting for death. In England, Florence Nightingale set up a process of carefully selecting and training women to nurse the sick. Strict standards concerning nursing procedures were set in place that ensured quality care for patients.

Florence Nightingale was much influenced by nursing care already in existence and offered by religious orders of Catholic nuns, such as the French Daughters of Charity and the Irish Sisters of Mercy. These women had pioneered nursing reforms at the beginning of the century. Nightingale was impressed by their work and modeled her own reforms on the quality of care and Christian principles she observed in these religious orders. For example, senior nurses became known by the title of Sister throughout the British Empire and wore veils and were encouraged not to press for higher wages.

It was from her early experience in the conditions of military hospitals during the Crimean War that Nightingale developed her skills in nursing: she nursed the wounded at Scutari in Turkey and then in the Crimea itself. Nightingale first went to these war zones in 1854 and took with her a group of Anglican sisters,[57] women belonging to the Catholic Sisters of Mercy and a number of laywomen. The nursing offered by these women, under Nightingale, drastically lowered the rate of death among the wounded. Returning to London, Florence Nightingale founded a school of nursing at St Thomas' Hospital. By the early 1870s, schools of nursing based upon her methods had spread throughout the world.[58]

During the American Civil War, both Catholic and Anglican religious sisters nursed the wounded in hospitals and on the battlefields. Abraham Lincoln (1809-65) saw to it that the Sisters of Mercy had ready access to the War Department for whatever they needed.[59] Also there were Protestant women who were nurses in the Civil War under Dorothea Dix (1802-87) who was in charge of nursing in the Union Army. Dix is best remembered for pioneering psychiatric nursing in the United States.

Catholic hospitals and schools became the two main works of pastoral care among the many religious congregations and orders that flourished in the nineteenth century. Some were established especially for nursing the sick and dying, such as the Little Company of Mary, founded by Mary Potter (1847-1913) at Hyson Green in the English diocese of Nottingham in 1877. These women were able to build upon the nursing reforms put in place by Florence Nightingale by having their sisters trained for the task. Mary Potter's Sisters opened their own nursing schools in many of the different countries in which they worked: England, Ireland, the United States, Australia, New Zealand, South Africa, Argentina, Malta and Italy. Some sisters specialized in the new field of psychiatric nursing while others worked in maternity care. Cardinal Manning was of the opinion that maternity nursing was unsuitable for religious women, a view reflected in the Rule of the Little Company of Mary prepared by Italian clerics who feared assistance at childbirth was 'capable of arousing the imagination and exposing modesty to danger'.[60] But the sisters were able to overturn such prudish restrictions placed by men upon their pastoral care. It was the vast number of women religious like these, the teachers and nurses who staffed the schools and hospitals, who selflessly carried out so much of the work of pastoral care in the Church of the nineteenth century. It was all to change after Vatican II in the second half of the following century when religious orders went into rapid decline and pastoral care again had to redefine itself to meet the new and fast changing conditions of the modern world.

# Chapter 9

# A Renewed Church

## Three Revolutions

On an April evening in 1917, as the long Russian winter was coming to an end, a zealous and potentially dangerous man emerged from the Finland Station in Petrograd. A band of workers was there to greet him. The Tsar had been forced to abdicate the previous month. Life in Petrograd had become tense and uncertain. Soldiers had been placed along the railway tracks in case of trouble and a military band struck up the *Marseillaise* as this shrewd and calculating revolutionary was welcomed back from exile in Switzerland. His name was Vladimir Ilyich Lenin (1870-1924). The Germans, keen for the destabilization of Russia that might force the country out of the First World War, had been only too happy to provide this crusading fanatic with safe passage across Germany to neutral Sweden and Finland. Lenin, with his Bolshevik followers, now began vigorously his campaign of 'All Power to the Soviets'.[1] Atheistic and dictatorial communism had arrived, founded upon the economic and social principles of Karl Marx that advocated a classless society.

Meanwhile, as the political, economic and social revolution gained momentum in Russia, a revolution of a very different kind had been unfolding in Vienna: a revolution of the mind. Wealthy, middle-class people were climbing the stairs of the apartment building on Berggasse 19 for psychoanalysis from Dr Sigmund Freud (1856-1939). This 'talking cure' was aimed at uncovering the unconscious and confronting the sexual and aggressive instincts believed to be at the root of human behavior. This revolution, too, was founded upon a materialistic view of human nature, with God seen as nothing more than a human projection.

A third revolution that shaped the twentieth century so definitively, although formulated in the previous century, was Charles Darwin's theory of evolution that grew out of his findings on the journey of the *Beagle* to the west coast of South America and to the Pacific Islands. The naturalist, Darwin, offered scientific evidence that all of life, including human life, is in constant change and development: the 'survival of the most fit'. Darwin had challenged the biblical accounts of creation. Apes, rather than Adam and Eve, were the source of human life. Nothing is fixed. Everything is in flux. All of reality is evolving.

These three revolutions, which so changed the modern world, became inextricably bound up with Christian pastoral care. Communism, with an evangelical fervor to spread its creed, promoted a way of life without God but with an accompanying crushing of human freedom. This the Christian Church opposed strenuously, seeing it as abhorrent to the dignity of the human person. But communism's economic theory, based on socialism, appeared hostile yet enticing: hostile, because it was godless and denied the freedom necessary for personal ownership and responsibility; yet enticing, because of its belief in the sharing of goods that seemed such a characteristic of the life of the early Christians. A Polish pope, John Paul II (1978-2005), helped bring about communism's final downfall yet he was also forthright in his criticism of the evils of unbridled capitalism. And liberation theology, with its pastoral strategy of empowering the people within the context of base ecclesial communities, was drawn to a Marxist analysis of oppression and injustice.

Freud freed sex from being a taboo subject. He saw sexual drives as an essential part of the human condition, even within infancy. Neurosis was largely the repression of unwanted sexual desires, assisted by a punishing superego molded from parental and societal restrictions learnt from earliest childhood. Human behavior was less the result of free choice and more the product of the unconscious. Persons could be freed from such troubling, inner conflicts through the greater self-awareness made possible by psychoanalysis. Religion only made people unhealthily dependent, went the Freudian doctrine. Christian pastoral care, which for so long had stressed free choice for one's actions, the value of repentant guilt, and the confession of sin, was under threat. Sexual sins, after all, were traditionally understood in Catholic moral thinking as dealing with 'grave matter'.

Christian pastoral care met the Freudian psychological revolution as it did the communist revolution: with ambivalence. Official Catholic pastoral teaching from the magisterium has remained firmly against sexual freedoms, interpreting the 'sexual revolution' as a purely materialistic view of human nature. Yet the call for a change in sexual ethics within pastoral care continues unabated in the Church. The issue of just how free one is psychologically when making decisions has led to a rethinking on moral culpability in the assessment of personal sin, as well as on the level of maturity which exists when it comes to such things as seeking marriage annulments. Sexual abuse is now generally understood as resulting from unresolved psychological issues involving power over others. Abuse, like so many other human aberrations, is more than just sin. Counseling, based on varying therapeutic techniques and psychological understandings of human nature, has become one of the most common means of pastoral care in the contemporary Church as it also has within the wider society. Modern means of pastoral care have, strangely, both rejected and embraced the Freudian revolution.

And the Darwinian revolution, too, has met with a mixed reception when it comes to pastoral care. A purely naturalistic view of life, without the transcendent, results in secularism, which has eroded the Christian life of faith in Western countries. Pastoral care in the twentieth century has had to direct much of its efforts in countering the effects of secularization. Darwin's studies also placed human beings firmly within the context of the rest of the natural world. Humanity forever after will be seen as interrelated with all forms of life on earth, a concept fundamental to the ecological challenge of caring for the environment. Human beings are part of the whole complex web of nature, not separate from it. As well, Darwin's ideas of an evolving understanding of reality have indirectly fostered more scientific ways of reading the Bible that call for biblical teachings to be placed within their own various literary and cultural contexts, as opposed to a fundamentalist interpretation of the Scriptures. A 'critical' reading of the Bible, using scientific tools of interpretation, meets with strong resistance from fundamentalist Christians who favor a pastoral response to life concerns based upon a literal reading of biblical texts. The other great divide in modern pastoral care that Darwin's ideas have alerted us to is that approach to Christianity which gives emphasis to an unchanging view of Church teachings, structures and practices, as against that which favors development and change: a static, versus an evolutionary, perspective on reality. This perhaps is the most divisive issue in contemporary pastoral care, namely, a restorationist versus a developmental view of Church life.

The story of these three revolutions, as they have affected pastoral care in the modern Catholic Church, we will see unfold more fully throughout the final two chapters of this book. But a fourth revolution, this time squarely within Catholicism itself, has also been at work. This revolution concerns the Second Vatican Council (1962-65) which sought to update Catholicism and its style of pastoral care in the new world order. Few in the Church, in particular, were prepared for the changes that were to happen following the Council. But Vatican II did not just appear from nowhere. The ground had been prepared by developments within the Church prior to the Council's commencement.

## Catholic Action

Direct lay involvement in the cause of the Church's mission became known as 'Catholic Action' in the earlier part of the twentieth century. In its European form, it was partly a response to the de-Christianization of society, especially among large sectors of the working class drawn to socialist movements that seemed to them to care more for their interests than did the Church. Catholic Action was encouraged by Pius XI (1922-39) in his encyclical *Quadragesimo Anno* (1931) to counter the effects of secularization and Marxist communism.

The aim of Catholic Action was for Catholic laypeople to become actively involved in working for the reform of social and economic structures to enhance people's lives. This was particularly the case in Belgium and France. Cardinal Joseph Cardijn (1882-1967) of Belgium began the *Jeunesse Ouvrière Chrétienne* (*Jocists*), known in English as the Young Christian Workers (YCW). It was based upon the principle of 'See, Judge, Act'. A counterpart organization for students became known as the Young Christian Students (YCS). Both these organizations spread widely throughout the Catholic world. In Italy, Catholic Action was an attempt to overcome much of the anticlerical feeling that had arisen from the Church's resistance to Italian nationalism in the nineteenth century. Catholic Action was about both the spiritual formation of its members and the building up of the kingdom of God in the world.

It was this idea of the Church's playing a dominant role in the world that led Pius XI to introduce the feast of Christ the King in 1928 to serve as the culmination of the Catholic liturgical year. But Catholic Action was not lay ministry in the more contemporary understanding of this term. Catholic Action was firmly under the control of the bishops from whom laypeople were to take their instructions. The layman or laywoman was seen as an extension of the bishop's pastoral role within the secular sphere. Catholic Action was the servant of episcopal holy orders rather than a lay ministry flowing directly from one's baptism. Catholic Action was thought of as a participation of the laity in the apostolate of the Church's hierarchy. By the 1950s the more generic term 'lay apostolate' came into increasing usage within pastoral care, founded upon the theological notion of the mystical body of Christ that Pius XII (1939-58) developed in the encyclical *Mystici Corporis* (1943).

## The Worker-Priest Movement

In 1943 a book appeared with the provocative title *France, pays de mission?* (France, a mission territory?) by Henri Godin and Yvan Daniel.[2] The authors put forward the thesis that France (traditionally Catholic) had seen most of its working-class people de-Christianized and that parish pastoral structures, with their bourgeois values and practices, were inadequate to meet such a critical change. The authors proposed small communities of priests and lay workers, instilled with missionary enthusiasm and the values of the gospel, live in the new industrial areas where working-class French Catholics resided and exercise an influence there. The Archbishop of Paris, Cardinal Emmanuel Suhard (1874-1949), read with both shock and enthusiasm this analysis of the state of the Church in France and the suggested novel responses put forward by Godin and Daniel. He committed himself immediately to this need for a new strategy of evangelization within his vast urban diocese, and, in response, developed the ideas and practices of Catholic Action by means of his pastoral plans known as the *Mission de Paris* and *Mission de France*, which relied on a team approach to ministry.[3] A special seminary to prepare priests to carry out a ministry outside of parish structures was opened at Lisieux. During their preparation students spent time in factories and other places of work and then reflected upon their experiences. It was an action-reflection model of priestly formation that was innovative for the time.

Out of the *Mission de France* the notion of 'worker-priests' of the late 1940s and early 1950s developed and many such priests graduated from the Lisieux seminary. Quite a number of these priests had been prisoners in Germany during the Second World War and forced to labor in factories. They knew first-hand of the miserable conditions of the laboring classes. Others had been actively involved in the French Resistance movement against the Nazi occupation of France and had been radicalized as a result of their experiences.[4] For the worker-priests, most of whom began their special style of mission as young men, it was manual labor that was to characterize their priesthood most. They worked on the docks in Marseille and in the factories of Paris and Lyon. Blue overalls had replaced the black cassock and white clerical collar. Their lives were a witness to poverty as they attempted to bring the message of the gospel to fellow laborers and their families by living and working alongside them. Some lived alone while others banded together in small groups. Their lives were characterized by simplicity and freedom from clericalism. Experiencing for themselves the injustices accompanying industrialization of that time, most of these men became activists in the trade union movement. Many were influenced by Marxism and the class struggle. But their lives as priests and their distinct methods of pastoral care gained theological support, especially through the writings of the distinguished Dominican theologian, Marie-Dominique Chenu (1895-1990).[5]

Some of these priests, like the workers to whom they had been sent, became disillusioned with the Church. And not a few in the Church became increasingly alarmed by the worker-priests whom they saw as betraying the very meaning of the Catholic priesthood and as being seduced by communist ideology. Pius XII brought the controversial worker-priest movement to an end in 1953.

### Catholic Action in North America: Dorothy Day and the Catholic Worker Movement

North America did not have the anticlerical sentiment that was to be found in many parts of Europe. Catholic Action in North America, prior to Vatican II, generally took on a more benign form. Daniel A. Lord (1888-1955), a Jesuit priest noted for his talents in theatrical and musical productions, along with an ability to write popular religious pamphlets, began a series of summer schools on Catholic Action in 1931, which revived the sodality movement among young Catholics.[6] The Legion of Decency went about recommending the movies coming out of Hollywood that were considered to be suitable for Catholics. Cardijn's pastoral strategy of 'See, Judge, Act' was incorporated into the Christian Family Movement (CFM), formed in the mid 1940s, which brought Catholic married couples together. It enjoyed great success in the following decades under the direction of Pat and Patty Crowley, popularly known as 'Mr and Mrs CFM'.

However, Catholic Action (but without episcopal control) showed its teeth in America in the Catholic Worker Movement founded by Dorothy Day (1897-1980) and Peter Maurin (1877-1949). On 1 May 1933, leftist groups had gathered in New York's Union Square to rally against Hitler's fascism and to demonstrate in support of socialist change. In the crowd was Dorothy Day, a woman in her late thirties, quietly selling the first edition of a newspaper called the *Catholic*

*Worker.* Born in Brooklyn into a lower middle-class family, Day had spent her younger years in the 1920s among radical intellectuals in the smoky cafes and seedy bars of Greenwich Village. Capitalist exploitation angered her. She was drawn by nature to the struggle of the poorer classes. Alongside this passion for justice to be done was a growing hunger within herself for a deeper, spiritual way of life. This she found in Catholicism. In 1927 she was baptized in the Catholic Church. Her common law husband whom she deeply loved, Forster Batterham, walked out on her. She was left alone to raise her only daughter, Tamar.

Dorothy Day was a journalist by profession. Five years after being received into the Catholic Church, she met the much older, French-born Peter Maurin, an eccentric intellectual who had migrated to Canada before settling in the United States. Maurin's mind was always full of ideas and he was ever ready to impose them. He made a deep impression upon Dorothy Day. With his obsessive personality, Maurin had immersed himself in the Catholic intellectual tradition. Together, Maurin and Day founded the *Catholic Worker* paper to spread their message. The *Catholic Worker* was founded upon four main principles: communitarian Christianity, personalist philosophy, non-violence/pacifism, and voluntary poverty.[7] It influenced the lives of a countless number of Catholics and others in its uncompromising stance for a more just and peace-loving world free of materialist values. The paper, and the movement that lay behind it, was firmly against nationalism, militarism and racial discrimination.

For all her radical ideas and utopian romanticism, Day remained firmly within the Catholic fold, too much so in the view of some of her liberal critics:[8] 'a loyal Catholic traditionalist'.[9] For her, no matter how 'rotten or corrupt' the Church might sometimes become, it 'had the mark of Jesus Christ on it'.[10] Day often angered bishops, but most of them, deep down, respected her. Her Houses of Hospitality sprung up around the country to offer shelter and dignity to those whose lives were enmeshed in misfortune. Many regard Dorothy Day as the most significant American Catholic laywoman of the twentieth century.

### Catholic Action in Australia: B.A. Santamaria and the Movement

By the late 1940s in Australia, Catholic Action in some quarters took on a militant anticommunist form, under the layman Bartholomew (Bob) Santamaria (1915-98), to rid the trade unions of communist leadership. Santamaria's organization became known as 'the

Movement' and was to become increasingly caught up in divisive party politics, splitting the Labor Party that had traditionally attracted the Catholic vote. This led a number of the bishops, especially in Sydney, to distance themselves from the Movement that had its power base in Melbourne under Irish nationalist Archbishop Daniel Mannix (1864-1963).

Removing himself more from the older Catholic Action principles of direct influence and ultimate control by the Church hierarchy, Santamaria went on to set up the National Civic Council (NCC) that had close links with the Democratic Labor Party. This political organization, with its outwardly Catholic flavor, espoused right-wing causes. Over time, followers of this organization became increasingly more concerned with internal Church controversies. Santamaria, with his characteristic pessimism and disposition to foster divisiveness, undoubtedly shaped much of the direction of pastoral leadership within the public forum in the Catholic Church in Australia during the Cold War years but, as Australian Catholic historian Edmund Campion notes, he remained 'unreconciled to the modern world'.[11]

## The Second Vatican Council

Without doubt the Second Vatican Council (1962-65) resulted in an extraordinary transformation of pastoral care within the Catholic Church: a transformation on a scale unprecedented in the Church's long history. Not only did the council result in remarkable changes in the way the Church went about doing pastoral care: there was a thorough re-examination of the theological assumptions upon which pastoral care is based. Pope John XXIII (1958-63), the rotund pontiff who won over the world with his warm and simple personality, called this council for the purpose of what he described as opening up the windows of the Church and letting in fresh air. Rigidity had come to characterize Catholicism and it was John's intention, in line with an optimism characteristic of the 1960s, to move the Catholic Church firmly in the direction of the modern world. The purpose of Vatican II, as the pope understood it, was not to condemn errors but to foster peace and unity within both Christianity and the world at large. He had no time for those whom he called prophets of gloom. While John XXIII did not live to see the council end its business, which spread over four sessions, Pope Paul VI (1963-78) took up what John had begun and directed the Church in implementing both the vision of the council and its decisions.

Vatican II moved Catholicism in a 'Darwinian' direction, from understanding reality, including the Church itself, in a static, unchanging way to seeing it as undergoing evolutionary transformation. Though the template of the Church's nature and pastoral mission remained intact, the Church was to occupy itself, in the context of a rapidly changing world, with a continuous and evolving task of transformation; this task came to be called *aggiornamento* (updating and renewal). The main issue experienced by those who shaped Vatican II and the mandate they bequeathed for doctrinal understanding and pastoral care was this: how a fidelity to the patrimony of the past becomes developmental continuity.[12]

## The Teachings of the Documents of Vatican II

Sixteen documents emerged from the Council.[13] The aftermath of Vatican II was a turbulent but exciting period for Catholics as they found themselves living in what seemed to be such a different Church from the one they had known for so long. Most Catholics came to welcome the new spirit that came upon their Church; others accepted the changes reluctantly; and a few resisted by refusing to move forward at all.[14]

The pastoral reforms of the Council were first experienced most directly in the liturgy; these reforms had been debated early in the proceedings of Vatican II. Soon Catholics found themselves celebrating the Mass and other sacraments in their own language rather than Latin. Active participation within the liturgy was encouraged. Liturgy, although perceived by many as having lost something of its transcendent nature, brought a new dynamism to pastoral life in the parishes.[15] Catholics were encouraged to become more familiar with the breadth and riches of the Scriptures as a foundation for their spiritual lives. The Bible, rather than the traditional Catholic devotions, took on a more prominent role in prayer, evangelization and education as the old fear and suspicion of Protestant, Bible-based Christianity receded. Scripture and tradition were but two harmonious expressions of the one word of God.[16] Other Christian Churches and communities were recognized as a means of salvation rather than as simply religious bodies that had deviated from the truth.[17] Non-Christian religions were praised for their capacity to be 'true and holy' by the way in which they 'often reflect a ray of that Truth which enlightens all people'.[18] The Catholic Church had been slow to enter into the ecumenical movement but, having done so, there was no turning back. Increasingly, pastoral care came to be done at many levels in an interdenominational way, including chaplaincy work in hospitals and other institutions; social welfare initiatives; theological education;

prayer and study groups; justice and peace initiatives; and evangelization. On several occasions, for instance, Pope John Paul II invited leaders from the world's great religions to gather with him in Assisi to pray for world peace.

Largely due to the work of the American theologian John Courtney Murray (1904-67), Vatican II rather belatedly affirmed the basic right of every person to religious freedom against the view that 'error has no rights', which might accept toleration in some circumstances but not liberty.[19] The dignity of the human person and the protection of human rights, through action on behalf of justice and peace, were recognized by Vatican II as being at the very heart of the Church's mission. The Council's Pastoral Constitution on the Church in the Modern World (*Gaudium et Spes*) affirmed these principles by offering an optimistic and systematic presentation of pastoral care for the present age of humanity: this task is about 'scrutinizing the signs of the times and of interpreting them in the light of the gospel', meaning to 'recognize and understand the world in which we live, its expectations, its longings, and its often dramatic characteristics'.[20]

Above all, it was a renewed theology of the Church that shaped the pastoral reforms of the Second Vatican Council, as developed in the Dogmatic Constitution on the Church (*Lumen Gentium*). The hierarchical theology of Church that was stressed in the previous century at Vatican I, with its doctrine of papal infallibility, was complemented at Vatican II by the more communal and biblical image of Church as being the People of God with its common 'priesthood of the faithful'. Only when one affirms the fundamental unity of all God's people within the Church, united in Christ, through the sacrament of baptism, can one speak of different Church offices and ordained ministries. Christopher Butler noted that no council had ever succeeded in presenting to the world so comprehensive an ecclesiology, a theology of Church, as had Vatican II;[21] it was a collegial vision that stressed shared authority and ministry. The Council reaffirmed the importance of the local church's freedom to express itself pastorally within its own culture, without losing sight of the essential unity of the Church focused upon the Bishop of Rome. As *Lumen Gentium* expressed it: 'This variety of local churches with one common aspiration is particularly splendid evidence of the catholicity of the undivided Church.'[22] This Council document taught that bishops in their local churches were not 'to be regarded as vicars of the Roman Pontiff' but as possessing a pastoral office in which 'the habitual and daily care of their sheep is entrusted to them completely'.[23] This tension in pastoral care between local autonomy and Roman centralization has gone on to be a characteristic feature of the post-Vatican II period, especially under the papacy of John Paul II. Whatever may be said about this, Richard McBrien has rightly pointed out that Vatican II recovered the idea of ministry as service, rather than as merely the assignment of ecclesiastical status.[24]

One of the most significant outcomes of the Second Vatican Council was the empowerment it gave to the laity for ministry. In the debate within the Council in preparation of the Decree on the Apostolate of the Laity (*Apostolicam Actuositatem*), Archbishop D'Souza of Bhopal, India, argued that it was high time for the Church to consider the laity as grown-ups. He spoke against the idea of Catholic Action that fostered a dependence of the laity upon the bishops when it came to exercising their mission.[25] Lay ministry received its endorsement at Vatican II not only from the document on the laity but, perhaps more importantly, from the renewed theology of Church that was at the basis of the conciliar documents as a whole, especially *Lumen Gentium* and *Gaudium et Spes*. The groundwork in providing the theological support for the laity's place in the life and mission of the Church had been done earlier in the pioneering work of the French Dominican, Yves Congar.[26]

### The Laity After Vatican II

Paul VI extended the work of the Council in *Ministeria quaedam* (1972),[27] a document that affirmed the ministry of the laity on the basis of their sharing in the priesthood of Christ, obtained through baptism. This same document opened up the ministries of lector and acolyte to laymen (but not laywomen), restricting them no longer to those preparing for diaconate and priesthood. Following the Synod of Bishops that met to consider the topic of evangelization, Paul VI provided a broad picture of lay participation in the ministry of the Church in the follow-up document to the synod, *Evangelii nuntiandi* (1975).[28] Pastoral care and other activities of the laity, when publicly endorsed by the Church, went beyond being regarded as apostolic works to being considered as ministry.

John Paul II directed the attention of the 1987 Synod of Bishops to the vocation and mission of the laity. While continuing to endorse and encourage lay ministry, the follow-up *Apostolic Exhortation on the Laity* (*Christifideles Laici*) (1988)[29] sounded a note of caution in the use of the word 'ministry'. There is a fear of confusing or softening the differences between the 'ministry' of the priesthood, belonging to all believers, and 'ministry' pertaining to the ordained priesthood. There is a hint in this document of the old idea of Catholic Action insofar as the legitimacy of lay ministry is said to arise from the official deputation given it by pastors and under the guidance of ecclesiastical authority. And there is a greater emphasis placed upon the laity's role in the world than within the inner life of the Church itself.

The place of the laity in ministry is treated with even more caution in the *Instruction on Certain Questions Regarding the Collaboration of the Non-Ordained Faithful in the Sacred Ministry of Priests* (1997), issued jointly in the names of a number of Vatican departments.[30] The teachings outlined in this instruction emphasize the unique position of ordained ministry and warn of various abuses when it comes to the collaboration of the laity in the mission of the Church. Yet the time has passed in the Church for lay ministry to be considered as little more than an emergency solution to the critical problem of the shortage of priests.

### The Permanent Diaconate

Vatican II, in *Lumen Gentium*, opened up the possibility for the restoration of the permanent diaconate for mature aged men who may be married, and for suitable young men for whom celibacy must remain a lifelong commitment.[31] Subsequently, Paul VI implemented the recommendation for this ministry of pastoral care in the Latin Church in *Sacrum Diaconatus Ordinem* (1967).[32] A year later, the episcopal conference of the United States approved the introduction of the permanent diaconate; the US is the country in which such ministry has been most widely adopted. It has been claimed that over ninety-five percent of all permanent deacons work in North America or Europe (though they are less numerous in Europe) while they are almost unheard of in Africa, Asia and Latin America.[33] Such uneven recognition of the value of the permanent diaconate stems from confusion over the role: is the role of the permanent diaconate one of charitable service? Or is it a predominantly liturgical role within the parish? Or do permanent deacons act as bishops' special representatives in some capacity or other?[34] But beyond such confusion as to the appropriate functions of the permanent diaconate ministry, a further reason many local churches are reluctant to introduce it is the fear of accentuating clericalism. There is also a lack of agreement concerning how extensive education and formation for diaconal ministry should be. A long, academic theological training program would deter many candidates. As well, in mission countries, catechists have long been exercising similar functions to those of deacons. Finally, there is a financial issue: should permanent deacons be paid a salary by the Church? Or ought they remain in their paid, secular employment? If they are retired, should they be expected to carry out their diaconal ministry unpaid?[35]

### New Spiritual Movements

New movements in evangelization came into prominence within Catholic life in the latter part of the twentieth century. They have been a source of exceptional vitality, high in energy, witnessing to the evangelical dimension within modern Catholicism. Although attracting only a minority within the Church, their influence has been powerful and their arrival into pastoral life has not been without controversy.

The Charismatic Renewal found its way into Catholic life soon after Vatican II. Although long a feature of Protestant Pentecostal Churches, Pentecostalism in its Catholic expression is said to have originated in 1967, among students and faculty at Duquesne University in Pittsburgh, Pennsylvania and, later, at the University of Notre Dame in Indiana and the University of Michigan in Ann Arbor. The Catholic Charismatic Renewal movement spread quickly in the 1970s, with prayer groups around the world drawing large numbers of adherents. Firmly grounded in the Bible, the Charismatic movement is ecumenical in tone and fosters the role of the laity in ministry. It stresses a healing ministry. Catholics flocked to be baptized in the Spirit, some joining covenant communities. Above all, this movement gives emphasis to the importance of religious experience; this has been its appeal.

More controversial has been *Opus Dei*, with its strong Catholic identity of an especially Spanish kind that had its birth in the context of the regime of General Francisco Franco (1892-1975), in the aftermath of the Spanish Civil War. Founded by the priest St Josemaría Escrivá de Balaguer (1902-75), as a pious association of laity and clergy, it emphasizes that sanctity can be found in one's everyday life and work. Escrivá's intention was to evangelize the professional and intellectual sectors of Spanish society who, in turn, were to exercise influence to further the aims of the Catholic Church. John Paul II canonized the group's founder in 2002, a move that ensured *Opus Dei* would have a strong place within Catholic evangelization.[36]

The Focolare Movement and 'Communion and Liberation' both have their origins in Italy. Focolare (meaning 'hearth' or 'family fireside') was founded in Trent in 1943 by a young schoolteacher, Chiara Lubich, to enliven the faith of individual Catholics. It has also been influential in promoting Christian values within the family and the world of business. At the core of the movement are men and women living celibate lives in small communities but engaged in secular employment.

The movement known as 'Communion and Liberation' was founded in the 1950s by a priest from Milan Archdiocese, Luigi Guissani. He was concerned over the decline in Catholic values in Italian cultural and social life and began a catechetical program in schools that extended into setting up study groups. 'Communion and Liberation' was closely associated for a long time with Italian politics but, following the collapse of the Christian Democrat Party, it claims to have pursued more spiritual values. Both Focolare and 'Communion and Liberation' have been active in the United Nations over issues such as birth and population control, abortion, reproductive rights, and the rights sought by homosexual persons.[37]

Founded in Madrid, Spain in 1964 by Kiko Arguello, an artist and convert from existential atheism, and by Carmen Hernandez, the Neocatechumenate movement works on the principle of the evangelization of already baptized adults through a series of stages resembling the pastoral and liturgical Rite of Christian Initiation for the unbaptized. Working through the whole sequence of stages may take from eight to ten years. Neocatechumens have been active in fostering vocations to the priesthood so that priest-members may work within parishes to spread the movement. Seminarians are frequently imported from other countries to set up a new house within a diocese. The movement's ministry focuses on evangelization, fostering a spirit of conversion and practical charity towards others.

Finally, there is the Community of Sant'Egidio (named after a church the community has been given in Rome), founded in 1968, by a teenager, Andrea Riccardi. He gathered a group of high school students who, together with him, were moved by the needs of the poor of Rome. They found inspiration in the first Christian communities of the Acts of the Apostles and Francis of Assisi. The Sant'Egidio movement has spread around the world, fostering friendship among people of different nations. Sant'Egidio identifies particularly with the marginalized in its humanitarian outreach: it offers support for such people as those experiencing disabilities, foreign immigrants, refugees, the imprisoned, and civilians in war-torn countries. The movement is particularly dedicated to the cause of world peace, engaging itself in ecumenical and interfaith dialogue.

These movements, and others like them, aim to bring vitality to the Church. It would be wrong to assess them all as being similar in theological outlook and in the style in which they do things. What distinguishes them though from many of the earlier movements in the Church is that they tend to stress personal renewal and charitable outreach among laity within everyday life. Unlike religious orders that have often set themselves apart from secular life with distinctive clothing and a vowed way of life, these movements generally encourage active engagement in the world but with the support of a strong faith community. Will they find wide acceptance among mainstream Catholics and bring new life to the wider Church beyond themselves, thus contributing significantly to its mission of evangelization? Or will they remain on the fringes of the Christian community? Are they divisive? Or do they express diversity, a catholicity that is one of the four characteristic marks of the Christian faith? Opinion is divided.

## Women and the Church

The combination of, on the one hand, the raising of awareness about women's experience of oppression at the hands of men and, on the other, women's efforts to change patriarchal beliefs and social structures that foster such oppression, was one of the defining characteristics of the second half of the twentieth century. Feminism, in opposing male dominance, sought to eradicate all forms of false consciousness standing in the way of women's freedom and equality, a dominance that feminists argue devalues women while, at the same time, dehumanizing men. Feminist theologian Anne Clifford proposes that the modern feminist movement came about in three stages.[38] First wave feminism is associated with the suffragette movement that emerged in the mid nineteenth century and carried through into the early twentieth century. It sought equality for women through the right to vote. Second wave feminism of the 1960s and 1970s, largely a North American and Western European phenomenon, dealt with the liberation of women through civil rights and gender equality. The more recent third wave type of feminism that began in the 1980s, argues Clifford, takes seriously the differences in women's experiences around the world and works for justice for all women with their own distinctive needs within the contexts of their vastly different cultures. It is an attempt to move away from interpreting women's needs from an exclusively Western perspective.

Women have attempted 'to find their own theological voices'.[39] Mary Daly, in her groundbreaking book, *The Church and the Second Sex* (1968),[40] was one of the earliest Catholic writers to offer a feminist analysis of the Church as being a sexist institution. Yet as the years went by, Daly became far more extreme in coming to believe the Christian Church to be beyond salvaging as an institution, whereas other more moderate Catholic feminist theologians, such as Elizabeth Johnson, attempt to recast doctrinal understandings and pastoral practices in a more gender-inclusive way. Johnson, for example, has written an analysis of an understanding of God drawing upon both feminine and masculine imagery within the Bible. Her book presents what she calls a 'right way' of speaking about God from within a woman's experience of reality.[41]

Much attention has been focused in more recent decades upon the question of the ordination of women to the diaconate, priesthood and episcopate, a practice adopted by sections of the Anglican Church and a number of other Protestant Churches. In 1976, the Congregation for the Doctrine of the Faith, with the ratification of Paul VI, issued a declaration, *On the Question of the Admission of Women to the Ministerial Priesthood (Inter Insigniores)*,[42] explaining the reasons for the Catholic Church's denying the sacrament of holy orders to women. Among the reasons were the following three principal ones: there is no basis for the practice in Christian tradition; Jesus called only male apostles to the priesthood; and the significance of the symbolism inherent in the maleness of Christ as head of the Church, which the priesthood represents in a sacramental way. In Anglicanism it has been a particularly divisive issue. John Paul II, in his apostolic letter of 1994, *On Ordination and Women (Ordinatio Sacerdotalis)*,[43] attempted to put an end to debate about the matter by reaffirming the teachings of Paul VI and declaring that the subject was now closed and not open to further debate. How the Catholic and Orthodox Churches, in opposing the ordination of women, will relate to other Churches who allow it is certain to remain a sensitive matter in ecumenical relations for some time to come.

Local Churches in different countries have sought to address the role of women in the Church. A particularly large research project was undertaken in the late 1990s on behalf of the Australian Catholic Bishops Conference. Its findings were published in 1999 and reflect the common experience of Catholic women in many parts of the world.[44] The research identified two broad approaches to the participation of women in the Catholic Church: one approach oriented towards maintaining the current forms of participation of women, or even returning to the style of participation operating before Vatican II; the other approach calling for a greatly expanded role for women.[45] Overall, it was found that the Church was perceived to be lagging behind the wider Australian society when it came to the equality of women. Particularly singled out was the limited participation of women in decision-making at all levels within the Catholic Church. The research project stated in its summary report that there was:

> … a strong sense of pain and alienation resulting from the Church's stance on women … It was perceived that little assistance and support were received from the institutional Church to undertake anything other than ancillary and support roles. Significant barriers to the full participation of women were experienced.[46]

Contemporary Australian women's experience of their role in the Church, uncovered by the bishops' research, highlighted the need for respectful dialog and action, something that undoubtedly resonates throughout the rest of the Catholic world. In 2004 the Vatican Congregation for the Doctrine of the Faith issued a *Letter on the Collaboration of Men and Women*.[47] The letter points to the unfortunate antagonism that can develop between women and men arising from suggestions of the gender subordination of women. It also laments an approach that seeks to minimize physical differences between men and women - as though it is all just a matter of history and culture - something that can overshadow the distinctiveness of the sexes and the complementarity that ought to exist between women and men. While recognizing motherhood as a key element in women's identity, the letter stresses that women should not be viewed from the sole perspective of procreation. Hence they should be able to seek entry into the world of work and have access to positions in public life which address political issues pertaining to economic and social problems within the world as a whole. Conscious of feminist critique about the way the Virgin Mary has sometimes been presented in pastoral life as devaluing sexuality and fostering feminine passivity, through the adoption of a docile and obedient nature, this letter teaches that imitation of Mary need not mean 'that the Church should adopt a passivity inspired by an outdated conception of femininity'.[48]

The role of women in society, and the way open to them for positions of influence and leadership within the Church, is a fundamental and pressing issue within contemporary pastoral care. It is a concern that will have to go on being recognized and addressed by Church leadership. The longer term effects from women who work as theologians and attain positions of ecclesial influence – things previously denied them - are yet to be seen. Feminist thinking is sure to continue to have a profound impact upon the Church in its teachings and structures, especially in relation to its pastoral mission.

## Marriage, Sex and Human Relationships

No issue has troubled pastoral care more in recent decades than sex and its manner of expression in human relationships. Long ago Freud freed sex from being a taboo subject and pointed to the consequence of its repression. His linking of sexuality with disturbed relationships in the earliest years of a person's life that result in enduring difficulties, ensured that the norms surrounding this fundamental aspect of humanity would never be the same. Not everything in the details of Freud's revolutionary ideas however has endured. Some even write off entirely the whole psychoanalytic understanding of human nature. But sexuality has come under renewed consideration in the modern world; it is no longer viewed suspiciously, and the Church has not been immune to such thinking.

### Marriage and the Family

Few would doubt the current crisis in marriage. By the beginning of the new millennium, most Western countries were experiencing somewhere between a third and a half of all first marriages ending in divorce. Single parent families are now common. An increasing number of people, especially women, experience abuse at the hands of their partners and churches have joined other organizations in providing temporary refuges for abused women and their children. The American bishops, at their national conference in November 2002, declared that women who are victims of violence ought not to think they must remain in abusive marriages.[49] More and more couples are choosing to cohabit, whether for a trial period or as a more lasting arrangement, rather than risk incurring the traumas their parents may have experienced through divorce. Life commitments that mean surrendering independence and autonomy have become more difficult in an age that places a high value upon freedom and women's emancipation. Rates of clinical depression and suicide continue to rise as family stability and support diminishes.[50]

Catholic teaching considers Christian marriage to be a sacrament in which Christ is symbolized and present in the love of the spouses for each other and their children. Permanent commitment and fidelity are expected. But there has been a shift in emphasis concerning the nature of marriage within Catholic teaching that reflects changes within the wider society. Marriage today is understood less as a legal contract - with accompanying social roles of the man as the breadwinner and head of the family, and the woman as the one with responsibility for the home and for seeing to the emotional needs of the children - and more about a relationship between equals. Such an understanding implies not only fidelity and commitment but also a quality of love expressed through good communication. What contributes today to the success of a marriage is primarily the quality of the relationship between the spouses and it is this factor that is recognized as nurturing fidelity and commitment between them and in relation to their children. Today women and men expect a lot more from the marriage relationship than did earlier generations and when this is poor the marriage gets into difficulties. John Paul II acknowledged these developments in 1981 in his *Apostolic Exhortation on the Family*. He wrote of the family as being 'a community of persons' founded upon human love.[51]

As a result, pastoral care has given increasing attention to assisting couples to value and develop good communication skills as a basis for their married love. Pre-marriage programs have been prepared to assist couples to have better understandings of themselves as persons. They aim to help couples to be more closely attuned to the needs of each person and to learn new skills of interpersonal communication based upon a Christian understanding of married love. Psychological knowledge and skills are incorporated into a sacramental theology of Christian marriage. The Marriage Encounter program was founded by a Spanish priest named Gabriel Calvo in Barcelona in the early 1960s and it soon spread throughout Latin America. It was introduced into the United States by Father Chuck Gallagher. Through a structured process of talks, given by team couples assisted by a priest; writing; and interpersonal verbal communication activities, during a live-in weekend, couples are led through a process from 'I' to 'We' to 'We and God' to 'We, God and the World'. Marriage Encounter is about enriching marriages rather than assisting troubled marriages.[52]

### Separation, Divorce and Remarriage

Pastoral care is often founded upon the assumption that the nuclear family is the norm. Yet the reality is that a great number of households include the divorced single parent or comprise the remarried living in blended families. It would be a mistake to look upon divorced and remarried Catholics as men and women who actively promote the rejection of the Church's teachings on the permanence and indissolubility of marriage. Usually such people do *not* actively promote divorce.[53] The breakdown of marriages is a common and sad reality in our times and there are many causes for it. Few families today remain unaffected.

Pastoral care for the divorced takes two forms. One is the marriage tribunal, which grants annulments where it can be demonstrated that a full and proper marriage was not a reality for the couple. The grounds for annulments have been extended to include psychological grounds relating to insufficient freedom and maturity. The other form of pastoral care for the divorced is that of healing support, often in groups, for persons experiencing the pain and grief of a relationship breakdown. James Young, a priest who was a pioneer in this kind of ministry, founded the North American Conference of Separated and Divorced Catholics in the early 1970s. 'The Beginning Experience' works as a support group that may also include people who have experienced the loss of a partner through death. The program known as 'Rainbows For All God's Children', is for children who have experienced parental loss through divorce or death.

A matter of pastoral controversy has been that of the Church's stance against Catholics in an irregular second marriage receiving the sacrament of Holy Communion. Yet, John Paul II made it very clear that Catholics who are divorced and in an irregular second marriage should not consider themselves separated from the Church, for as baptized persons they share in its life.[54] With the large numbers of divorced and remarried Catholics in parishes today the matter of the reception of the Eucharist has become a pastoral issue of some magnitude.

### Birth Control

When Paul VI finally issued the encyclical *Humanae Vitae* in 1968,[55] reaffirming the Church's constant teaching against using artificial means of birth control, a storm was unleashed within Catholicism. Large numbers of Catholics began questioning, for the first time in the modern era, the Church's official teaching as it applied to their personal lives. In some respects, the controversy over birth control was more about authority than about the ethics of sexual behavior. *Humanae Vitae* resulted in Catholics more and more making up their own minds about morality than following, without question, the official teachings of their Church. John Paul II was quick to recognize this crisis in authority and he was a consistent and ardent supporter of Catholic teaching concerning the regulation of birth. It was *Humanae Vitae*, as he was only too well aware, that stimulated so much independence of thinking and behavior in Catholic life after Vatican II, something that he sought to reverse in his pontificate. Dissent from Church teaching continues to trouble the Church in the vexed issue concerning theological pluralism and the role of conscience.

## Abortion and Life Issues

While the debate over Catholic teaching on contraception was confined largely within the Church, the moral teaching opposing abortion was felt on a far broader canvas. The 'Roe v. Wade' decision of the Supreme Court in the United States in 1973 removed restrictive policies on abortion in most states and resulted in its decriminalization throughout the country. Similar legislation has since been passed in many other countries. But whether abortion can be debated at all by Catholics is a controversial issue. Feminists, whether approving or disapproving of abortion, are generally united in their conviction that the reality of pregnancy must be looked at from the woman's point of view.

In 1972 the United States bishops began their 'Respect for Life' program. Cardinal Joseph Bernardin (1928-96), the Archbishop of Chicago, vigorously opposed abortion but within the wider framework of what he called a 'consistent ethic of life', the 'seamless garment'. It came to characterize his pastoral role as a bishop-teacher and was influential. This idea Bernardin first presented in a public lecture at New York's Fordham University on 6 December 1983. In the 'consistent ethic of life' he attempted to link a whole range of life issues that he saw as under threat. It was a theme to which he continually returned throughout the remainder of his life.

> Each of the issues I have referred to this evening – abortion, war, hunger and human rights, euthanasia and physician-assisted suicide, and capital punishment – is treated as a separate, self-contained topic in our public life. Each is indeed distinct, but an ad hoc approach to each one fails to illustrate how our choices in one area can affect our decisions in other areas. There must be a public attitude of respect for all of life, if public actions are to respect life in concrete actions.[56]

## Ministry Among Gays and Lesbians

The 1973 police raid on the Stonewall Inn in lower Manhattan's Greenwich Village is usually regarded as the event that triggered the

Gay Rights Movement. Since that time there has been a growing acceptance of homosexuality within wider society as gay men and lesbian women have struggled for social acceptance and equal rights within the law. In the Catholic Church the pastoral care of gay and lesbian Catholics has remained an explosive issue. In 1986 the Congregation for the Doctrine of the Faith issued a lengthy *Letter to the bishops of the Catholic Church on the pastoral care of homosexual persons*.[57] This letter reaffirmed past Church teaching[58] that homosexual acts are 'intrinsically disordered', while recognizing that the 'the particular inclination of the homosexual person is not a sin'. But the letter also went much further than previous documents of the magisterium when it asserted that the homosexual orientation, not just homosexual acts, 'is a more or less strong tendency ordered towards an intrinsic moral evil; and thus the inclination itself must be seen as an objective disorder.'[59] This moved the ethical debate on homosexuality to a new level.

The recognition of same-sex unions as the legal equivalent to marriages, along with the legal possibility of same-sex couples' adoption of children, has become part of the political agenda in many Western countries in more recent years. The move has been strongly opposed by the Vatican in a statement, *Same-Sex Unions Harmful to Society*, issued by the Congregation for the Doctrine of the Faith in 2003,[60] a statement endorsed the following year by the United States Conference of Catholic Bishops, in their *Statement on Marriage and Homosexual Unions*, and by the Canadian bishops.[61] There is the concern to reject same-sex unions, so as to preserve the traditional understanding of marriage. Yet there is also concern to respect the dignity of homosexual persons, and to condemn all forms of unjust discrimination, harassment or abuse against them, this latter issue being more pronounced in the American Bishops' document.

Organizations for the pastoral care of gay and lesbian Catholics are now common in the Catholic Church, sometimes recognized officially within dioceses and sometimes not. The issue of their public recognition by dioceses is usually dependent upon the level of their conformity with official Church teaching on homosexuality. Such groups involved in this kind of ministry include 'Courage', 'Dignity' and 'New Ways Ministry', in the United States, 'Dignity' in Canada, 'Quest' in the British Isles, and 'Acceptance' in Australia. Beyond Catholicism, the Metropolitan Community Church (MCC) was founded in 1968 by Troy Perry for a ministry directed expressly towards gay and lesbian Christians. What Christians with a homosexual orientation do want from their respective Churches is that their experience not simply be spoken about without their involvement: they want it to be discussed with them.[62]

The particular needs of parents of gay or lesbian children are acknowledged in the 1997 pastoral statement of the United States Bishops, *Always Our Children*.[63] The statement offers practical guidelines for parents, amidst their anxiety and struggle, to be 'accepting and loving' of their gay or lesbian child as a gift of God. The bishops advise parents to urge their son or daughter 'to stay joined to the Catholic faith community'.

## HIV/AIDS

No other epidemic in human history has resulted in the death of so many human beings as that caused by the human immunodeficiency virus (HIV) responsible for the condition known as AIDS. AIDS is now the leading cause of death by infection and the fourth leading cause of death worldwide.[64] With the appearance of AIDS in the 1980s and its devastating impact especially upon gay men and injecting drug users, the Church was quick in its pastoral response to provide spiritual assistance and nursing care for those suffering from the disease. The Catholic Church dismissed outright any idea that AIDS was a punishment from God for immoral behavior, an idea that was being put about by some fundamentalist Christians.[65] Joseph Bernardin cautioned against treating our encounter with people having AIDS as an occasion primarily to speak about moral principles of behavior,[66] while Cardinal Basil Hume in England (1923-99) rejected any 'merciless and self-righteous moral backlash' and instead pleaded for a 'moral reawakening' as 'society's best hope'.[67] Controversy remains within Churches as to whether they ought to endorse 'safe sex' education programs that encourage chastity - while recognizing that the reality of many people's sexual behavior does not always live up to that ideal - and provide knowledge about the use of condoms in a context where human life itself is at stake.

Most HIV/AIDS infection is now in developing countries, affecting women and children as well as men. It is as much a justice issue as a sexual issue. The social and sexual subordination of women and children, along with poverty, are factors at work in the spread of HIV/AIDS in the poorer nations of the world. Here pastoral care relating to AIDS ought to be seen as being as much about the Church's working for the removal of poverty, and the restoration of the full and equal dignity of women and children, as much as being about chastity and charitable assistance.[68]

## Sexual Abuse

No issue in pastoral care has given rise to as much frustration, anger and pain as that of the sexual abuse of minors, as well as of adults, by persons working in the name of the Church as priests, religious or laypersons. The public image of the Church has been very badly damaged not only by the actions of those guilty of abuse but also by the way so many bishops and religious superiors have failed to prevent such abuse from being repeated by offenders or have attempted to keep it quiet with so called 'hush money'. Throughout much of the Church there has been a crisis of confidence in its leadership and a widespread public suspicion about priests and religious, in general. A willingness by Catholics and others outside the boundaries of Catholicism to look to the Catholic Church as a source of moral leadership has been eroded. Child abuse has resulted in the recognition of the lamentable abuse of power and trust by many of those entrusted with pastoral care.

Those who have been abused are often psychologically damaged and may suffer depression, anxiety, uncontrollable fears, suicidal thinking, difficulties with forming stable relationships, eating disorders and a wide range of other emotional disturbances and behaviors. Following their historic and much publicized meeting in Dallas in June 2002 to deal with sexual abuse within the Church, the United States Conference of Catholic Bishops, in their *Charter for the Protection of Children and Young People*, stated that the first obligation to victims is that of healing and reconciliation; this might include the provision of counseling, spiritual assistance, support groups and other social services. Of particular importance in the pastoral care of victims, state the bishops, is 'to listen with patience and compassion to their experiences and concerns'.[69] Also needed are clear mechanisms to respond promptly to allegations of sexual abuse by persons employed by the Church that take into consideration due process for both victims and alleged perpetrators.

Arising out of their historic meeting in Dallas, the American Bishops commissioned a lay panel of experts to report on the causes and context of the sexual abuse crisis. This National Review Board published its findings two years later. It claimed that four per cent of priests in ministry over the last half century committed acts of sexual abuse upon minors. While careful to state that neither the discipline of celibacy nor the presence of homosexually oriented priests caused the crisis, the Board maintained that it was not possible to understand the abuse crisis without reference to these issues. Among its recommendations, the

Board encouraged enhanced screening, formation and oversight of candidates for the priesthood; increased sensitivity in responding to allegations of abuse; greater transparency and accountability of bishops and church leaders; improved interaction with civil authorities; and far more openness to the participation by the laity in the life of the Church.[70]

The Australian Catholic Bishops Conference and Major Religious Superiors issued *Towards Healing*, a document that offers detailed guidelines and procedures for dealing with allegations of abuse, in 1996.[71] An accompanying document sets out professional standards for those working for the Church. Both the Canadian and Irish Bishops have also issued guidelines for dealing with allegations of abuse by clergy.[72]

As Stephen Rossetti points out, what victims want most of all 'is a Church which cares and which acknowledges their pain'.[73] The sexual abuse scandal in the Catholic Church has resulted in the demand for a Church that is far more accountable than previously in its pastoral structures and practices.

## Pastoral Counseling and Spiritual Direction

In modern times the role of the minister has undergone a profound change in emphasis when it comes to pastoral care as the 'cure of souls': a change in emphasis from penitential confessor to spiritual counselor. The focus has moved from sin to suffering, from forgiveness to healing. This change has come about largely as a result of the Freudian revolution, which has drawn attention to the psychological underpinnings of human nature. This erosion of a sense of human sinfulness and a conviction that psychology has replaced the perspective of faith leads some within the Church to view with deep suspicion the counseling approach to pastoral care. On the other hand, those within the pastoral counseling movement argue that the salvation offered by Christ through divine grace, and mediated through ministry, has to be grounded within contemporary understandings of human nature, its flaws and its possibilities for change. How neurosis is connected to human sinfulness and how healing relates to our reconciliation with God and neighbor are matters that have characterized more recent theological understanding and practice of Christian ministry.[74]

Pastoral care using counseling methods, 'cure by talk', is to be found in the pioneering work of Anton Boisen (1867-1966), a chaplain in a psychiatric hospital. In 1925 he began a training program for

Protestant theological students in the Worcester State Hospital in Massachusetts. Student chaplains kept detailed written records of their observations, conversations and subsequent reflections upon individual patients. These were then discussed in small groups under the guidance of experienced chaplain-supervisors. This case study approach to pastoral education sought to bring together the disciplines of theology, psychology, medicine and social work to improve the pastoral care of patients. It was the beginning of what came to be called 'Clinical Pastoral Education' (CPE). Instead of relying on an educational methodology based primarily upon books, Boisen insisted that the primary teacher was the patient, 'the living document': an action-reflection model of learning. CPE was adapted later to other pastoral settings beyond that of hospitals, and its goals and methodologies have been used increasingly in both Catholic and Protestant schools of theology in preparing students for ministry.[75] Accused of over-emphasizing psychology, CPE has incorporated in more recent decades a stronger theological base.

Pastoral counseling flourished initially within Protestantism, especially in North America, in the 1950s and 1960s, and soon found its way into Catholic circles by the late 1960s and 1970s. Since then, ministry education has come increasingly to offer basic counseling skills, while some pastoral ministers have become more highly trained in the discipline, enabling them to function as specialist pastoral counselors. Initially dominated by psychoanalytic counseling theory, pastoral counseling later moved more in the direction of the non-directive therapeutic methods of Carl Rogers (1902-87), known as 'person-centered therapy'. The focus in such therapy was on 'becoming the self that one truly is'. Rogers had a strong Evangelical Protestant background though he reacted against this in later life. His style of helping, which placed stress upon empathic listening, genuineness in the helper and non-judgmental acceptance of the client, found ready acceptance within pastoral care.[76] With the proliferation of different theories of counseling and psychotherapy, a wider range of interventions are now used within pastoral counseling. Illness, anxiety, addictions, vocational issues, relationship difficulties and bereavement are but some of life's many experiences that receive attention in pastoral counseling.

What makes pastoral counseling distinct from more secular forms of counseling is a question that has preoccupied pastoral theology. It is recognized that pastoral counseling must have distinct aims and methods resting upon a firm foundation of Christian faith. But a well-developed theory of pastoral counseling, grounded upon a sound theological framework, is in need of more work, especially within Catholic theology. In Protestantism, Howard Clinebell's liberation-growth approach, emphasizing spiritual wholeness and Christian ethics, is one of the most developed models of pastoral counseling that has appeared.[77]

There are two broad approaches to counseling within ministry that are distinct in their aims. First, there is what usually goes by the explicit name of 'Christian counseling'. It is typically associated with Protestantism of a more evangelical or fundamentalist kind.[78] It draws upon the usual counseling methods of warmth, acceptance and empathy and is familiar with the different theories of psychotherapy. The aim, however, is quite intentional. It is to lead the person to a predetermined code of behavior and thinking that aims at Christian conversion. It rests upon a theology that sees human nature as basically flawed and in need of redemption that can come about by only an explicit affirmation of Christ as one's savior. In this approach to counseling, there are strict polarities: righteousness and wickedness, truth and error. 'Christian counseling' is regarded as effective only if it leads a person to a deep and genuine faith in Jesus Christ. As such, it is a specialized form of evangelism. It is really a variation of the behaviorist model of counseling that works on a process of subtle but overt persuasion using techniques designed towards predetermined outcomes.

What usually goes by the name of 'pastoral counseling' – the second approach - has a different emphasis and goals. While working out of a definite framework of Christian beliefs and values, the pastoral counselor remains more focused on the person's particular experience and needs and emphasizes the empowerment of the person to come to his or her decisions. Like the 'Christian counselor', the 'pastoral counselor' holds out the possibility of faith in Christ but there is not the same pressure as in the former approach to push the person to this. There is a greater readiness to recognize that faith has its stages, with accompanying moments of readiness for each person at any time during life. This style of counseling avoids the all or nothing approach to faith, for God's grace is not understood to be confined by human-imposed boundaries. While not ignoring the reality of human sinfulness and its recognition, the 'pastoral counselor' has a more positive theological view of human nature: growth, rather than rescue.

There is also the distinction between a supportive pastoral care relationship, which is able to draw upon interpersonal skills, and pastoral counseling of a greater depth, and usually longer duration, requiring more specialized skills. And counseling is but one form of pastoral care, not the total picture. Counseling, teaching, evangelization and sacramental penance are each distinct types of ministry with their own particular goals and methods.

Spiritual direction, as widely practiced today, is closely related to pastoral counseling. While in earlier times spiritual direction was primarily a ministry among clergy and religious sisters and brothers, it has increasingly become a form of pastoral care sought after by many laywomen and men. Its special focus remains a person's attention to the mystery and presence of God in one's life and a response to this intimacy with God and its consequences for personal relationships.[79] At the heart of spiritual direction is the desire to lead a person into a more contemplative spirituality that consists of quiet meditation and attentiveness in listening to God speaking in the circumstances of one's life. Carolyn Gratton stresses the idea of attention being awakened to a participation in the Mystery within spiritual direction.[80]

We are living in a time of increasing interest in matters of the 'soul', especially forms of meditation. Many people in the secularized Western world, estranged from their roots within Christianity but dissatisfied with a purely material basis for life, are seeking the journey inwards in some form or other. Hence the contemporary interest in Eastern religions, New Age movements and Jungian psychology. Yet we have already seen that Christianity has its own rich spiritual tradition. This can nurture and shape spiritual direction. There are distinct Benedictine, Carmelite and Jesuit spiritualities, for example, which have arisen out of the Catholic religious orders. Both Eastern and Western streams of Christianity have an abundant mystical literature that is being rediscovered by people seeking to foster the inner life. Spiritual direction has various names: spiritual guidance, spiritual companionship, or having a soul friend. As Jean Stairs notes in an excellent book on spiritual direction within the Reformed tradition, the Protestant emphasis on Scripture alone led to a certain wariness of being advised or directed by another. Protestant Churches, she writes, are now scrambling to respond to this renewed interest in matters of the soul.[81] The quest for what Kenneth Leech calls 'God-consciousness' is at the heart of this ever-growing ministry of spiritual direction.[82]

Two Catholic writers who have been particularly influential in spiritual guidance in our time have been Thomas Merton (1915-68) and Henri Nouwen (1932-96). Merton's spirituality is firmly rooted in the monastic and mystical tradition yet his writings are recognized as speaking with particular eloquence to the experiences of people in the secular world. Merton's interest in Eastern spirituality, especially Zen Buddhism, and his attention to the relationship of the spiritual life to the social issues of peace and nonviolence, have contributed to his appeal.[83] As for Nouwen, his spirituality is primarily relational: with God, with self, and with others.[84] Like Merton, Nouwen had the ability to recognize the spiritual hungers of our time and offered hope to a world afflicted by disillusionment. His small book, *The Wounded Healer*, influenced a whole generation of people working in pastoral care.[85] Fostering spirituality has taken on an ever increasing importance in the pastoral life of the Church, reflecting a movement within the wider society as people today hunger for greater depth in their lives.

# Chapter 10

# A Global Mission

One Sabbath day, in the stone synagogue at Nazareth, Jesus announced that he had been anointed by God '... to bring good news to the poor. He has sent me to proclaim release to the captives and recovery of sight to the blind, to let the oppressed go free' (cf. Lk 4:16-18). Jesus understood his task in life to be one of ushering in the reign of God into this world, of enhancing the lives of women, men and children. All around him he saw his people being oppressed by the harsh power of the ancient Roman Empire that ruled his land and by the restrictive customs of the Jewish religious law that too often crushed genuine human values. For him, religion was more about how people lived than cultic purity. Yet life in this world could be improved only if it were to be seen through the eyes of God. Jesus was no mere political reformer. At the heart of his message was God's commandment of love for all. That day his message was not well received. His listeners wanted to drive him out of his own town.

Today the Church continues in its pastoral mission to work towards making the reign of God that Jesus first announced in the Nazareth synagogue more obvious. Its efforts are not always welcomed. Amidst global poverty and hunger, religious and political fanaticism fuelling terrorism, millions of persons being displaced from their homelands, and irreversible ecological devastation, the task of pastoral care takes on new dimensions in a world that is increasingly realized to be intimately interconnected. As never before in its long history, the Church's mission has become truly global. It is in turning to the broader and universal issues confronting contemporary life that we conclude the Church's story of pastoral care.

## Social Justice, Communism and Liberation Theology

### The Social Teachings of the Church

While the women's liberation movement gained momentum in the West, another form of liberation was taking shape in Latin America and in some countries of the so-called 'Third World'. It was a movement in the quest for economic and political justice inspired by liberation theology. Liberation theology is not just about ideas. It is theological thinking that is directed towards pastoral action. This movement for social justice within liberation theology, despite its leanings towards Marxist analysis, has firm roots within official Catholic social teaching that go back to Leo XIII's encyclical *Rerum Novarum* ('The Condition of Labor')[1] from the end of the nineteenth century. Throughout the twentieth century the popes have been untiring in their teaching on social issues. Communism, with its expansionist militancy, was seen as the great threat to human freedom and religion. Its promise of a more just society through the equal sharing of material goods, as against the dangers of capitalist greed, posed a particular challenge to Christian social thought and pastoral action. Catholic social teaching has attempted to combine a more just sharing of wealth (the positive side of socialism) with free enterprise and the freedom to possess private property (the positive side of capitalism).

In 1931, during the time of the effects of the Great Depression, Pius XI issued *Quadragesimo Anno* ('After Forty Years'),[2] which stressed the responsibility of the state to reform the social order and protect workers' rights. Pius introduced the concept of the principle of 'subsidiarity', by which problems should be resolved initially on more local levels. In 1937 the same pope wrote *Divini Redemptoris* ('The Divine Redeemer') against communism, and four days after issuing that document, priests in Germany were ordered to read from the pulpit *Mit brennender Sorge* ('With burning concern') in which the pope exposed the errors of the Nazi doctrines of National Socialism. The papal document had been smuggled into Germany and secretly printed and distributed. Controversy continues to surround Pius XII's silence, throughout the dark days of the Second World War, concerning Hitler's atrocities of the Final Solution that resulted in the Jewish Holocaust.[3] At the height of the Cold War between communism and the West came Pope John XXIII's encyclical *Mater et Magistra* ('Mother and Teacher')[4] in 1961. Poverty was no longer primarily a problem between rich and poor classes but between rich and poor nations. The pope pointed directly at the spending involved in the nuclear arms race as contributing to poverty and threatening world peace. The Church's pastoral teaching on poverty became internationalized. With the erection of the Berlin Wall by the communists in August 1961 and the threat of nuclear war posed by the Cuban Missile Crisis in October 1962, this encyclical again addressed the pressing issue of peace that could be maintained only through respect for human rights and by nations attending to their responsibilities.

By the latter part of the 1960s the concept of development began to take hold within a world where the gap between rich and poor countries was ever widening. Paul VI's encyclical, *Populorum Progressio* ('On the Development of Peoples') in 1967 endorsed the work of aid agencies and taught that 'the superfluous goods of wealthier nations ought to be placed at the disposal of poorer nations'.[5] Global solidarity had now become an essential feature of pastoral care. The Vietnam War was at its height and numerous African countries were in the midst of violent wars, seeking independence. More radical ideas were laid out in 1971 by Paul VI in *Octogesima Adveniens* ('A Call to Action').[6] To combat injustice and discrimination, political as well as economic action was needed. As the world was verging on recession, and riots relating to various causes had broken out in cities around the world, such as the cause concerning civil rights in the United States, the pope addressed new problems, such as marginalization arising with urbanization. Injustices must be challenged. In the same year, as a result of the Synod of Bishops, Paul VI wrote of justice as 'a constitutive dimension of preaching the gospel' in the document *Justice in the World*.[7]

John Paul II, with his experience of having lived in communist Poland, saw social justice as central to the agenda he laid down for the pastoral mission of the Church. Upon becoming pope he immediately aligned himself with the Solidarity movement in Poland, under the Gdańsk trade union leader, Lech Walesa, a movement that was to be instrumental in bringing communism to its knees in that country and eventually throughout the Eastern European Soviet bloc. Criticizing communism and capitalism, John Paul's *Laborem Exercens* ('On Human Work')[8] in 1981 interpreted work and the conditions of employment as central to the measure of human dignity. With increasing numbers of people on the move around the globe, the Pope noted that migrant workers, in particular, had become victims of exploitation. Ten years later, in 1991, in *Sollicitudo Rei Socialis* ('On Social Concern')[9] John Paul addressed the problems arising from global debt and the economic gap between the Northern and Southern Hemispheres. The West was targeted for its selfish isolation while the East was criticized for its failure to alleviate human misery and to respect human rights. All sides of a divided world were guilty for the evils of the arms race. A hundred years after *Rerum Novarum*, John Paul delivered *Centesimus Annus* ('On the Hundredth Year')[10] in 1991. Following the then recent collapse of the Berlin Wall, the Pope discussed the evils of both communism and capitalism. Communism is degrading because of its atheistic view of humanity while capitalism, which can foster consumerism and greed, is prone to cheapen human beings and ultimately destroy the planet. In *Evangelium Vitae* ('The Gospel of Life')[11] John Paul spoke in 1995 of the need to reverence life and attacked the 'culture of death' in modern society that threatens life in so many different ways, such as through abortion or warfare.

From this brief survey of some of the more important papal social teachings it is obvious that social justice took on ever-increasing importance in the Catholic Church's program of pastoral care throughout the twentieth century. These universal teachings aimed to cultivate action, and local Churches have labored to bring them into the context of their own countries. In the United States the bishops entered into a new mode of teaching on social issues through pastoral documents that were written after wide consultation with people from different areas of expertise and viewpoints, and for the nation as a whole: *The Challenge of Peace* (1983) and *Economic Justice for All* (1986) are two examples.[12] A similar process was followed by the Australian bishops in *Common Wealth for the Common Good* (1992)[13] and in England and Wales with publication of the bishops' *The Common Good and the Catholic Church's Social Teaching* (1996).[14] These pastoral documents of national Churches all involve a theological reflection upon scripture and Church teachings but are accompanied by a social analysis of contemporary experience that draws upon the insights of sciences such as economics, political science, demography, sociology and others. Conclusions are then drawn for a practical response in action: a re-working of Cardijn's pastoral method of 'See, Judge, Act'. It is the methodology of that area of theology known as practical theology[15] that is meant to shape and guide pastoral practice.

## Communism

On 1 December 1989 an extraordinary meeting took place in Rome that was to signal that history had taken a dramatic new turn. The Russian General Secretary, Mikhail Gorbachev (b.1931), and the Polish Pope, John Paul II, met in the Vatican's Apostolic Palace to exchange greetings and discuss the new world order following the collapse of the Berlin Wall just weeks earlier. Communism throughout Eastern Europe was about to collapse.[16] During the years of the Cold War the Church had suffered badly under communism. In communist countries, some of which stretched beyond Eastern Europe to include China and Cuba, pastoral care was largely a matter of assisting Christians simply to survive and practice their faith. Levels of religious freedom varied from country to country and frequently two Churches existed side by side: the Church recognized and controlled by the state and the underground Church that refused accommodation with the communists, as in China. Many Catholic bishops and lay people were arrested and jailed for speaking out against the Communist party. Among them were Archbishop Alojzije Stepinac (1898-1960) of Croatia, and Cardinal József Mindszenty (1892-1975) of Hungary, both of whom attracted wide publicity.

In 1931 Pius XI had denounced communism in his encyclical letter *Quadragesimo Anno* but it was Pius XII who set the Catholic Church firmly against Moscow and its satellite states. Pius XII, through a decree from the Vatican's Holy Office, excommunicated communists and denied the sacraments to Catholics who 'helped these enemies of God'. During the 1950s devotion to the Virgin Mary intensified among Catholics around the world and became associated with prayers to the Virgin for the conversion of communist Russia. Fatima, the Marian shrine in Portugal where Mary is said to have appeared to three shepherd children in 1917, warning them of impending world disasters, became a particular focus for anti-communist feeling among Catholics. The Blue Army of Mary was the organization that helped spread the Fatima devotion. And the anti-communist cause was also helped by the Irish-born American priest, Father Patrick Peyton (1909-92) in his crusade to get Catholic families to recite the Rosary daily in their homes. His slogan reached the lips of millions of Catholics: 'The family that prays together stays together.' Peyton spoke at rallies in more than forty countries and his Rosary Crusade became a central feature of pastoral care promoted by clergy during the 1950s and early 1960s.[17]

During the pontificate of Paul VI the Vatican's attitude towards communism began to move from outright confrontation to efforts at diplomatic dialog, in an attempt to gain concessions for Catholics living under Marxist states. Cardinal Agostino Casaroli (1914-98) engaged in a series of missions of diplomacy arising out of his conviction that if the Church was to survive, then some form of accommodation with communism was necessary.[18] That all changed under John Paul II, who believed in working from a position of strength and resistance, especially within his native Poland. Communism in Eastern Europe finally came down but in these lands a new threat arose in the 1990s that had to be faced through pastoral care, namely, secularist materialism, offered by the freedoms of Western-style democracy.

## Liberation Theology and Base Ecclesial Communities

In 1976 the National Conference of the Bishops of Brazil issued a pastoral message. It sums up the essential spirit of liberation theology, which for a time formed the essential basis of pastoral care in much of Latin America and other countries of the developing world, such as the Philippines. The bishops of Brazil addressed the following words to their people:

> There was a time when our preaching to the people advised mainly patience and resignation. Today, without ceasing to do this, our words are also addressed to the great and powerful, to indicate to them their responsibility for the suffering of the poor. The Church has attempted to take up the defense of the rights of the weak, the poor, the Indians, and the children yet to be born. Today, however, it no longer asks for the people an alms consisting of leftovers falling from the table of the rich, but rather a more just distribution of goods.[19]

Eight years earlier, in 1968, the Latin American Bishops Conference had met at Medellín, Colombia to consider the consequences of the Second Vatican Council for their part of the world. The year 1968 saw protest movements, especially by students, on the streets in many parts of the world with, for example, demonstrations against the Vietnam War and capitalism, and demonstrations for civil rights, for black Americans, and for women's rights. In much of Latin America at that time, leftist groups, aligning themselves with Marxist ideology, were involved in violent struggles against repressive regimes linked with the right, which upheld neo-capitalist policies that did little to assist the populous underclass struggling just to exist. Injustice and oppression were rife in many of the Latin American countries that were predominantly Catholic. The Catholic hierarchy had always been closely aligned with the wealthy, ruling class.

Medellín endorsed a theology of liberation as did the Third General Council of Latin American Bishops in Puebla in 1979. Yet at Medellín there were two distinct orientations to the question of injustice.[20] Gregory Baum has described them as the 'soft' meaning and the 'hard' meaning of liberation.[21] The 'soft' meaning of liberation, particularly evident in Medellín's chapter, *On Justice*, is of the liberal, reformist understanding of social change prominent in the documents of Vatican II, especially *Gaudium et Spes*. It involves an optimistic view of human society, which sees it as capable of evolving towards greater justice. Baum argues that this is the understanding of justice from the capitalist West. On the other hand, the 'hard' meaning of justice, namely liberation, is to be found in Medellín's chapter, *On Peace*. Here there is an analysis of the concrete conditions of oppression.

The systemic causes of human misery are named. Justice requires a certain rupture of the present order, not simply an evolution, as in the 'soft' meaning of the term. In this 'hard' view, justice will not result simply from the conversion of individual persons. The oppressed must take social action to overcome injustice.

Gerard Kelly has explained that the assumption behind doing theology from a liberation perspective is that there exists a gap between people's understanding of God arising from their faith, and the realities that they face within their historical situation and its associated ideologies.[22] Liberation theology, while having expressed itself in different ways, first received its most complete and familiar presentation in Gustavo Gutierrez's book, A Theology of Liberation, published in English in 1973.[23] Whereas more traditional theologies are more concerned with individual life and repentance, liberation theology is social in its orientation. It stresses the social dimension of sin, conversion, and grace. It is a reading of the Scriptures from the perspective of society's victims. Liberation from all forms of bondage is salvation. The reign of God involves God's redemptive presence in bringing change to this world.

There are a number of characteristics of liberation theology, including the de-privatization of the gospel. The concern is less with a rational interpretation of the world and more with a desire to change it. Truth statements can be understood only in their relationship to action or what is called 'liberating praxis'. There is a preferential option for the poor, as theology must uncover the ideologies present in religion and the wider social order. Liberation theology, always contextual, is essentially a political act that seeks social change. The Church and its teachings are considered irrelevant unless they can work for the improvement of concrete historical circumstances.[24]

Liberation theology, as a basis for pastoral care, found its clearest expression within the base ecclesial communities. By the 1970s these small communities were firmly established in Brazil but quickly emerged and grew elsewhere. Dom Helder Câmara (1909-99), the Archbishop of Olinda and Recife, Brazil - and known as 'the bishop of the poor'- was a strong supporter. In part, the base ecclesial communities were a response to the shortage of clergy, especially in rural areas. They combined social activism with prayer and reflection upon the Scriptures. Their aim was to connect the gospel message with the realities of people's lives. For the poor, these communities became their most immediate experience of Catholicism.

The base ecclesial communities drew upon the educational methods developed by Paulo Freire (1921-97). Freire achieved fame in Brazil during the 1950s teaching illiterate adults to read. The core of Freire's method was the teacher's entering into the lived world of the student and engaging her or him in dialog. From the dialog emerged 'generative' words and themes about which people felt a degree of passion. The Freire method was intended to help people become active participants, rather than passive recipients, in their learning. The technique and philosophy underlying it came to be known as 'conscientization'. Yet Freire's method of education, developed most famously in his book, *Pedagogy of the Oppressed*,[25] was intensely political, aiming at empowering the socially and economically oppressed poor in Latin America. Its publication resulted in his expulsion from Brazil for many years. Supported by the World Council of Churches and UNESCO, Freire devoted his talents to the education and liberation of the poor in various countries of Latin America, Africa and Asia, and influenced a great number of educators while teaching in the United States. Paulo Freire was a close friend of Dom Helder Câmara and his educational methods were a guiding force within the base ecclesial communities.[26]

Oscar Romero (1917-80), the Archbishop of San Salvador, remains one of the best known and admired figures in Latin America in contemporary times for his voice on behalf of the poor. It was to cost him his life. He was gunned down by right-wing extremists while celebrating Mass in a hospital chapel. Romero had been a traditional, conservative cleric until he was changed by a new willingness to open his eyes to the suffering, injustices and assassinations experienced by the poor and their supporters within El Salvador, especially those who worked on the coffee plantations in his diocese. He pleaded with American President Jimmy Carter for the cessation of all foreign military aid to his beleaguered country. He was accused by other bishops in El Salvador of staining the Church with politics.[27] Oscar Romero, together with civil rights activist and American Baptist minister Dr Martin Luther King Jr (1929-68), who was shot dead in Memphis, and Anglican Archbishop Desmond Tutu (b.1931) of Capetown in South Africa, who led the fight against apartheid, are some of the public faces within a liberationist approach to pastoral care that cuts across denominational differences.

But liberation theology, and the pastoral structure of the base ecclesial communities through which this theology found practical expression, came under mounting pressure. Because of liberation theology's heavy reliance upon Marxist methods of social analysis, in 1984 the Vatican Congregation for the Doctrine of the Faith issued a lengthy *Instruction on Certain Aspects of the 'Theology of Liberation'*.[28] It listed what it saw as the many dangers within liberation theology. These included an overemphasis on earthly realities; misreading the Bible in identifying the kingdom of God with politics and human liberation movements; and an over-reliance on atheistic Marxism as a tool of social analysis, which, the Vatican asserted, cannot be separated from the overall ideology of atheistic Marxism. John Paul II had little sympathy for Marxist-inspired communism. A follow-up document two years later, *Instruction on Christian Freedom and Liberation*,[29] was more positive in tone. But a new wave of Latin American bishops appointed by John Paul II ensured that liberation theology and the base ecclesial communities would diminish in influence.

Liberation theology that had its origins in Latin America focused on the poor but it has inspired other marginalized groups and causes to develop their own theological reflection. Black theology, feminist theology, gay and lesbian theology, ecological theology, and a theology concerned with the experiences of people with physical and intellectual disabilities all look to liberation theology for their methods of drawing into dialog the elements of lived experience, the human sciences and the Christian tradition, all for the purpose of radical social change. All have deeply affected the direction of pastoral care.

### Mother Teresa

While social justice teaching and liberation theology seek to assist the poor and marginalized by empowering them to change what it is that oppresses them (the quest for justice), Mother Teresa (1910-97) is the best known representative of an alternative method that concerns itself with a hands-on form of practical care in alleviating human suffering (the practice of charity). Mother Teresa has won the admiration of people everywhere for the work of her Missionaries of Charity around the world in caring for the poorest of the poor. Her fame came as a result of a television program in the 1960s about her life and work by the British journalist Malcolm Muggeridge. Before then she was not widely known.

Albanian-born Agnes Bojaxhiu left her home in Skopje in 1928 to join the Sisters of Loreto in Ireland. She was sent as a novice to Darjeeling in the foothills of the Himalayas and the following year taught in a Loreto school in Calcutta. After almost twenty years as a sister in the Loreto Order, she felt a call to serve the poor. She chose to live and work in the slums of Calcutta where she cared for the destitute and the dying. She had taken the religious name of Teresa. Her Missionaries of Charity were approved as a new religious order in 1950, her sisters dressed in their distinctive blue and white saris. The Missionary Brothers of Charity were established in 1963.

Mother Teresa opened a house for the dying, called *Nirmala Hriday* (Pure Heart), alongside Calcutta's well-known Kalighat Temple. Some devout Hindus protested that her shelter for the dying defiled the temple. To these objections the local police commissioner responded: 'I promised to get this woman out of here, but until you can bring your mothers and sisters to do the work she is doing I cannot keep my promise. In the temple you have a stone goddess, but here is the living one.'[30] The complaints abruptly came to an end when she took in one of the Hindu priests dying of cholera. She opened a center to care for abandoned children in Calcutta as well as a home to look after leprosy patients with funds raised from the raffle of a white Ford Lincoln car given to her by Pope Paul VI. Her Sisters of Charity devoted their lives to care for all kinds of people in desperate need, including drug addicts, alcoholics and people afflicted with AIDS.[31]

With her wrinkled face and rough peasant features, Mother Teresa was a familiar figure in high places and was loved by the media. She turned up everywhere, whether at Harvard University to accept an honorary doctorate or at the United Nations to address the General Assembly. She won the Nobel Peace Prize in 1979. She was always a welcome visitor to the Vatican. A fierce and vocal opponent of abortion, Mother Teresa was able to speak with authority when it came to issues about life and death. She was beatified by her close friend and admirer, John Paul II, on 20 October 2003. Despite her critics, who claim she neglected to introduce modern medicine into her institutions, it would be unreasonable to doubt that this woman has contributed immensely to making the world a more humane and loving place. Perhaps more than anyone else in the twentieth century, she reminded people everywhere of the need to serve and love the poor and dying – those in whom she always saw Christ himself.

### The Church and Globalization

#### *A Globalized World*

Globalization is a term that has come to characterize our contemporary experience of living in a shrinking world. In its economic meaning, globalization refers to the rapid shift of capital, goods, and labor around the world for maximum profitability to shareholders. It relies on fast transport, computer technology, taxation policies, interest and exchange rates, environmental and other forms of regulation that lead to the collapse of national borders in business. Internationalism, speed and quick adaptation are the keys to globalization. Political globalization takes into account the increasing interdependence of countries throughout the world in both war and peace, as exemplified in the workings of the United Nations. A broad understanding of globalization takes into account the decline in local culture due to greater global uniformity fostered by large multinational conglomerates that influence a country's way of life in regard to such things as dress, food, language, architecture, music, movies and television programs, and the insatiable urge for consumer goods.

Globalization is not necessarily all bad news. In many countries globalization, through investment, has helped reduce poverty and has led to more prosperity among a growing, more educated middle class; and information technology has allowed greater access to information, ideas and communication. Also, there has been far more communication and understanding among cultures, countries and religions; increased awareness of human suffering around the world, resulting in compassion and practical assistance for victims of natural disasters, wars and civil unrest; increased awareness about campaigns for human rights, especially the rights of women and children; and increased pressure applied to governments to be more accountable for their policies.

But globalization also has it costs: uneven development, and exploitation of poorer countries by richer countries; Western domination of more traditional societies, which breeds resentment; the entrance and exodus of short-term capital from countries at lightning speed; the growth of a consumer culture that has changed the perception of the worth of human beings, seeing them as dependent on possessions; the gradual and often rapid erosion of local culture; the spread of disease, especially AIDS; a rise in international crime from drug trafficking, corruption and money laundering; and a rise in international terrorism.[32] A shrinking world is not all good news.

Yet from its beginnings at Pentecost, the Church has always understood its mission in global terms. Christianity is a universal faith confined neither to one place nor one culture for no single culture can capture the full reality of the gospel. Beginning with Paul VI, and continuing even more with John Paul II, the modern papacy has sought actively to reach out to the peoples of diverse culture that make up the human race by engaging in extensive travel to all continents of the globe. In terms of the universal Church and the local Church, as spoken of at Vatican II, the Church seeks to be unified yet, at the same time, to integrate itself into the distinct styles of life in local communities. But a balance between the one and the many has not always been easy to achieve, and in an increasingly globalized Church it inevitably leads to tension. How much ought the center intervene in the way the local Church goes about its affairs?

Globalization today, with its push towards uniformity, is happening at the same time as a revival in religion that is linked with resurgent nationalism and the assertion of particular cultural identities. This is especially true within Islam. We have seen religious nationalism linked to violence involving many peoples. For example, people in the Balkan, Chechnyan, Indonesian and Sudanese conflicts have been so involved, adversely affecting relations between Islam and Christianity; Jews in Israel have been involved, with adverse effects on their Palestinian neighbors; and Tibetan Buddhists have been involved, in their struggle against the communist Chinese government in Beijing. Anwar Ibrahim even argues that religion will become 'the single most important force' in resistance against the move to uniformity brought on by globalization.[33] In pastoral terms, the challenge is whether religion turns towards violence or reconciliation in this task.

### Reconciliation and Peace

Religion is in a unique position to contribute to the peace of the world. Each of the great religions, including Christianity, has a rich ethical tradition and spiritual notion of human happiness and dignity. Religion can bring to the world stage a vision for humanity that extends beyond economics and the domination of one culture over another. But religions have to turn away from the tribal appeal of closed-minded fundamentalism to that of tolerance, harmony and mutual understanding. No doubt, conflicts will always exist. But in a globalized world, as the religions of the world encounter each other more closely, the opportunity is there for religion to contribute to reconciliation. Religion not only has an ethical and spiritual message to offer. It has rituals of reconciliation that touch the lives of their adherents at a deep level. In the Catholic tradition, for example, to what extent has the sacrament of reconciliation been utilized as a pastoral means of reconciliation in racial and religious conflicts in those parts of the world where such disharmony is markedly present? As well, religion has within itself the capacity to create communities of peace and reconciliation. Robert Schreiter notes that these three dimensions of religion – ethics/spirituality, rituals and community - have the power to transform memories from hurt to healing if used in a creative way.[34] These three tasks religions can do within their own traditions as communities of faith but the different religions can also work at these tasks together, in solidarity with one another. Such co-operation will require a commitment to interreligious dialog. Of course, the reality is that Churches and religious traditions often identify closely with the political aspirations of their own people. It can be difficult for a religious institution to take a non-partisan view in conflicts that divide people. Reconciliation has to be more than the use of conflict resolution techniques. It is about spiritual renewal and this includes religions themselves examining critically their own sinfulness that is in need of repentance and change of heart.[35] Also on a practical level, religions share a common heritage of commitment to assist the poor and suffering. Christianity, through its charitable institutions and international networks, can witness to reconciliation powerfully through its aid work.

What has been the more recent history of the Catholic Church, in particular, concerning the work of peace? The Christian peace movement, *Pax Christi*, traces its origins to 1945. It was Marthe Dortel-Claudot, a teacher in the south of France, who was moved to begin a campaign of prayer for a spirit of reconciliation between France and Germany following the Second World War. In 1950 *Pax Christi* was formally constituted as The International Catholic Movement for Peace. In England the organization was set up in 1971 and has been a powerful voice for nonviolence and justice, especially through the untiring efforts of Bruce Kent (b.1929). The organization, placing emphasis upon a spiritual basis for peace, has been successful in acting as a bridge between the Church and the secular peace movement. Pope John XXIII's 1963 encyclical *Pacem in Terris* (Peace on Earth),[36] issued in the atmosphere of the possibility of nuclear annihilation in the Cold War years, instructed humanity that war was no longer a suitable means of resolving conflicts. The pope called for an end to the arms race and for a progressive disarmament.

In the United States it was Dorothy Day's *Catholic Worker* that kept alive and inspired the Catholic peace movement. Eileen Egan was closely associated with the *Catholic Worker* in New York and founded the organization *Pax*. While there was general support at the time for America's dropping of atomic bombs over Hiroshima and Nagasaki to bring the Second World War in the Pacific to a conclusion, James Gillis, Paulist priest and editor of *Catholic World*, believed that the United States had delivered 'the most powerful blow ever delivered against Christian civilization and moral law'.[37]

The years of the Vietnam War marked the time when peace activism reached a climax. In the 1960s many of the American bishops, such as New York's Cardinal Francis Spellman (1889-1967), who had established a tradition of visiting American troops abroad each Christmas, were outspoken in their support of the war. But as the conflict dragged on, this support began to diminish. Daniel and Philip Berrigan, brothers and priests, actively opposed American involvement in the Vietnam War and took their protest outside the law. The Catonsville Nine, which included the two Berrigan priests, stole files from the draft board and, with accompanying prayers, publicly burnt them with napalm in Catonsville, Maryland while waiting to be arrested. They had invited the media to be present to ensure maximum publicity for their actions. Their methods were copied around the country. Blood was poured over draft cards. Philip and Daniel eventually were both jailed.[38] As would be expected, such actions by pastoral ministers caused deep division within both the Church and country.

Aid distributed to developing countries from Church organizations has become an increasingly important mark of the pastoral care offered by most denominations. Famine, war, political oppression, adverse climatic conditions, rapid population growth, poverty, lack of education, racial conflicts, natural disasters and disease have placed at risk the lives of millions of people around the globe. Church organizations, such as the Catholic Fund for Overseas Development (CAFOD) in England and Wales, Catholic Relief Services in the United States, and Australian Catholic Relief, represent pastoral care on a worldwide scale aimed at alleviating human misery in developing countries. Education in social justice among donor Churches and advocacy for social change have assumed increasing importance within the mission goals of such national bodies. In the age of globalization, pastoral care finds itself reaching out to a larger and ever-widening humanity.

### Refugees and Asylum Seekers

In New York Harbor the Statue of Liberty stands as a symbol of welcome and hope for a better way of life. On it is the inscription:

'Give me your tired, your poor, your huddled masses yearning to breathe free.' And, as we have seen earlier, millions of people accepted the invitation to emigrate to the United States and many other countries around the world that were eagerly looking for people to populate their lands. Today the situation has changed: what are we to do with those millions of displaced persons officially declared as refugees and those who turn up uninvited at airports or on coastlines in small, rusty boats - the asylum seekers? These people are the casualties of war, famine, oppressive regimes and natural disasters. The new, globalized world has seen people on the move on a scale never known in history. Vast numbers of people are displaced and few, if any, countries seem particularly to want them. The words inscribed on the Statue of Liberty don't apply to them. There is the difficult balance between the rights of countries to ensure border protection, choosing who should come and who should go, and the need for humanitarian assistance that shares the burden among the richer and more stable nations. Poorer countries are often the first place of asylum, such as Thailand and Indonesia, putting unfair burdens on these nations already overstretched economically. The responsibilities of nation-states towards refugees is set down in the United Nations 1951 Convention and in the 1967 Protocol. Refugees enjoy the right under these regulations not to be returned to a country where they may be persecuted.

Refugees and asylum seekers inevitably touch the nerve of a country's sense of security, whether they be from Afghanistan or Haiti. Where will it all stop, if we open wide the doors? And what will happen as a result, in regard to national employment, and to racial and religious harmony? And there is the issue of deciding who are genuine refugees and who are simply in search of a better life. Countries have different ways of responding to asylum seekers in search of visas offering them official refugee status. Often it is a policy of allowing asylum seekers to live in the general community under some form of supervision. Australia adopted the most restrictive of methods by locking up men, women and children in detention centers, usually in isolated places, for the entire time it takes to process their refugee application. In some cases this can take several years. It is designed as a deterrent to others and to stamp out the lucrative business of people smuggling.

Jesuit priest and asylum seekers' advocate, Frank Brennan, reminds us of the need for 'considered moral discourse' between governments and their people that goes beyond political considerations when it comes to legislating just and humane policies concerning people in search of asylum.[39] Former Australian diplomat, John Menadue, argues for this greater sense of morality in public life:

> Without morality in public life, we have only rules and laws to fall back upon. Important as they are, laws are not sufficient. A law-based society can go down many slippery paths: towards a totalitarian society where anything that is not legal is forbidden, as in the USSR; or a society where what is legal is right.[40]

The experience of refugees and asylum seekers is often traumatic. Fleeing peril in their homeland, they find themselves in an unknown environment where they are prone to many deeply painful experiences: great insecurity about an unknown future concerning their fate; frustration, that can lead to a lack of hope, over protracted processes in visa application; public expression of racism and hostility towards them; poverty; language difficulties and cultural alienation; loneliness and grief over loss of homeland and family members; sometimes the lack of freedom to work which makes them dependent on welfare; and mental health problems, especially among those experiencing a long period of detention.

Pastoral care faces an enormous challenge in responding to this new outcome of globalization. The Jewish and Christian Scriptures have been shaped very much by refugee experience: the wanderings of Abraham and Moses in search of a new homeland; the exile of the Jewish people in Babylon, and the prophetic literature that responded to this situation; the diaspora experience of Jews in the ancient pagan Greek and Roman worlds; the flight into Egypt by Mary, Joseph and the child Jesus; and the expulsion of the first generations of Jewish Christians from the Synagogue. The biblical heritage is a rich resource for pastoral theological reflection.

What are the possibilities for a pastoral response to the plight of refugees and asylum seekers, in fostering what the Vatican *Instruction on the Love of Christ Towards Migrants* (2004) names 'a culture of solidarity', which 'offers a providential opportunity for the fulfillment of God's plans for a universal communion'?[41] The first element in a pastoral response comprises practical assistance to help resettle these people. Dioceses, parishes and other groups can help with housing, language skills, schooling, employment possibilities, and with simply providing a sense of welcome in a new and strange environment. A second element is to ensure that arrangements are made to obtain the necessary government permissions to visit people in detention centers and to provide religious services and care for them, whatever their faith. Third, advocacy and legal assistance for particular individuals or groups is required to process their claims for residence. And finally, public campaigning and education to raise awareness about the need to protect the rights, including the humane treatment, of refugees and asylum seekers, is necessary. The Church has a role to share these tasks with others in the broader society, so helping to shape a society that is more tolerant, inclusive and welcoming.

### Interreligious Dialog or Fundamentalism?

The Churches have now long been engaged in the task of ecumenism, that is, in seeking greater unity within the world of Christianity itself. By contrast, the quest for increased understanding and cooperation between the diverse religions of the world is more recent. Globalization has brought the great religions into closer contact with each other both internationally and through the experience of people of different faiths living alongside each other in those countries that have become increasingly multicultural in their population composition. Interreligious dialog offers possibilities not just for the mutual enrichment of the religions but also for peace in a world divided by conflicts fueled by fundamentalist religious beliefs.

And there is the issue of the aims and methods of Christian mission. Whereas nineteenth, and early twentieth, century Catholic missionary activity aimed at mass conversions in developing countries, by the latter part of the twentieth century there were new emphases: a proclamation of the gospel that links redemption with the pursuit of justice, and a Christian presence that replaces conquest with partnership and interreligious dialog and understanding. But such emphases create uneasy tension for Christian mission. On the one hand, there is the desire to spread the belief that God has been revealed and offers salvation in a unique and definitive way in Jesus Christ. On the other, there is the wish to avoid old forms of cultural and religious imperialism that set limits on God's power to save and that see foreign cultures and their religions as being nothing other than primitive and pagan, in need of replacement.[42] David Bosch has written: 'A Christian is not simply somebody who stands a better chance of being "saved", but a person who accepts the responsibility to serve God in this life and promote God's reign in all its forms.'[43]

But, as we already have seen, it is not just a new approach to Christian mission that has given rise to interreligious dialog. The modern world has seen a migration of peoples around the globe on a scale never known before. On the streets of large multicultural cities, such as Chicago, London, Toronto or Melbourne, churches, synagogues, temples and mosques are all to be found. In apartment blocks, schools, offices, factories and shopping malls, we find Christians, Jews, Buddhists, Sikhs and Muslims living and working alongside each other. Differences in language, dress and religion can threaten social harmony - and the terrorism of Islamic extremists often leads to others' suspicion, and even acts of violence, towards ordinary and good people, especially Muslims. Governments and community groups have the task of promoting racial tolerance and harmony; and interreligious dialog has its role to play. At both universal and local levels, religion has a unique capacity to foster harmony and peace in our world, just as it can also, perversely, promote hatred and killing. Following the horrifying events associated with the terrorist acts of '9/11', an argument could be mounted that interreligious dialog is one of the most pressing and vital tasks facing pastoral care in our new globalized, but fractured, world. It is far more than just a theoretical and speculative exercise about abstract beliefs. Cardinal Francis Arinze has written that if the major religions do not address realities affecting the world in its quest for reconciliation and peace, then 'religion would be presenting itself as an interesting philosophy, but one that is wholly detached and unconcerned with the sometimes beautiful, sometimes harsh realities of human existence on earth.' Religion, then, Arinze declares, 'would be declaring itself marginal in life'.[44]

There are three broad approaches in theology for Christian understandings and attitudes towards other religions. The first is termed 'exclusivist'. In this approach, salvation requires an explicit, personal faith in Jesus Christ. Other religions are viewed primarily from the point of view of error and falsehood and there is little to be gained from dialog. The most one can expect is tolerance and respect. At the other end of the spectrum is the 'pluralist' approach. This maintains that, within the universe, there are many roads to salvation of which Christianity is but one. Salvation through Jesus Christ is not the only path. But contemporary Catholic teaching adheres to a third broad approach, the 'inclusivist', which maintains that all salvation is through Jesus Christ but the saving grace of Christ is universal and can reach all people, irrespective of their religion. This theological approach is open to seeing aspects of other religions as having the possibility to be good and positive; it is an understanding that can be found in the teaching of Vatican II.[45] Whether salvation, brought to us by Christ, can actually be mediated through these other religions themselves is nowhere stated in the teachings of the Second

Vatican Council. But whether a door has been opened slightly to this understanding of 'participated mediation' by Church teachings since Vatican II, is open to interpretation.[46] In the long run, as S. Wesley Ariarajah of the World Council of Churches cautions: 'An inhospitable theology cannot produce hospitable people.'[47]

Some of the more practical implications arising from interreligious dialog have to do with the form of our pastoral responses to several phenomena, such as marriages across religious traditions, and the subsequent religious upbringing of children of such unions - something that has now become increasingly common in multicultural societies; strongly held differences of belief between religions concerning human rights, especially in regard to women; the explicit role of religion in politics, society and law; responses to conversion from one religion to another; forms of shared prayer on public civic occasions and in schools which reflect the makeup of the population; and ways of conducting prayer in common on non-civically related occasions. The question raised by such occasions is whether such prayer should be conducted in common at all or whether adherents of different faiths may pray together, as happened at Assisi and the Vatican after John Paul II's invitation to world religious leaders to pray together for peace. For the sake of world peace, religions can no longer afford to ignore, let alone generate, antagonism toward one another. Pastoral care in the form of interreligious dialog has become an urgent priority.

But to turn our attention to fundamentalism. Religious fundamentalism is a broader phenomenon than particular beliefs associated with individual religions, such as creationism, in opposition to the theory of evolution, among Christian fundamentalists; strict adherence to the Islamic law of *Sharia*; or the belief held by some Jews that all land in Israel was given by God to the Jewish race for all time and that there can be no compromise concerning land for peace. No: fundamentalism is something deeper and all embracing. As Richard Antoun has argued so clearly, fundamentalism is an orientation to the modern world that is common across all the major religious traditions:[48] fundamentalist believers of whatever faith have more in common than they often realize. Fundamentalism, in its various guises: protests against change; teaches dogmatism; values certainty; dwells on a mythic past; presents a total way of life which demands total commitment; clings to a clearly defined identity among its followers; and appeals to revered religious documents that are adhered to in a strict and literal way. Put simply, fundamentalism is a deeply felt reaction to the modern, secularized world that has distanced religion from public life. It is a minority struggle against what are seen as the forces of evil: a 'them versus us' mentality. Fundamentalism breeds conflict, with suspicion and hostility directed towards the outsider. Of course, it can express itself at different levels of intensity. It typically has appeal among young people who are prone to be idealistic; who feel cut off from the benefits of the consumer society; or who feel alienated and insecure in a world today where there are few certainties.

Fundamentalism is a tremendous challenge to pastoral care. In one sense, it is the very opposite of reconciliation. Yet its offer of certainties and its appeal to unswerving commitment seduces religions eager to attract followers in an increasingly secular world. Fundamentalism inevitably divides groups. As we have seen throughout this history of pastoral care, new movements have continuously arisen within the Church, bringing with them reform and energy. The same is true within all the great religions. Did not Christianity itself begin in this way as a reform movement within Judaism before enlarging and finding its own distinct identity? How we may discern between reformist groups that bring life and energy, on the one hand, and fundamentalist groups that generate narrow and separatist paths, on the other, is a continuous challenge for adherents of all religions, if not for the human race as a whole, in its deepest desire for world peace.

### Planet Earth and the Environment

A case might be made that the pastoral issue of most consequence facing the Church today and in the immediate future is that of our treatment of the environment. Yet is ecology really a pastoral care concern, a matter affecting the lives of human beings, one might ask? Thomas Berry believes it is. He wrote some years ago:

> The future of the Catholic Church in America, in my view, will depend above all on its capacity to assume a religious responsibility for the fate of the earth... After we burn our lifeboat, how will we stay afloat? What will then be the need of religion, Christianity, or the church?'[49]

As we come to the end of this survey of pastoral care over the two thousand year history of the Church, the matter of our care (or lack of care) for the earth assumes an importance and magnitude like no other issue we have been considering. At stake is the continued existence of the biosphere itself and our place within it. With the advent of the industrial revolution in the nineteenth century, the dignity of human life was put at risk through unscrupulous labor practices and pollution that disfigured much of the land. The toll on human life and the natural world has now reached crisis proportions because of pollution and global warming brought on by modern industrial practices. The 1997 Kyoto meeting on global warming made clear the direct link between forest destruction and global warming. Weather patterns are affected by global warming, leading to cyclones and a rise in ocean levels that threatens, for example, the very existence of atolls and low lying islands that are home to many people of the Pacific. This is due partly to the melting of iceshelves in the polar regions of the planet. The loss of Antarctica's 1500 square mile Larsen B iceshelf on the east coast of the Antarctic peninsula, in 2002 (an event fictionalized in the climate change film, *The Day After Tomorrow*), resulted in the release of hitherto land-bound glaciers, which subsequently will cause ocean levels to rise and will threaten the existence of many land and marine animal species, such as the polar bear.[50] The ecosystem is extremely fragile. Deforestation, especially in developing countries, and the rapid increase in urbanization everywhere, has already seen the destruction of the habitats of countless species of animal life.

The *Putting Life before Debt* statement (1999), endorsed by the Irish Bishops, emphasized how foreign debt puts enormous pressure upon poorer countries.[51] The 2000 Jubilee campaign around the world encouraged Christians to lend their support to the call for freeing poor nations from the crippling burdens of repaying foreign debts which, of course, hinder their social and economic progress and predispose the environment to devastating degradation. Yet rich nations, in turn, are tempted to resist calls to reduce their greenhouse gas emissions if poorer countries are not doing the same. The Rio Earth Summit in 1992 called for sustainable development, namely, the generation of wealth and use of the earth's resources within the limits of ecological possibility – good ecology is good business, it was argued. To what extent overpopulation threatens the future of the earth's resources remains a pastoral concern for the Church to consider in the debate as to whether contraception or education and economic development provide the best means for lowering the birth rate in the developing world. And there is the issue of world peace as the earth's resources become more scarce and fought over. It is the relationship between peace and respect for the environment that John Paul II wrote about at length in *Peace With God the Creator, Peace With All Creation* (1990).[52] The American bishops have also written at length on the environment, stating the need for a conversion of heart in regard to our use of the earth's resources to save the planet for our children and future generations.[53]

Christianity has a rich tradition to draw upon in its pastoral task of care for the earth, especially the Scriptures. In the book of Genesis, God chooses Noah to ensure that human and animal life are preserved from the destruction of the great flood. God later enters a covenant with Noah, symbolized by the rainbow, and 'never again shall all flesh be cut off by the waters of a flood, and never again shall there be a flood to destroy the earth' (Gen 9:11).

The Christian Creed begins with the biblical belief in God the Father, creator of heaven and earth. In the fourth and fifth centuries, when the creeds of the Church were formulated, we have seen how debate raged over the human and divine natures of Christ and the relationship of the three Persons of the Trinity to one another. In our own day of greater ecological awareness, theological interest in the Trinity addresses new concerns. To what extent have we chosen to deny the creator God, our Father, by exploiting life in all its forms? In our increasingly secularized age, in which God has been pushed aside, have we lost our sense of the sacredness and giftedness of creation and of our limited place in it? Have we plundered the garden of paradise? We are part of the ecosystem; we do not stand apart from it. And the salvation brought to us by Christ is key to our understanding of the Trinity. Medieval Christians were obsessed with salvation in terms of what happened to them in life after death, with life on earth being understood as of little significance and merely transitory. Eschatology is Christian belief about the future, the fulfillment brought by Jesus Christ. Belief in the trinitarian Christ as savior ought not to mean a diminished concern for life in this world for nothing is lost in the absolute future of Christ. It is the world itself that is consummated. What we humans do in the world and to the world has eschatological significance. Separating earth from heaven is eschatologically indefensible.[54] Denis Edwards writes how ecology, with its understanding of how interrelated systems support life on earth, is related to the Spirit of God whose role is to draw creatures into communion with the divine Persons of the trinitarian God. The Spirit's work is to bring each creature into relationship with other creatures in a global ecological system. In this process of ongoing creation, the Spirit enables each creature to be in communion with the trinitarian God. All creation is held in God's love for the Spirit is in all things.[55]

Creation spirituality addresses how God is revealed to us in the material world which is to be held sacred. It is a spirituality rooted in the tradition of St Francis of Assisi who saw God by means of the animals and the natural world. Liturgy is a means of awakening us to the sacredness of creation. The liturgical celebrations of the sacraments use natural elements such as water, oil, bread and wine to put us in contact with the grace of the divine. Prayer, song, flowers, incense, fire, vestments, exhortation and art have the potential to raise our awareness of the beauty of the earth and to expand our imagination. To participate in the Church's rituals celebrating Christ's victory over sin and death, and then to go forth destroying water, air, soil, plants and animals 'is a contradiction that is hypocritical and deeply pathological'.[56] The Church has a pastoral responsibility to care for life on earth in all its forms. Can there be anything more important for us to attend to at this moment in our globalized and fragile world?

## Conclusion

Pastoral care, in our own times, finds itself existing in the world of postmodernism, that is, amidst ways of seeing the world which reject the Enlightenment principles of rationality and objectivity built upon empirical verification and which adhere, by contrast, to the perspective of the self only. For, it argues, there is no independent truth:[57] there is only individual interpretation. Reality is read differently by everyone. Emotions and intuitions are as valid a part of knowing as reasoning; everything is historically and culturally conditioned. The universe, in the thinking of deconstructionist philosophers, such as Jacques Derrida (1930-2004), is not 'out there' waiting to be discovered. No, reality is entirely relative. This is the new ethos that may significantly shape our culture in which pastoral care is to be offered. The issues that have been discussed in the final two chapters of this book can be fully understood only within this world of postmodernism. For none of us are immune from our cultural surroundings, so that they affect us all, including the ways in which we respond to the reign of God, for better or worse. In some respects postmodernism is at the heart of the Church's present conflicts within its own walls and outside them. In every age - as we have seen throughout the Church's story from its beginnings - the Church's pastoral life and concerns inevitably reflect the philosophical assumptions and values of the time in which it lives. The task is to sort out what can be accepted and what needs to be rejected.

Today, religious fundamentalism is in the ascendancy and Christianity is not exempt from this phenomenon. Religion can be oppressive or it can be freeing. Religion can be divisive and intolerant or it can be a source of reconciliation and harmony. Pastoral care can be of a kind that listens to the voices of those who, in so many different ways, feel marginalized, or it can simply dictate from within the confines of its own walls and learn nothing. Pastoral care - and the theological reflection that must accompany it - has the task of putting the Christian tradition in dialog with the world. Both Church and world can critique and learn from each other to promote the more humane and enriched life which God intends for us all. The Christian voice has a right to be heard in public but it will be heard only when there is an openness to talk, not just a desire to confront. Belligerent behavior in the name of God, as the history of the Church has frequently demonstrated, always ends with tragic results. For in the long run, actions speak louder than words. As in every age of its long history, it will be Christianity's practical kindness and compassion to the sick, poor and neglected that will be most noticed. This book has shown us something of that story.

Religious identity, mixed with an intolerance of other faiths, is used all too frequently as an offensive weapon for political ends. Increasingly, this has taken the form of international terrorism. While religion may not be the simple cause of conflicts and wars, often it is the medium and ideology through which such ends are pursued. The great religions of the world today, in this age of globalization, are faced with a stark choice: either work together for harmony and peace within the human family, or remain separate and apart in a way that fuels intolerance and hostility. This choice is of the utmost importance in the way the Church goes about choosing its priorities and deciding its methods of pastoral care. Our understanding in faith as to how Christianity relates to other religions is a crucial theological and pastoral question in this early part of the third millennium. The future of world peace rests heavily on the outcome.

# Bibliography

Bernier, Paul. *Ministry in the Church: A Historical and Pastoral Approach.* Mystic, Connecticut: Twenty-Third Publications, 1992.

Bosch, David J. *Transforming Mission: Paradigm Shifts in Theology of Mission.* Maryknoll, New York: Orbis Books, 1991.

Brown, Peter. *The Rise of Western Christendom.* Malden, Massachusetts: Blackwell, 1997.

Carey, Patrick W., ed. *American Catholic Religious Thought: The Shaping of a Theological and Social Tradition.* New York: Paulist Press, 1987.

Chadwick, Henry. *The Church in Ancient Society: From Galilee to Gregory the Great.* Oxford: Oxford University Press, 2001.

Clebsch, William A., and Charles R. Jaekle, *Pastoral Care in Historical Perspective.* New York: J. Aronson, 1983.

Coleman, John A., ed. *One Hundred Years of Catholic Social Thought: Celebration and Challenge.* Maryknoll, New York: Orbis Books, 1991.

Cooke, Bernard. *Ministry to Word and Sacraments: History and Theology.* Philadelphia: Fortress Press, 1976.

Dolan, Jay P. *The American Catholic Experience: A History from Colonial Times to the Present.* Garden City, New York: Doubleday, 1985.

Duncan, Bruce. *The Church's Social Teaching: From Rerum Novarum to 1991.* North Blackburn, Victoria: Collins Dove, 1991.

Evans, G. R., ed. *A History of Pastoral Care.* London: Cassell, 2000.

Green, Vivian. *A New History of Christianity.* New York: Continuum, 1996.

Harries, Richard, and Henry Mayr-Harting, eds. *Christianity: Two Thousand Years.* Oxford: Oxford University Press, 2001.

Hastings, Adrian, ed. *A World History of Christianity.* London: Cassell, 1999.

Hunter, Rodney J., ed. *Dictionary of Pastoral Care and Counseling.* Nashville: Abingdon, 1990.

Kelly, Joseph F. *The World of Early Christianity.* Collegeville, Minnesota: The Liturgical Press, 1997.

MacCulloch, Diarmaid. *Reformation: Europe's House Divided 1490-1700.* London and New York: Penguin, 2004.

McClelland, V. Alan, and Michael Hodgetts, eds. *From without the Flaminian Gate: 150 Years of Roman Catholicism in England and Wales 1850-2000.* London: Darton, Longman and Todd, 1999.

McGrath, Alister E. *Historical Theology: An Introduction to the History of Christian Thought.* Oxford: Blackwell, 1998.

McNeill, John T. *A History of the Cure of Souls.* New York: Harper and Row, 1951; reprinted Harper's Ministers Paperback Library, 1977.

Mullett, Michael A. *The Catholic Reformation.* London: Routledge, 1999.

Niebuhr, Richard H., and Daniel D. Williams, eds. *The Ministry in Historical Perspectives.* 2d ed. New York: Harper and Row, 1983.

Norman, Edward. *The English Catholic Church in the Nineteenth Century.* Oxford: Clarendon Press, 1984.

Oden, Thomas C. *The Care of Souls in the Classic Tradition.* Philadelphia: Fortress Press, 1984.

O'Farrell, Patrick. *The Catholic Church and Community in Australia.* West Melbourne: Thomas Nelson, 1977.

Osborne, Kenan B. *Lay Ministry in the Roman Catholic Church: Its History and Theology.* New York: Paulist Press, 1993.

Patton, John., ed. *The Blackwell Reader in Pastoral and Practical Theology.* Oxford: Blackwell, 2000.

Rademacher, William J. *Lay Ministry: A Theological, Spiritual, and Pastoral Handbook.* New York: Crossroad, 1991.

Reardon, Bernard M. G. *Religious Thought in the Reformation.* 2d ed. London: Longman, 1995.

Rynne, Xavier. *Vatican Council II.* 2d ed. Maryknoll, New York: Orbis Books, 1998.

Thomson, A. F. *The Western Church in the Middle Ages.* London: Arnold, 1998.

Volz, Carl A. *Pastoral Life and Practice in the Early Church.* Minneapolis: Augsburg Fortress, 1990.

# Notes

## Chapter 1: Jews and Gentiles

[1] Homer, *Iliad*, 2.570.

[2] Victor Paul Furnish, *II Corinthians,* The Anchor Bible, vol. 32A, ed. William Foxwell Albright and David Noel Freedman (New York: Doubleday, 1984), 7.

[3] Philo, *Legatio ad Caium, xxxvi*, 281.

[4] Jerome Murphy-O'Connor, 'Introduction: The First Letter to the Corinthians', in *The New Jerome Biblical Commentary,* ed. Raymond E. Brown, Joseph A. Fitzmyer, and Roland E. Murphy, (London: Geoffrey Chapman, 1990), 788.

[5] Furnish, 13.

[6] It was at Ephesus, especially, that the cult of the Virgin Mary became popular. The Council of Ephesus in 431 declared Mary to be 'the mother of God', *Theotokos*, thus elevating her importance within Christian doctrine and devotion. The Christian Virgin had replaced and surpassed the pagan fertility goddess Artemis. There exists a tradition that Mary went to Ephesus where, it is believed, she died.

[7] Large numbers of clay votive offerings representing different body parts have been excavated at Corinth (ears, arms, legs, breasts, feet, genitals, etc.). Furnish notes how Paul's imagery of the many parts of the human body to depict the Church (1 Cor 12:12-30) would have had special meaning for his Corinthian readers as they were very familiar with the shrine of Asclepius - see Furnish, 17. At Pergamum, in modern Turkey, there are particularly well-preserved ruins of such a shrine to Asclepius. The snake, symbol of the medical profession, has its origins in the healing cult of Asclepius who was thought to dwell in the animal. In the Old Testament, the snake was understood as a symbol of healing. During the Exodus, as told in the book of Numbers, the people of Israel were instructed to gaze upon the image of the bronze serpent held up by Moses on a pole if they were to survive a snake bite (Num 21:6-9).

[8] For a detailed examination of the social setting for Paul's preaching, see Ronald F. Hock, *The Social Context of Paul's Ministry: Tentmaking and Apostleship* (Philadelphia: Fortress Press, 1980).

[9] David G. Horrell, *The Social Ethos of the Corinthian Correspondence: Interests and Ideology from 1 Corinthians to 1 Clement,* Studies of the New Testament and Its World, ed. John Barclay, Joel Marcus and John Riches (Edinburgh: T and T Clark, 1996), 91-101.

[10] Horrell, 114-5.

[11] Horrell, 117.

[12] In the latter years of the first century, some decades after Paul's martyrdom, the Christian community at Corinth voted out the presbyter-bishops of the community and installed new pastors to lead their community. Those ejected from office had a small following and this group appealed to the Church in Rome for help. The Roman Church, in a letter addressed to its sister Church in Corinth, stressed the

need for proper order and supported those who had been thrown out of office. The new leaders were encouraged to step down and engage in an act of penance. It seems the letter was composed in the name of the whole Roman Church but a second century source attributed its authorship to Clement, the letter now being known as *1 Clement*. Henry Chadwick offers an interpretation of this letter whereby authority in office is assured by due succession. The Corinthians, Chadwick writes, were 'grateful that the Roman community gave a strong lead'. See Henry Chadwick, *The Church in Ancient Society: From Galilee to Gregory the Great* (Oxford: Oxford University Press, 2001), 59-64.

[13] Horrell, 102-5. Horrell draws upon the theories of G. Theissen, *The Social Setting of Pauline Christianity*, ed and trans. Hohn Schütz (Edinburgh: T and T Clark, 1982; and P. Lampe, 'Das korinthische Herrenmahl im Schnittpunkt hellenistisch-römischer Mahlpraxis und paulinischer Theologia Crucis (1 Kor 11, 17-34)', *ZNW* 82 (1991):183-213.

[14] Horrell, 105-9.

[15] Most contemporary commentators on 2 Cor would agree on this point. For a summary of the discussion upon the matter, see Raymond E. Brown, *An Introduction to the New Testament* (New York: Doubleday, 1997), 548-51.

[16] See James D. G. Dunn, *The Theology of Paul the Apostle* (Grand Rapids, Michigan / Cambridge, U.K.: William B. Eerdmans, 1998), 294-315.

[17] Dunn notes that the distinctiveness of early Christian belief in the return of Christ should not be underrated. He states that Elijah's reappearance on earth was already firmly believed at the time of Paul, and Enoch was probably linked with Elijah in regard to this. But the resurrection of Jesus and the claim that, as Messiah, he would return to the earth was unheard of in Judaism of the time. Yet the coming again of a great hero was compatible with Jewish thought. Dunn sums up by claiming that 'we should see this very early line of Christian reflection as part of the developing theological reflection within Second Temple Judaism and contributing to it', 295-6.

[18] Raymond E. Brown, John R. Donaghue, Donald Senior, and Adela Yarbro Collins, 'Aspects of New Testament Thought' in *The New Jerome Biblical Commentary*, 1363.

[19] John Rogerson, Howard Clark Kee, Eric M. Myers and Anthony Saldarini, *The Cambridge Companion to the Bible* (Cambridge: Cambridge University Press, 1997), 475.

[20] Bart D. Ehrman, *The New Testament: A Historical Introduction to the Early Christian Writings* (New York: Oxford University Press, 1997), 278.

[21] Dunn, 672.

[22] Quoted in Dunn, 297.

[23] Bernard Cooke, *Ministry to Word and Sacraments: History and Theology* (Philadelphia: Fortress Press, 1976), 343.

[24] John P. Meier, *A Marginal Jew: Rethinking the Historical Jesus* (New York: Doubleday, 1994).

[25] Ibid., 617.

[26] Ibid., 726.

[27] Ibid., 970.

[28] Joachim Jeremias, *Jerusalem in the Time of Jesus* (London: SCM, 1969), 126-33.

[29] Joseph F. Kelly, *The World of Early Christianity* (Collegeville, Minnesota: The Liturgical Press, 1997), 142-3.

[30] See, for example, Brown, *An Introduction to the New Testament*, 639, and Jerome D. Quinn, *The Letter to Titus*, The Anchor Bible, vol. 35, ed. William Foxwell Albright and David Noel Freedman (New York: Doubleday, 1990), 18-9.

[31] Robert A. Wild, 'Introduction: The Pastoral Epistles', in *The New Jerome Biblical Commentary*, 892, and Quinn, *The Letter to Titus*, 17-9.

[32] For a more detailed examination of the development of church ministries within early Christianity, see Raymond E. Brown, *Priest and Bishop: Biblical Reflections* (London: Geoffrey Chapman, 1970).

[33] Raymond E. Brown, *The Churches the Apostles Left Behind* (London: Geoffrey Chapman, 1984), 33.

[34] Susanne Heine, *Women and Early Christianity: Are the Feminist Scholars Right?* (London: SCM, 1987), 89.

[35] Elisabeth Schüssler Fiorenza, *In Memory of Her: A Feminist Theological Reconstruction of Christian Origins*, 2d ed (London: SCM, 1995), 184.

[36] Rogerson, Kee, Myers and Saldarini, 498.

[37] James Tunstead Burtchaell, *From Synagogue to Church: Public Services and Offices in the Earliest Christian Communities* (Cambridge: Cambridge University Press, 1992), 279.

[38] James D. G. Dunn, *The Parting of the Ways Between Christianity and Judaism and the Significance for the Character of Christianity* (London: SCM, 1991), 60-71.

[39] Ibid., 19.

[40] Ehrman, 33.

[41] Raymond E. Brown, *The Community of the Beloved Disciple* (New York: Paulist Press, 1979). His reconstruction of the Johannine community in this book is summarized in Brown, *An Introduction to the New Testament*, 374-405.

[42] Dunn, *The Parting of the Ways*, 158.

[43] Justin, *Dialogue* 47-8.

[44] Chadwick, 58.

[45] Dunn, *The Theology of Paul the Apostle*, 506.

[46] Tacitus, *Hist.* 5.5.2.

[47] Josephus, *War* 2.184-203; Philo, *Legat.* 184-338; Tacitus, *Hist.* 5.9.

[48] For a detailed description and meaning of sacrifice as practiced in ancient Judaism, see Roland de Vaux, *Ancient Israel: Its Life and Institutions* (London: Darton, Longman and Todd, 1961), 415-56 and Roland de Vaux, *Studies in Old Testament Sacrifice* (Cardiff: University of Wales Press, 1964).

### Chapter 2: Martyrs, Sinners and Heretics

[1] Quoted in Henry Chadwick, *The Early Church*, rev.ed., The Penguin History of the Church (Harmondsworth: Penguin, 1993), 29.

[2] Tacitus, *Annals* XV. 44.

[3] Pliny, *Letters* X. 96-117.

[4] Lucian, *The Death of Peregrinus*, 13.

[5] Vivian Green, *A New History of Christianity* (New York: Continuum, 1996), 18.

[6] See Peter Brown, *The Cult of Saints* (Chicago: University of Chicago Press, 1981) and Peter J. Lynch, *Not Without Hope: Christian Traditions of Grieving* (Sydney: Catholic Institute of Sydney, 1989), 11-9.

[7] *Martyrdom of Polycarp*, 2.3.

[8] Text translated with commentary in Joyce E. Salisbury, *Perpetua's Passion: The Death and Memory of a Young Roman Woman* (New York: Routledge, 1997).

[9] Salisbury, 136.

[10] Tertullian, *Spectacles*.

[11] Salisbury, 140-1.

[12] J. José Alviar, *Klesis:The Theology of the Christian Vocation according to Origen* (Dublin: Four Courts Press, 1993), 13.

[13] Rowan A. Greer, trans. and ed. *Origen*, The Classics of Western Spirituality (New York: Paulist Press, 1979), 17.

[14] Alviar, 171-5. In these pages the author summarizes Origen's theology in *An Exhortation to Martyrdom*.

[15] Quoted in Chadwick, *The Early Church*, 31.

[16] See Arthur J. Droge and James D. Tabor, *A Noble Death: Suicide and Martyrdom among Christians and Jews in Antiquity* (San Francisco: Harper and Row, 1992).

[17] Ignatius, *To the Romans*. Quoted in Droge, 130. See also G. W. Bowersock, *Martyrdom and Rome* (Cambridge: Cambridge University Press, 1995), 4.

[18] Bowersock, 4.

[19] The more fanatical members of the Donatists would commit religious suicide, particularly by throwing themselves into ravines of the Aures Mountains or by drowning themselves. In a sermon at Cyprian's grave, Augustine asked why they never employed a rope as a more comfortable means of taking their own lives. He went on to remark that they preferred to follow the methods of the devil in their suicidal behavior rather than his disciple, Judas. See F. Van der Meer, *Augustine the Bishop: The Life and Work of a Father of the Church*, trans. B. Battershaw and G. R. Lamb (London: Sheed and Ward,1978), 83-4.

[20] Augustine, *The City of God* 1,19.

[21] This summary of the catechumenate relies primarily upon Aidan Kavanagh, *The Shape of Baptism: The Rite of Christian Initiation* (New York: Pueblo, 1978), especially 35-78. For a more detailed examination of early Church documents concerning baptismal rites, see Thomas M. Finn, *Early Christian Baptism and the Catechumenate: West and East Syria*, Message of the Fathers of the Church Vol. 5; *Early Christian Baptism and the Catechumenate: Italy, North Africa, and Egypt*, Message of the Fathers of the Church Vol. 6 (Collegeville, Minnesota: The Liturgical Press, 1992).

[22] Henry Chadwick, *The Church in Ancient Society: From Galilee to Gregory the Great* (Oxford: Oxford University Press, 2001), 115.

[23] Cyprian, *On the Lapsed*, 8; *Letter* 59.10. Commented upon in W. H. C. Frend, *The Early Church: From the Beginnings to 461*, rev.ed. (London: SCM Press, 1991), 98-9.

[24] Robin Lane Fox, *Pagans and Christians* (Harmondsworth, Middlesex: Viking, 1986), 455-7.

[25] Fox, 459.

[26] Cyprian, *On the Lapsed*.

[27] Cyprian, *Letter* 55.6, 17.

[28] Joseph A. Favazza, *The Order of Penitents: Historical Roots and Pastoral Future* (Collegeville, Minnesota: The Liturgical Press, 1988), 178-83.

[29] Frend, 101-3.

[30] Norbert Brox, *A History of the Early Church*, trans. John Bowden (London: SCM Press, 1994), 45.

[31] Monika Hellwig, *Sign of Reconciliation and Conversion: Sacramental Penance for Our Times* (Wilmington, Delaware: Michael Glazier, 1982), 31.

[32] *Hermas* 1.3; 9.5; 31.2,6; 42.2; 51.5; 100.4.

[33] Irenaeus, *Against Heresies.*

[34] Tertullian, *On Repentance*, 7, 9.

[35] David M. Coffey, *The Sacrament of Reconciliation* (Collegeville, Minnesota: The Liturgical Press, 2001), 42.

[36] Tertullian, *On Purity*. The work is an intemperate attack on Callistus, Bishop of Rome, for his lenient policy in dealing with sexual sins.

[37] John T. McNeill, *A History of the Cure of Souls* (New York: Harper and Row, 1951); repr. Harper's Ministers Paperback Library, 1977, 89.

[38] The process of ecclesial penance attested to by Cyprian is found scattered throughout his treatise, *On the Lapsed* and in the *Letters*. See Favazza, 202-32 for a more detailed discussion of Cyprian's writings on ecclesial penance.

[39] Coffey, 42.

[40] Kenan B. Osborne, *Reconciliation and Justification: The Sacrament and Its Theology* (New York: Paulist Press, 1990), 64.

[41] Coffey, 45-6.

[42] Brox, 111.

[43] Lucian, *On the Death of Peregrinus,*12,13. Quoted in Brox, 83.

[44] 2 *Clement*, 16.4.

[45] Chadwick, *The Early Church*, 56.

[46] Cyprian, *On Works and Alms.*

[47] Cyprian, *Letters* 35, 36.

[48] Clement of Alexandria, *The Instructor* 3.4.

[49] Tertullian, *Apology,* 39.16.

[50] F. L. Cross and E. A. Livingstone, eds. *The Oxford Dictionary of the Christian Church* (Oxford: Oxford University Press, 1997), s.v. 'Parabalani'.

[51] Robert M.Grant, *Early Christianity and Society: Seven Studies* (London: Collins, 1978), 142-5.

[52] John Chrysostom, *Homily* 21.6.

[53] Reference to be found in Rowan A. Greer, *Broken Lights and Mended Lives: Theology and Common Life in the Early Church* (University Park, Pennsylvania: State University Press, 1986), 131.

[54] Chadwick, *The Early Church,* 60.

[55] Gregory of Nyssa, *On the Deity and the Son and the Holy Spirit*. Quoted in Carl A. Volz, *Pastoral Life and Practice in the Early Church* (Minneapolis: Augsburg Fortress, 1990), 57.

[56] John Julius Norwich, *Byzantium: The Early Centuries* (London: Viking, 1988): 52-6.

[57] Chadwick, *The Church in Ancient Society,* 197.

[58] The intrigue that occurred amidst the political and theological struggles surrounding the Arian controversy is described in more detail in Frend, 146-77.

[59] Chadwick, *The Church in Ancient Society,* 528.

[60] Ibid., 529.

[61] See Adrian Hastings, ed. *The Oxford Companion to Christian Thought* (New York; Oxford University Press, 2000), s.v. 'Nestorianism', by John McGuckin.

[62] Chadwick, *The Church in Ancient Society*, 530.

[63] Ibid., 530.

[64] Ibid., 535.

[65] McNeill, 41. In chapters 2 and 5 of this work McNeill discusses the pagan and patristic consolation literature in some depth.

[66] Jerome's letters of consolation include: Letter 39, *To Paula, Concerning the Death of Blesilla*; Letter 60, *To Heliodorus*; Letter 77, *To Oceanus, on the Death of Fabiola*.

[67] Peter Brown, *The Body and Society: Men, Women and Sexual Renunciation in Early Christianity* (London: Faber and Faber, 1990), 318-9.

[68] Neil B. McLynn, *Ambrose of Milan: Church and Court in a Christian Capital* (Berkeley, Los Angeles: University of California Press, 1994), 237.

[69] Ibid., 225.

[70] Augustine, *The Confessions*, trans. Maria Boulding, The Works of Saint Augustine, ed. John E. Rotelle (Hyde Park, New York: New City Press, 1997), 231-2.

### Chapter 3: Monks, Barbarians and Pastors

[1] The *De Principiis* is the main theological work of Origen that brings together and develops his central ideas. In the *Apology*, Origen deals with a series of anti-Christian themes current at the time. As well, there are a whole series of scriptural, moral and spiritual essays.

[2] Peter Brown, *The Body And Society* (London: Faber and Faber, 1989).

[3] Ibid., 168. For this story, Brown draws on Eusebius, *Ecclesiastical History*, 6.8.2-3. Eusebius' account of Origen's castration is based on an oral tradition. Epiphanius, on the other hand, maintained Origen sought to preserve his celibacy with the help of drugs. See Henry Chadwick, *The Church in Ancient Society: From Galilee to Gregory the Great* (Oxford: Oxford University Press, 2001), 139-40 where Chadwick outlines Origen's ideas on sexuality and the body as found in his *Homilies*.

[4] Ibid.,165.

[5] Origen, *Homily on Numbers*, 6.3.

[6] Origen, *Homily on Genesis*, 5.4.

[7] Origen, *Homily on Leviticus*, 9.2; *Homily on Exodus*, 4.8.

[8] Augustine's literary output was immense. The principal treatises in which Augustine refuted the teachings of Pelagius are the *Merits of Sinners* and the *Baptism of Children*. It is in his works *The Spirit and the Letter* and *Nature and Grace* that Augustine sets out and develops his Catholic doctrine.

[9] There is an immense literature relating to Augustine's thought. Two more recent works are Gareth B. Matthews, ed. *The Augustinian Tradition* (Berkeley, Los Angeles: University of California Press, 1999) and John M. Rist, *Augustine: Ancient Thought Baptized* (Cambridge: Cambridge University Press, 1994). For Augustine's ideas about women, see Kim Power, *Veiled Desire: Augustine's Writing on Women* (London: Darton, Longman and Todd, 1995). Augustine's theology about human nature, grace and predestination are well summarized in the classic biography of Augustine by Peter Brown, *Augustine of Hippo: A Biography* (London: Faber and Faber, 1967). See also Gerald Bonner, *St Augustine of Hippo: Life and Controversies* (Norwich: The Canterbury Press, 1986), 352-93. For a more concise presentation, in a helpful work that seeks to summarize the history of Christian theology, see Alister E. McGrath, *Historical Theology: An Introduction to the History of Christian Thought* (Oxford: Blackwell, 1998), 79-85.

[10] James E. Goehring, *Ascetics, Society and the Desert: Studies in Egyptian Monasticism*, Studies in Antiquity and Christianity (Harrisburg, Pennsylvania: Trinity Press International, 1999), 20.

[11] Louis Bouyer, *A History of Spirituality: Vol.1: The Spirituality of the New Testament and the Fathers* (Tunbridge Wells: Burns and Oates, 1968), 313.

[12] Benedicta Ward, 'Pastoral care and the monks', in *A History of Pastoral Care*, ed. G. R. Evans (London: Cassell, 2000), 79.

[13] Richard Woods, *Christian Spirituality: God's Presence through the Ages* (Chicago: The Thomas More Press, 1989), 82.

[14] Douglas Burton-Christie, *The Word in the Desert: Scripture and the Quest for Holiness in Early Christian Monasticism* (New York: Oxford University Press, 1993), 4.

[15] The issue concerning the physical place of the desert as the dwelling place of the Eastern monks is argued at length by Goehring, 75-89.

[16] Anthony Meredith, *The Cappadocians* (London: Geoffrey Chapman, 1995), 28-9.

[17] W. H. C. Frend, *The Early Church: From the Beginnings to 461*, rev.ed. (London: SCM Press, 1991), 194.

[18] Basil, *Letter* 94.

[19] Gregory of Nazianzen, *Oration* 43.63. Quoted in Carl A. Volz, *Pastoral Life and Practice in the Early Church* (Minneapolis: Augsburg Fortress, 1990), 85.

[20] Rousseau discusses Basil's hospital within the broader context of his teaching and charitable practices. See Philip Rousseau, *Basil of Caesarea* (Berkeley: University of California Press, 1994), 139-44.

[21] The earliest surviving manuscript of Benedict's *Rule* is probably one written for Anglo-Saxon England about the year 750. It is housed in the Bodleian Library, Oxford.

[22] Adrian Hastings, Alistair Mason and Hugh Pyper, eds. *The Oxford Companion to Christian Thought* (Oxford: Oxford University Press, 2000), s.v. 'Benedictine thought', by Margaret Truran.

[23] Joseph H. Lynch, *The Medieval Church: A Brief History* (London: Longman, 1992), 33. See also John A. F. Thomson, *The Western Church in the Middle Ages* (London: Arnold, 1998), 31.

[24] Terence Kardong, *The Benedictines* (Wilmington, Delaware: Michael Glazier, 1988), 21.

[25] Ludo J. A. Milis, *Angelic Monks and Earthly Men: Monasticism and its Meaning to Medieval Society* (Woodbridge, Suffolk: The Boydell Press, 1992), 41-67. Chapter 4 of this book addresses medieval monasticism's attitude towards people with attention given to the works of mercy. This author argues that charitable assistance held little importance for monasticism at this time because of its overall concern for heavenly salvation. At best, practical assistance to the needy was of marginal concern.

[26] Lynch, 45-7.

[27] Richard Sharpe, 'Churches and communities in early medieval Ireland: towards a pastoral model', in *Pastoral Care Before the Parish: Studies in the Early History of Britain*, ed. Nicholas Brooks (Leicester: Leicester University Press, 1992), 99-102.

[28] Ibid., 101-2.

[29] Arian places of worship from this period, with their splendid mosaics, can still be seen today in Ravenna. Theodoric the Goth was responsible for the building of the Arian baptistery and the church of S. Apollinare Nuovo. The church of S. Vitale, with its celebrated mosaics depicting the Emperor Justinian and Empress Theodora surrounded by their imperial retinue, was begun by the Arian Goths but completed by the Byzantines in the middle of the sixth century. When Justinian's general

Belisarius captured Ravenna in 540 from the control of the Arian Goths, the emperor issued a decree granting to Catholics all Arian church property. Hence the glorification of the Byzantine court in S. Vitale.

[30] Lynch, 40.

[31] Vivian Green, *A New History of Christianity* (New York: Continuum, 1996), 49.

[32] Bede, *Ecclesiastical History of the English People*, trans. Leo Sherley-Price, rev. trans. R. E. Latham. rev. ed. (London: Penguin, 1990).

[33] Margaret Truran, 'The Roman Mission', in *Monks of England: The Benedictines in England from Augustine to the Present Day*, ed. Daniel Rees (London: SPCK, 1997), 19.

[34] C. H. Lawrence, *Medieval Monasticism: Forms of Religious Life in Western Europe in the Middle Ages* (London: Longman, 1984), 51-2.

[35] From his monastery at Jarrow, Bede wrote his *Ecclesiastical History of the English People* in 731. The magnificently illuminated codex of the four Gospels, known as the *Lindisfarne Gospels*, came from this tradition of Celtic Christianity in Britain.

[36] Lawrence, 58.

[37] Truran, 46-7.

[38] Nikola Proksch, 'The Anglo-Saxon Missionaries to the Continent', in Rees, ed., 53.

[39] Peter Brown, *The Rise of Western Christendom* (Malden, Massachusetts: Blackwell, 1997), 272.

[40] Hugh Connolly, *The Irish Penitentials And Their Significance for the Sacrament of Penance Today* (Dublin: Four Courts Press, 1995), 21. Connolly states that these vices were first listed by Evagrius Ponticus (d.399) in his *Antirhetikos*. It was followed later by Pope Gregory the Great's well-known teaching of the seven capital sins.

[41] Ibid., 30-6.

[42] Ibid., 3-4.

[43] Ibid., 13-7.

[44] John T. McNeill, *A History of the Cure of Souls* (New York: Harper and Row, 1951); repr. Harper's Ministers Paperback Library, 1977, 116.

[45] Connolly,14.

[46] Ibid., quoted on p. 154.

[47] Kenan B. Osborne, O.F.M., *Reconciliation and Justification* (Mahwah, New Jersey: Paulist Press, 1990), 89.

[48] Ibid., 93.

[49] McNeill, 122-4.

[50] James A. Coriden, *The Parish in Catholic Tradition: History, Theology and Canon Law* (New York: Paulist Press, 1997), 18-30.

[51] The link between asceticism and charity in the *Pastoral Rule* is examined by Conrad Leyser, 'Experience and Authority in Gregory the Great: The Social Function of "Peritia" ', in *Gregory the Great: A Symposium*, ed. John C. Cavadini (Notre Dame: University of Notre Dame Press, 1995), 38-61.

[52] Carole Straw, *Gregory the Great: Perfection in Imperfection* (Berkeley: University of California Press, 1988), 22.

[53] Gregory the Great, *Pastoral Care*, trans. Henry Davis, in Ancient Christian Writers Series, ed. Johannes Quasten and Joseph C. Plumpe, No.11 (Westminster, Maryland: The Newman Press, 1950), 1.1.

[54] Thomas C. Oden, *Care of Souls in the Classic Tradition* (Philadelphia: Fortress Press, 1984), 59.

[55] R. A. Markus, *Gregory the Great and His World* (Cambridge: Cambridge University Press, 1997), 27-9.

[56] Gregory the Great, *Pastoral Care*, 4.

### Chapter 4: Friars, Pilgrims and the Diseased

[1] Kenneth Hudson, *Exploring Cathedrals.* (Sevenoaks, Kent: Hodder and Stroughton, 1978), 1.

[2] C. H. Lawrence, *The Friars: The Impact of the Early Mendicant Movement in Western Society* (London: Longman, 1994), 6.

[3] R. W. Southern, *Western Society and the Church in the Middle Ages*, The Pelican History of the Church, vol. 2 (Harmondsworth, Middlesex: Penguin, 1970), 285.

[4] Alexander Murray, 'The Later Middle Ages', in *Christianity: Two Thousand Years*, ed. Richard Harries and Henry Mayr-Harting (Oxford: Oxford University Press, 2001), 98.

[5] Lawrence, 105-7.

[6] Ibid., 126.

[7] For a discussion on the function of monastic schools in the Middle Ages, see George Ferzoco and Carolyn Muessig, eds. *Medieval Monastic Education* (London and New York: Leicester University Press, 2000).

[8] Joseph H. Lynch, *The Medieval Church: A Brief History* (Longman: London, 1992), 89-93; 239-48.

[9] Alister E. McGrath, *Historical Theology: An Introduction to the History of Christian Thought* (Oxford: Blackwell, 1998), 104-5. Scholasticism owes its origins particularly to a work known as the *Sentences* of Peter Lombard, compiled 1155-8. The work, divided into four books, utilizes the method of dialectical analysis and offers a coherent presentation of the doctrines of the Christian faith. It is a rational exploration of revelation.

[10] Bernard Cooke, *Ministry to Word and Sacraments: History and Theology* (Philadelphia: Fortress Press, 1976), 123.

[11] John T. McNeill, *A History of The Cure of Souls* (New York: Harper and Row, 1951), repr. Harper's Ministers Paperback Library, 1977, 145-7.

[12] Jonathan Sumption, *Pilgrimage: An Image of Medieval Religion* (London: Faber and Faber, 1975), 15.

[13] S. G. F. Brandon, *The Judgment of the Dead* (London: Weidenfeld and Nicholson, 1967), 166.

[14] Rosalind Brooke and Christopher Brooke, *Popular Religion in the Middle Ages* (London: Thames and Hudson, 1984), 14-5.

[15] Sumption, 29.

[16] R. N. Swanson, *Religion and Devotion in Europe, c.1215-c.1515* (Cambridge: Cambridge University Press, 1995), 163-4 and Benedicta Ward, *Miracles and the Medieval Mind: Theory, Record and Event 1000-1215* (Aldershot, Hampshire: Wildwood House, 1987), 35-6.

[17] J. G. Davies, *Pilgrimage Yesterday and Today: Why? Where? How?* rev. ed. (London: SCM Press, 1988), 7-18.

[18] Sumption, 104.

[19] Diana Webb, *Pilgrims and Pilgrimage in the Medieval West* (London: I. B. Tauris, 1999), 64-5.

[20] Philippe Ariès, *The Hour Of Our Death*, trans. Helen Weaver (New York: Vintage Books, 1982), 72.

[21] Sumption, 198.

[22] Ibid., 199.

[23] Ibid., 211.

[24] A detailed historical account tracing the development of the doctrine of purgatory can be found in Jacques Le Goff, *The Birth of Purgatory*, trans. Arthur Goldhammer (Chicago: University of Chicago Press, 1984).

[25] Ariès, 174-81.

[26] Ibid., 166.

[27] More, *Workes*, 79. Quoted in Eamon Duffy, *The Stripping of the Altars: Traditional Religion in England c.1400-c.1580* (New Haven, Connecticut: Yale University Press, 1992), 361.

[28] Medieval chantry chapels can still be seen in many cathedrals. Westminster Abbey, for example, contains many notable chantries. Often they were vandalized or destroyed during the Protestant Reformation.

[29] Swanson, 231.

[30] M. Francis Mannion, 'Stipends and Eucharistic Praxis', *Worship* 57 (1983):194-214.

[31] The first recorded outbreak of the Black Death occurred at the Sicilian port of Messina in 1347, thought to have been brought in by Genoese ships returning from the Crimea on the Black Sea. It has been generally believed that the Black Death was a bubonic plague bacterium spread by rat fleas. More recent scientific research rejects this traditionally held belief by claiming that the Black Death was an Ebola-like virus in which the disease was transferred directly from person to person rather than through rats. See the newspaper article in *The Independent* (London), 23 July 2001. For a discussion of the biomedical issues of the Black Death and the way it affected society, see Norman F. Cantor, *In the Wake of the Plague: The Black Death and the World it Made* (New York: Simon and Schuster, 2001).

[32] Ariès, 108-10.

[33] Ibid., 110-6.

[34] Swanson, 118.

[35] Lawrence, 6; 15.

[36] Swanson, 119.

[37] Ibid., 117.

[38] The place of the Beguines in medieval religious life is discussed in Herbert Grundmann, *Religious Movements in the Middle Ages*, trans. Steve Rowan (Notre Dame, Indiana: University of Notre Dame Press, 1995), 139-52.

[39] Otto Gründler, 'Devotio Moderna', in *Christian Spirituality: High Middle Ages and Reformation, Vol II*, ed. Jill Raitt (London: SCM, 1988), 176-93.

[40] *New Catholic Encyclopedia, Vol. 7*, 2nd ed (Detroit: Gale/Thomson Learning in association with The Catholic University of America, Washington, D.C., 2003), s.v. 'Hospitals, History of', by E. Nasalli-Rocca.

[41] *New Catholic Encyclopedia, Vol. 7* (New York: McGraw-Hill, 1967), s.v. 'Hospitals, History of', by A. B. McPadden; s.v. 'Hospitallers and Hospital Sisters', by L. Butler.

[42] Catherine Peyroux, 'The Leper's Kiss', in *Monks and Nuns, Saints and Outcasts: Religion in Medieval Society*, ed. Sharon Farmer and Barbara H. Rosenwein (Ithaca: Cornell University Press, 2000),174-6.

[43] Malcolm Barber, *The New Knighthood: A History of the Order of the Temple* (Cambridge: Cambridge University Press, 1994), 41.

[44] Alan Forey, 'The Military Orders, 1120-1312', in *The Oxford Illustrated History of the Crusades*, ed. Jonathan Riley-Smith (Oxford: Oxford University Press, 1995), 208.

[45] Ibid., 198.

[46] Malcolm Barber, 'The Charitable and Medical Activities of the Hospitallers and Templars', in *A History of Pastoral Care*, ed. G. R. Evans (London: Cassell, 2000), 154.

[47] Jonathan Riley-Smith, *Hospitallers: The History of the Order of St John* (London: Hambledon Press, 1999), 25.

[48] C. H. Lawrence, *Medieval Monasticism: Forms of Religious Life in Western Europe in the Middle Ages* (London: Longman, 1984), 173.

[49] James L. Empereur, *Prophetic Anointing: God's Call to the Sick, the Elderly, and the Dying*, Message of the Sacraments, Vol. 7 (Wilmington, Delaware: Michael Glazier, 1982), 22-3.

[50] Charles W. Gusmer, *And You Visited Me: Sacramental Ministry to the Sick and the Dying*, Studies in the Reformed Rites of the Catholic Church, Vol. VI (Collegeville, Minnesota: The Liturgical Press, 1990), 11.

[51] Ibid., 26.

[52] Empereur, 51-3.

[53] 'Rite of Anointing and Pastoral Care of the Sick', in *The Rites of the Catholic Church as Revised by Decree of the Second Vatican Council and Published by Authority of Pope Paul VI*, trans. The International Commission on English in the Liturgy (New York: Pueblo, 1976).

[54] Gusmer, 38-40.

### Chapter 5: Protesters and Reformers

[1] Despite the popular tradition, there is debate as to whether Luther actually posted the ninety-five theses on the university church door. Haile suggests Luther may merely have sent them to bishops in the area of Wittenberg for consideration. At least one of these clerics would have been responsible for the sale of indulgences. See H. G. Haile, *Luther: A Biography* (London: Sheldon Press, 1981), 74.

[2] Owen Chadwick, *The Reformation*, rev.ed., The Pelican History of the Church, vol. 3 (Harmondsworth, Middlesex: Penguin, 1972), 50.

[3] Bernhard Lohse, *Martin Luther: An Introduction to His Life and Work* (Edinburgh: T and T Clark, 1987), 92.

[4] Heiko Oberman, *Luther: Man between God and the Devil* (New Haven, Connecticut: Yale University Press, 1989), 187.

[5] Quoted by David Cornick, 'The Reformation Crisis in Pastoral Care', in G. R. Evans, *A History of Pastoral Care* (London: Cassell, 2000), 232.

[6] Ibid., 184.

[7] Bernard M. G. Reardon, *Religious Thought in the Reformation*, 2nd ed (London: Longman, 1995), 63.

[8] Ibid., 65.

[9] Melanchthon was Luther's colleague in Wittenberg and was the first to systematize early Lutheran theology, especially through his *Loci Communes* (1521) and his *Apology for the Augsburg Confession.*

[10] Luther outlined his views on the sacraments in the polemical tract, *The Babylonian Captivity of the Church,* published in 1520.

[11] Chadwick, 73.

[12] Reardon, 100-2. Luther's teachings on the Eucharist can be found especially in *The Babylonian Captivity of the Church* (1520), *The Misuse of the Mass* (1521) and *The Abomination of the Secret Mass* (1525).

[13] Alister E. McGrath, *Historical Theology: An Introduction to the History of Christian Thought* (Oxford: Blackwell, 1998), 189.

[14] Ibid., 189-90.

[15] Daphne Hampson, *Christian Contradictions: The Structures of Lutheran and Catholic Thought* (Cambridge: Cambridge University Press, 2001), 52.

[16] Reardon, 97.

[17] Ibid., 93-5.

[18] Ibid., 141.

[19] James Kittleson, 'Martin Bucer and the Ministry of the Church', in *Martin Bucer: Reforming Church and Community* (Cambridge: Cambridge University Press, 1994), 94.

[20] Gottfried Hammann, 'Ecclesiological motifs behind the creation of the "Christlichen Gemeinschaften" ', in *Martin Bucer: Reforming Church and Community,* 134.

[21] Chadwick, *The Reformation,* 80-1. The understanding of the manner of Christ's presence in the Eucharist within the thought of the Protestant Reformers is examined in detail in Paul H. Jacobs, *Christ's Eucharistic Presence: A History of the Doctrine,* American University Studies, Series VII, Theology and Religion, Vol. 157 (New York: Peter Lang, 1994), 117-67.

[22] William J. Bouwsma, *John Calvin: A Sixteenth Century Portrait* (New York: Oxford University Press, 1988), 217.

[23] Calvin, *Institutes,* IV, iv-ix.

[24] Bernard Cottret, *Calvin: A Biography* (Grand Rapids, Michigan: William B. Erdmans, 2000), 166.

[25] Reardon, *Religious Thought in the Reformation,* 186.

[26] Chadwick, 85.

[27] Calvin, *Institutes,* IV, xv, 20. This matter is discussed in Reardon, 187.

[28] Cottret, 295.

[29] Ronald S. Wallace, *Calvin, Geneva and the Reformation* (Edinburgh: Scottish Academic Press, 1988), 171-2.

[30] Ibid., 172-3.

[31] Calvin, *Institutes,* III, xxiv, 3.

[32] Calvin, *Institutes,* III, xxi, 5,7.

[33] Reardon, 191.

[34] The nineteenth century sociologist Max Weber argued that the rise of Protestantism contributed in a significant way to the rise of modern capitalism. Protestant asceticism, with its sense of divine calling, provided a religious motivation for a worldly work ethic. See Max Weber, *The Protestant Ethic and the Spirit of Capitalism,* trans. Talcott Parsons (New York: Charles Scribner's Sons, 1930).

[35] For an analysis of how the Protestant Reformation altered Christian understanding of work, poverty and wealth, see Carter Lindberg, *Beyond Charity: Reformation Initiatives for the Poor* (Minneapolis: Fortress Press, 1993).

[36] For an account of the dissolution of the religious houses during the English Reformation, see David Knowles, *Bare Ruined Choirs* (Cambridge: Cambridge University Press, 1976). This work is an abridged version of Knowles' final volume of his three volume work, *The Religious Orders in England* first published by Cambridge University Press in 1959.

[37] Chadwick, 121.

[38] Diarmaid MacCulloch, *Thomas Cranmer* (New Haven and London: Yale University Press, 1996), 511. The author discusses the influences upon the development of the 1552 Prayer Book, 504-13.

[39] A. G. Dickens, *The English Reformation* (London: B. T. Batsford, 1964), 215.

[40] John Foxe, as a martyrologist, compiled large scale accounts of the English Protestant martyrs. His *Acts and Monuments* was first published in English during the reign of Elizabeth I in 1563. Foxe's standards of accuracy are not those of modern historical scholarship. See Dickens, 26; 305.

[41] Christopher Hibbert, *The Virgin Queen: The Personal History of Elizabeth I* (London: Penguin, 1992), 91.

[42] Chadwick, 248.

[43] Vivian Green, *A New History of Christianity* (New York: Continuum, 1996), 146-7.

[44] Eamon Duffy, *The Stripping of the Altars: Traditional Religion in England c.1400-c.1580* (New Haven, Connecticut: Yale University Press, 1992), 4.

[45] R. Po-Chia Hsia, *The World of Catholic Renewal 1540-1770*, New Approaches to European History Series (Cambridge: Cambridge University Press, 1998), 80.

[46] Christopher Haigh, *English Reformations: Religion, Politics, and Society under the Tudors* (Oxford: Clarendon Press, 1993), 264.

[47] Ibid, 264.

[48] Po-Chia Hsia, 82.

[49] The closing years of the eighteenth century brought about significant changes for Catholics in England. The *Relief Act* of 1791 authorized the celebration of Mass in registered chapels. The arrival of more than five thousand priests from France fleeing the Revolution assisted the growth in Catholic life as did the large number of immigrants coming from Ireland. The 1829 *Act of Emancipation* restored to Catholics their full rights as citizens, enabling them to be eligible for government office and to sit in Parliament. With the restoration of the Catholic hierarchy in 1850, Cardinal Nicholas Wiseman (1802-65) became the first Cardinal-Archbishop of Westminster.

[50] The term 'Counter-Reformation' first appeared during the 1770s and gained general acceptance by the 1830s. Today it is generally agreed that it is no longer helpful to interpret the Council of Trent and its aftermath as solely a reaction to Protestantism. The term 'Catholic Reformation' is one that is now commonly used. For a discussion on the subject, see the Introduction in David M. Luebke, *The Counter-Reformation: The Essential Readings*, Blackwell Essential Readings in History (Oxford: Blackwell, 1999), 3.

[51] Hubert Jedin, *A History of the Council of Trent, Vol. I, The Struggle for the Council*, trans. Ernest Graf (London: Thomas Nelson and Sons, 1957), 548.

[52] For a summary of Trent's teaching on justification, see Reardon, 291-92. For a full account of Trent's deliberations on the subject, see Hubert Jedin, *A History of the Council of Trent, Vol. II, The First Sessions of Trent 1545-47,* trans. Ernest Graf (Thomas Nelson and Sons, 1961), 283-316.

[53] On 31 October 1999, The Catholic-Lutheran Joint Declaration on the Doctrine of Justification was signed in Augsburg, Germany, by the Catholic Church and the Lutheran World Federation, which represents the vast majority of Lutherans around the globe. In this Joint Declaration there is agreement on a common doctrinal core while allowing for different theological approaches. Allowance was made for variations in theological understanding concerning, for example, the degree of human cooperation with God's grace and the effect upon the redeemed person of Christ's gift of saving grace. The full text of the Joint Declaration was published, prior to it being signed, in *Origins* 28 (July 16, 1998): 120-7.

[54] The disagreement over the role of contrition in obtaining God's forgiveness was an issue of dispute between Protestants and Catholics as to whether it was a kind of 'good work'. Luther subsequently recognized the value of confession as a pastoral aid for troubled consciences, but not in a sacramental sense as Trent affirmed. See Michael A. Mullett, *The Catholic Reformation* (London: Routledge, 1999), 50-1.

[55] Bernard Cooke, *Ministry to Word and Sacraments: History and Theology* (Philadelphia: Fortress Press, 1976), 7-8.

[56] Jedin, *A History of the Council of Trent, Vol. II,* 321.

[57] Ibid., 367.

[58] It is generally agreed that the immediate inspiration for seminaries established by Trent came from seminary legislation promulgated for England in 1556 by Cardinal Pole. See *New Catholic Encyclopedia* (New York: McGraw-Hill, 1967). s.v. 'Seminary', by J. A. O'Donohoe.

[59] John B. Tomaro, 'San Carlo Borromeo and the Implementation of the Council of Trent', in *San Carlo Borromeo: Catholic Reform and Ecclesiastical Politics in the Second Half of the Sixteenth Century,* eds. John M. Hedley and John B. Tomaro (Washington: Folger Books, 1988), 67.

[60] Po-Chia Hsia, 106-10.

## Chapter 6: Spiritual Enthusiasts

[1] Kenneth Clark, *Civilisation: A Personal View* (London: British Broadcasting Corporation and John Murray, 1969), 167.

[2] Michael A. Mullett, *The Catholic Reformation* (London: Routledge, 1999), 90.

[3] John W. O'Malley, *The First Jesuits* (Cambridge, Massachusetts: Harvard University Press, 1993), 71-2.

[4] Mullett, 94.

[5] William V. Bangert, S.J., *A History of the Society of Jesus,* rev. ed. (St Louis: The Institute of Jesuit Sources, 1986), 27.

[6] O'Malley, 197-8.

[7] Ibid., 167-74.

[8] Quoted in Georgina Masson, *The Companion Guide to Rome,* 6th ed. (London: Collins, 1980), 167.

[9] O'Malley, 178-87.

[10] For a recent biography of Philip Neri, see Paul Turks, *Philip Neri: The Fire of Joy,* trans. Daniel Utrecht (Edinburgh: T. and T. Clark, 1995).

[11] Mullett, 70.

[12] Ibid., 70.

[13] Ibid., 72-4.

[14] Mullett, 104; R. Po-Chia Hsia, *The World of Catholic Renewal 1540-1770*, New Approaches to European History (Cambridge: Cambridge University Press, 1998), 29.

[15] Mullett, 107-9.

[16] Po-Chia Hsia, 36.

[17] Jennifer J. Cameron, *A Dangerous Innovator: Mary Ward (1585-1645)* (Strathfield, New South Wales: St Pauls, 2000), 199.

[18] For a general presentation of the history, ideas and impact of Jansenism, see William Doyle, *Jansenism*, Studies in European History (New York: St Martin's Press, 2000).

[19] Having been already suppressed in several European countries, in 1773 Pope Clement XIV suppressed the Society of Jesus overall in the Brief *Dominus ac Redemptor*. However, in some places the Jesuits continued to teach, as in Austria and Germany. They found the support of Catherine the Great of Russia and, in England, carried on their work. In the United States their mission in Maryland remained unaffected. The Society was formally restored in 1814 by Pius VII, in the papal bull *Sollicitudo omnium ecclesiarum*.

[20] Adolf Darlap, ed. *Sacramentum Mundi: An Encyclopedia of Theology*, Vol. 3. (New York: Herder and Herder, 1969), s.v. 'Jansenism', by Konrad Hecker.

[21] Quoted in Mullett, 166.

[22] For an examination of the quarrel over penitential ethics within the French Catholic community of the seventeenth century as a result of Jansenist teaching, see Alexander Sedgwick, *The Travails of Conscience: The Arnauld Family and the Ancien Régime* (Cambridge, Massachusetts: Harvard University Press, 1998), 126-7.

[23] Louis Dupré, 'Jansenism and Quietism', in *Christian Spirituality: Post Reformation and Modern*, eds. Louis Dupré and Don E. Saliers (London: SCM, 1990), 126.

[24] R. A. Knox, *Enthusiasm: A Chapter in the History of Religion* (Oxford: Clarendon Press, 1950), 212-3.

[25] Frederick M. Jones, *Alphonsus de Liguori: The Saint of Bourbon Naples 1696-1787* (Dublin: Gill and Macmillan, 1992), 203-8.

[26] Ibid., 281-2.

[27] Ibid., 283-4.

[28] H. Richard Niebuhr and Daniel D. Williams, eds. *The Ministry in Historical Perspectives* (San Francisco: Harper and Row, 1983), 108-9.

[29] Michael Baigent and Richard Leigh, *The Inquisition* (London: Viking, 1999), 62.

[30] Bernini's marble statue for an altar in the small church of St Maria della Vittoria in Rome depicts Teresa in a state of heavenly rapture in which an angel of God has just pierced her heart with a golden flaming arrow, resulting in accompanying feelings of pain and bliss. It is as though the saint is in a state of spiritual orgasm. Mullett (pp.141-4) remarks that spiritual achievements described by mystics, such as this, may well reflect the interior sexual struggles of women within the religious environment of enclosed convents. But is it more than that? Certainly, mystical language often brings together the body and soul into an indescribable unity.

[31] Kieran Kavanaugh, ed. *John of the Cross: Selected Writings*, The Classics of Western Spirituality (New York: Paulist Press, 1987), 33.

[32] William M. Thompson, ed. *Bérulle and the French School: Selected Writings*, The Classics of Western Spirituality, trans. Lowell M. Glendon (New York: Paulist Press, 1989), 77.

[33] Michael Cox, *Handbook of Christian Spirituality* (San Francisco: Harper and Row, 1985), 185.

[34] Raymond Deville, *The French School of Spirituality: An Introduction and Reader*, trans. Agnes Cunningham (Pittsburgh, Pennsylvania: Duquesne University Press, 1994), 86.

[35] Ibid., 81.

[36] *New Catholic Encyclopedia, Vol.12*, 2nd ed (Detroit: Gale/Thomas Learning in association with The Catholic University of America, Washington, D.C., 2003), s.v. 'Sacred Heart, Iconography of', by J. U. Morris.

[37] Deville, 172-7.

[38] Mullett, 164.

[39] David Hugh Farmer, *The Oxford Dictionary of Saints,* 3rd ed (Oxford and New York: Oxford University Press, 1992), 345.

[40] Quoted in Elisabeth Stopp, 'François de Sales', in *The Study of Spirituality*, eds. Charles Jones, Geoffrey Wainwright and Edward Yarnold, S.J. (London: SPCK, 1986), 380.

[41] For a brief account of the life of St Vincent de Paul, see Hugh O'Donnell, 'Vincent de Paul: His Life and Way', in Frances Ryan and John Rybolt, eds. *Vincent de Paul and Louise de Marillac: Rules, Conferences, and Writings,* The Classics of Western Spirituality (New York: Paulist Press, 1995), 13-38.

[42] For a brief account of the life of Louise de Marillac, see Louise Sullivan, 'Louise de Marillac: A Spiritual Portrait', in Ryan and Rybolt, eds., 39-64.

[43] *The Philokalia: The Complete Text,* 3 vols, eds. St Nikodimos of the Holy Mountain and St Makarios of Corinth, trans. G. E. H. Palmer, Philip Sherrard and Kallistos Ware (London and Boston: Faber and Faber, 1979-84).

[44] Timothy Ware, *The Orthodox Church,* rev.ed. (Harmondsmith: Penguin, 1981), 236-42.

[45] Mullett, 97.

[46] Bangert, 35.

[47] Ibid., 186-8.

[48] Bamber Gascoigne, *The Christians* (London: Jonathan Cape, 1977), 191.

[49] Mullett, 160.

[50] Bangert, 153.

[51] Andrew C. Ross, *A Vision Betrayed: The Jesuits in Japan and China, 1542-1742* (Maryknoll, New York: Orbis Books, 1994), 43.

[52] Quoted in Vivian Green, *A New History of Christianity* (New York: Continuum, 1996),182-3.

[53] Ross, xvi.

[54] Green, 178.

[55] James Hennessy, S.J., *American Catholics: A History of the Roman Catholic Community in the United States* (New York: Oxford University Press, 1981), 20.

[56] Jay P. Dolan, *The American Catholic Experience: A History from Colonial Times to the Present* (Garden City, New York: Doubleday, 1985), 24.

[57] Hennessy, 21.

[58] Dolan, 35-6.

[59] Jane Shaw argues that current historical thinking suggests that the ideas of the French Enlightenment occurred first in England and related to the 'scientific revolution' and ideas on religious toleration following the Civil War that occurred there. See Jane Shaw, 'The Late Seventeenth and Eighteenth Centuries', in *Christianity: Two Thousand Years*, ed. Richard Harries and Henry Mayr-Harting (Oxford: Oxford University Press, 2001), 163-8.

[60] Ulrich Im Hof, *The Enlightenment*, The Making of Europe Series, trans. William E. Yuill (Oxford: Blackwell, 1994), 72.

[61] Frank Whaling, ed., *John and Charles Wesley: Selected Writings and Hymns*, The Classics of Western Spirituality (New York: Paulist Press, 1981), 21.

[62] Quoted in Green, 215.

[63] Whaling, 25.

[64] Whaling, 37.

[65] Robert Bruce Mullin, 'North America', in *A World History of Christianity*, ed. Adrian Hastings (London: Cassell, 1999), 423.

[66] Green, 222.

[67] Mullin, 429.

[68] Cynthia Lynn Lyerly, *Methodism and the Southern Mind 1770-1810* (New York: Oxford University Press, 1998), 58.

[69] Shaw, 182.

### Chapter 7: Liberals, Workers and Missionaries

[1] Christopher Hibbert, *The French Revolution* (London: Penguin, 1982), 232; Richard and Charles Winston, *Notre-Dame De Paris* (New York: Newsweek Books, 1971), 115-6.

[2] Simon Schama, *Citizens: A Chronicle of the French Revolution* (London: Viking Penguin, 1989), 491.

[3] Hibbert, 227-30.

[4] Vivian Green, *A New History of Christianity* (New York: Continuum, 1996), 227.

[5] The scene was immortalized in Jacques Louis David's (1748-1825) neoclassical painting of the event. David, and others like him, believed they were living in heroic times within the history of civilization.

[6] H. Daniel-Rops, *The Church In An Age of Revolution*, trans. John Warrington (London: J. M. Dent and Sons, 1965), 74.

[7] Ibid., 204.

[8] Ibid., 206-7.

[9] Norman Davies, *Europe: A History* (London: Pimlico, 1997), 796.

[10] Ibid., 679.

[11] Christopher Hibbert, *Queen Victoria: A Personal History* (London: HarperCollins, 2001), 215.

[12] John A. Coleman, 'Introduction', in *One Hundred Years of Catholic Social Thought: Celebration and Challenge*, ed. John A. Coleman (Maryknoll, New York: Orbis Books, 1991), 4.

[13] Paul Misner, *Social Catholicism in Europe: From the Onset of Industrialization to the First World War* (New York: Crossroad, 1991), 42.

[14] Ibid., 130-2.

15 Ibid., 134-5.

16 Ibid., 44-6.

17 Bruce Duncan, *The Church's Social Teaching: From Rerum Novarum to 1991* (North Blackburn, Victoria: Collins Dove, 1991), 41.

18 Quoted in Misner, 54.

19 Duncan, 41.

20 Misner, 73. By the latter part of the twentieth century, the St Vincent de Paul Society began to broaden its mission by delving more into social activism through lobbying on behalf of the poor and marginalized. Raising social consciousness has become an important characteristic of its work alongside that of its more long-standing mission of charitable assistance. Women's conferences were organized separately throughout the world from 1856 as the 'Woman's Society of St Vincent de Paul', with headquarters in Bologna, Italy. It was eventually amalgamated with the men's society in 1967.

21 Ibid., 67-9.

22 Quoted in Daniel-Rops, 250.

23 Michael Schäfers, 'Rerum Novarum – The Result of Christian Social Movements "From Below" ', in *Rerum Novarum: A Hundred Years of Catholic Social Teaching*, ed. John Coleman and Gregory Baum, trans. John Bowden (*Concilium* 1991, no. 5 – London: SCM, 1991), 11.

24 John Molony, *The Worker Question: A New Kind of Historical Perspective on Rerum Novarum* (North Blackburn, Victoria: Collins Dove, 1991), 19-20.

25 Duncan, 34. See also Hunter Schmidt and Edward Cornelius Bock, 'Wilhelm von Ketteler: the social bishop', *Social Justice Review* 76 (July-August, 1985): 99-103.

26 Ibid., 55

27 Molony, 57.

28 Patrick W. Carey, ed. *American Catholic Religious Thought: The Shaping of a Theological and Social Tradition* (New York: Paulist Press, 1987), 226.

29 David Newsome, *The Convert Cardinals: Newman and Manning* (London: John Murray, 1993), 329.

30 Ibid., 333.

31 Ibid., 329.

32 Hogan argues that in the latter part of the nineteenth century, despite most Australians belonging to the working class, the hierarchy and clergy did little in the way of supporting a labor movement concerned for the rights of workers. Their message was generally one of conformity and obedience to the social system of the time. It was not until Cardinal Moran's arrival in the country that a more socially active Catholicism began to emerge in Australia. See Michael Hogan, *The Sectarian Strand: Religion in Australian History* (Ringwood, Victoria: Penguin, 1987), 138-40.

33 Moran's speech, in an attempt to reach as wide an audience as possible, was remarkable insofar as he chose to deliver it in a masonic hall. Only seven years earlier Leo XIII had issued the encyclical, *Humanum Genus*, in which he had outlined the evils of Freemasonry, which he saw as a threat to the stability of society and the Church. In Italy, the organization was a particular enemy of the papacy.

34 Duncan, 162-9.

35 Ibid., 76.

[36] David J. O'Brien, 'A Century of Catholic Social Teaching: Contexts and Comments', in Coleman, *One Hundred Years of Catholic Social Thought: Celebration and Challenge*, 17.

[37] Modernism was condemned by Pius X in his decree, *Lamentabili*, and the encyclical, *Pascendi*, of 1907. Three years later a *motu proprio* introduced the anti-Modernist oath to be taken by clerics and those teaching in Catholic institutes of higher learning. Modernism aimed at bringing Catholic teaching into closer relation to contemporary philosophical, historical, social and scientific developments of the time. It first emerged towards the end of the nineteenth century. Among other things, it encouraged a more critical examination of the Bible by subjecting it to scientific study; and it encouraged a more experiential approach to the discovery of truth, unlike the intellectualist approach of scholastic theology, such as Thomism. Among the leaders in the Modernist movement were A. Loisy, M. Blondel, F. von Hugel and G. Tyrrell.

[38] Roy Hattersley, *Blood and Fire: William and Catherine Booth and Their Salvation Army* (London: Abacus, 2000), 2.

[39] Ibid., 197-202.

[40] Ibid., 285-9.

[41] Ibid., 366.

[42] See Colm Kerrigan, *Father Matthew and the Irish Temperance Movement 1838-1849* (Cork: Cork University Press, 1992).

[43] David J. Bosch, *Transforming Mission: Paradigm Shifts in Theology of Mission* (Maryknoll, New York: Orbis Books, 1991), 301.

[44] A. Camps, 'The Catholic Missionary Movement from 1789 to 1962', in *Missiology: An Ecumenical Introduction*, ed. A. Camps, L. A. Hoedemaker, M. R. Spindler, and F. J. Verstraelen (Grand Rapids, Michigan: William B. Erdmans, 1995), 230-1.

[45] *Oxford Dictionary of the Christian Church*, 1997 ed., s.v. 'Carey, William'.

[46] A. Wind, 'The Protestant Missionary Movement from 1789 to 1963', in Camps, 241-3.

[47] Stephen Neill, *A History of Christian Missions* (Harmondsworth, Middlesex: Penguin, 1964), 400.

[48] *New Catholic Encyclopedia, Vol.7*, 2nd ed (Detroit: Gale/Thomson Learning in association with The Catholic University of America, Washington, D.C., 2003), s.v. 'India, Christianity in', by K. Pathil.

[49] Kenneth Scott Latourette, *A History of the Expansion of Christianity, Volume VI: The Great Century in North Africa and Asia* (London: Eyre and Spottiswoode, 1944), 16.

[50] William Burridge, W.F., *Destiny Africa: Cardinal Lavigerie and the Making of the White Fathers* (London and Dublin: Geoffrey Chapman, 1966), 106-8.

[51] Ibid., 114-5.

[52] Ibid., 120.

[53] Ibid., 18; 128-30.

[54] José de Arteche, *The Cardinal of Africa: Charles Lavigerie Founder of the White Fathers*, trans. Mairin Mitchell (London and Glascow: Sands, 1964), 161-2. In the nineteenth century the trade in slavery was enormous, especially from West Africa. By 1850, twenty-five thousand people were exported annually to South America through Mozambique alone. In the British Empire, through the efforts of philanthropists, such as William Wilberforce, the slave trade was made illegal in 1807, but full emancipation came in only 1833. Holland declared slavery illegal in its territories

in 1814. In 1848 slavery was suppressed in all French colonies but it was not until 1864 that France formally made the trade in slavery illegal. In the United States, slavery came to an end through a constitutional amendment in 1865, following the Civil War. Despite prohibitions, the slave trade continued to persist on the African continent. See Peter Hinchliff, 'Africa', in *The Oxford Illustrated History of Christianity*, ed. John McManners (Oxford and New York: Oxford University Press, 1990), 469-70.

**Chapter 8: Migrants, Teachers and Nurses**

[1] Peter Herring, *Ultimate Train* (London and New York: Dorling Kindersley, 2000), 50, 60.

[2] James Hennesey, *American Catholics: A History of the Roman Catholic Community in the United States* (New York/Oxford: Oxford University Press, 1981), 117, 173.

[3] Jay P. Dolan, *The American Catholic Experience: A History from Colonial Times to the Present* (Garden City, New York: Doubleday, 1985), 137.

[4] Dolores Liptak, *Immigrants And Their Church* (New York: Macmillan, 1989), 62.

[5] O'Farrell argues that, in Ireland before the 1840s, about only a quarter of the Catholic population regularly attended Mass. A great change in devotional fervor and church attendance came about between 1850 and 1875 due largely to a revived Church led by Cardinal Paul Cullen (1803-78) of Dublin. See Patrick O'Farrell, *The Catholic Church and Community in Australia* (West Melbourne: Thomas Nelson, 1977), 9, 83.

[6] Dolan, 130.

[7] Ibid., 137.

[8] Liptak, 114-7.

[9] Ibid., 131-2.

[10] Patrick W. Carey, *The Roman Catholics*, Denominations in America Series, Number 6 (Westport, Connecticut: Greenwood Press, 1993), 43-4. In the seven provincial councils of Baltimore (1829-49), neither slaves nor African Americans in general were mentioned.

[11] Liptak, 172-3.

[12] Cyprian Davis, *The History of Black Catholics in the United States* (New York: Crossroad, 1991), 146-52.

[13] Ibid., 161.

[14] Ibid., 172-4.

[15] Dolan, 166.

[16] Philip Gleason, *Keeping the Faith: American Catholicism Past and Present* (Notre Dame, Indiana: University of Notre Dame Press, 1987), 41-4.

[17] Carey, 62.

[18] Quoted in Carey, 62.

[19] In England, Catholic religious practice was tolerated after 1791 but the official *Emancipation Acts* were not enacted until 1829.

[20] Patrick O'Farrell, *The Irish in Australia* (Kensington, New South Wales: New South Wales University Press, 1987), 41.

[21] O'Farrell, *The Catholic Church and Community in Australia*, 24.

[22] O'Farrell, *The Irish in Australia*, 105.

[23] Ibid., 42.

[24] Bruce Elder, *Blood on the Wattle: Massacres and Maltreatment of Australian Aborigines since 1788* (Frenchs Forest, New South Wales: Child and Associates, 1988), 39.

[25] In 1843 Polding arranged for four Passionist priests - three Italians and a Frenchman - to come to Sydney to work among the Aboriginal people. But they moved north to Queensland where they set up a mission for Aborigines on Stradbroke Island, near Brisbane, which failed. For an account of this mission, see Ralph M. Wiltgen, *The Founding of the Roman Catholic Church in Oceania 1825 to 1850* (Canberra: Australian National University Press, 1981), 358-67. In South Australia the Jesuits began a mission to Aborigines in 1882 but it was unsuccessful and finally closed in 1899. The Plenary Council of the Australian Church in 1885 spoke out against the shocking treatment of Aboriginal people and arranged an annual collection for missionary work among them.

[26] Naomi Turner, *Catholics in Australia: A Social History, Vol. 1* (North Blackburn, Victoria: Collins Dove, 1992), 123-5.

[27] Quoted in O'Farrell, *The Catholic Church and Community in Australia*, 84-5.

[28] For an account of Caroline Chisholm's life, see Joanna Bogle, *Caroline Chisholm: The Emigrants' Friend* (Leominster, Herefordshire: Gracewing, 1993).

[29] For a history of the Catholic Church in New Zealand see Michael King, *God's Furthest Outpost: A History of Catholics in New Zealand* (Auckland: Penguin, 1997).

[30] Edward Norman, *The English Catholic Church in the Nineteenth Century* (Oxford: Clarendon Press, 1984), 7.

[31] The Oxford Movement that flourished in the years 1833-45, also known as the Tractarian Movement because of the series of tracts written upholding religious truth and Church reform, was led by an Anglican clergyman and a Fellow of Oriel College Oxford, John Keble (1792-1866). Edward Pusey (1800-82) and John Henry Newman (1801-90) were among its prominent supporters. The Tractarians embraced and fostered the theology and practices of High Church Anglicanism by emphasizing a Catholic style of worship and drew heavily upon the writings of the early Church Fathers of the patristic period. Many in the movement were drawn to Rome. There were at least five hundred converts from Oxford and two hundred from Cambridge who followed Newman into the Catholic Church, shortly after 1845. Very few of them had any contact with the local Catholic clergy. See V. Alan McClelland, 'The Formative Years, 1850-92', in *From Without the Flaminian Gate: 150 Years of Roman Catholicism in England and Wales 1850-2000*, ed. V. Alan McClelland and Michael Hodgetts (London: Darton, Longman and Todd, 1999), 14.

[32] Quoted in Ian Ker, *John Henry Newman: A Biography* (Oxford and New York: Oxford University Press, 1990), 342.

[33] Quoted in Norman, 118.

[34] David Meara, 'The Catholic Context', in *A. W. N. Pugin: Master of Gothic Revival*, ed. Paul Atterbury (New Haven and London: Yale University Press, 1995), 60.

[35] Eamon Duffy, *Saints and Sinners: A History of the Popes* (New Haven and London: Yale University Press, 1997), 230.

[36] Ibid., 266.

[37] Ibid., 229.

[38] Harold A. Buetow, *Of Singular Benefit: The Story of Catholic Education in the United States* (New York: Macmillan, 1970), 110.

[39] Harold A. Buetow, *The Catholic School: Its Roots, Identity, and Future* (New York: Crossroad, 1988), 24.

[40] Dolan, 267.

[41] Buetow, *Of Singular Benefit: The Story of Catholic Education in the United States*, 114.

[42] Dolan, 270.

[43] The first Catholic institution in the United States to offer graduate education for higher degrees was the Catholic University of America, established in 1884.

[44] Dolan, 272.

[45] Ibid., 277.

[46] O'Farrell, *The Catholic Church and Community in Australia*, 143.

[47] Ronald Fogarty, *Catholic Education in Australia 1806-1950, Vol. 1: Catholic Schools and the Denominational System* (Carlton, Victoria: Melbourne University Press, 1959), 179.

[48] After intense lobbying over this issue of funding to denominational schools - what was called State Aid - the federal government of Australia in 1964 began to offer limited money to the states to fund privately run schools. Grants have since expanded, allowing Catholic schools to grow in number.

[49] Ibid., quoted on page 190.

[50] Margaret M. Press, *Julian Tenison Woods: 'Father Founder'*, new ed. (Strathfield, New South Wales: St Pauls, 2004), 247.

[51] Ibid., 171.

[52] Quoted in Edmund Campion, *Australian Catholics: The Contribution of Catholics to Australian Society* (Ringwood, Victoria: Viking Penguin, 1987), 50.

[53] See Paul Gardiner, *Mary MacKillop: An Extraordinary Australian* (Newtown, New South Wales: E. J. Dwyer and David Ell Press, 1993).

[54] Maurice Whitehead, 'A View from the Bridge: The Catholic School', in *From Without the Flaminian Gate: 150 Years of Roman Catholicism in England and Wales 1850-2000*, ed. V. Alan McClelland and Michael Hodgetts, 230.

[55] Norman, 174.

[56] Ibid., 182.

[57] A number of religious orders dedicated to nursing were established within the Church of England around this time: the Anglican Sisters of Mercy (1850); All Saints Sisterhood (1851); and Sisters of St Margaret (1854).

[58] William J. McDonald, ed. *New Catholic Encyclopedia, Vol. X* (New York: McGraw-Hill, 1967), s.v. 'Nursing, History of', by C. M. Frank.

[59] Jo Ann Kay McNamara, *Sisters: Catholic Nuns Through Two Millennia* (Cambridge, Massachusetts: Harvard University Press, 1996), 624.

[60] Patrick Dougherty, *Mother Mary Potter: Foundress of the Little Company of Mary* (London and Glasgow: Sands and Co., 1961), 237.

**Chapter 9: A Renewed Church**

[1] Richard Pipes, *The Russian Revolution 1899-1919* (London: Fontana Press, 1992), 392.

[2] Henri Godin and Yvan Daniel, *France, pays de mission?* (Paris: Abeille, 1943).

[3] Olivier de la Brosse, ed. *The Responsible Church: Selected Texts of Cardinal Suhard* (London: Geoffrey Chapman, 1967), 27-8.

[4] Oscar L. Arnal, *Priests in Working Class Blue: The History of the Worker-Priests (1943-54)* (New York: Paulist Press, 1986), 58-66.

[5] Ibid., 113.

[6] James Hennesey, *American Catholics: A History of* the *Roman Catholic Community in the United States* (New York and Oxford: Oxford University Press, 1981), 258.

[7] Nancy L. Roberts, *Dorothy Day and the Catholic Worker* (Albany: State University of New York Press, 1984), 7.

[8] William D. Miller, *Dorothy Day: A Biography* (San Francisco: Harper and Row, 1982), 276.

[9] Roberts, 105.

[10] Quoted in Roberts, 26.

[11] Edmund Campion, *Australian Catholics* (Ringwood, Victoria: Viking Penguin, 1987), 170.

[12] Stephen Duffy, 'Catholicism's Search for a New Self-Understanding', in *Vatican II: Open Questions and New Horizons,* ed. Gerald M. Fagin, Theology and Life Series, Vol. 8 (Wilmington, Delaware: Michael Glazier, 1984), 19.

[13] Austin Flannery, ed. *The Basic Sixteen Documents of Vatican Council II: Constitutions, Decrees, Declarations* (Northport, New York: Costello Publications, 1996).

[14] French Archbishop Marcel Lefebvre (1905-91) was opposed to the changes introduced into the Catholic Church as a result of the Second Vatican Council that he viewed as entirely corrupt. He founded a seminary at Econe, Switzerland and the Society of St Pius X to further his ideas. Refusing to recognize the liturgical guidelines in the new Order of the Mass, and ordaining bishops without papal approval, he was finally excommunicated in 1988.

[15] Vatican II, Constitution on the Sacred Liturgy (*Sacrosanctum Concilium*).

[16] Vatican II, Constitution on Divine Revelation (*Dei Verbum*).

[17] Vatican II, Decree on Ecumenism (*Unitatis Redintegratio*).

[18] Vatican II, Declaration on the Relationship of the Church to Non-Christian Religions (*Nostra Aetate*), n. 2.

[19] Vatican II, Declaration on Religious Freedom (*Dignitatis Humanae*). Murray's theology of religious freedom is well summarized in Charles Curran, *American Catholic Social Ethics: Twentieth-Century Approaches* (Notre Dame, Indiana: University of Notre Dame Press, 1982), 172-232.

[20] Vatican II, Pastoral Constitution on the Church in the Modern World (*Gaudium et Spes*), n. 4.

[21] Christopher Butler, *Theology of Vatican II,* rev. ed. (London: Darton, Longman and Todd, 1981), 52.

[22] Vatican II, Dogmatic Constitution on the Church (*Lumen Gentium*), n. 23.

[23] Ibid., n. 27.

[24] Richard P. McBrien, *Ministry: A Theological, Pastoral Handbook* (San Francisco: Harper and Row, 1987), 42-4.

[25] Xavier Rynne, *Vatican Council II,* 2nd ed. (Maryknoll, New York: Orbis Books, 1999), 324-5.

[26] Congar, prior to Vatican II, laid the theological foundations concerning the role of the laity within the Church based upon their sharing in the sacrament of baptism. See Yves Congar, *Lay People in the Church: A Study for a Theology of the Laity,* trans. Donald Attwater (London: Geoffrey Chapman, 1959).

[27] Paul VI, 'Motu Proprio on Reforming Minor Orders' (*Ministeria quaedam*), *Origins* 2 (21 September 1972): 203-5, 216-7.

[28] Paul VI, Evangelization in the Modern World (*Evangelii Nuntiandi*) (Homebush, New South Wales: St Paul, 1976).

[29] John Paul II, 'Apostolic Exhortation on the Laity' (*Christifideles Laici*), *Origins* 18 (February 9, 1989): 561-95.

[30] The document was issued on 15 August 1997 by the Congregation for the Clergy, Pontifical Council for the Laity, Congregation for Divine Worship and Discipline of the Sacraments, Congregation for Bishops, Congregation for the Evangelization of Peoples, Congregation for Institutes of Consecrated Life and Societies of Apostolic Life, and the Pontifical Council for the Interpretation of Legislative Texts.

[31] *Lumen Gentium*, No. 29.

[32] Paul VI, General Norms for Restoring the Permanent Diaconate in the Latin World (*Sacrum Diaconatus Ordinem*) (Washington, D.C.: United States Catholic Bishops Conference, 1967).

[33] Fritz Lobinger, 'Why No Diaconate in the South', *East Asian Pastoral Review* 35 (No.3/4, 1998): 392-401.

[34] Avril Keely, 'The Permanent Diaconate and the Service Model of Diaconal Ministry', *Australasian Catholic Record* 77 (July 2000): 299-306.

[35] In 1998 the Vatican issued guidelines on the permanent diaconate. See Congregation for Catholic Education, 'Basic Norms for the Formation of Permanent Deacons', *Origins* 28 (27 August 1998):181-91; and Congregation for the Clergy, 'Directory for the Ministry and Life of Permanent Deacons', *Origins* 28 (27 August 1998): 191-204.

[36] A sociological study of *Opus Dei* can be found in Joan Estruck, *Saints and Sinners: Opus Dei and Its Paradoxes* (New York and Oxford: Oxford University Press, 1995).

[37] Gordon Urquhart, ' Movements on the March,' *The Tablet* (26 June, 1999): 877-8.

[38] Anne M. Clifford, *Introducing Feminist Theology* (Maryknoll, New York: Orbis Books, 2001), 5.

[39] Ibid., 329.

[40] Mary Daly, *The Church and the Second Sex* (San Francisco: Harper and Row, 1968).

[41] Elizabeth A. Johnson, *She Who Is: The Mystery of God in Feminist Theological Discourse* (New York: Crossroad, 1992).

[42] Paul VI, Declaration on the Question of the Admission of Women to the Ministerial Priesthood' (*Inter Insigniores*), *Origins* 6 (3 February 1997): 517-31.

[43] John Paul II, 'Apostolic Letter on Ordination and Women' (*Ordinatio Sacerdotalis*), *Origins* 24 (9 June 1994): 49-52.

[44] Research Management Group for the Australian Catholic Bishops Conference, Bishops Committee for Justice, Development and Peace, Australian Catholic University and the Australian Conference of Leaders of Religious Institutes, *Woman And Man: One in Christ Jesus – Report on the Participation of Women in the Catholic Church in Australia* (Sydney: HarperCollins, 1999), Executive Summary, vii-ix.

[45] Ibid.,

[46] Ibid.,

[47] Congregation for the Doctrine of the Faith, 'Letter on the Collaboration of Men and Women', *Origins* 34 (May 31, 2004): 169-76.

[48] Ibid., Section IV.

[49] See United States Catholic Bishops, 'When I Call for Help: A Pastoral Response to Domestic Violence Against Women', *Origins* 32 (November 21, 2002): 399-403.

[50] Jack Dominian, 'How Marriage Works', *The Tablet* (6 February 1999): 162.

[51] John Paul II, 'Apostolic Exhortation on the Family' (*Familiaris Consortio*), *Origins* 11 (24 December 1981): 437-68, n. 18.

[52] The movement is explained in Fr. Chuck Gallagher, *The Marriage Encounter: As I Have Loved You* (New York: Doubleday, 1975).

[53] Gerald D. Coleman, *Divorce and Remarriage in the Catholic Church* (New York: Paulist Press, 1988), 5.

[54] 'Apostolic Exhortation on the Family', n. 84.

[55] Paul VI, 'On the Regulation of Birth' (*Humanae Vitae*) (Homebush, New South Wales: St Paul, 1968).

[56] Joseph Bernardin, 'The Consistent Ethic of Life, Annual Helder Câmara Lecture. Archdiocese of Melbourne, Australia, 23 February 1995,' in Alphone P. Spilly, ed. *Selected Works of Joseph Cardinal Bernardin, Volume 2 – Church and Society* (Collegeville, Minnesota: The Liturgical Press, 2000), 137.

[57] Congregation for the Doctrine of the Faith, 'Letter to the Bishops of the Catholic Church on the Pastoral Care of Homosexual Persons', *Origins* 16 (13 November 1986): 377-82.

[58] Congregation for the Doctrine of the Faith, 'Declaration On Certain Questions Concerning Sexual Ethics', *Origins* 5 (22 January 1976): 485-94.

[59] 'Letter to the Bishops of the Catholic Church on the Pastoral Care of Homosexual Persons', n. 3.

[60] Congregation for the Doctrine of the Faith, 'Considerations Regarding Proposals to Give Legal Recognition to Unions Between Homosexual Persons', *Origins* 33 (14 August 2003): 177-82.

[61] Administrative Committee of the United States Conference of Catholic Bishops, 'Statement on Marriage and Homosexual Unions', *Origins* 33 (25 September 2003): 257-9; the Permanent Council of the Canadian Conference of Catholic Bishops, 'Marriage and Same-Sex Unions', on internet site: http://www.cccb.ca/PublicStatements.html.

[62] Peter J. Liuzzi, *With Listening Hearts: Understanding the Voices of Lesbian and Gay Catholics* (New York: Paulist Press, 2001), 7-10.

[63] United States National Conference of Catholic Bishops' Committee on Marriage and Family, 'Always Our Children', *Origins* 27 (9 October 1997): 285-91.

[64] World Health Organization, *World Health Report* (Geneva, 1999). Quoted by John D. Fuller, and James Keenan, 'Introduction: At the End of the First Generation of HIV Prevention', in *Catholic Ethics on HIV/AIDS Prevention*, ed. James F. Keenan (New York: Continuum, 2000), 32.

[65] The Australian bishops, for example, wrote that 'AIDS should not be presented as a divine judgment on a sexually permissive society'. See Australian Catholic Bishops, *The AIDS Crisis: A Message to the Australian People*, 1987.

[66] Cardinal Joseph Bernardin, 'Pastoral Letter: The Church's Response to the AIDS Crisis', *Origins* 16 (13 November 1986): 385.

[67] Cardinal Basil Hume, 'AIDS: Time for Moral Renaissance', *The Times*, 7 January 1987.

[68] AIDS as a justice issue is argued by Lisa Sowle Cahill, 'AIDS, Justice, and the Common Good', in Keenan, *Catholic Ethics on HIV/AIDS Prevention*, 282-93. See also Kevin T. Kelly, *New Directions in Sexual Ethics: Moral Theology and the Challenge of AIDS* (London and Washington, D.C.: Geoffrey Chapman, 1998).

[69] United States Bishops, 'Charter for the Protection of Children and Young People, Revised', *Origins* 32 (28 November 2002): 412. The Charter and 'Essential Norms for

Diocesan/Eparchial Policies Dealing with Allegations of Sexual Abuse by Priests or Deacons, Revised' were revised slightly from those issued immediately after the Bishops' June meeting of 2002 following discussions with Vatican officials. See *Origins* 32 (28 November 2002): 409-18 for the full text of both revised documents.

[70] National Review Board, 'Report: Causes and Context of the Sexual Abuse Crisis', *Origins* 33 (11 March 2004): 653-8.

[71] The document *Towards Healing* was first published in 1996 and revised in 2000 by the Catholic Bishops and Major Religious Superiors in Australia. It is a set of procedures to be followed in instances of complaints of sexual abuse by Church personnel. In 1999 the same body published a document of professional and ethical guidelines for clergy and religious known as *Integrity in Ministry*.

[72] Canadian Conference of Catholic Bishops, *From Pain to Hope: Report from the CCCB Ad Hoc Committee on Child Sexual Abuse* (Ottawa: Canadian Conference Catholic Bishops, 1992); Irish Catholic Bishops Advisory Committee on Child Sexual Abuse by Priests and Religious, *Child Sexual Abuse: Framework for a Church Response*. (Dublin: Veritas Publications, 1996).

[73] Stephen Rossetti, 'Child Sexual Abuse: A Conversion of Perspective', *The Tablet* (21 January, 1995): 74. See also Stephen J. Rossetti, *A Tragic Grace: The Catholic Church and Child Sexual Abuse* (Collegeville, Minnesota: The Liturgical Press, 1996).

[74] A helpful introductory text as to how psychology can assist Christian ministry in its many dimensions can be found in Fraser Watts, Rebecca Nye and Sara Savage, *Psychology for Christian Ministry* (London and New York: Routledge, 2002).

[75] Rodney J. Hunter, ed. *Dictionary of Pastoral Care And Counseling* (Nashville: Abingdon, 1990), s.v. 'Pastoral Care Movement', by E. B. Holifield.

[76] See Carl R. Rogers, *Client-Centered Therapy: Its Current Practice, Implications and Theory* (Boston: Houghton Mifflin Company, 1951).

[77] Howard Clinebell, writing within a Protestant tradition, has offered what is perhaps the most developed theological foundation for pastoral counseling. He describes his approach as a wholistic-liberation-growth model. See Howard Clinebell, *Basic Types of Pastoral Care and Counseling: Resources for the Ministry of Healing and Growth* (Nashville: Abingdon, 1984). For a summary of the developments within the modern pastoral counseling movement, see Clyde J. Steckel, 'Directions in Pastoral Counseling', in *Clinical Handbook of Pastoral Counseling, Vol. 1, Expanded Edition*, ed. Robert J. Wicks, Richard D. Parsons, and Donald Capps (New York: Integration Books/Paulist Press, 1993): 26-35.

[78] Lawrence Crabb is a well-known representative within evangelical 'Christian Counseling'. See Lawrence J. Crabb, *Understanding People: Deep Longings for Relationship* (Grand Rapids, Michigan: Zondervan, 1987).

[79] For a discussion of the aims and methods of spiritual direction see William A. Barry and William J. Connolly, *The Practice of Spiritual Direction* (New York: Seabury Press, 1982).

[80] Carolyn Gratton, *The Art of Spiritual Guidance: A Contemporary Approach to Growing in the Spirit* (New York: Crossroad, 1992), 13.

[81] Jean Stairs, *Listening for the Soul: Pastoral Care and Spiritual Direction* (Minneapolis: Fortress Press, 2000), 3.

[82] Kenneth Leech, *Soul Friend: Spiritual Direction in the Modern World*, new and rev. ed. (London: Darton, Longman and Todd, 1994), 181.

[83] See Christine M. Bochen, ed., *Thomas Merton: Essential Writings*. Modern Spiritual Masters Series (Maryknoll, New York: Orbis Books, 2000).

[84] Deirdrie La Noue, *The Spiritual Legacy of Henri Nouwen* (New York and London: Continuum, 2000), 146-7.

[85] Henri Nouwen, *The Wounded Healer: Ministry in Contemporary Society* (New York: Doubleday, 1972).

### Chapter 10: A Global Mission

[1] Leo XIII, 'The Condition of Labor' (*Rerum Novarum*) in David J. O'Brien and Thomas A. Shannon, *Catholic Social Thought: The Documentary Heritage* (Maryknoll, New York: Orbis Books, 1992), 14-39.

[2] Pius XI, 'After Forty Years' (*Quadragesimo Anno*), in *Catholic Social Thought: The Documentary Heritage*, 42-79.

[3] The issue is discussed at length in John Cornwell's controversial book, *Hitler's Pope: The Secret History of Pius XII* (New York: Viking/Penguin, 1999). Cornwell, in pages 268-77, lists a number of possible reasons often cited for the silence of Pius XII concerning the Holocaust: timidity; indecisiveness; bias towards the Nazis, anti-Semitism; justifiable prudence for fear of consequences; a desire to remain impartial so as to be in a position to be a peace broker; unclear information at hand; a fear of the spread of communism at the expense of the 'lesser' evil of fascism; a piety and theology that distanced itself from social responsibility outside the boundaries of the Catholic Church.

[4] John XXIII, 'Mother and Teacher' (*Mater et Magistra*), in *Catholic Social Thought: The Documentary Heritage*, 83-128.

[5] Paul VI, 'On the Development of Peoples' (*Populorum Progressio*), in *Catholic Social Thought: The Documentary Heritage*, 240-62, n. 49.

[6] Paul VI, 'A Call to Action' (*Octogesima Adveniens*), in *Catholic Social Thought: The Documentary Heritage*, 265-86.

[7] Paul VI, 'Justice in the World' (Synod of Bishops), in *Catholic Social Thought: The Documentary Heritage*, 288-300, n. 6.

[8] John Paul II, 'On Human Work' (*Laborem Exercens*), in *Catholic Social Thought: The Documentary Heritage*, 352-92.

[9] John Paul II, 'On Social Concern' (*Sollicitudo Rei Socialis*), in *Catholic Social Thought: The Documentary Heritage*, 395-436.

[10] John Paul II, 'On the Hundredth Year' (*Centesimus Annus*), in *Catholic Social Thought: The Documentary Heritage*, 439-88.

[11] John Paul II, 'The Gospel of Life', *Origins* 24 (6 April 1995): 689-727.

[12] The full text of both documents *The Challenge of Peace* and *Economic Justice for All* of the United States Catholic Bishops can be found in *Catholic Social Thought: The Documentary Heritage*, 571-680. *Economic Justice for All* received much criticism from certain groups in the United States. They questioned the wisdom and practicality of bishops defining economic policy. The *Wall Street Journal* remarked that the bishops had come up with 'poor policy'. See George E. McCarthy and Royal W. Rhodes, *Eclipse of Justice: Ethics, Economics, and the Lost Traditions of Catholicism* (Maryknoll, New York: Orbis Books, 1992), 11.

[13] Australian Catholic Bishops Conference, *Common Wealth for the Common Good: A Statement on the Distribution of Wealth in Australia* (Blackburn, Victoria: Collins Dove, 1992).

[14] Catholic Bishops Conference of England and Wales, *The Common Good and the Catholic Church's Social Teaching* (Manchester: Gabriel Communications, 1996). An abbreviated version of the document can be found in *The Tablet* (26 October 1996): 1421-6.

[15] Much has been written on the different approaches to practical theology. One of the most comprehensive studies of practical theology, outlining its methodology and theoretical foundations, is that of Gerben Heitink, *Practical Theology: History, Theory, Action Domains: Manual for Practical Theology*, trans. Reinder Bruinsma (Grand Rapids, Michigan and Cambridge, U.K.: William E. Eerdmans, 1999). See also John Patton, ed. *The Blackwell Reader in Pastoral and Practical Theology* (Oxford: Blackwell, 2000).

[16] Many reasons have been offered for the fall of communism. These include political deadlock, economic implosion, ideological breakdown, technological advance, democratic ideas, and Western pressure. See Jonathan Luxmoore and Jolanta Babiuch, *The Vatican and the Red Flag: The Struggle for the Soul of Eastern Europe* (London and New York: Geoffrey Chapman, 1999), xii.

[17] *New Catholic Encyclopedia, Vol. 11*, 2nd ed (Detroit: Gale/Thomson Learning in association with The Catholic University of America, Washington D.C., 2003), s.v. 'Peyton, Patrick Joseph', by R. Krieg.

[18] See Jonathan Luxmoore, 'The Cardinal and the Communists', *The Tablet* (2 September, 2000): 1152-4.

[19] Quoted in Alvaro Barreiro, *Basic Ecclesial Communities: The Evangelization of the Poor*, trans. Barbara Campbell (Maryknoll, New York: Orbis Books, 1984), 50.

[20] 'Medellín Conclusions', in *The Gospel of Peace and Justice: Catholic Social Teaching since Pope John*, ed. Joseph Gremillion (New York: Orbis Books, 1976), 445-54.

[21] Gregory Baum, *Theology and Society* (New York: Paulist Press, 1987), 8-12.

[22] Gerard Kelly, 'Basic Christian Communities: A Study in the Church's Self-Understanding' (MTh Dissertation, Catholic Institute of Sydney, 1985), 18.

[23] Gustavo Gutierrez, *A Theology of Liberation*, trans. Sr Caridad Inda and John Eagleson (Maryknoll, New York: Orbis Books, 1973).

[24] Roger Haight, *An Alternative Vision: An Interpretation of Liberation Theology* (New York: Paulist Press, 1985), 29.

[25] Paulo Freire, *Pedagogy of the Oppressed* (New York: Seabury Press, 1968).

[26] An obituary that outlines Freire's life and achievements can be found in *The Tablet* (17 May 1997): 647-8.

[27] Marie Dennis, Renny Golden, and Scott Wright, *Oscar Romero: Reflections on His Life and Writings*, Modern Spiritual Masters Series (Maryknoll, New York: Orbis Books, 2000), 12-4.

[28] Congregation for the Doctrine of the Faith, 'Instruction on Certain Aspects of the "Theology of Liberation" ', *Origins* 14 (13 September 1984): 193-204.

[29] Congregation for the Doctrine of the Faith, 'Instruction on Christian Freedom and Liberation', *Origins* 15 (17 April 1986): 713-28.

[30] Quoted in Benny Aguiar, 'Something Beautiful for God', *The Tablet* (13 September 1999):1149.

[31] Ibid.

[32] Chandra Muzaffar, 'Globalization and Religion: Some Reflections', in Joseph A. Camilleri and Chandra Muzaffar, eds. *Globalisation: The Perspectives and Experiences of the Religious Traditions of Asia Pacific* (Selangor Darul Ehsan, Malaysia: International Movement for a Just World, 1998), 181-6.

[33] Anwar Ibrahim, 'Globalisation and the Cultural Re-Empowerment of Asia', in *Globalisation: The Perspectives and Experiences of the Religious Traditions of Asia Pacific*, 3.

[34] Robert J. Schreiter, *The Ministry of Reconciliation: Spirituality and Strategies* (Maryknoll, New York: Orbis Books, 1998), 127-30.

[35] Gregory Baum, 'A Theological Afterword', in Gregory Baum and Harold Wells, eds. *The Reconciliation of Peoples: Challenge to the Churches* (Maryknoll, New York: Orbis Books, 1997), 186-9.

[36] John XXIII, Peace on Earth (*Pacem in Terris*), in *Catholic Social Thought: The Documentary Heritage*, 131-62.

[37] Quoted in Hennesey, 281 from *Catholic World* 161 (1945): 449-52.

[38] Curran, 239-40.

[39] Frank Brennan, *Tampering with Asylum: A Universal Humanitarian Problem* (St Lucia, Queensland: University of Queensland Press, 2003), 27.

[40] John Menadue, 'Morality and public policy in Australia', in Frank Brennan, Jim Carlton, Hilary Charlesworth et al., eds. *Refugees, Morality and Public Policy* (Ringwood, Victoria: David Lovell, 2002), 76.

[41] Pontifical Council for the Pastoral Care of Migrants and Travelers, *The Love of Christ Toward Migrants*, n. 9. For the full text of this Instruction, see *Origins* 34 (12 August 2004): 145-68.

[42] The dialectical relationship between interreligious dialog and proclamation of the Gospel within the one evangelizing mission of the Church is discussed in the encyclical of John Paul II, 'The Mission of the Redeemer' (*Redemptoris Missio*), n. 55, *Origins* 20 (31 January 1991): 541-68.

[43] David J. Bosch, *Transforming Mission: Paradigm Shifts in Theology of Mission* (Maryknoll, New York: Orbis Books, 1991), 488.

[44] Francis Cardinal Arinze, *Religions for Peace: A Call for Solidarity to the Religions of the World* (New York: Doubleday, 2002), 11.

[45] Vatican II, Declaration on the Relationship of the Church to Non-Christian Religions (*Nostra Aetate*), n. 2.

[46] See Pontifical Council for Interreligious Dialog and the Congregation for the Evangelization of Peoples, *Dialog and Proclamation: Reflections and Orientations on Interreligious Dialog and the Proclamation of the Gospel of Jesus Christ*, in *Origins* 21 (19 May 1991): 121-35. Jacques Dupuis comments on 'participated mediation' as reflected in this Church document in Jacques Dupuis, *Christianity and the Religions: From Confrontation to Dialog*, trans. Phillip Berryman (Maryknoll, New York: Orbis Books, 2002), 72.

[47] S. Wesley Ariarajah, *Not Without My Neighbour* (Geneva: World Council of Churches (WCC) Publications, 1999), 98.

[48] Richard T. Antoun, *Understanding Fundamentalism: Christian, Islamic and Jewish Movements* (Walnut Creek, California: Altamira Press, 2001).

[49] Thomas Berry, 'Ecology and the Future of Catholicism', in Albert J. LaChance and John E. Carroll, eds. *Embracing Earth: Catholic Approaches to Ecology* (Maryknoll, New York: Orbis Books, 1994), xi.

[50] Andrew Darby, 'Breaking up is hard on Antarctica', *The Sydney Morning Herald*, 23 September 2004, 1,8.

[51] International Cooperation for Development and Solidarity (CIDSE) and Caritas International, 'Putting Life before Debt', can be found on internet site: http://www.cidse.org/pubs/finaldebteng.html .

[52] John Paul II, 'Peace With God the Creator, Peace With All Creation', *Origins* 19 (14 December 1989): 465-8.

[53] United States Catholic Bishops, 'Renewing the Earth: An Invitation to Reflection and Action on the Environment in the Light of Catholic Social Teaching', *Origins* 21 (12 December 1991): 425-32. In October 2003 the Social Affairs Commission of the Canadian Conference of Catholic Bishops issued a document on the environment, 'A Pastoral Letter on the Christian Ecological Imperative', see internet site: http://www.cccb.ca/files/pastoralenvironment.html .

[54] Gregory Brett, 'A Timely Reminder: Humanity and Ecology in the Light of Christian Hope', in Denis Edwards, ed. *Earth Revealing, Earth Healing* (Collegeville, Minnesota: The Liturgical Press, 2001), 166-8.

[55] Denis Edwards, 'For Your Immortal Spirit Is in All Things: The Role of the Spirit in Creation', in Edwards, 45-66.

[56] Marc Boucher-Colbert, 'Eating the Body of the Lord', in LaChance and Carroll, 116.

[57] For an introductory analysis of Postmodernism and its implications for Christianity, see Stanley J. Grenz, *A Primer On Postmodernism.* (Grand Rapids, Michigan /Cambridge, U.K.: William B. Eerdmans, 1996).

# Index